Memoirs of a Soviet Ambassador

THE WAR: 1939-43

Books by Ivan Maisky

Memoirs of a Soviet Ambassador

THE WAR: 1939–43

Ivan Maisky

SOVIET AMBASSADOR TO THE UNITED KINGDOM
1932-43
MEMBER OF THE ACADEMY OF SCIENCES
OF THE USSR

TRANSLATED FROM THE RUSSIAN BY
Andrew Rothstein

CHARLES SCRIBNER'S SONS
New York

First published in the United States in 1968

First published in Russia as
VOSPOMINANIA SOVETSKOGO POSLA: VOINA 1939-1943
(Izdatelstvo 'NAUKA', Moscow 1965)

A-2.68 [v]

Printed in the United States of America

LIBRARY OF CONGRESS CATALOG CARD NUMBER 68-12501

Contents

Part Three

GERMANY'S ATTACK ON THE USSR

Part Four

THE STRUGGLE FOR THE SECOND FRONT

Part Five

RETURN TO MOSCOW

Preface

THIS book, a continuation of my previous reminiscences, deals with my diplomatic work in London during the second world war.

In preparing it, I sought to reproduce genuine historical truth. The events of 1939-43 described in the following pages represent a particularly important period in our epoch, and consequently an account of them should be particularly accurate.

In acquainting the reader with various historical personages, I have tried to make use of neither black nor white alone. Real life is complex, real people are varied and changeable. If these circumstances are not taken into account, the pen of the writer of memoirs may produce not history, but the falsification of history.

The recollections offered here are based not only on what has been recorded in memory (a very important but not always reliable source) but also on the much more objective voice of facts and documents. During the years of my work in Britain as Ambassador I wrote a regular, though not daily, diary, and in addition made separate records of particular occasions. Fairly often I also exchanged letters with my friends and comrades in diplomacy. Today I am able to make use of all such materials for my memoirs. In this book I sometimes make precise quotations from them. But even when I am recounting conversations or impressions without any such special reference, they are usually based on documents of this kind.

I was aided also by sources of another kind—parliamentary reports, reference works on people and events, Soviet and foreign monographs, collections of documents, memoirs of military men, politicians and diplomats of various nationalities. Not infrequently I have in my memoirs to dispute the statements of foreign authors, correct their mistakes, expose their inventions or distortions.

In the long run this book is an attempt, to the best of my ability, to present the point of view of a Soviet citizen on the events which it describes. It may also serve as one of the primary sources for future research into the foreign policy of the USSR on the eve of, and during, the second world war.

IVAN MAISKY

Part One

*

The Phoney War

I

Germany's Attack on Poland

At 5.30 a.m. on 1 September 1939, without any preliminary ultimatum or formal declaration of war, Hitlerite Germany attacked Poland. At 5.40 a.m. Hitler addressed a broadcast to his army, stating that the Polish Government had rejected a peaceful settlement of questions in dispute, and therefore he was obliged to appeal to arms. Simultaneously the divisions of the Wehrmacht crossed the frontiers of Poland from East Prussia, Pomerania, Poznan and Slovakia, while the German Air Force attacked Polish cities with all its strength. On the same day, 1 September, Foerster, the Nazi leader at Danzig, proclaimed the annexation of that city to the Third Reich.

These events at once faced the Governments of Britain and France with the dread question, what was to be done?

The formal reply to this question was very simple. On 31 March 1939 Britain and France had given Poland a unilateral guarantee of its integrity and independence. On 6 April the same year, by a statement of Beck, Polish Minister for Foreign Affairs, this unilateral guarantee was made bilateral, with the provision that later a formal pact of mutual assistance would be signed by Poland and Britain (such a pact between Poland and France was already in existence). In fact, on 24 August 1939 Poland and Britain concluded a pact of this kind. Thus on 1 September 1939, when Hitlerite Germany attacked Poland, Britain and France, in keeping with the letter and the spirit of the agreements mentioned, should have immediately and unreservedly acted, arms in hand, in defence of their ally...

Should have! But just at this point there began to be revealed those submerged reefs which were diverting the foreign policy of Britain and France from the path of wisdom and honour and were pushing it on to the path of stupidity, hypocrisy and treachery.

I have described in detail elsewhere[1] how the stubborn sabotage by the Governments of Chamberlain and Daladier prevented the conclusion on the eve of the war of a triple pact of mutual assistance by the USSR, Britain and France—the only measure which could have hindered Hitlerite aggression and prevented Germany's attack on Poland. I also described the insane political blindness and thoughtlessness of the 'Government of Colonels' in Warsaw, which had boastfully declared that it did not require aid from the USSR to defend itself against Hitlerite Germany. I shall not repeat all this here. It will be sufficient to say that on 1 September 1939 the same Chamberlain and Daladier who had just prevented the conclusion of a triple pact of mutual assistance were still in power in Britain and in France. This was why the first thought of the British and French Prime Ministers, when they heard the news of the awful events in Poland—a thought which, of course, was not openly expressed but which dominated their consciousness—was: could they not in some way avoid performing the obligations they had undertaken to Poland? I speak frankly of the existence of such a thought in the minds of Chamberlain and Daladier because, as we shall soon see, their actions during the month that followed represented the exact fulfilment of the idea in practice.

Formally events developed as follows. On 1 September at 9.40 a.m. the British and French Ambassadors in Berlin handed to Ribbentrop, the German Minister for Foreign Affairs, a statement from their Governments which essentially was an ultimatum: if Germany did not immediately cease military operations and recall its troops from Poland, Britain and France would carry out their treaty obligations to Poland.

Twelve hours before this, on the evening of 31 August, Mussolini, who officially still remained 'neutral', had proposed that the German-Polish conflict should be settled by mediation: a 'Five-Power Conference' (Germany, Italy, Britain, France and Poland) should be urgently assembled, to decide the issues in dispute around a table. The Italian dictator was clearly dreaming of a new 'Munich'. Chamberlain and Daladier eagerly seized on Mussolini's proposal, and began putting off the fulfilment of their obligations towards their ally who had been attacked. It was just

1. *Who helped Hitler?* (Hutchinsons, 1964).

because of this that for 54 hours after Germany's attack on Poland they did not declare war. In all probability, they would have waited even longer, in the hope of settling by 'Munich' means the German-Polish conflict. But here Hitler upset the calculations of the appeasers. He demanded as a preliminary for the 'Five-Power Conference' the cancelling of the Anglo-French ultimatum of 1 September. Chamberlain and Daladier did not venture to accept this: the wave of anger against Hitlerite aggression had risen too high in their countries for this.

As a result, Mussolini's attempt failed. The war proceeded with its iron footfalls.

Information about these backstairs moves and counter-moves penetrated into the press and political circles. They aroused great excitement among the peoples. This excitement found an exceptionally vivid reflection at a meeting of the House of Commons on the evening of 2 September.

After Chamberlain, at monotonous and tedious length, had reported that the British and French Governments had not yet received a reply from Hitler to their statement of 1 September, and that they could not recognise the unilateral infringement of the status of Danzig laid down by the Versailles Treaty, Arthur Greenwood impetuously rose from the Labour Opposition benches. He was temporarily acting as Leader of the Opposition (its regular leader, Attlee, was ill), and was now in a state of extreme indignation. At that moment, from the Conservative benches where there also could be felt very great tension, Amery, turning to Greenwood, cried: 'Speak for England!'

Amery was a furious imperialist and reactionary, but he considered that loyalty to the pledge given was a matter of Britain's national honour. He was no less indignant than Greenwood at Chamberlain's delay in fulfilling the obligations to Poland, and wanted Greenwood to speak now not only as representative of the Opposition Party but as representative of the whole nation. The House expressed its loud approval of Amery's remark.

'I believe the whole House is perturbed by the right hon. Gentleman's statement,' Greenwood began. 'An act of aggression took place 38 hours ago. The moment that act of aggression took place one of the most important treaties of modern times automatically came into operation . . . There are many of us on all sides of this House who view with the gravest concern the fact that hours went by and news came in of bombing operations . . . I wonder how long we are prepared to vacillate . . . Every minute's delay now means the loss of life, imperilling our national interests . . . imperilling the very foundations of our national honour . . . Delay is dangerous . . . I believe that the die is cast.'

The Opposition benches expressed their loud approval of the speaker, and on the Conservative benches many did not conceal their satisfaction. Greenwood expressed what the nation was feeling at that critical moment, and his words became historic.

Chamberlain was embarrassed, sought to justify his action, referred to the difficulties of telephone negotiations between London and Paris, but finally was obliged to promise that not later than the following morning the Government would tell the people of a quite definite decision.[1]

The result of the scene I have described, and also of the ever-growing indignation of the masses, was that on Sunday, 3 September, at 9 a.m., Nevile Henderson, the British Ambassador in Berlin, handed the German Government a Note which stated that if Hitler did not agree within two hours to the withdrawal of German troops from Poland, Britain would declare war on Germany. A similar démarche was made by the French Ambassador in Berlin as well, with only this difference, that the period of the French ultimatum expired not at 11 a.m. but at 5 p.m. on 3 September.

Hitler, of course, left the 'final appeal' by Britain and France unanswered, and at 11.15 a.m. Chamberlain in a brief broadcast was forced to announce that a state of war existed between the two countries.

The same morning there was a session of Parliament. The Prime Minister was depressed and pitiable. His voice was hollow and broken.

'This is a sad day for all of us', said Chamberlain, 'and to none is it sadder than to me. Everything that I have worked for, everything that I have hoped for, everything that I have believed in during my public life, has crashed into ruins.'

I was sitting in my place in the Diplomatic Gallery and thinking: 'You are only gathering the fruits of your own stupidity and malice. The chariot of justice moves slowly, but still it moves, and now you have fallen under its wheel. The pity only is that great masses of the people will have to pay for your crimes.'

Greenwood in the name of the Labour Party promised the

1. *Parliamentary Debates. House of Commons*, 2 September 1939.

Government full support in the struggle against Hitlerite Germany. Archibald Sinclair, on behalf of the Liberal Party, did the same. Lloyd George declared that, although in the past he had often criticised the foreign policy of the Government, now, in the situation that had been created, he considered it his duty to help in bringing the war to a victorious conclusion.

Churchill also spoke at this meeting. He warned against treating the war lightly.

'We must not underrate the gravity of the task which lies before us or the temerity of the ordeal,' he said. 'We must expect many disappointments and many unpleasant surprises, but we may be sure that the task which we have freely accepted is one not beyond the compass and the strength of the British Empire and the French Republic.'[1]

In conclusion Gallacher, the only Communist in the House, declared that he desired 'the speedy and effective defeat of the Nazi régime as a sure way of bringing about hope for a lasting peace for the peoples of the world'.

I was following attentively all that went on at this historic meeting of the House of Commons, and there was constantly turning over and over in my mind the thought: 'Chamberlain and Daladier have failed their examination in preventing a war; how will they stand up to the examination of at any rate fulfilling their obligations to Poland?'

There was not long to wait.

We now know precisely that Hitler had thrown against Poland fifty-seven of his best divisions (including eight mechanised divisions), that the German Air Force which was attacking the Polish cities numbered 2,000 of the most up-to-date machines of that day, and that a vast number of tanks, armoured cars and guns had impetuously burst into Polish territory. To this terrible blow Poland could oppose only thirty-one divisions (including only two mechanised brigades), 800 planes of which only about half could be reckoned as of modern types, a fairly modest number of guns and quite a small number of tanks. True, Poland had eleven cavalry brigades, but what could they do against tanks and armoured cars?

In fairness to the Polish Army, it should be said that the soldiers and many officers fought most bravely, but the Germans had too great an advantage in numbers and armament. The Polish High

1. *Ibid.*, 3 September 1939.

Command displayed its complete incapacity, and did not even bother to prepare any central reserves. The strategic disposition of the Polish forces was extremely inadequate, and the greater part of the Polish Air Force was destroyed by the Germans while it was still grounded on its own aerodromes.

At that time I did not know all these details. Probably the British and French Governments were not completely aware of them either. However, from the very first day of the German-Polish war it was clear that vast forces had descended on Poland, far exceeding her own, and that Hitler was relying upon the notorious *Blitzkrieg* about which the Nazis had been shouting so much in the preceding months. In such circumstances, one might have thought, the very greatest speed and energy were necessary in affording assistance to the victim of aggression. Britain and France, one might have thought, should most urgently have diverted to the West, to themselves, at least a part of the German forces operating in Poland. One might have thought that they should immediately and seriously have attacked the Siegfried Line and poured bombs on the German fortifications and cities. But what took place in fact?

Here are some extracts from the notes I made in the first months of the war:

'*4 September*. Chamberlain has broadcast a speech in German, to the German people. The British Air Force has bombed German warships at Wilhelmshafen and Brunsbüttel. Damage has been done. The Germans did not reply. British planes have dropped six million leaflets over Germany.

'*5 September*. British planes have dropped three million leaflets over the Ruhr region.

'*6, 8 and 9 September*. British planes have again dropped leaflets over Germany.

'*24–25 September*. The British planes have again dropped leaflets over Germany; in all, eighteen million leaflets have been dropped since the war broke out.'

The French behaved no better. Here are a few characteristic extracts from the same entries:

'*4 September*. The first French war communiqué: "Operations have begun on land, at sea and in the air."

'*5 September*. The second French communiqué: "French troops have entered into contact with the enemy along the whole line between the Moselle and the Rhine."

'*6 September*. The third French communiqué reports crossings of the frontier by French troops in the region of "no man's land" (the name given to a strip from three to twelve miles wide, separating the Maginot Line from the Siegfried Line).

'*10–16 September*. The French communiqués report the systematic advance of French troops in the region of "no man's land".

'*22 September*. From the Western Front are reported increased artillery activity and local engagements south of Saarbrücken.

'*24 September*. The French communiqué states that during the night numerous local attacks by the enemy on "our advanced positions" in the Saar region were beaten off; and then it adds that in "authoritative French circles" the situation on the Western Front is described as "a position of strategic anticipation".'

All this was taking place when Poland was on fire, when the German armies were tearing its territory to pieces, when the German Air Force was hurling bombs on its cities, and when not only days, but even hours and minutes were important! The behaviour of British and French ruling quarters seemed direct mockery of their ally fallen on evil days, and in more sincere persons in both countries this aroused a blush of shame for their Governments. I remember meeting Greenwood in Parliament in the middle of September. We talked of the German-Polish war. Greenwood was in utter confusion.

'It is terrible, terrible!' he said loudly. 'Our Government gave the most solemn promises to come to the help of Poland in the event of a German attack—and what are we doing? Surely the British and French loan of eight-and-a-half million pounds to the Polish Government is not help! We haven't sent a single plane to Poland, and we are using our own planes to drop useless leaflets over Germany!'

Greenwood was one of the best representatives of the Labour Party leadership, and I did not doubt his subjective sincerity. But this had no practical significance: the whole policy of the Labour Party for many years past made it an accomplice of the ruling group in the country. Even now the Labour Party could not escape responsibility for the betrayal of Poland which was being carried out by the British Government.

On another occasion I met the Liberal M.P. Mander in the Lobby. He was in despair.

'I don't understand the policy of our Government,' he said bitterly. 'It is in complete contrast with all our traditions and our conceptions of honour and dishonour! I am really ashamed to look at the world.'

The result is well known. Churchill in his war memoirs writes: 'In two days the Polish air power was virtually annihilated . . . The second week was marked by bitter fighting, and by its end the Polish Army, nominally of about two million men, ceased to exist as an organised force.'[1]

On 17 September the Polish President, Moscicki, together with the 'Government of Colonels' headed by Beck, fled from their country to Rumania.

The Polish State set up by the Versailles Conference had ceased to exist. On its territory there remained individual centres of resistance, of which the most important was Warsaw. Surrounded on all sides by Germans, it fought on heroically until 28 September, but in the end fell under the blows of the enemy.

When all this was over, and Poland lay finally crushed, the Pope on 30 September, receiving representatives of the Polish clergy, delivered an 'emotional' oration, in which among other things he said: 'Christ, who shed tears over the death of Lazarus, will one day reward you for the tears you are shedding for your dead and for Poland.' It is difficult to conceive an example of greater hypocrisy! . . . Had not the Vatican by all its policy in the pre-war years facilitated the growth of Nazism in Germany? And had not the Vatican, like the Governments of Britain and France, not betrayed Poland in September 1939? . . .

In such circumstances the entry of the Red Army into the eastern part of Poland on 17 September 1939, i.e. when the Polish State had ceased to exist, represented genuine salvation for the Ukrainians and Belorussians living there from all the horrors of the Nazi invasion[2]. At the same time there opened before the western Ukrainians and Belorussians the possibility of coming to gether with Soviet Ukraine and Belorussia in a single national unit, which in effect did take place at the end of 1939.

1. *The Second World War*, Vol. I, 1955, pp. 396–7.

2. Owing to the stubborn sabotage by the British and French Governments which banked on a conflict between the USSR and Hitlerite Germany, the triple pact of mutual assistance between the USSR, Britain and France against Fascist aggression, offered by the Soviet Government in April 1939, could not be concluded. The negotiations went on for about four months, and in August 1939 finally reached a dead end, for which the British and French Governments were guilty. There was a danger that Chamberlain and Daladier, then at the head of the London and Paris Governments, might in one form or another support Hitlerite aggression against the USSR. Anticipating this danger, and seeking to postpone the possible attack by

Churchill in his war memoirs thought it necessary to dispatch some poisoned arrows in this connection at the Soviet Union.[1] It is strange, however, that he found it possible in the same memoirs to pass in silence by the betrayal of Poland by Britain and France. Why? Was it not because in September 1939 Churchill was a member of the British Government and, consequently, himself bore responsibility for the crime committed by that Government?

It is characteristic likewise that in the official history of the foreign policy of Britain in the period of the war[2] you cannot find one word about what the British Government was doing in September 1939. There is the story of how Britain declared war on Germany, which ends on 3 September. There is the story also of Britain's reaction to Hitler's peace proposals on 6 October (when Poland had already been crushed). But what the British Government thought, wrote, said, and did between the two dates mentioned, when the tragedy of Poland was being played out, remains unknown. Yet that month was filled with the most important events, to which Britain should have reacted day by day. But you will find no comments in Woodward. Once again, is it not because the behaviour of the British Government in September 1939 bears a too vivid impress of perfidy, and its apologists don't want to recall it?

By 1 October 1939 it had become perfectly clear that Chamberlain and Daladier had failed in their examination on fulfilment of their obligations to Poland, perhaps to an even greater extent than in their examinations on the averting of war.

1. *Op. cit.* pp. 398–9.
2. Sir Llewellyn Woodward, *British Foreign Policy in the Second World War*, H.M. Stationery Office, 1962.

Hitler on the USSR if only for a time, the Soviet Government on 23 August 1939 concluded a pact of non-aggression with Germany. As in the situation which had arisen then the Soviet Union was not in a position to save the whole of Poland from Hitlerite aggression, it demanded that the German Government should at least not transfer military operations to Eastern Poland, inhabited by Ukrainians and Belorussians. For more details see the author's *Who Helped Hitler?*

2

'Business as Usual'

The six months which followed the crushing of Poland—it was the winter of 1939–40—were the period of the so-called 'Phoney War'. It is usually considered that this period includes also September 1939—thirty days fateful in the history of Poland. It seems to me, however, that this is not quite right. September 1939 fully deserves another title—*the month of betrayal of Poland by the Governments of Britain and France*—and only the next six months, up to the beginning of April 1940, could be described as the 'Phoney War'.

What was the essence of the 'Phoney War'? And what were its roots?

The essence was that formally Britain and France were waging war against Germany but, in fact, were not waging it. And not because London and Paris, preparing some vast offensive operations, were obliged to put up with temporary calm at the front, but because London and Paris in general did not want to fight. They considered the declaration of war on Germany which they had made on 3 September 1939 to be a grievous misunderstanding, imposed on them by force of external circumstances, and were striving in every possible way to end it as rapidly as possible. They did not accept, they did not wish to accept, the idea that they were at the very beginning of a gigantic world conflict which it was now too late to arrest: and that it was now impossible to return the West to the condition of peace (perhaps a bad peace, but still peace) which had been maintained until 3 September. In this there spoke their historic short-sightedness and their mood, so well expressed in the well-known words: 'The wish is father to the thought.' Hence, naturally, there followed the general line of conduct of the London and Paris Governments: not to do anything which could in the least degree promote the sharpening and extension of the war.

Such was the essence of the 'Phoney War'. And where lay its roots?

The roots were to be found in that policy of 'appeasing' the aggressors, and Hitler first and foremost, in that conception of 'Western security' which constituted in the pre-war years the political credo of the 'Cliveden set' in Britain, and of the notorious '200 families' in France who cried 'Better Hitler than the Popular Front.' Their passionate desire was to push Germany and the Soviet Union into conflict and, after both these countries were bled white in their mutual struggle, themselves to step out into the historical limelight and establish such an order in Europe as would completely answer to their interests. Chamberlain and Daladier had been stubbornly aiming at this objective in the period of the tripartite negotiations between the USSR, Britain and France in 1939. Thanks to the skill of Soviet diplomacy, Chamberlain and Daladier had not then succeeded in impelling Germany against the USSR. On the contrary, they themselves had fallen into the pit which they had been digging for the land of Soviets. London and Paris were trying (and up to the present day are still trying) to shift to Moscow the responsibility for their political miscalculations.

However, even having formally declared war on Germany, Chamberlain and Daladier did not wish to renounce the conception of 'western security' so dear to their hearts. They considered that on 3 September 1939 there had been an unfortunate accident: in the twilight of the international situation friends had not recognised one another, and had taken to fisticuffs against one another. But this unpleasant incident could and must be settled as soon as possible, after which there would once again be established normal, and maybe even friendly relations, between Germany and the Anglo-French bloc. The 'Phoney War', as conceived by Chamberlain and Daladier, had its purpose precisely to bring about reconciliation between the two sides in the shortest possible time And then there would open up the broad highway for all kinds of anti-Soviet machinations and intrigues, which had been engaging the energies of those conducting British and French policy so fully on the eve of the war.

On one occasion, in November 1939, I had a meeting with Lloyd George. The old man, unlike many others who had turned their backs on the Soviet Embassy after the pact with Germany, continued to maintain his friendly relations with me. We had a long talk on the situation which had arisen. Towards the end Lloyd George said:

'If you think that recent events have taught Neville anything, you are making a bad mistake. Neville is incorrigible, and besides he is also terribly obstinate . . . I know for a fact that he is ready even now to make a deal with the Germans if they give him to understand that they are ready to attack you . . . You may be sure that he is not thinking of a real war with Germany for a moment.'

Lloyd George himself considered Chamberlain's policy stupid and dangerous for Britain, but with an eloquent gesture said that for the time being nothing could be done against him.

I was following very attentively everything that was then going on, and unwillingly came to the conclusion that Lloyd George was right: no one in official political circles (with very few exceptions) was thinking of a serious war with Germany, or was preparing for it. On the contrary, most people in these circles believed that in some miraculous way the war would finish at any moment, and meanwhile the principle of 'business as usual' should be maintained. I well remember, when on 1 August 1914 the first world war began—I was then a political emigrant in London—everyone was saying: 'The war will be over by Christmas.' And now public opinion—from the Prime Minister to the rank and file man in the street—was cherishing the illusion: 'The war will be over by the spring' (1940). All the statements and actions of official political circles bore the stamp of such moods.

And in fact, how did matters stand?

Of course, when war was declared, Chamberlain had to create a 'new' Government. Simple political decency required this. But if he had seriously been thinking of war, he would at once have formed a Government of a 'national' character, on the broadest possible coalition basis, and in any case with the essential participation of the second main party—the Labour Party. But what did Chamberlain do?

He left all the most important posts in the hands of the most die-hard 'Munichites'. Halifax remained Foreign Secretary, Simon Chancellor of the Exchequer, Anderson Home Secretary, Stanley President of the Board of Trade, Kingsley Wood Secretary for

Air, Samuel Hoare Lord Privy Seal, Euan Wallace Minister of Transport, etc. The only change in comparison with the past was that Chamberlain took into his Government representatives of the Conservative 'opposition'—Churchill as First Lord of the Admiralty and Eden as Dominions Secretary. I will remark in passing that the latter appointment to no small degree was due to Chamberlain's striving for support on the part of the Empire, and therefore he gave Eden this particular post as a man most popular in Britain's overseas dominions. In this way Chamberlain's 'new Government' was in substance the old Government, the Government of Conservative 'appeasers', ever so faintly touched up in anti-Hitlerite colours, and could not in any way pretend to be called 'national'.

The Labour Party as before remained in the condition of 'His Majesty's Opposition'. And here too, there was a particular purpose: age-old tradition decrees that Britain should be headed by a government of one of the main parties, and that it should be faced by the opposition of the other main party. Chamberlain argued that this had been so, this would be so, and this must be so today as well. It should be said that the Labour Party leadership in the first months of the war also stood by this 'doctrine'. It likewise did not believe in the seriousness of the war, it likewise strove to preserve the usual standards and customs. There were exceptions, but not very often. Hence the Labour Party, when the Government was being reorganised, displayed no activity in the sense of creating a genuine national Cabinet. In justification of such a policy the usual argument was: 'We don't want to bear responsibility for Chamberlain's stupidities; let him get out of it as best he can.' The only concession made by the Labour Party was to promise support for the Government without joining it, and observance of a party electoral truce during the war.

Approximately the same position was taken up by the trade unions at their Bridlington Congress on 4 and 5 September, and also at a meeting of the Executive Committee of the Amsterdam Trade Union International held in Paris on 13 and 14 October. The following characteristic fact also bore witness to the determination of the Labour leaders to proceed on the principle of 'business as usual': on 20 March 1940 a well-known M.P., D. N. Pritt, K.C., was expelled from the Labour Party for his 'too friendly attitude to the USSR'. Oh yes! Everything went on as usual. In this respect the war had changed nothing.

In addition to the formation of his 'new Government', it was very important for Chamberlain to display to the whole world, and to Germany in particular, that the Empire supported him. This would have raised his chances in the event of a deal with Hitler. This task proved more easily accomplished than was expected by many, both in Britain and beyond her borders. The reason was comprehensible. If Britain had declared war on some country of bourgeois democracy, the Dominions and colonies would probably have thought long over what should be their attitude. But Britain had declared war on a Fascist state, which completely rejected all the principles of democracy (bourgeois as well) and was applying a policy of the most bestial racialism. Thereby the choice for Britain's overseas possessions was greatly simplified.

In effect, Australia and New Zealand declared war on Germany simultaneously with Britain on 3 September, and Canada on 10 September. In spite of apprehensions in London, the Union of South Africa also decided very quickly in favour of Britain. Before the war there was in power a Government of the Boer Nationalist Hertzog, which in many respects (especially on the racial question) sympathised with Hitlerite Germany. Hertzog therefore declared for a policy of neutrality in the war between Britain and Germany, but was defeated in Parliament. On 5 September he was replaced by the well-known Anglophile, Field-Marshal Smuts, whose Government declared war on Germany. Egypt and Iraq, which *de jure* were independent States, but in fact at that time were still British semi-colonies, did not venture to do the same, because the Fascists had a powerful 'Fifth Column' there: however, they none the less broke off diplomatic relations with Germany. In India Britain encountered certain difficulties, to which reference in more detail will be made below: but here too in the end all went off with comparative success.

The sole exception was Eire (the Irish Free State). The age-old hostility of the Irish to their British oppressors brought about the result that, already on 2 September 1939, Eire officially declared its neutrality in the war between Britain and Germany. An extremely strange situation arose: even at the most critical moments of the war, when it was a question of Britain's life or death, there existed in Dublin, barely a hundred miles from the British shores, Fascist diplomatic missions—German, Italian and Japanese—which carried on large-scale espionage and diversion against London.

However, in one form or another, the formal mobilisation of the Empire against Hitlerite Germany was achieved in general at the very beginning of the war.

The international situation, too, was comparatively favourable for Britain and France. In the course of September and October 1939 the Scandinavian countries, Belgium, Holland, the States of the American continent, Iran and Siam declared their neutrality in the war which had begun. Their neutrality in most cases bore a friendly character, though out of fear of Germany they did not venture to demonstrate this too openly. Italy, Spain and Japan for the time being took up a position of neutrality—true, not friendly but one of temporising hostility—but still it was neutrality. The USSR also declared its neutrality.

Of great importance for Britain and France was the conduct of the United States of America. Here, however, they had nothing to fear. President Roosevelt before the war and during the war more than once publicly attacked the aggressive aspirations of the Fascist Powers and afforded Britain and France all the aid possible for a neutral State. The publication on 4 November 1939 of a new Neutrality Act, the essence of which will be set forth later, was particularly weighty in this regard.

Chamberlain needed also to show that he was doing something to prepare for military operations and for strengthening the armed forces. The broad mass of the people were after all in an anti-Fascist mood, and they expected practical steps by the Government to fight Germany. The Premier began with the easiest task of all. On 7 September General Gort was appointed Commander-in-Chief of the British Expeditionary Corps in France (although that Corps as yet did not yet exist), and General Ironside —militarily a complete mediocrity, but in return a furious opponent of the USSR—was appointed Chief of the General Staff. Samuel Hoare, one of the leading 'Munichites', became chairman of the special Defence Committee.

However, all these were generals without an army. An army was needed, but in creating it the Government displayed astonishing tardiness and sloth. A General Military Service Act had been adopted some time before the war (on 27 April 1939); but for all practical purposes it remained for a long time on paper. Now an order was issued that all men between the ages of eighteen and forty-one were subject to call-up, and in case of necessity could be transferred to any part of the world. Mobilisation also began. All this took place very slowly, just as though the Government was expecting that at any moment those called up would not be required and could be sent home. It is sufficient to say that even young men of twenty-four were requested to attend the calling-up centres only in March 1940, i.e. six months after the outbreak of war.

Certain measures of a military character were also taken in internal affairs. A blackout at night was introduced. The Government was given powers to issue war loans. Trade with enemy countries was prohibited, and a postal censorship for overseas services established. Rationing of foodstuffs began, starting with bacon and butter. A special committee of representatives of the trade unions and employers' organisations, under the chairmanship of the Minister of Labour, was set up for the purpose of 'advising the Government on questions affecting both sides'. The evacuation of women and children from large cities to rural areas was begun: it was considered that there they would be in greater safety in the event of German air raids. For treatment of the wounded 200,000 beds were got ready and 70,000 nurses trained.

Talk went on in Parliament about the necessity of putting industry on a war basis, but the reorganisation itself went on at a snail's pace, and with constant anxiety over the private interests of individual firms and concerns. Endless debates were aroused by the problem of whether it was necessary to set up a Ministry of Supply, but somehow no definite decision could be arrived at. All the activities of the Government bore the stamp of extreme hesitation, half-heartedness, unwillingness to introduce any serious changes in the traditionally established pattern of things. And this was not surprising: the spirit of 'business as usual' predominant in ruling circles penetrated everywhere, and exercised its pernicious influence on everything.

As regards the Western Front, a real farce continued there. The newspapers daily reported 'patrol actions', 'contacts between reconnaissance parties', 'encounters between scouts', and small 'exchanges of artillery fire' in which there were hardly any victims. On 22 December 1939 Daladier proudly announced in the Chamber that the total losses of France during the first four months of the war amounted to only 1,500 men! He added that this was to be explained by the existence of the 'Maginot Line'. After all, in the first world war France in the same period had lost

450,000 men! Of course the reason was not the 'Maginot Line'. The reason was that in 1939 France was carrying on a 'phoney war', i.e. was not willing to carry on any war at all against Hitlerite Germany.

The British, who by the middle of October had landed an expeditionary corps numbering about 160,000 men in France, were naturally following the example of their French allies, and also doing nothing at the front. Their losses were insignificant. There was no air war either from one side or the other. The Germans were 'mysteriously' silent. Many explained their behaviour by their worry about the USA. It is possible that this played a certain part, but the main cause was another. As we now know, Hitler had already, in October 1939, issued his directive for preparation of an attack on the Western countries (the so-called Plan Yellow); from January 1940 onwards this preparation became really serious, and the Germans naturally had no reason to dissipate their energies before the moment of attack. It was important also to lull the vigilance of their adversary, in order to preserve the element of surprise when the attack came.

The war at sea went on somewhat more actively. But in the first stages the British were clearly unfortunate. True, in a short time they managed to put an end to German shipping on the high seas: but in revenge the Hitlerites succeeded during the first four months of the war in sinking British and allied vessels with a total tonnage of 810,000, and in addition during that period inflicted two shrewd blows on Britain's naval pride.

The first blow was the following: on 14 October a German submarine, displaying unusual skill and courage, penetrated into the principal British naval base at Scapa Flow, and sank the battleship *Royal Oak* (29,000 tons) which was lying at anchor there. There was a terrible scandal. Churchill, as First Lord of Admiralty, had to live through some very unpleasant days: but then the necessary steps were taken to avert anything similar for the future.

The second blow was of a somewhat different character. At the end of August 1939, on the very eve of the war, the German pocket battleship *Admiral Graf Spee* secretly left Wilhelmshafen and proceeded to the Southern Atlantic, with instructions to develop a piratical campaign against British commercial vessels directly war began between Britain and Germany. Hitler was evidently inspired by the example of the famous German raiders of the first world war, the *Goeben* and the *Breslau*, and now wanted to repeat the same operation. Over the period from September to December 1939 the German pirate succeeded in sinking ships totalling about 60,000 tons, but then a British cruiser squadron was sent out after him. There followed a prolonged and not very skilful chase of the *Admiral Graf Spee* by the British warships. In the end the British succeeded in inflicting some damage on the pocket battleship, and in driving it into the mouth of the River Plate, near Montevideo. However, the *Admiral Graf Spee* did not surrender to its enemy, but was blown up by its crew on 17 December 1939. The German pirate perished, but not at all in any way which could give British sailors a sense of pride and satisfaction.

On 27 November 1939 I made the following entry in my diary:

'When you look at Britain at the present day, you can't help getting the impression of a powerful and vigorous man dressed in a semi-military uniform and equipped with extremely primitive weapons. He is energetically marking time, and trying to throw out his chest like a champion. It seems as though he is bursting to go into the attack: but in reality he desperately doesn't want to fight, and is only waiting for the first suitable occasion to throw off this unusual disguise, put on a dressing gown and sit down by the fire to read the evening paper . . . Oh no! there's no smell of a warlike spirit in Britain today. In the ruling group, because with very few exceptions it is still seeking an agreement with Hitler against the USSR: among the masses, because they have still not grasped the situation and are waiting for events to develop. Many believe that the war will soon be over. And perhaps the most obvious evidence that there is nevertheless a war on is the nets of the barrage balloons, hanging night and day in the London sky since 3 September to prevent dive-bombing by German planes which have not yet appeared, but which are awaited—or which people make a show of awaiting.'

3

Political Twilight

WHEN I recall the early months of the war, and the moods then prevalent in Britain, I involuntarily think of the expression: political twilight—a twilight in which all things and events assumed a kind of unclear, floating, indeterminate outline.

I will begin with the Government. I was aware that within the Cabinet there was not complete unity of views on the character of the war and its further development. True, the overwhelming majority of the Ministers followed Chamberlain, but there was a minority very critical in its attitude to the Prime Minister. This minority formally consisted of two persons, Churchill and Eden, but to a greater or lesser extent it attracted some other Ministers, who would not openly attack Chamberlain, but found much that was negative in his policy, and much that was positive in the policy of Churchill. Among them were such men as Walter Elliot, the Minister of Health, Leslie Hore-Belisha, the War Minister, de la Warr, President of the Board of Education, and one or two more. A struggle went on between the two groups, and although as yet Chamberlain unquestionably was master of the situation, the future could not be guaranteed in the circumstances of wartime. In fact, as will soon appear, Chamberlain's authority fell sharply in the spring of 1940, while the role of Churchill rose to a high degree.

Chamberlain considered that Hitler did not wish seriously to fight Britain, and that Britain had no reason seriously to fight Germany, while all that was going on in the West after the defeat of Poland was no more than reciprocal manoeuvring in order to occupy the most advantageous positions possible for concluding a 'reasonable compromise' between the two sides. This could be seen from all the actions of the Government, and it slipped out even in the open speeches of Chamberlain himself and of Foreign Secretary Halifax. Thus, in a broadcast on 7 November 1939 Halifax defined Britain's war aims in the following terms:

'We are fighting in defence of freedom; we are fighting for peace; we are meeting a challenge to our own security and that of others; we are defending the rights of all nations to live their own lives. We are fighting against the substitution of brute force for law as the arbiter between nations, against the violation of the sanctity of treaties and disregard for the pledged word.'

In just the same way the Prime Minister himself, in a broadcast on 26 November which dealt with the aims pursued by Britain in this war, declared:

'Our desire . . . would be to establish a new Europe; not new in the sense of tearing up all the old frontier posts and redrawing the map according to the ideas of the victors, but a Europe with a new spirit in which the nations which inhabit it will approach their difficulties with good will and mutual tolerance.'

All these were general phrases and fine words which opened up the possibility for the most differing interpretations, and did not in any way prevent the conclusion of peace with Germany. Fairness requires it to be said that now, after so many disappointments, even Chamberlain was not inclined to believe in the stability of agreements signed with Hitler. Therefore more than once he said in his speeches that peace was impossible, so long as Hitler remained in power in Germany. But already many indications led me at that time to the conclusion that Chamberlain was least of all thinking of overthrowing Hitler by force of arms, but was seeking other ways, much more akin to his spirit, for achieving his object, i.e. for the conclusion of a 'reasonable compromise' between Britain and Germany. Today we have irrefutable proofs that the suspicions we entertained at the end of 1939 were justified. Chamberlain's biographer Keith Feiling reproduces these words of the Prime Minister at the time to which I refer:

'What I hope for is not a military victory—I very much doubt the feasibility of that—but a collapse of the German home front. For that it is necessary to convince the Germans that they cannot win.'[1]

The best means for achieving this, Chamberlain considered, was

1. *Life of Neville Chamberlain* (Macmillan, 1946), p. 418.

the blockade of Germany, and he supposed that the desired effect would become apparent by the spring of 1940. Chamberlain dreamed of the 'extremists', headed by Hitler, being removed under the influence of the blockade and replaced by more 'moderate' elements (in other words, by the German generals), with whom it would be possible to agree on a peace based on a 'reasonable compromise'. Chamberlain was convinced that in Germany too such moods were powerful, and that therefore there was no need to expect the development of a real war in the West. Very curious evidence on this is supplied by Field-Marshal Montgomery. He tells the following in his memoirs:

'I well remember the visit of Neville Chamberlain to my division' (which was then in France. I.M.); 'it was on the 16th December 1939. He took me aside after lunch and said in a low tone so that no one could hear: "I don't think the Germans have any intention of attacking us. Do you?"'[1]

That was the conception which the men of the Cliveden Set took as their point of departure in their anticipations of the immediate future—and it was they who determined British policy in the first months of the war!

The other group within the Government, the Churchill group, looked at things much more realistically and correctly. Thus, in a broadcast on 12 November 1939, Churchill bluntly stated:

'No one in the British Isles supposed this was going to be a short or easy war.'[2]

'No one in the British Isles' . . . This was an obvious exaggeration, or the tribute of politeness to the Prime Minister which Churchill was bound to pay, in view of his position as a member of the Cabinet.

In conversation with me on 6 October Churchill expressed himself much more frankly.

'Chamberlain', he said, 'still thinks he can go for a ride on the tiger or on his successors . . . That's nonsense! . . . And all Neville's hopes of finishing the war by the spring are stupid too . . . The war will be long and cruel. In the not distant future Britain will have to fight for her life . . . There can be no "reasonable compromises" with Germany.'

I was also deeply impressed by a conversation with War Minister Hore-Belisha which took place at the beginning of

1. *Memoirs of F.M. The Viscount Montgomery of Alamein* (Collins, 1958), p. 58.
2. *Times*, 13 November 1939.

November 1939. My relations with him were somewhat peculiar. Being a Liberal National, part of the group headed by Simon, Hore-Belisha avoided visiting the Soviet Embassy. But whenever we met in some neutral spot he willingly talked with me, and did not restrain himself in assessing things and people that he did not like. Hore-Belisha was a clever man, one of great initiative, and that was just why he was not very well liked by the Cliveden set. On that occasion I met him at a diplomatic reception and asked what he thought of the prospects of the war. Hore-Belisha made an irritable gesture, as though beating off a persistent fly, and took me aside. He said:

'The prospects of the war? . . . As yet I see nothing favourable ahead . . . We're always too late, too hopelessly late . . . Look, we now announce with pride that Britain and the Empire have a million men under arms; first of all, that's not enough, and secondly it's late . . . We should have had a million under arms two years ago, then we should have had by now a trained army of a million men: while now all we have are a million untrained recruits . . . Could they stand up against the German army?'

Hore-Belisha stopped for a moment, and then went on bitterly:

'We are being governed by old men, who don't understand the situation and the needs of the time. What is the Government doing? Writing various papers which nobody needs! The Prime Minister assures us that there will be no war, and that by the spring we shall be signing peace with Germany . . . What nonsense! We are faced with the greatest test in our history, we ought to be most urgently mobilising all fit men, replacing the men in industry by women, and generally preparing for a long and painful war—but the Government won't hear of it. They say: "Don't let's provoke Hitler" . . . But I feel in my bones that Hitler will present us with a terrible surprise, and in not so distant a future either.'

Hore-Belisha was a lively character, and there was much truth in his words. But just because of that he did not suit Chamberlain's Government, and on 5 January 1940 was forced to resign.

However, all these arguments and differences about the further course of the war bore a somewhat unreal character, because there was one other very important factor in the game—Hitlerite Germany. What were her plans and intentions? Yes, at present she was silent, and displaying astonishing passivity at the front. But was this a serious policy, or a military stratagem? No one could reply with exactness to this question, and therefore both

Chamberlain's hopes and Churchill's anticipations remained for the time being only misty accumulations of contradictory ideas.

Opinions outside the Government were also imbued with twilight colours. The Labour leaders were displaying no independence or originality. In essence, they were simply dragging at the tail of the Government, confining their criticism to particular questions and petty details. On 8 November 1939 the Labour Party leader, Clement Attlee, put forward a programme of Labour's war aims at a meeting of the Parliamentary Labour Party. In all essentials it coincided with what Chamberlain and Halifax were saying on the same subject, with one difference: Attlee demanded 'abolition of imperialism' and 'equal rights for all nations in access to markets and sources of raw material'. Attlee, however, did not say how this could be achieved, while the whole past of the Labour Party made one suppose that the demand quoted was only a piece of demagogy, intended to calm to some extent the excitement among the workers.

They were indeed excited, and at the same time confused. Ordinary people—those whom the British call 'the man in the street'—are much more sincere and straightforward than high 'politicians'. When war was declared, they thought that war would really begin. I remember, on one occasion in October 1939, having a talk with the driver of a taxi who had brought me home. He was completely at a loss.

'What sort of a war is this?' he asked, with a gesture of helplessness. 'Last war there were big battles right at the start, the Germans invaded France and nearly got to Paris . . . But what's going on now?' He stopped for a moment, and then continued: 'My son has gone into the army, and says there's going to be a war . . . Others say that there won't be any war; the soldiers will be at the front up to the spring, and then will come home . . . What's your guess?'

On another occasion I went in to a democratic Lyons restaurant for a cup of coffee. The waitress, a young girl, proved talkative, and told me all about her 'dilemma'. She had a young man, and they intended to get married soon.

'Directly everything is ready', she added confidentially, '—but we haven't bought all the furniture yet . . .'

In Britain it's the custom (even among the workers) to marry only when all the 'outfit' for the family nest has been acquired, up to the table napkins and the handkerchiefs.

'We reckoned on buying everything by next spring, and now there's a war and my Jimmy has been called up . . . So we don't know what to do . . . Jimmy says: "Let's get married now, even if everything is not ready . . . If anything happens to me at the war, at least you'll get a pension" . . . And I tell him: "Well, but there's a lot we have to buy yet . . . Let's wait . . . Everybody says there won't be any war" . . . So we go on arguing about it . . . What do you think, will there be a war or not?'

From local Labour parties and trade unions news began to reach me that there was confusion among the workers too. As a matter of fact, from the end of October some trades councils (at Glasgow, Edinburgh, Aberdeen, Birmingham, etc.) began adopting anti-war resolutions but they were, all the same, exceptions. In the main the mass of the workers 'were silent' and, like the Lyons waitress, were wondering whether there would be a war or no.

The dominant mood in the country was one which very much resembled a state of surprise. In his speech of 26 November Chamberlain had frankly admitted that so far the war was very little like what had been expected. And my old acquaintance Walter Elliot, the Minister of Health, whom I had got to know many years before at the house of Bernard Shaw, explained this phrase of the Prime Minister in the following way.

'Many thought', he said over a cup of tea, 'that Hitler would immediately fall on France, yet he is still keeping quiet. Many thought that the Germans would immediately begin bombing our cities, yet so far there's not been a single German plane over London . . . On Hitler's part this may be a trick, but possibly it is not a trick. I don't exclude the possibility that he is hoping to create a united capitalist front against your country . . .'

I smiled, and Elliot hastened to add:

'Of course we wouldn't accept that, but Hitler may be cherishing illusions . . . you know his attitude to communism.'

I replied: 'You personally, Mr. Elliot, maybe won't agree to a united front with Hitler against the USSR, but don't go bail for your Prime Minister.'

Elliot began saying something about the force of public opinion which would never tolerate an alliance between Britain and Hitlerite Germany: but I interrupted him to ask how matters stood with the mobilisation of the British forces for war.

He replied that here, too, 'things have turned out better than we have hoped for . . . First and foremost, the Government has succeeded in building up a united national front within the country: the Liberals and Labour men are supporting it. Of course, among the Labour M.P.s there is a small group of pacifists like Lansbury, who are against the war and for peace at any price, but their influence is insignificant. Besides, the Government has managed to get the Empire on its side'. And Elliot briefly repeated what I knew already about the reaction of the Dominions and colonies to Britain's declaration of war on Hitlerite Germany.

'And last but not least', continued Elliot, 'during the first three months of the war our international position has become considerably stronger.' He gave me a quizzical glance, and added: 'Without wishing to, you've rendered us a good service.'

'What do you mean?' I asked.

'Well, you see' explained Elliot, 'your pact of non-aggression with Germany has aroused some dissension between Germany on the one hand and Italy, Spain and Japan on the other. It's strengthened the inclinations of Mussolini and Franco to maintain neutrality in the war for the time being, and consequently our communications through the Mediterranean with India and the other British possessions in the East are so far secure. It's become easier for us in the Far East as well . . . It's an ill wind that blows nobody any good! Then as you know the French and ourselves signed in October a pact of mutual assistance with Turkey: that assures us, apart from anything else, at least the friendly neutrality if not the support of the whole Moslem world in North Africa, the Near East and India . . . Now the USA have just adopted the new Neutrality Act.[1] Vast opportunities are now opening for acquiring arms and ammunition from America. Roosevelt has become our unspoken ally . . . Oh yes, our situation today is much stronger than it was three months ago.'

Almost rubbing his hands with satisfaction, Elliot gave me to understand that the neutrality of the USSR was also a positive

1. In 1935 the USA adopted a Neutrality Act under which neither the US Administration nor American private firms could sell arms to countries which were at war. No distinction was made between aggressors and the victims of aggression. Thus, when for example Italy attacked Ethiopia immediately after the adoption of this Act, the USA refused to sell arms to Ethiopia. But on 4 November 1939, after the second world war had begun, the US Congress adopted a new Act, under which both the government and private firms were entitled to sell arms to belligerent countries, on condition however that payment was made in cash and the arms were transported not on American vessels but on the purchaser's ships. This Act in common parlance received the title of 'Cash and Carry'. It had in mind, first and foremost, the supplying of American arms to Britain and France.

factor from the British point of view. It made the international situation much more healthy.

Elliot was right in underlining a certain reinforcement of Britain's position towards the close of the third month of war. It was just this that explained the negative attitude of the British Government to Hitler's 'peace offensive' which opened after the defeat of Poland, and also to the attempts at mediation undertaken by the King of the Belgians and the Dutch Queen in November 1939. In British ruling circles there was no group similar to that of Laval, Bonnet and others which existed in France, and which was demanding immediate peace on any terms. The British Government wanted peace on the basis of a 'reasonable compromise', and therefore thought it necessary for the time being to manoeuvre—all the more because a number of internal and external factors made that possible.

And one thing more. The British Government at that time pinned great hopes to the time factor. Even the 'Clivedenites' argued approximately in this way: the resources of the British Empire and France were immeasurably greater than those of Germany, but the Germans had entered the war with their resources already mobilised, while Britain and France had not yet had time to do this. Britain and France needed a certain period of time to bring their forces and resources into a state of battle readiness: the longer the time they could take over this, the more decisive would be their advantage over Germany. Now when this advantage became quite unquestionable, the time would come to open negotiations with Germany for the purpose of reaching a 'reasonable compromise'; meanwhile they must wait, and squeeze the Third Reich more and more firmly with a ring of blockade and hunger. Did not blockade and hunger bring the Kaiser's empire to its knees at the end of the first world war?

In all these plans and calculations there was much *naïveté* and historical blindness—but then those were characteristic features of the 'Munichites', both before the war and during the war. Hence followed the profound conviction of Chamberlain that events would not go beyond the framework of a 'phoney war', and that by the spring of 1940 peace would be re-established in the West. Small but extremely characteristic symptoms of this confidence were the two following facts: at the end of December 1939 British troops in France were allowed leave to spend their Christmas at home, while in January 1940 many women and children previously evacuated to rural areas were allowed to return to London.

No, Chamberlain was not thinking at all of any serious development of the war. He did not expect any direct threat from Germany. His political blindness, which was the consequence in the long run of his hatred for the land of Socialism, was truly phenomenal. What took place in reality some three months later was a complete surprise for the British Prime Minister.

4

Britain and the USSR

THE general attitude of the rulers of Britain to the Soviet Union had always been hostile and negative since 1917. This was dictated by the class interests of her bourgeoisie, by the basic antagonism between capitalism and socialism. However, against this general background there were periods when under the influence of various factors, internal or external, there were temporary periods of thaw or freezing-up in Anglo-Soviet relations. Needless to say, the first were fewer than the second.

Within the ruling class itself there were two main groupings on the question of the attitude to the USSR. One regarded the USSR as its principal enemy, and put up with difficulty even with coldly formal relations between the two countries. The other, although in principle no less hostile, displayed more elasticity and was ready to co-operate with the USSR in the sphere of trade. The first grouping, headed in the thirties by Neville Chamberlain, was much more numerous and influential than the second, the leaders of which were Churchill and Lloyd George. However, external circumstances sometimes brought about a situation in which the first grouping was obliged to take serious account of the second.

The winter of 1939–40 was of a very stormy character in Anglo-Soviet relations. It was distinguished by three waves of anti-Soviet fury, separated by small intervals of calmer mood.

The first wave rose immediately after the conclusion of the Soviet-German pact of non-aggression on 23 August 1939. It was due to the extreme irritation of the ruling circles in Britain and France at the fact that they had emerged from the tripartite negotiations of 1939 for a pact of mutual assistance most ingloriously, for which Chamberlain and Daladier should have blamed only themselves.[1] Instead, they attacked the USSR, accusing it of a 'double game' and of 'insincerity'. In essence, there lay at the foundation of the anti-Soviet campaign which then broke out the resentment of the Western politicians at Soviet diplomacy having proved more sensible than that of Britain and France, and at the USSR as a result not having fallen into the pit which they had been digging for it. The then Under-Secretary for Foreign Affairs, R. A. Butler, to whom I shall have later to refer a good deal, on one occasion gave me a fairly transparent hint of this. However, the first anti-Soviet wave subsided very quickly, because on 1 September, exactly a week later, the second world war began, and both the British and French Governments had to turn their attention to very different affairs. One of the consequences of the first campaign was the cancellation by British firms of Soviet orders for machine tools, machinery and equipment which had been placed in Britain long before the war, but which still had not yet been completed by British works. All the firms had one and the same excuse: 'There's a war on, and now we need all this ourselves.' There could be no doubt that the Government was behind the firms in this respect.

The second and now much higher, wave arose after the Soviet forces on 17 September 1939 had crossed the Polish frontier in order to save the working people of Western Ukraine and Western Belorussia from the threat of German occupation. In the press, on the BBC, in Parliament, from the church pulpit there were outcries about a 'stab in the back' for the Poles, about a new 'partition of Poland' between Germany and Russia, about the 'perfidy' of the Bolsheviks and so forth. However the second wave, too, did not roar for long: substantially it had subsided by 1 October. A striking symptom of this was a broadcast by Churchill on that very day. Touching on events in Eastern Europe, Churchill said: 'Russia has pursued a cold policy of self-interest . . . That the Russian armies should stand on this line was clearly necessary for the safety of Russia against the Nazi menace. At any rate, the line is there, and an Eastern front has been created which Nazi Germany does not dare assail.'

After hearing Churchill's speech, I came to the conclusion that somewhat different breezes, more favourable for the USSR, were evidently blowing in the British political atmosphere. I wished to

1. See the present writer's *Who Helped Hitler?*

test this, and I telephoned to Churchill. For several years before the war we had maintained a good acquaintance, but from the moment of his entry into Chamberlain's Cabinet in September 1939 I refrained from attempts to see him, not knowing how my initiative would be received. Now Churchill responded to my telephone call in an extremely friendly fashion, and invited me to call at the Admiralty where, as First Lord, he had his official residence. I remember that meeting very well.

When, about 5 p.m. on 6 October, I found myself before the vast and ponderous building of the Admiralty, there was a thick fog in the streets of London, one in which street lighting was quenched and the shades of night fell fast. Churchill received me in his ministerial office. At first the conversation bore a light and semi-social character. Then Churchill went on to memories which were bound up with that very study in which we were sitting. It was exactly a quarter of a century ago, during the first world war, that he had sat in this room, also as First Lord, and he had even left here some 'relics', preserved up to that day. Here Churchill rose, went up to the wall behind his armchair at the desk (we were talking in another corner of the study, sitting on a settee) and threw open the wooden panels. Behind them was a large naval chart with various marks and symbols.

'It was on this chart that I used then to follow the movements of the German fleet', remarked Churchill.

Then the conversation proceeded to more serious subjects. Churchill expressed his regret that our countries were now not together engaged in struggle against Hitlerite Germany. I replied that, as he well knew, this was not our fault. and that the responsibility for this lay on the Prime Minister of the Government in which he was now participating.

'I know, I know,' hastily said Churchill, 'but it's not worth while recalling the past... All that is a stage that is over.'[1]

Churchill continued:

'Today we must think not of the past but of the future.'

And then he began to set forth his own views to me. The differences between Britain and the USSR were a melancholy misunderstanding. In substance, the interests of Britain and the USSR at the present time coincided. The USSR could not desire

1. During the tripartite negotiations of 1939 Churchill energetically supported the idea of a pact of mutual assistance between the USSR, Britain and France and combated the sabotage of such a pact by Chamberlain and Daladier.

the strengthening of Hitlerite Germany, its annexation of the Baltic seaboard, or its entry into the Balkans and the Black Sea. This would contradict the interests of the security of the Soviet Union, and the whole past history of the struggle between Slavs and Teutons. But Britain and France likewise could not suffer Hitler to seize Rumania, Yugoslavia, Bulgaria and particularly Turkey. Thus there was a community of very important interests between the Soviet Union, Britain and France. Yes, at the present time on account of Chamberlain's mistakes last summer, Russia and the Anglo-French bloc were at variance; but he, Churchill, was certain that in the further course of the war they would meet once more, and would carry on a common struggle with Nazi Germany. For that very reason Churchill was opposing in every possible way the inflaming of anti-Soviet passions in British political quarters, and was recommending the 'Ministers of the Crown' to keep cool heads and follow the dictates of 'common sense'. In particular he, Churchill, had recently been demonstrating to some of his cabinet colleagues that Britain should not object to the setting up of Soviet military and naval bases on the Baltic. Such bases were directed against Germany, and could only be useful from the point of view of British interests.

My position during this conversation was a very delicate one. I was a supporter of the German-Soviet pact because in the situation which had been created I saw no other way out for the USSR: but I considered this pact a bitter necessity imposed on us by the criminally stupid policy of Chamberlain and Daladier. I also did not believe in the durability and stability of the agreement with Germany. I considered that we should be constantly on our guard, and should not exclude the later possibility of a rupture with Germany and an alliance with Britain and France. Of course I could not develop all these considerations before Churchill, and therefore, after listening to the warm monologue of the First Lord, I cautiously replied:

'I won't venture to judge what may happen in the more or less distant future. Time will show. At present, however, I am quite satisfied with the fact that the USSR has taken up the position of a neutral Power and may therefore stand aside from all the horrors of war.'

Churchill smiled and said, not without a note of sarcasm: 'Oh yes, time will show.'

After this meeting with Churchill, I became during October and

November something like a rich bride with many suitors. The ring of cold hostility which had encompassed our Embassy after the entry of Soviet troops into Poland broke up and gradually disappeared. I began to be invited everywhere, and people of the most varied views and conditions sought contact with me. During some seven weeks I met Halifax, Eden, Churchill (once more), Butler, Elliot, Stanley and other members of the Government. All of them gave me to understand that the past was a closed book, that a new page in Anglo-Soviet relations should be opened and that there should be an effort to improve them as rapidly as possible. Speaking in the House of Lords on 26 October, Halifax now quite officially, on behalf of the Government, declared that one must see the difference between the actions of Germany and the USSR in Poland, and that the new Western frontier of the USSR coincided with the 'Curzon Line'. At the same time Stanley, President of the Board of Trade, made us a proposal for commercial exchanges in 1940, and hinted that he was ready to go to Moscow to conclude an appropriate agreement. Soundings were made of me as to whether Britain ought not to recall her Ambassador Seeds from the USSR—as a person too closely connected with the tripartite negotiations of sad memory—and replace him by someone else more acceptable to the Soviet Government.

What aroused this change of attitude towards the USSR?

It was founded on the desire to isolate Germany to the maximum, weaken her and thereby facilitate the conclusion with her of a peace based on 'reasonable compromise'.

In this respect the British Government had a minimum and a maximum programme.

The minimum programme was that the USSR for the duration of the war should observe *simple neutrality*, taking up the same attitude to both sides in the conflict.

The maximum programme was that Soviet neutrality should be gradually transformed into *neutrality friendly to Britain and France* like the neutrality of the USA, which in effect recalled something like slightly veiled military co-operation.

There were people (among them Churchill) who thought it conceivable that the USSR might even be transformed into an ally of Britain and France, but these were a comparatively rare exception in the first months of the war.

Such was the real background of that unexpected attention of which I became the object in October and November 1939.

In connection with the events of these two months there necessarily arises in my memory the figure of Stafford Cripps, and it will not be out of place to characterise this interesting man here, even if briefly.

The son of Lord Parmoor, an outstanding lawyer and politician who at the end of his life became a member of the first Labour Government, Stafford Cripps went through a public school and became at an early age one of the most brilliant advocates in Great Britain. Like his father, he joined the Labour Party, which got him elected to Parliament. But in his character Cripps did not resemble the typical Labour man, closely linked with the trade unions and valuing higher than anything else the peaceful channel of the 'happy mean'. Perhaps because Cripps came from intellectual circles and was a widely cultivated man, there was always something original in him, which would not fit into the framework of the standard and the commonplace. He had his own views on many questions of ideology and current politics, which often drew him into quarrels with the official leadership of the party and made his career a stormy and interrupted one. Cripps's name was widely known far beyond the bounds of his own party: he undoubtedly was a 'national' figure and, even when later expelled from his party, managed to occupy 'national' posts—thanks, in the main, to his own authority as a public figure.

When at the beginning of the thirties I made the acquaintance of Cripps, he immediately made a deep impression on me. Tall and thin, with a long face and lively sharp eyes, Cripps was a most strict vegetarian and consumed only certain vegetables and nuts. He ate nothing that was boiled. It was always a puzzle for my wife how to feed Cripps when he used to come to lunch with us. He spoke willingly and interestingly. It was not only pleasant but useful to listen to him, because the breadth of his information and connections was vast. This, however, did not exclude a considerable muddle in his head.

Cripps presented himself to me as a left-wing Socialist but not a Marxist. In questions of current policy he really did follow a leftward course, and the best proof of this was that he was a warm supporter of the united front of all left-wing forces, including the Communists. For the orthodox Labour leaders such views were equivalent to mortal sin, and it was just because of this Cripps had been expelled from the Labour Party not long before the war. Another vivid proof of his left-wing opinions was his extremely friendly attitude to the Soviet Union. He demonstrated this in practice in 1933, in connection with the Anglo-Soviet conflict after the so-called 'Metro-Vickers case', which led to the temporary rupture of economic relations between Britain and the USSR.[1] At the same time Cripps was inspired by an ideology which could only be described as Christian Socialism. He said on one occasion to me that a strong religious instinct was alive among the mass of the workers, and that it should be made use of in the interests of Socialism. In Cripps's opinion this was quite possible, since the strivings and actions of primitive Christianity contained much that was Socialist and even Communist. For this reason Cripps maintained close links with the more left circles of British churchmen (there were and are such), and sometimes himself spoke from the pulpit, calling on the masses to bring about a true 'Kingdom of God' on earth. Cripps and I formed very good personal relations: he was often at our Embassy, I sometimes visited him in the small country house belonging to his family, and we always had most interesting conversations, often sharpened with ideological polemics, but never leading to mutual estrangement.

During the days of October-November 1939 which I have described, Cripps took an active part in the attempts to improve relations between Britain and the USSR. One must say frankly that

1. In March 1933, when negotiations for the conclusion of a new trade agreement between the USSR and Britain were at their height, six British engineers from the firm of Metropolitan-Vickers, working in the USSR under a technical assistance agreement with that firm, were arrested in Moscow on a charge of espionage and wrecking. All of them were sent for trial. The British Government demanded their immediate liberation without investigation or trial, asserting without the slightest evidence that the engineers were entirely guiltless. This was direct intervention in the internal affairs of the USSR, and produced a sharp rebuff by the Soviet Government. In its effort to exercise pressure on the USSR, the British Government demonstratively interrupted the trade negotiations, and introduced a Bill into Parliament giving it the right, should the Soviet Government refuse to carry out the British demands, to impose an embargo on Soviet imports into Britain. The Labour Party opposed this Bill, and their main speaker on this question was Cripps. Nevertheless the Bill was adopted by the Conservative majority of the House of Commons. Despite all the efforts and threats by the British Government, the six engineers were tried, and the Court sentence on 18 April 1933 sent two of them to prison for two and three years, expelled three from the USSR, and acquitted one. The following day, 19 April, the British Government prohibited the importation of Soviet goods into Britain. The USSR replied by imposing an embargo on the importation of British goods into the Soviet Union. A commercial war began between the two countries, and continued for over two months. Finally the conflict was settled on 1 July 1933 by negotiations between M. M. Litvinov, at that time People's Commissar for Foreign Affairs, and the British Government during the World Economic Conference in London, in the summer of 1933.

he did not like everything in our actions at that time. He was shocked, for example, by the German-Soviet non-aggression pact, though in conversation with me he recognised that it was inevitable and legitimate in the situation created by the Anglo-French sabotage of the tripartite negotiations. He did not like the establishment of Soviet military bases in the Baltic States, which was taking place just at that time. But I could not notice any essential difference, as compared with the past, in his general attitude to the Soviet Union and in his striving to promote co-operation between Britain and the USSR, both in the economic and in the political spheres. Possibly that striving had grown even stronger under the influence of wartime considerations. Cripps understood very well that the agreement between the USSR and Hitlerite Germany could be only provisional, and that in the further course of the war the USSR and Britain might find themselves in the same camp. As a true Englishman, Cripps considered that the best lubricant in relations between countries is trade, and therefore was now making great efforts for its restoration, after the *de facto* rupture caused by the outbreak of war. Cripps turned out to have personal connections with the President of the Board of Trade, Stanley. This made it easier for him to mediate to a certain extent in this question between the British Government and the Soviet Embassy.

But Cripps was not able for long to occupy himself with the problem of improving Anglo-Soviet relations. Just at this time the British Government entrusted him with another important undertaking. With the outbreak of war the situation in India, Britain's most important colony at that time, became very complicated. The question arose in all its acuteness, whether India would or would not support Britain in the war against Hitlerite Germany?

In those days India in the main was divided into two parts: the provinces governed by the British Crown and the possessions of the individual Indian Princes. All the Princes immediately promised Britain their support. But in the provinces which had a certain measure of self-government, under the constitution of 1935, very much depended on the attitude of the main political party of the country—the Indian National Congress, then headed by Gandhi and Nehru. That party laid down as a condition for co-operating with Britain in the war the recognition of the principle of independence of India. The British Government did not wish to accept such a condition, and was seeking for some less radical solution. On 26 October 1939 there was a big debate in Parliament about the present and future condition of India, and Cripps spoke in the course of it. He demanded the urgent establishment of an All-India Parliament, and the formation by it of a central government which would act in wartime as the Viceroy's Executive Council. Furthermore India should be promised complete self-determination after the war.

In November 1939 the situation in India became more acute. The Indian National Congress, as a sign of its refusal to co-operate with Britain, recalled its Governments then existing in several of the provinces. The watchword of civil disobedience was in the air. Gandhi thought that even more resolute action was possible. The British Government was very perturbed, and was seeking for some means of reducing the tension in India: and the War Cabinet decided to make use of Cripps for this purpose. Shortly before this, as I mentioned earlier, he had been expelled from the Labour Party and thus was an 'independent'. At the same time, he was a 'left-winger'. He was also a 'national' figure. All this made Cripps a very suitable emissary to India for negotiations with the National Congress. The Cabinet took its decision accordingly. It had fairly weighty justification. But why did Cripps agree to accept the proposal of the Cabinet? He explained it to me in the following way:

'The present war is a war against German Nazism, and my duty as a Socialist is to support it. For the successful prosecution of the war the unity of the British Empire is essential during the war period. The attitude of India is particularly important. We should come to an understanding with her. It is easier for me to do this than for the Viceroy with all his staff. However, I don't intend to suggest the maintenance of the *status quo* up to the end of the war. The British Government should even now meet to the maximum the national demands of India. And I want to try and work out with the leaders of the Indian National Congress a platform which would make it possible for India and Britain to join forces against Hitler.'

It was clear to me that Cripps' mission was of an essentially imperialist character, and I gave him to understand my opinion in general terms: but it seemed to me not tactful at that moment to dwell too deeply on this theme.

Cripps left for India and, although a description of his activity there is not within the scope of my narrative, I can say briefly that he spent several months in India, had prolonged negotiations with the leadership of the Indian National Congress, worked out various plans for its temporary reconciliation with the British Government, but in the end failed to find any compromise acceptable to both sides.

I return, however, to my struggle in London for the improvement of Anglo-Soviet relations.

From the end of November there began to be noticeable a 'disillusionment' in Government circles as regards that policy of 'taming' the USSR which had been carried on during the preceding two months. The politicians in London had evidently calculated that the Soviet Government at the first kindly smile on their part would immediately melt and throw itself on their neck. However the Soviet Government, which always pursued an independent policy and in addition remembered very well the behaviour of the British and French in the tripartite negotiations of 1939, maintained an attitude of tranquil anticipation. This aroused a certain irritation in London, and ever more frequently there began to be heard voices asserting that the USSR had adopted an obviously hostile attitude to the 'Western democracies', that it was obviously impossible to change that attitude, and that therefore it was better openly to admit the fact and draw the necessary practical conclusions from it. Undoubtedly there was no small element of bluff in this talk, aimed at psychologically 'intimidating' the USSR: but it is beyond doubt also that the talk was nourished by the profound hostility of the ruling circles of Britain to the Soviet Union, hostility which had in addition been greatly strengthened by the events of the past three months. The situation was becoming very explosive, and the first suitable pretext was sufficient for a new outbreak of the anti-Soviet campaign on a large scale. Such a pretext was the Soviet-Finnish war, which began on 30 November 1939.

5

An anti-Soviet storm

DURING the previous seven years of my work in London as Ambassador of the USSR I had lived through quite a number of anti-Soviet storms, but that which followed 30 November 1939 broke all records. The reasons for this were complex: but at bottom they sprang from the desire of the ruling British (and French) circles to 'switch' the war, i.e. to replace the war with Hitler which was so unpleasant for them by the much more attractive war with 'Soviet Communism'. In secret these leading quarters reckoned that if there were such a reorientation they would sooner or later succeed in making a united front with the Nazis, and with their common effort crush the 'Bolshevik revolution' which was causing the West such anxieties.

There were certain other circumstances, too, operating in the same direction. Finland was one of the main suppliers of timber to Great Britain, and was very popular there as a 'model democracy' of the Scandinavian type. This was to no small degree facilitated by the close links between the Finnish Social Democrats and the Labour Party, and likewise the participation of the Social-Democrats in some Finnish Governments in the pre-war years. There was some importance also in the fact that the extreme right-wing Finnish Social-Democrat, Vaino Tanner, for a number of years had been President of the International Co-operative Alliance.

Such was the terrain on which there blew up the storm connected with the Soviet-Finnish war.

The storm was begun by Chamberlain's speech on 30 November in Parliament, in which he made a violent attack on the USSR and supported Finland. No less violently did Halifax attack the USSR in the House of Lords on 5 December. At the same time Roosevelt proclaimed a 'moral embargo' of the Soviet Union, while ex-President Hoover even demanded that the American Ambassador should be recalled from Moscow. Then followed in the USA a noisy anti-Soviet campaign in the press, on the radio, and in the churches. This campaign afforded powerful support to the enemies of the USSR in Britain and France, and inspired them to undertake a number of actions with the objective of launching war against the Soviet Union.

It was precisely the influence of the USA that imbued Britain, France and the Latin American countries with the courage to organise the expulsion of the USSR from the League of Nations (14 December 1939). It was precisely the influence of the USA that encouraged Daladier at the Anglo-French Supreme Council on 19 December to propose a rupture of relations with the USSR, but this was not adopted because of opposition by the more cautious British. However, Chamberlain did not exclude the possibility of a rupture, he only preferred that it should take place in some other form, best of all on the initiative of the Soviet side. Chamberlain was even ready to help in such a course of events, as is attested by the following curious fact.

At the end of December it was announced that Seeds, the British Ambassador in Moscow, was going home 'on leave'. Immediately rumours began to circulate in political quarters that he would not return from his 'leave' to the USSR. At the same time information 'from reliable sources' began to appear in the British press to the effect that Ivan Maisky, the Soviet Ambassador in London, was being recalled and would soon leave the country. Some correspondents with time on their hands even asserted that they had seen the Ambassador's luggage being taken out of the Embassy and sent to the railway station. This obviously inspired fuss in the press was supplemented by reports spread in political circles that Maisky, 'disappointed' in the results of his work in Britain, himself did not wish to stay any longer in London and was striving to return home as soon as possible.

The Soviet Government interpreted the campaign which had begun in the following way: the British Government was preparing for a rupture of relations between the two countries, and this would be more easily effective if there were no Ambassadors in Moscow and London, and their place were taken by much less influential and authoritative chargés d'affaires. From this a practical conclusion was drawn: when at the beginning of January 1940 Seeds really did appear in London, and when the Foreign Office was waiting for the Soviet Government, out of considerations of 'prestige', to recall me to Moscow, it did nothing of the kind. To the great disappointment of the Foreign Office, I remained in London and made my contribution to the struggle against a rupture of relations between Britain and the USSR.

The anti-Soviet storm was not confined to purely official circles. It assumed a wider character. The Labour Party leaders played a particularly prominent part in this. In January 1940 they sent a special delegation to Finland, headed by Walter Citrine, secretary of the General Council of the TUC. On its return it published a report full of the most violent attacks on the Soviet Government.[1] Some of my Labour Party acquaintances at that time even stopped noticing me when we met. Léon Blum in France declared that help should be given to Finland at all costs, even if this should lead to war with the USSR. Quite understandably, the Socialist International and the Amsterdam Trade Union International vigorously attacked us.

It is hardly necessary to add that all the national press day by day hurled buckets of filth and slander at the Soviet Union, that an icy void came into existence around our Embassy, and that at many diplomatic receptions people avoided my wife and myself as they would the plague. Were it not for old personal connections built up in more favourable years—connections which made it possible for me even in this exceptionally hostile environment to learn something of what was going on—the position of the Soviet Embassy in London would have been very difficult.

The storm aroused by the Soviet-Finnish war had another aspect too. In hurling their anathemas at the USSR, the ruling groups in Britain and France strove in every possible way to support the Finnish reactionaries. Some hotheads demanded an immediate declaration of war on the Soviet Union. The British and French Governments energetically supplied the Finnish reactionaries with arms[2] and encouraged in their countries the recruiting of volunteers to fight on the Finnish side. Large-scale collections for

1. Sir Walter Citrine, K.B.E., *My Finnish Diary* (Penguin Books Ltd., 1940)

2. Information published after the end of the Soviet-Finnish war showed that Britain and France had sent Finland 405 planes, 960 guns, 5,224 machine guns and a large quantity of munitions.

the Finnish Red Cross, and for a fund in aid of the poor in Finland, went on. The British Queen demonstratively sent a subscription to this fund. Grippenberg, the Finnish Minister in London, became the hero of the hour: he was photographed, interviewed, invited to all kinds of receptions and in general given every possible assurance of sympathy and support.

Even more dangerous plans began to be formed in the minds of the British and French Ministers: they began to think of sending their own regular military units to help Finland under the guise of 'volunteers', and even made certain preparations in this direction. But such units could be sent, and supplies to them maintained, only over the territory of Norway and Sweden. The British and French Governments approached them with requests to this effect—but the requests were rejected. The Scandinavian countries had taken up an official attitude of neutrality (true, one extremely friendly to Finland) in respect of the Soviet-Finnish war, and did not wish to infringe it by such an act as permitting the transit of British and French troops through their territory. The British and French several times attempted to win them over, promising them aid in the event of any complications with the USSR or Germany, but were unsuccessful. The experience of Poland, which had just perished after Britain and France had given her their well-known guarantees, spoke too loudly for itself. Thus the military expedition planned in London and Paris did not take place.

Here it should be noted that during the Soviet-Finnish war France took up an even more aggressive attitude than Britain in relation to the USSR. The roots of such a state of mind in France went back to the time of the October Revolution, which had annulled the loans granted by the bankers of Paris to the Tsarist Government. The bankers could not forgive the Soviet Government for such 'sacrilege', and on every convenient occasion brought out their complaints in order to inflame an anti-Soviet atmosphere in France. Some part was also played by the difference between the British and French temperaments. In Paris politicians were fonder of noisy and dramatic gestures than their counterparts in London. All this found its expression in practical politics.

On 15 September 1939, twelve days after the beginning of the war with Germany, Daladier, who had been Premier before the war as well, formed a new Government vividly reactionary in hue. By 26 September this Government had prohibited the French Communist Party. On 9 February 1940 all the Communist deputies were expelled from Parliament, and at the beginning of April were sent to prison for four and five years, with loss of civil and political rights for five years after their release. At the same time there was let loose a frenzied anti-Communist and anti-Soviet campaign, in which a most active part was played by the leaders of the French Socialists and the General Confederation of Labour. On 8 February 1940 the Paris police raided the Soviet Trade Delegation in France, on 15 March the French Government declined to prolong the Franco-Soviet Trade Agreement on its expiry, and finally on 26 March, seizing on a petty and chance incident, the French Government proclaimed Y. Z. Suritz, the Soviet Ambassador in Paris, *persona non grata* and demanded his recall from France.

Not surprisingly, the Daladier Government during the Soviet-Finnish war sought in every possible way to sharpen the relations of Britain and France with the USSR and worked out the most adventurist plans for 'aiding' Finland. Among them was also a scheme (the details of which became known to us later) to arrange air attacks through Turkey and Iran on the oil wells at Baku. However, both these countries revealed no desire at all to be dragged into a war with the USSR, while cooler heads in Britain and France realised the military stupidity of such an operation. As a result, it did not take place, any more than the dispatch of British and French troops to Finland through Scandinavia. This exceptional impetuousness of the French somewhat shocked the British; but they took no effective action to moderate it, and therefore bear full responsibility for everything that then went on.

6

The USSR and Finland

THE entry of the Soviet Union into war with Finland was a step to which it was compelled. Alarmed at the anti-Soviet policy of the reactionary Government of Finland, and concerned for the security of its frontiers, the USSR strove to prevent the utilisation of Finland as a jumping-off ground for war against the USSR. In the course of 1938 and 1939 the Soviet Government repeatedly declared to the Government of Finland the urgent necessity of improving Soviet-Finnish relations and taking steps to reinforce the security both of the USSR and of Finland. Encouraged by the Western countries, including Fascist Germany, the ruling circles of Finland took up an irreconcilable position.

My purpose does not include a detailed account of events during the Soviet-Finnish war, with which I was not directly concerned: but there was one personal aspect which forced me to follow with particular attention everything that was going on in that part of Europe at the end of 1939 and the beginning of 1940.

In 1929–32 I was the Soviet plenipotentiary representative in Finland. It was a very difficult time in the history of Soviet-Finnish relations. The 'Lapua movement' (the Finnish variety of Fascism) was at the crest of its wave in Finland; hostile demonstrations used to be organised in front of the building of the Soviet Mission in Helsinki; there was a large-scale agitation for a 'Greater Finland', to include Leningrad and Karelia; the Lapuans wanted to kidnap me, as the Soviet representative, and deport me to remote forests; any attempt on the Soviet side to improve relations between the two countries was met at bayonet-point. The enemies of the USSR in the West, principally in Britain and

France, strove to make use of this unfavourable situation in their own interests, pouring oil on the bonfire of Finnish anti-Soviet passion.

During my years of work in Helsinki I more than once thought with a sigh: 'What a pity that anti-Soviet and anti-Russian feelings are running so high in Finland just now! If this people became our friend, it would be a true and reliable one. It would be worth while working for such an objective.' In spite of all complications and obstacles, I tried to promote such an outcome. Not many Finns at that time were inclined to talk on such subjects: but there were fortunate exceptions, among whom the most outstanding undoubtedly was Paasikivi, later the well-known President of the Finnish Republic. At that time he was director of one of the Finnish banks and a prominent leader of the Coalition Party, which was on the right flank of political life in the country. Nevertheless, unlike many other Finnish politicians, Paasikivi willingly maintained relations with the Soviet Mission. We often met and talked on various subjects, but particularly on the prospects of Soviet-Finnish relations.

My usual theme was that there were two real facts which no one could change: the first, that the USSR and Finland were neighbours, and the second that the USSR had 150 million inhabitants (the Soviet population about 1930), while Finland had 3·5 millions. Arising from these two facts, every effort must be made to promote good neighbourliness between the two countries. And this was not at all difficult. The USSR had no designs, and did not intend to have any, on the integrity and independence of Finland. All it wanted was that there should be normal political and economic relations between the two countries, that Finland should not serve as a wasps' nest which the imperialist enemies of the Soviet State could make use of at any moment for their own purposes. Moreover, if such normal relations existed, a large and profitable Soviet market would be opened to Finland, and its international status would become much stronger. Paasikivi shared my views, and himself more than once developed them, clothing them in concrete facts and possibilities. Yet towards the end he would make a helpless gesture and add:

'But you understand that in the present atmosphere there are very few who will take this point of view, and still less who would risk publicly expressing it . . . All the same, I will try and open the eyes of at any rate those few people who are capable of listening to the voice of common sense.'

And Paasikivi really did do this. Today, many years later, I reflect with great satisfaction that it was he who succeeded in playing such a great part in establishing good neighbourly relations between Finland and the USSR, relations about which one could only dream at that time.

But I return to depicting the course of events. By January 1940 there already began to appear a gradual change in the balance of forces at the front which was unfavourable for the Finnish reactionaries. At the same time the aid promised them from the West, in spite of all the anti-Soviet clamour which surrounded it, fell behind more and more. In these circumstances the Rüti-Tanner Government began unofficially to sound out the possibility of concluding peace with the USSR. In January the well-known Finnish writer Hella Vuolioki, who was always friendly to the idea of a Finnish-Soviet *rapprochement*, visited Stockholm and met Alexandra Kollontay, the Soviet Ambassador in Sweden; it was a question of the speediest restoration of peace between the two countries. On 23 February President Kallio of Finland approached the British and French Governments with a request to afford their assistance in putting an end to the Soviet-Finnish war.

Just at that time the Soviet Government took a step which greatly facilitated the fulfilment of this wish of the Finnish side.

Before recounting this, I should dwell for a moment on the personality of Richard Butler. A son of a high British official in India, he was born there and spent his early childhood in India. Then he had the customary public school education of boys of the ruling class, and passed through Cambridge. At the age of twenty-seven he became a Conservative M.P., and at thirty Under-Secretary for India. When we met in 1938, he was Under-Secretary of State at the Foreign Office, representing his Department in the House of Commons, since Halifax, as a member of the House of Lords, could only speak in the Upper House. This gave Butler an important status, since the House of Commons in Britain is regarded as more important than the House of Lords.

Butler undoubtedly was a clever and widely cultivated man. His mind was always full of ideas which sometimes were rather unusual for the ordinary Conservative. Thus he considered that if the Conservatives wanted to retain their position as the main British party, they should listen to the dictates of the modern age, and particularly should attend to social problems.

In the sphere of foreign policy, Butler on the whole followed the 'Cliveden' line (it was not in vain that he was Halifax's deputy), but displayed much more flexibility and ingenuity than his chief, and held the opinion that diplomats existed in order to 'rub away' difficulties and complications arising between countries. It was just for this reason that, even in the circumstances of the anti-Soviet storm aroused by the Soviet-Finnish war, he maintained good relations with me, was always extremely obliging and courteous and constantly said: 'We ought to meet and talk more often.'

To meet this wish, on 16 February 1940 I invited Butler to luncheon at the Embassy. I wanted to talk with him more frankly, and therefore there were only three at table: Butler, my wife and myself. The conversation very quickly became relaxed, and Butler began putting to me the questions which interested him. What was the nature of Soviet-German relations—an alliance or not an alliance? What was the USSR seeking in Finland? What were the intentions of the USSR in relation to Norway and Sweden?

I replied that there was no alliance between Germany and the USSR, that our country was carrying on its own, perfectly independent foreign policy, and that in the war between Germany on one side and Britain and France on the other we maintained the position of neutrality. We had no claims at all on Sweden and Norway, all we wanted was that they should remain neutral in the Soviet-Finnish war. We had no intention of annexing Finland, but we could not put up with the fact that the rulers of that country were ready to serve every enemy of the USSR. My words had the effect of calming Butler. Evidently growing bolder, he put me the direct question:

'Can't the Soviet-Finnish war be ended by mediation?'

I immediately cabled to Moscow about my conversation with Butler, and received a reply on 22 February. The same day I asked to see him, and told him the contents of the instructions I had received. Their substance was the following: the Soviet Government was giving the British Government the most reassuring undertakings as to the nature of Soviet-German relations and as to the absence of any claims of the Soviet Union on the Scandinavian countries, and then declared its readiness to end the war with Finland as rapidly as possible. With this, Moscow indicated the peace terms which were acceptable to it, providing for the maintenance of the complete independence of Finland, and invited Britain to take part in the establishment of peace between the USSR and Finland.

Butler heard me out with great attention, and even with a certain excitement, and said when I had finished:

'What you have told me is of exceptional importance. You understand that I can decide nothing myself. I must report about it all to the Government. Afterwards we shall see one another again.'

When I was leaving Butler I saw how he at once went quickly, almost ran, to Halifax's office. On the evening of the 23rd Butler telephoned to me and said that he would like to see me next morning.

At the appointed hour I came to see him. He began by apologising that he was receiving me, not Halifax, as should have been the case in view of the exceptional importance of the question involved. But Halifax that day was out of London, and the Government did not want to delay handing over its reply until Monday (the 24th was Saturday). Butler then with somewhat unusual solemnity stated that the Cabinet had received with great satisfaction the declaration of the Soviet Government regarding Sweden and Norway, the nature of Soviet-German relations and the general line of conduct of the USSR in the larger war. The Cabinet considered that these declarations would facilitate a considerable improvement of the atmosphere between London and Moscow.

Matters were otherwise on the question of Finland. The British Government welcomed, of course, the readiness of the USSR to end the war and conclude peace with the Rüti-Tanner Government, but it did not think it could participate in negotiations, because it found the terms of peace we had put forward too harsh. The British Government, however, did not see why the USSR could not make its peace offer to Finland directly.

It was clear that the Chamberlain Government did not wish to commit itself in any way, and preferred to keep its hands free to be able, if necessary, to attack the USSR. I expressed my regret at the attitude of the British Government and gave it to understand that this attitude would not be well thought of in Moscow.

Two days later I learned that the British refusal to mediate was partly to be explained by strong pressure from Paris, where the wave of anti-Soviet fury still stood very high. More than that, Daladier behind Chamberlain's back had promised Finland every possible military aid if it continued the war with the USSR.

But it was already too late. On 23 February the Finnish Government informed Moscow that it was ready to begin peace negotiations, and the Red Army's piercing the Mannerheim Line at the beginning of March finally decided the outcome of the war. On 12 March 1940 the treaty of peace between the USSR and Finland was signed in Moscow.

Thereafter the anti-Soviet storm in Britain and France began gradually to die down, and the general atmosphere returned to its 'normal' state—the kind of normality which, to use the language of a later day, could be described as the atmosphere of 'cold war'.

In concluding the account of the Soviet-Finnish war, I would like to make one observation of a general character.

The bourgeois world has always maintained, and still maintains, an attitude of extreme hostility to the Soviet State. One of the consequences is its half-conscious, half-instinctive readiness to believe everything derogatory to the USSR. In the first years after the revolution it believed such stupid fairy tales as the 'nationalisation of women'. Later it believed in the incapacity of the Bolsheviks to master modern technique and to build a powerful industrial machine. In the 'thirties it believed in the organic weakness of the Red Army and called it 'a colossus on feet of clay'. Every piece of positive evidence about Soviet affairs, with the obsequious assistance of the capitalist press, was rapidly and easily forgotten, while everything that was negative was taken up on a big scale and for long remembered. Such was the general psychological inclination not only of our enemies but also of neutral elements. An atmosphere of this kind had a certain influence even on our friends abroad. I remember how, in the middle of the 'thirties, one of the best Labour Party friends of the Soviet Union came up to me at a diplomatic reception in London. We talked about the May Day demonstration which had just taken place in Moscow. My friend was very pleased that there was a powerful demonstration of the Soviet Air Force at the military parade on that occasion.

'Our diehards will have to think again', he said with satisfaction. But then, unexpectedly leaning towards me, he added almost in a whisper: 'I understand, of course, that to make an air demonstration in the capital you had to assemble planes from all over the country, but that is quite a legitimate military trick when you are up against the capitalist world.'

I explained to the Labour man that we hadn't assembled planes from anywhere for the Moscow demonstration, that on 1 May there had flown over the Red Square only those planes which were permanently stationed near Moscow, and that air demonstrations had taken place simultaneously in the other largest centres of the USSR. Our friend was amazed, and took a lot of assuring that I was speaking quite seriously.

In the second half of the 'thirties the reputation of the Red Army as a serious military force had begun gradually to make its way in the West. But now, after the Soviet-Finnish war, that reputation received a serious set-back. Of course, the more thoughtful and objective people in the West, guessing instinctively the reasons for our initial reverses, were inclined to assess more truly the real state of affairs: but at that time they were few. It was not only broad 'public opinion', but also statesmen and military experts, yielding to the organic prejudices of bourgeois society of which I spoke about, who after the Soviet-Finnish war finally adopted the conclusion that the Red Army was really 'a colossus on feet of clay'. The consequences of such an obviously slanderous assessment of the military strength of the Soviet Union showed themselves later on both in Britain, France and the USA, and in Germany. From this assessment there followed a sequence of measures taken by these Powers, which played a most serious part in the course of the second world war.

7

Chamberlain Marks Time

WHEN the Soviet-Finnish war was over and the passions aroused by it had burned themselves out, the Governments of Chamberlain and Daladier found themselves no better off than they were at the start. They had not succeeded in 'switching' the war. Nothing had come of the united front with Hitler against the USSR. The French and British armies still stood face to face with the Germans, and both London and Paris were faced as before, perhaps even with greater urgency than before, with the fatal question: what was to be done? I well remember the state of mind which prevailed at that time among the rulers of Britain. On 4 March, still on the eve of the Soviet-Finnish peace, but when it was clearly rapidly approaching, I visited Butler to talk about various current questions. Butler was even more amiable than usual, and after all the questions on the agenda had been dealt with, began himself to talk about the prospects of the war:

'We are not at all clear about the immediate future . . . We don't know whether the war with Germany will go on, and if it does, what form it will take . . . We don't intend to take the offensive ourselves . . . Our information is that Hitler is not inclined to push ahead and expand the war either . . . It would seem that a possibility of peace is arising; but will there be any chance of agreement about the terms?'

Butler made an indefinite gesture. He was not alone in his state of mind. His remarks were a good reflection of the general atmosphere prevailing in March 1940 in British ruling circles.

I quote here the following entry in my diary made on 30 March 1940:

'Six months have passed since the beginning of the European war, and when I now try to sum up all that I see, hear, observe and learn from various sources, the picture I get is approximately as follows.

'The four strong points on which the British Government took its stand at the end of November last year still, on the whole, preserve their essential significance at the present day, i.e. three months later. The united national front within Britain has not been shaken. True, the mass of the workers are emerging more and more from the state of confusion and amazement in which they were plunged at the very outbreak of the war, but the trade union and Labour Party "machine", which entirely supports the Government, has not been shaken at all.

'The united front of the Empire also stands firm. True, Eire maintains a demonstratively neutral attitude, while in India the National Congress recently (1 March) has demanded complete independence of India as a condition for co-operating with Britain; but nevertheless all the British possessions beyond the seas continue to a greater or lesser extent to support Britain in her struggle against Germany.

'No essential changes have taken place in the international situation either. In the USA isolationist feelings have somewhat increased, it is true; Turkey, in spite of the £90 million she got from Britain and France, is stubbornly resisting efforts to drag her into the war; Italy, whom Britain has all the winter tried to retain in a condition of neutrality by various economic concessions (including permission for German coal to be brought to her ports) is displaying more and more independence and waywardness; all the same, the diplomatic situation even now arouses no serious apprehensions in Britain and France.

'Things are a little worse as regards the time factor. Three months ago the British rulers were firmly convinced that time was working in their favour. After all, the resources of the British and French Empires are immeasurably greater than the resources of Germany and her satellites. Give us time to mobilise them, the British said, and then . . . Now the rulers of Britain (and of France too) are much less confident in the accuracy of their previous calculations. Why? Because the blockade of Germany on which Chamberlain and Daladier pinned such great hopes has proved in reality only a "semi-blockade", with all the attendant consequences.

'Such a situation makes the question of British-Soviet relations more acute. In particular the "Vladivostok problem" is arising. As a consequence of losing the British market for machinery, and for various other reasons, we have increased our purchases of machine tools and equipment in the USA. Our ships are transporting them from American ports on the Pacific to Vladivostok. And now British cruisers are intercepting these ships on the high seas and taking them to Hong Kong. At present, for example there are two Soviet steamers there, the *Selenga* and the *Mayakovsky* which have been arrested by the British. I have been asking Butler for several weeks for them to be released, but he keeps on putting me off with promises and excuses. The fact of the matter is that the British are afraid that the cargoes of the *Selenga* and the *Mayakovsky* may be destined for Germany.

'Summing up, one can assert that the situation has changed somewhat for the worse for Britain and France during these three months, but still the position of the Chamberlain Government is as yet sufficiently stable, if . . . if, of course, there are no sudden changes at the front.

'But what about the war? How will that go? Chamberlain and Daladier would most of all like to see it ended. But that does not depend on them alone. And since the war still continues, they must willy-nilly think about the forms in which it is to be carried on. Of course one need not anticipate a large-scale offensive of the British and French by land. They are afraid—particularly France—of letting loose a great air war, since the Germans undoubtedly would reply in full measure. Evidently things will reduce them selves to attempts at intensifying the blockade by imposing quotas on the neutrals, withdrawing export surpluses from the Balkan markets and stopping Germany's access to Swedish iron ore. But that makes little difference to the present situation. The "phoney war" is continuing, and one of the characteristic symptoms of the state of mind of the top rulers of Britain is the fact that once again leave from the front, which had stopped in January, was renewed on 16 March. How characteristic it is, too, that the whole of the Government (including Butler) has broken up and gone to its country estates for the Easter holidays.'

As can be seen from this entry, the British ruling class even six months after the beginning of the second world war, still did not want to take the war seriously, and continued to think about it as it would about a football match or a game of cricket. Evidence of this also was a conversation which I had with Butler on 18 March.

On 17 February 1940 Sumner Welles, the American Under-Secretary of State, had on Roosevelt's instructions gone to Europe. He was to visit Paris, Rome, Berlin and London in order to ascertain whether an end of the war and conclusion of peace were possible. When I met Butler on 18 March I asked what he could tell me about this important diplomatic act. Butler was outspoken, and told me that according to Sumner Welles, who had had a detailed discussion with Hitler, the latter was ready to conclude peace on the following conditions: the creation of a small Poland, which would not be 'dangerous' to Germany; the establishment of an autonomous Bohemia and Moravia; the return of the former German colonies; the right of Germany, without obstruction by other States, to establish a great economic empire in Europe, on the basis of customs preferences which would embrace Scandinavia, Central and South-Eastern Europe. Hitler anticipated also a large development of economic relations with the USSR. Having set forth his 'peace plan', Hitler added that if it did not prove possible to come to an arrangement with Britain and France on this basis in the most immediate future, he would set about the war in real earnest, and would completely crush them within six months: he possessed, he alleged, new weapons which would give the Germans a decisive superiority in the struggle.

When listening to Butler's account, I was thinking willy-nilly: 'If Hitler ventures to say all this openly to the official representative of the American President, what must be his real aims?' I never believed that the German-Soviet pact could be long-lived, but at that moment I felt acute alarm for the immediate future of our country . . .

I asked what were Sumner Welles's impressions of his talks with Mussolini. Butler replied that the demands of the Italian dictator in the main amounted to handing over the port of Djibouti in Ethiopia to Italy, a place for her in the Council of the Suez Canal, a settlement of the status of the Italians in Tunis, financial aid from the City and the internationalisation of Gibraltar. After recounting Mussolini's desires, Butler added somewhat contemptuously:

'All these are comparatively petty details, and could be easily settled, except for one thing: the internationalisation of Gibraltar is absolutely unacceptable for us.'

'Well, but what do you think about Hitler's "peace programme"?' I asked.

Butler shrugged his shoulders and replied:

'Any "peace programme" must be approached without prejudice, with an open mind so to speak . . . Of course in its present form Hitler's "programme" contains a number of points which would arouse sharp opposition on the part of British public opinion. But I don't think this programme is his last word. Much could be changed in the course of negotiations . . .'

And so it was clear that the British Government was ready even now to conclude a 'reasonable compromise' with Germany. More accurately, not the whole Government but its 'Chamberlainite' majority. Those elements in the Government which sympathised with Churchill had somewhat different views. I think this because the very next day after my talks with Butler—on 19 March—I was at lunch with Lord Beaverbrook, who was connected with the Conservative 'opposition' to Chamberlain, and heard from him quite a different assessment of Hitler's 'peace programme'.

'What, Hitler wants the return of the colonies? He wants in fact to hold all Europe? But what would then happen?' Beaverbrook cried almost with fury. 'He would perpetually hang over Britain and France like the sword of Damocles. He would dictate his will to us! No, that's quite impossible!'

But in those days comparatively few of the Conservatives thought in that way. The 'Clivedenites' were patiently getting ready for a deal with Hitler, and were even thinking that they had big trumps in their hand. Thus, when Chamberlain spoke on 4 April at the Central Council of the Conservative Party, he demonstrated at length to his own satisfaction that at the beginning of the war Hitler had a great advantage over Britain, because she was quite unprepared for war, but that now, seven months later, the situation had radically changed to Britain's advantage. In conclusion the Prime Minister said that one thing at any rate was now clear: 'Hitler has missed the bus!'

It is difficult to decide what there was more of in this declaration—stupidity or quite phenomenal conceit?

Literally five days later Hitler showed that it was just Chamberlain and Daladier who had missed the bus.

8

The German Offensive and the fall of Chamberlain

At 5 a.m. on 9 April 1940 the German Ministers in Copenhagen and Oslo presented memoranda to the Danish and Norwegian Governments which stated that henceforth Germany was undertaking the military defence of Denmark and Norway from Anglo-French aggression, and for this purpose was introducing her troops into their territory.

Simultaneously Nazi armed forces crossed the frontier of Denmark and made unexpected landings in the most important ports of Norway. On the evening before, German merchant vessels had arrived there, and now German sailors and soldiers hidden in their holds made a sudden appearance. Denmark did not resist. Her King and her Social-Democratic Prime Minister Stauning even issued an appeal to the people to maintain calm and not to resist the Germans in any way. By midday on 9 April the whole of Denmark was occupied by the Nazis, and transformed into one of the provinces of the Third Reich.

Things proved somewhat different in Norway. The Norwegian Government rejected the German demand, and together with King Haakon VII left Oslo for a remote part of the country in order to organise the struggle against the Nazi invasion. Nevertheless by the evening of 9 April all the most important ports of the country—Oslo, Bergen, Trondheim, Stavanger—were in the hands of the Germans, while on the following day the Government of Norwegian traitors, headed by the notorious Quisling, which they had created, was already functioning.

This was a classic model of the 'lightning war', prepared in such secrecy that its victims did not even suspect the peril which was hanging over them.

I recall that on 8 April, the eve of the fatal day, I met Colban, the Norwegian Minister in London. He was a very cultivated and well-read man, who had worked for long at the League of Nations, and we were on friendly terms. For several days there had been stubborn rumours that the clouds were gathering over Norway, and I asked Colban to what extent they were well-founded. Colban waved his hand, and cried with deep conviction:

'All that is nonsense! . . . We have the most categorical assurances from Germany that she will respect our neutrality.'

And then, dropping his voice somewhat, he added:

'If I am afraid of anything just now, it is some rash actions on the part of our British friends . . . You are aware, of course, that the Swedish iron ore which Germany is receiving gives them no rest. The ore goes to Germany from Sweden by two routes: directly across the Baltic and the longer way round through the Norwegian port of Narvik and then along our Atlantic coast, within Norway's territorial waters . . . I have heard that Churchill has long been insisting on the mining of our territorial waters: if that were done, the German ships bringing iron ore from Narvik would have to go outside territorial waters, and there they would be captured by the British . . . So far Chamberlain has been successfully resisting Churchill—after all, mining the territorial waters of a neutral State would be a breach of international law . . . But who knows how things will go in the future?'

Colban's doubts were not unfounded. On the very day we were talking, 8 April, British warships did, in fact, lay mines at three points in Norwegian territorial waters. However, it would be wrong to think that the German action on 9 April was only a reply to the British action: it would have been impossible to prepare within 24 hours such a complicated operation as the lightning seizure of Denmark and Norway (we know now that the plan for this was finally worked out by the Germans in December 1939). But Colban as late as 8 April was firmly convinced that on the part of Germany no direct danger was threatening Norway.

Two days after Hitler's 'leap' into Scandinavia I had occasion to see Count Reventlow, the Danish Minister in London. He was in a complete state of despair—not only because his country had been occupied by the Nazis, but also because of other more personal reasons.

'Just imagine', he said bitterly, 'only last week I sent my wife and children to stay with my parents in Denmark, they sent me a telegram that they had arrived safely . . . And now . . . What will become of them? When will I see them again? Will I ever see them? . . .'

I began to ask Reventlow how it could happen that his family left for Denmark on the very eve of the Hitlerite invasion? Were there really no preliminary symptoms of the advancing danger?

'Just imagine, there were none!' said Reventlow throwing up his hands. 'No symptoms! No signals! Everything took place absolutely unexpectedly, as though it had fallen from heaven . . .'

Yes, the Scandinavian operation was carefully prepared and carried out by Hitler. It would undoubtedly later have been extended to Sweden as well, if on 13 April the Soviet Government had not informed the German Government that it was interested in the maintenance of Swedish neutrality.

The events in Scandinavia were a terrible blow for Britain and France. So the 'phoney war', to which Chamberlain and Daladier had grown so accustomed, had sharply come to an end! War had begun in all seriousness, that war about which they had least of all wanted to think. The inexorable logic of events, over which the 'Munichites' had no control, had entered into force. London and Paris were forced to act . . .

And what did they do?

I have already mentioned that the King and Government of Norway had not capitulated, but had retreated into the depth of the country with the resolution to resist. From the very beginning it was clear, of course, that they could not hold out for long with their own forces alone. All over Britain and France there rose the single cry: 'Aid for Norway!' The Governments of Chamberlain and Daladier set about organising the aid. If they really wanted to afford serious support to the fighting Norwegians, and at the same time to retain an important strategic base for themselves, the greatest audacity and speed were necessary. But what took place in reality? It is difficult to imagine a picture of greater incapacity, muddle, confusion, lack of discipline, insufficient co-ordination and stupid rivalries between persons and institutions than that which was revealed during the Norwegian campaign in Britain and France. The direct object of this campaign was to drive the Germans out of the Atlantic ports of Norway, and first of all to seize Trondheim and Narvik. For three weeks British and French troops attempted to bring this about, but by the beginning of May were obliged to recognise their failure and to evacuate their forces from southern Norway. The Allies tried to console themselves by the fact that Germany's naval losses during these battles were considerably larger than the British, and that therefore the general relationship of forces between the two sides at sea had changed in their favour; but the impotence displayed by the British and French on land was so visible that it only facilitated the further strengthening of the myth of the invincibility of the German army.

These events aroused a tremendous excitement in Britain. It was becoming more and more clear that the Chamberlain Government was incapable of carrying on the war. If the country wanted to avoid disaster (and this it certainly did want) resolute measures were urgently necessary. It was in such an atmosphere that there took place a stormy two days' debate in Parliament (7 and 8 May), entirely devoted to discussing the course of the war. I was present, and will here quote one more entry in my diary which I made at that time:

'During the last seven years I have more than once had occasion to be present at 'big days' in the House of Commons, but I have never yet seen anything like this. When I entered the Chamber and sat down in my place in the "Ambassadors' Gallery" I was struck at once by the atmosphere of general tenseness and anxious anticipation. All the M.P.'s benches were packed, all the Members were very excited, turning to each other, discussing something feverishly. There was no room for some of them, and they were crowded in the gangways and in the public galleries[1]. The Leaders of the Opposition were already sitting in their places on the Front Bench to the left of the Speaker. The Government entered, and the Ministers took their place opposite. Chamberlain rose to make a

1. At the beginning of the nineteenth century there were 450 places in the House of Commons. This corresponded to the number of M.P.s in the seventeenth century. By the beginning of the last century the number of Members had grown to 600, and on days of important meetings many M.P.s had to sit in the galleries or stand in the gangways. However, out of respect for 'traditions of the past', they were unwilling to reconstruct the Parliament building. In 1834 Parliament was burnt to the ground in a big fire. A new building was put up —that which stands on the bank of the Thames today—but out of respect for the same 'traditions of the past' there still turned out to be places for only 450 M.P.s in the House of Commons. During the second world war German bombs destroyed the Chamber. A new one was built after the war, but once again places were provided only for 450, although the number of M.P.s then exceeded 600, as it does today. A vivid example of British conservatism.

report on the course of the war, concentrating his attention on the Norwegian operations. The Prime Minister was never a good speaker. This time he spoke worse than usual. He talked at very great length, very boringly, submerging himself in too great detail. During his speech, the Conservatives dutifully wanted to support him, sometimes calling out: "Hear, hear", but they were doing so languidly, and clearly only for form's sake. When the Prime Minister at last sat down, the temperature among the Conservatives fell to zero. All were deeply disappointed.

'After Chamberlain the first to speak was the Labour leader Attlee. He also cannot be counted among the brilliant orators, but this time, evidently warmed up by the passions boiling around him, Attlee spoke vividly and sharply. He accused Chamberlain of fearing to face the facts. It was necessary frankly to recognise, said the Leader of the Opposition, that in Norway they had suffered a reverse. The Prime Minister said that Germany had planned this expedition with very great care over a long period. Attlee wanted to know what care was exercised in planning the means for defeating that stroke if it should come . . . They were informed on 19 March that there was a force of 100,000 men ready to go to Finland . . . What he did not understand was the rapid dispersal of all these troops . . . He had heard stories of some boys being sent there, quite young, and having very little training . . . It was unbelievable that in Norway and Denmark the landing preparations that had gone on for many months could have passed without any indication. He wanted to know whether they got intelligence, and whether such intelligence, if they did get it, was properly used . . . The gravamen of his attack on the Government was that it did not seem that there was a thinking out of the British plan beforehand, that there was not adequate Intelligence, that there was not the necessary concentration on the essential objective . . . He was not in the least satisfied, despite all the Prime Minister had said, that the present War Cabinet was an efficient instrument for conducting the war . . . People were saying that those mainly responsible for the conduct of affairs were men who had had an almost uninterrupted career of failure. Norway followed Czechoslovakia and Poland. In a life-and-death struggle they could not afford to have their destinies in the hands of failures or men who needed a rest.

'Attlee's speech was repeatedly interrupted by loud cries of "Hear, hear", and made a deep impression on the House.

'Archibald Sinclair, the Liberal leader, also sharply criticised the Government, but was much milder than Attlee, and demanded a smaller War Cabinet, a War Cabinet free from departmental responsibility, thinking, planning and imparting drive and thrust to the war effort.

'After the speeches of the official Opposition leaders many other M.P.s spoke, the vast majority of them criticising the Government. A particularly powerful impression was made by the Conservative Amery. He attacked Chamberlain without restraint for his methods of government and conducting the war, and ended his speech in these words:

'"The time has come for a real National Government . . . I have quoted certain words of Oliver Cromwell. I will quote certain other words. I do it with great reluctance . . . This is what Cromwell said to the Long Parliament when he thought it was no longer fit to conduct the affairs of the nation: *You have sat too long here for any good you have been doing. Depart, I say, and let us have done with you. In the name of God, go.*"

'Amery's words produced a storm of approval, and not only on the Opposition Benches. Among the Conservatives there could also be heard cries of approval. Many M.P.s jumped up and, turning to the Government Bench, were loudly shouting: "In the name of God, go!" For some minutes there was chaos in the House. Passions were heated to the extreme. For the first time the atmosphere in the Chamber began to lead to a clear conclusion: an end had come to the Chamberlain Government.

'Next day, 8 May, the debate continued. The first to speak was one of the Labour Party leaders, Herbert Morrison, a sharp-tongued and clever man, an excellent speaker in a venomously sarcastic style. He subjected the Government to merciless criticism, and when touching on the Norwegian operations, put a number of searching questions to it. He asked:

'"Was there a plan in operation for unity of command between the various forces in Norway? . . . Is it the case that anti-aircraft guns were sent without predictors? Is it the case that other guns were sent without ammunition? Is it the case that machine-guns were sent without spare barrels? . . . Is it a fact that the military force was not supplied with snow-shoes, the consequences being that the troops were stuck on the roads and were bombed there? Is it a fact that Territorial brigades were sent . . . which were second Territorial Army units that had never had even brigade training? . . . The fact is that before the war and during the war we have felt that the whole spirit, tempo and temperament of at least some Ministers have been wrong, inadequate and unsuitable. I am bound to refer in particular to the Prime Minister, the Chancellor of the Exchequer and the Secretary of State for Air. Just as they lack courage, initiative, imagination, psychological understanding, liveliness and self-respect in the conduct of foreign policy, so I feel that the absence of those qualities has manifested itself in the actual conduct of the war. I have the genuine apprehension that if these men remain in office, we run grave risk of losing this war."

'In view of the exceptional danger hanging over the country, the Labour Party had decided at the end of the debate to raise the question of confidence in the Government. Morrison called on every member of Parliament honestly and dispassionately to give his assessment of the activity of the Cabinet.

'Scarcely had Morrison ceased to speak than Chamberlain rose and in great agitation asked to reply. The demand of a vote of confidence had obviously made him beside himself. The Prime Minister still did not wish to understand that his day was over, and convulsively was snatching at any straw which, it seemed to him, could keep him afloat. And here, hastily and in an attack of irritation, Chamberlain made a big tactical mistake. Answering Morrison, he cried: "I accept the challenge. I welcome it indeed. At least we shall see who is with us and who is against us, and" (turning to the Conservative benches) "I call on my friends to support us in the Lobby tonight!"

'Something like a gasp passed through the ranks of the M.P.s. There was particular agitation among the Conservatives. I should say so! On the agenda was the dread question of whether Britain was to be or not to be, a question which required a genuine attitude of principle on the part of every member, free from every personal element: but Chamberlain found nothing better to do than to appeal to the friendly feelings of his Conservative colleagues. This shocked many, and only underlined once more the unsuitability of Chamberlain as Prime Minister in such a difficult historic situation.

'In fact, the following speakers who criticised the Government, particularly the Conservative Duff Cooper and the Liberal Lloyd George, very skilfully made use of this lapse by Chamberlain. The attempts of Air Minister Samuel Hoare and Winston Churchill, who closed the discussion, somehow to soften the hostile atmosphere created around the Prime Minister, had no success. Lloyd George as ever was razor-sharp, and ended his indignant speech with the words:

'"He has appealed for sacrifice . . . I say solemnly that the Prime Minister should give an example of sacrifice, because there is nothing which can contribute more to victory in this war than that he should sacrifice the seals of office."

'The Chamber resounded with loud outcries of "Hear, hear".

'I followed Churchill with a particular feeling while he was ending the two days' debate on behalf of the Government. During the preceding months information had reached me about the struggle which he was carrying on against Chamberlain within the Cabinet. Yet now, as the official representative of the Cabinet, sharing the responsibility for all its activity, Churchill had to defend it or, at any rate, explain the mistakes which had been made and find extenuating circumstances for them. This was not an easy task for him, and probably because of this his speech was unnecessarily long, and was not distinguished by the vividness and wit usually characteristic of his speeches. Churchill called on all the parties to unite, and opposed the question of confidence being put: but this was only the Parliamentary game, canonised by age-old traditions.

'Late that evening there was the vote. 281 votes were cast for the Government and 200 against it. Formally, therefore, the Government had won a victory, and the party discipline of the Conservatives had played its part: but in effect, after all that had taken place in the debate, it meant a defeat. Its significance was all the deeper because thirty-three Conservatives had voted against the Government, including such prominent figures as Amery, Duff Cooper, Boothby, Harold Macmillan,[1] Lord Winterton, General Spears, and others. The Liberal-National Hore-Belisha and the National Labour Harold Nicholson were with the Opposition, as well as the whole group of orthodox Liberals headed by Sinclair.

'The result of the voting aroused stormy applause on the part of the Opposition. The supporters of the Government behaved with great restraint. There was a feeling in the air that something exceptionally important, of truly historic significance, had occurred.

1. The future Prime Minister.

'While leaving Parliament, I met Greenwood, the Deputy Leader of the Labour Party. He was terribly excited and smiling. "Well," he cried, "at last we have got rid of Chamberlain!"

'And he warmly shook my hand.'

In fact, on 10 May the Chamberlain Government resigned.

Part Two

*

The German - British Duel

1

The Churchill Government

On 10 May 1940, without any warning, Germany attacked Holland, Belgium and Luxemburg. Everything was carried out in Hitler's usual manner. At 3 a.m. units of the Wehrmacht suddenly crossed the frontier into the territory of Holland and Belgium, while the German air force began bombing their cities. Only a few hours later did the German Ministers at The Hague and Brussels present identical 'memoranda' to Van Kleffens, the Dutch Minister for Foreign Affairs, and Spaak, the Belgian Minister for Foreign Affairs, which stated that Britain and France were making preparations to infringe the neutrality of these countries and attack the Ruhr region through their territory, and that in view of this Germany was obliged to occupy them in order to 'assure their neutrality' by these means. The war was clearly spreading and becoming more complex. It was quite clear that France's turn would be next. Chamberlain's fantasies about Hitler's 'unwillingness' to attack the West were disintegrating one after another, like rotten thread...

It was in such circumstances that the new British Government had to be formed. It was considered unquestionable that only Churchill could be head of the Government, and that it would include the Labour and Liberal parties together with the Conservatives. It was also considered unquestionable that this 'National Government' should be set up immediately, without allowing more than a few hours to pass. The roar of German guns on the fields of Flanders left no alternative. In fact, the composition of Churchill's War Cabinet was out by the evening of 10 May. In addition to Churchill himself, it included two more Conservatives—Chamberlain as Deputy Prime Minister and Halifax as Foreign Secretary—and two Labour Party men—Attlee as Lord Privy Seal and Arthur Greenwood as Minister without Portfolio. At the same time it was stated that Anthony Eden (Conservative) was appointed Secretary for War, A. V. Alexander (Labour) First Lord of the Admiralty and Sir Archibald Sinclair (Liberal) Secretary for Air. All three had naturally to work in the closest possible contact with the War Cabinet. This group of eight, composed of four Conservatives, three Labour Party men and one Liberal, became the highest authority in the country and was in charge of all military operations. The presence of Chamberlain and Halifax in it aroused various unpleasant recollections among the mass of the people, and the retention of Halifax as Foreign Secretary was particularly disliked. However all understood that, in creating a 'National Government', Churchill was obliged to manoeuvre, and to include in it representatives of the Munichites (who had now lost a great part of their influence) as well, and therefore the new Cabinet met with universal approval.[1]

Between 11 and 15 May all the other Ministerial posts not included in the War Cabinet were filled. There were twenty-six of them, distributed among the parties as follows: seventeen Conservatives, five Labour men, three National Liberals (the Simon group) and one National Labour (the Macdonald group). The numerical balance was not entirely favourable for the Labour opposition, because the Simon and Macdonald groups in the past had always gone together with the Munichites. This defect found partial compensation in the Labour Party being given three posts which were very important in war time—those of the Minister of Supply (Herbert Morrison), Economic Warfare (Hugh Dalton) and Labour (Ernest Bevin), and also by the fact that among the Conservatives there were some striking representatives of the 'opposition' within the Conservative Party. Thus Duff Cooper was appointed Minister of Information, Amery Secretary for India and Lord Beaverbrook Minister of Aircraft Production. The latter appointment was of particular importance.

In the year preceding the war the British aircraft industry had had a considerable development, but a somewhat unhealthy one. There were too many private firms in the country, producing too

1. Many opponents of the Munichites consoled themselves with the thought that, as was known, Chamberlain was a sick man and would soon have to resign. In fact he left the Government at the beginning of October, and on 9 November 1940 he died of cancer.

many varied types of planes. This was the operation of the natural law of the capitalist economic system, multiplied moreover by the special individualism of the British. There was no mass production of any definite types. Yet now, in anticipation of a severe air war with Germany, the British Government needed at any price rapidly to organise the mass production of a minimum number of types of planes—fighters, bombers, reconnaissance machines, etc. A radical re-organisation of the aircraft industry was needed, the closing down of some factories and the extension of others, the amalgamation of some firms and the dividing up of others, a complete refashioning of all their plans and intentions. This was a very difficult problem, and it was not by chance that Churchill entrusted Lord Beaverbrook with its solution.

Beaverbrook was a man of tremendous energy and initiative, and in addition a powerful newspaper king who feared no one. He justified Churchill's expectations. He really carried out a revolution in British aircraft construction, one which was necessitated by the requirements of war time. If Britain in the autumn of 1940 survived the air 'blitz' which Hitler launched against her (I shall tell of this in detail later), if the British air force on that occasion succeeded in beating off the Nazi offensive, this was to no small degree due to Beaverbrook. His actions were hard and severe—and what war could be won in white gloves? But he achieved his object, which was to inflict a blow on the enemy. What his methods were like can be well illustrated by the following example about which John Maynard Keynes, the well-known British economist, told me in the summer of 1940.

Beaverbrook had come to the conclusion that, in order to develop mass production of a particular type of plane, it was essentail to combine Lord Nuffield's aircraft factory at Oxford with one of the Vickers plants. It was late at night, but Beaverbrook did not wish to put off an important measure to the morning. He summoned a secretary and said: 'Go to Oxford immediately and inform Lord Nuffield that as from tomorrow his factory is being amalgamated with the Vickers plant.'

The secretary was horror-struck: 'But surely Lord Nuffield won't give his consent... He is so stubborn and... so wealthy!... Nothing will make him submit to a decision of the Ministry of Aircraft Production!'

'That's my business,' replied Beaverbrook. 'Don't you hang about, get off to Oxford at once!'

The secretary, who wasn't at all pleased at the thought of meeting the sharp-tongued and arrogant aristocrat, and especially on such an unpleasant errand, tried to avoid the journey by pointing out that the last train for Oxford had already left.

'Take a car,' Beaverbrook ordered.

'But I won't reach Oxford by car before half-past twelve!' argued the secretary despairingly. 'Lord Nuffield will be asleep...'

'Never mind, wake him up,' Beaverbrook continued inexorably. 'Tell him that as from tomorrow he's being amalgamated with Vickers.'

Then the secretary threw down his last card—and, as it seemed to him, a trump card: 'But there hasn't yet been a Government decision about the amalgamation! The Prime Minister has not signed one yet!'

'Calm down', Beaverbrook consoled the secretary. 'By the time you arrive at Oxford there will have been a Government decision too.'

The secretary left, and Beaverbrook at once rang up the Prime Minister. A quarter of an hour later a Government decision to amalgamate the two factories had been signed.

The affair was over—but it's not difficult to imagine Nuffield's feelings, and his views on Lord Beaverbrook.

I cannot go bail for all the details of this story, although I heard it from a man as serious as Keynes: but it very well reproduces the whole spirit of Beaverbrook's management of the Ministry of Aircraft Production. Later on I more than once observed similar cases myself...

However, I have anticipated somewhat, and will return to a chronological account of events.

On 13 May Churchill presented his new Government to Parliament. I was present at this session, and well remember the solemn and severe mood which dominated the Chamber of the House of Commons. There was not the usual hubbub, there were neither conversations nor jokes among the members. All seemed tense, concentrated, filled with one feeling, one anticipation, and were looking impatiently at the Government Front Bench, or more precisely at the solid figure of the Prime Minister sitting in the middle of the bench.

Churchill rose and began to speak. There was always something of an actor in his make-up. I saw this and felt it when I had diplomatic or personal contacts with him. Churchill usually wrote his Parliamentary speeches when he had the time. But on this occasion he was really and sincerely agitated. His voice even broke from time to time. The Prime Minister's words were brief but full of deep significance.

'I would say to the House', said Churchill, 'as I said to those who have joined this Government: "I have nothing to offer but blood, toil, tears and sweat." We have before us an ordeal of the most grievous kind. We have before us many, many long months of struggle and of suffering. You ask what is our policy? I will say: it is to wage war, by sea, land and air, with all our might and with all the strength that God can give us: to wage war against a monstrous tyranny, never surpassed in the dark, lamentable catalogue of human crime . . . You ask, what is our aim? I can answer in one word: victory—victory at all costs, victory in spite of all terror, victory, however long and hard the road may be; for without victory, there is no survival. Let that be realised: no survival for the British Empire, no survival for all that the British Empire has stood for, no survival for the urge and impulse of the ages, that mankind will move forward to its goal...'

I was listening to Churchill as I sat in the diplomatic gallery, and thought: 'Yes, this is the whole Churchill, a British imperialist to the marrow of his bones—yet at this turn of history he is doing a great service.'

When it came to voting on the question of confidence in the new Government, something without precedent in the annals of the British Parliament took place: for confidence there were 381 votes, against none. The Churchill Cabinet was accepted unanimously. This was a vivid demonstration of its strength. And strength the Cabinet needed very badly: it was faced with problems of exceptional importance and exceptional difficulty.

It was essential first of all to react quickly to the events in Belgium and Holland. Here the situation was extraordinarily complicated and perilous.

If Britain and France, in the years following the advent of Hitler to power in Germany, had conducted the policy on which people like Churchill had insisted, and reinforced this policy by concrete action, Belgium and Holland would long ago have been included in the system of Anglo-French defence against the menace of Nazi aggression. In that event the 'Maginot Line' would probably, in one form or another, have been continued to the shores of the North Sea, and would have covered not only France but equally Belgium and Holland. In that event Germany would have had to solve a very difficult military problem.

After the overthrow of France there was much ridicule of the 'Maginot Line', but without sufficient justification. For given the technique of warfare in 1939, this Line had it been extended to the sea, would have represented a powerful fortification and a very serious obstacle on the way to the conquest of France—on condition, of course, that France really wanted to carry on a struggle against Nazism and defend her independence. Had such a condition existed, it is doubtful whether Hitler would have decided to attack her at all: too great would have been the sacrifices in overcoming a barrier so powerful from the military point of view. But it was just this basic and decisive condition that did not exist either in France or in her ally, Chamberlainite Britain. Hence followed quite a number of exceptionally important political and strategic consequences.

The political consequences were summed up in the infatuation of the leading circles in Britain and France with the notorious conception of 'Western security' (i.e. with the calculation that war could be promoted between the USSR and Germany), with the policy of 'appeasing' the aggressors and, ultimately, 'Munich'. For the sake of their stupid and criminal fantasies the leading circles in Britain and France sacrificed Austria, Spain and Czechoslovakia, and completely undermined any faith among other nations in their capacity to withstand the Fascist dictators. This aroused profound dissensions in the smaller European countries, part cularly in Belgium and Holland.

The strategic consequences of the same fact reduced themselves to the impossibility of establishing the 'Maginot Line' from Switzerland to the shores of the North Sea. Seeing what had happened to Austria, Spain and Czechoslovakia, Belgium and Holland did not venture to bind up their fate with that of Britain and France. On the contrary, they began to be afraid of such a connection, because they feared that it might 'provoke' Hitler to hostile action against them. Therefore there grew stronger and stronger in Belgium and Holland the view that it was more advantageous to follow a policy of strict neutrality. Such a policy, the leading circles in these two countries thought, was more likely to assure their security than an open alliance with Britain and

France. Of course, such a hope in the circumstances of Europe at the end of the thirties was just as senseless an illusion as the Anglo-French conception of 'Western security'. But bourgeois politicians often suffer from amazing short-sightedness.

The result of the policy of strict neutrality on the part of Belgium and Holland was that the Maginot Line ended at Longwy, i.e. 35 miles to the south of the Belgian frontier. Further to the north there were no serious fortifications either on the France-Belgian frontier or all the more on the Belgian-Dutch frontier with Germany. Thus to the north of the Maginot Line there was a large unfortified stretch through which the Germans could always outflank, and in fact did outflank, the main line of the French defences. The position was even worse because the military leaders of France (and in particular Pétain), being prisoners of the strategic conceptions of the first world war, thought for some reason that the Ardennes were impassable for the German army. and therefore found it unnecessary to build a Maginot Line on that sector. In those days only de Gaulle understood that the development of military technique would bring entirely new forms of a future war, and would open to the enemy quite different possibilities from those of 1914–18. But de Gaulle at that time had only the modest rank of Colonel, and did not enjoy any influence among the leaders of the French army.

If all the foregoing be taken into account, it will become comprehensible that, when on 10 May 1940 Hitlerite Germany fell upon Belgium and Holland, the destruction of these countries was inevitable. The Dutch attempted to resist, blew up bridges, flooded parts of their territory, but all this hardly retarded the advance of the Nazi armies. Making large-scale use of the air-force, of parachutists, of the 'Fifth Column', the Germans advanced rapidly. They inflicted particularly heavy blows on Rotterdam. Three days after the beginning of military operations, the Dutch Queen Wilhelmina landed in England with all her family, and on 14 May General Winkelmann, the commander-in-chief of the Netherlands armed forces, gave a cease-fire order to his troops and called upon the population not to offer resistance to the German invaders.

Belgium resisted somewhat longer. This was explained by the fact that the Belgian Government, while remaining neutral, had nevertheless mobilised an army of 600,000 since the beginning of the war, and also by the fact that immediately after the German attack British and French forces (particularly in the air) were sent to help the Belgians. There was also some importance in the circumstance that during the months of the 'phoney war' the British and French had managed to build up certain fortifications on the Belgian-French frontier, which were not as strong as on the Maginot Line, but did nevertheless create some difficulties for an enemy advance. For these reasons the Germans moved forward in Belgium more slowly than in Holland. Only on the seventh day, 17 May, did the Nazis enter Brussels, which obliged the Belgian Government to evacuate itself to Ostend. On 18 May Antwerp fell. Battles went on for another ten days in various parts of the country, and only on 28 May did the King of the Belgians, Leopold III, proclaim capitulation. However, the Deputies and Senators of the Belgian Parliament who had retreated to France met at Limoges, where they annulled this capitulation and repudiated their King. After this the Pierlot Government announced its resolve to continue the war together with Britain and France. When France fell, the Pierlot Government moved to London, where it remained to the end of the second world war.

However important all these events might be, there appeared in the British press on 15 May a report which disturbed me even more. It was clear from this report that the Germans had broken through precisely those same Ardennes which the French generals had considered impassable for the German army, and had appeared near Sedan. The very name 'Sedan' sounded most sinister. It was here, in 1870, that France had suffered a severe defeat at the hands of Prussia, and the French army headed by Napoleon III had capitulated. And now Hitlerite Germany at this very place had given a visual demonstration of its superiority not only over the French army but also over the military conceptions of the leading circles in France. This aroused in me not a little anxiety, since during the preceding months there had been coming from France a great deal of information about the profound internal dissension which dominated the country.

I remember how on one occasion, not long before the events described, I had a very arresting conversation with my old acquaintance Sir Sidney Clive, who for a number of years had been Marshal of the Diplomatic Corps at the British Court. He was a man of Conservative views, but intelligent and observant. We were on good terms, and Clive often talked with me very frankly. At the beginning of the war he had gone to work in the

Red Cross, spent some months in France and had now only just returned to London.

'I don't understand these French,' Clive said in perplexity. 'I spent the last few weeks in the house of a very big French manufacturer. Everything went very well, but I was shocked by some of my host's views. He was against the war with Germany—well, that I can understand . . . I regret the war with Germany myself . . . But he didn't want a French victory . . . How could that be? Once war has begun, you have to win it! . . . Then my host kept on saying that the worst danger for France was the Popular Front . . . Better let the Germans rule France . . . That I couldn't understand . . . What would then become of France, her people, her ancient culture? . . . I noticed generally that the feeling of patriotism had been almost completely atrophied in my host and the friends who often visited him . . . It looks as though some kind of serious breakdown has taken place in the very psychology of the French.'

Clive was right in noticing that breakdown: only he did not understand that it was not the French people which was suffering from it, but the upper set of the French bourgeoisie.

For me the news about the German breakthrough near Sedan had quite a special significance. If France were crushed (and such a possibility could not be excluded) how would Britain then conduct herself? Would she sign peace with Hitlerite Germany, or would she continue the war alone? Much depended on this. If Britain accepted peace, then we must expect that Hitler would already in the summer of 1940 turn eastward against the Soviet Union. But if Britain remained in a state of war with Germany, the breathing space created by the German-Soviet Pact of non-aggression would still continue. The reply to the question which worried me was of the most serious importance for our country, for the Soviet Government, for all its immediate plans and actions.

I expected that I would receive an appropriate inquiry from Moscow: but Moscow was silent.

I considered it, however, my duty, the duty of an Ambassador of the USSR in London, independently of the conduct of the People's Commissariat for Foreign Affairs, to express my opinion on the question of what would be Britain's attitude in the event of the fall of France. My opinion, I thought, might facilitate the adoption by the Soviet Government of a correct decision at such a critical time. And today, many years later, I think with satisfaction of what I reported to Moscow about the prospects then opening.

However, before sending a telegram to my Government, I wanted finally to be convinced that my assessment of the situation was correct.

My general impression was that Britain, even in the event of the fall of France, would continue the war. I thought of it in this way. The mood of the mass of the workers was very anti-Fascist. The seizure of Belgium and Holland by the Germans was bound to bring to their feet all the petty bourgeois, intellectual and even big capitalist elements (apart from the 'Clivedenites') who had grown up in the traditional conviction that it was dangerous for Britain if the shores of those countries were in the hands of too powerful a State. Churchill was now in power, and he would not make a deal with Hitler, because he acutely felt the contradiction between the imperialist interests of Britain and Germany at this stage in history. Thus there seemed to be no forces within the country which might push Britain into peace with Germany. Nevertheless, I decided once more to test my impressions, and for this purpose to make contact with 'the earth of England itself'. i.e. to have a talk with people who might be considered authoritative interpreters of the views and moods of the British, particularly in the leading circles of the country.

I began with Eden. At that moment, as mentioned earlier, he occupied the post of Secretary for War, and if he had wished could on formal considerations have avoided talking to me on matters of foreign policy. But I reckoned on our good relations established in preceding years, and was not mistaken.

I began with asking him about the state of affairs at the front. Eden set forth in much detail what was going on there, but there was nothing particularly new in his words, compared with the reports in the newspapers. Then I put him the direct question: would the French hold out?

Eden strove to demonstrate that they would, but from a number of almost imperceptible symptoms I felt that he was not fully confident of this. After hearing him out, I said:

'In politics realism is essential, and one has to plan one's actions not only for events turning to the best, but also to the worst . . . Suppose France does not hold out, and capitulates to Germany: what then? What will be Britain's position?'

I added that if Eden considered my question out of place, I

would not be offended should he refuse to reply: but if he did not so consider it, I should be very grateful for any information on this question which interested me.

'I have nothing to hide', Eden responded, 'because the position of our Government on the question you raise is quite definite . . . I hope, I very much hope, that the worst will not happen . . . But if there were a misfortune, and France really did not hold out, Britain would all the same continue the war alone. We cannot accept peace with Hitler.'

Eden's words were firm, and their tone aroused confidence.

I left the Secretary for War with a feeling of considerable relief, but nevertheless not completely reassured. Against my will doubts turned over and over in my mind: was Eden sincere with me to the bitter end? Were not his words only an official version, behind which quite different intentions might be concealed? After all, Eden was a member of the Government, and was naturally bound by collective responsibility in his conversations with foreign Ambassadors. In particular, with the Ambassador of the Soviet Union, which the British Government now regarded with great suspicion. I decided therefore to continue my investigation, and without any delay.

The same day I went to see Lloyd George in his country house, Bron-y-de, where as always he received me very kindly. The old man himself began talking about the war. He was rather excited. Only the previous day he had seen one of his friends who had returned from the French front. What he had heard from him was simply amazing.

'This is an unprecedented kind of war!' cried Lloyd George. 'On the German side you don't see any men, you understand me, no officers, no soldiers . . . Only machines! . . . Tanks, armoured cars, lorries, motorcycles . . . And of course planes, very many planes . . . The German air force has a colossal superiority over the French and British! . . . There has never been anything like this before . . . This war is quite unlike the last war.'

Lloyd George's words led straight to the question which most of all interested me: would France hold out?

'I don't know . . . I am not sure . . .,' answered Lloyd George. 'In the last war France, in spite of all her faults, was magnificent . . . She fought like a lioness . . . And she had leaders like Foch and Clémenceau . . . Present-day France is not like what she was then . . . Her spirit is different . . . And somehow you don't see any outstanding leaders... Yet the enemy today is much more dangerous than in 1914.'

'But if France falls', I began, 'what will England do?'

I had hardly finished the phrase when Lloyd George cried: 'Fight, fight and go on fighting! . . . The English are not easily frightened. I am a Welshman, you know,' said the old man with a smile, 'and I can judge the English objectively. Yes, the English won't put up their hands even if the Germans were to land on British soil. The English will fight stubbornly and defend their positions . . . Perhaps without any brilliant display, but as firmly as bulldogs... That's what the people are like here.'

I asked what were the grounds for Lloyd George's confidence. It was now clear that Hitlerite Germany had a big military superiority over France. If France were to fall, the Germans would have a big military superiority over Britain as well. Wouldn't the 'Clivedenites' raise their head again in such conditions, wouldn't they again come to power?

Lloyd George's bright blue eyes sparkled even more brightly, and he began explaining the position to me with a kind of passionate fury:

'They are finished with! The bigger the danger, the less chance they have. We can't sign peace with Hitler. We can't! . . . Judge for yourself. Germany always was and always will be stronger than us on land—that is history. Germany at present is stronger than us in the air as well. The only way in which she is inferior to us is on the sea, in her navy . . . But supposing we conclude peace with her. What can be the basis of such a peace at the present time? Obviously by giving Hitler complete freedom of action on the continent of Europe. What will then happen? Hitler will seize all the countries on the Continent except yours, and will harness all their economic, financial and industrial resources. As a result, Hitler in perhaps five years' time will have a navy stronger than the British, and he will become master on the sea as well . . . What will then become of us? What will become of these islands, and of our Empire?'

An expression of terror passed over Lloyd George's lively countenance, and involuntarily he clenched his fists.

'No, no!' he ended with profound conviction. 'Peace with Germany now is absolutely impossible. Even a man like Chamberlain understands that.'

So Lloyd George's opinions confirmed what I had earlier heard from Eden. These opinions were all the more convincing because they were expressed by a man who held no ministerial post, and was in opposition to the Conservatives.

However, I was still not satisfied, and decided to make one last test. Straight from Lloyd George I went to see the Webbs, as their house at Passfield Corner was not far from Bron-y-de.

Sidney and Beatrice Webb at that time had no official posts. They were living peacefully in their country house and writing interesting books: in particular, in 1935 they had published a large work about our country entitled *Soviet Communism*. They were extremely remote from the ideas of Communism, but were favourably disposed to the USSR, and their work played an important propaganda part in the 'thirties in labour and democratic circles of the West. The couple excellently knew and understood the psychology of the British ruling class: Beatrice came from a wealthy bourgeois family while Sidney had worked for many years as an official in the Civil Service. At difficult moments, when I had to ascertain how the British Government would conduct itself in any particular circumstances, I often sought a resolution of my doubts from the Webbs. They gave their forecast willingly, and I don't remember a single occasion on which they were mistaken. Now, too, I decided to listen to their opinion on the question of how Britain would behave in the event of the fall of France.

As I was on very intimate and simple terms with the Webbs, I immediately and frankly on my arrival put the question that was worrying me to them. We were sitting by the fire in their small drawing room, and Beatrice, as always, was sitting on the fireguard with her back to the fire. Her slender hands were clasped about her knees, and she listened closely to what I was saying Beatrice was eighty-two at the time, but her mind worked splendidly.

She reacted at once and without the slightest hesitation to my question.

'Why, of course we shall continue the war.' She said this as though it were something self-understood, just as one might say that every night people go to bed. Sidney supported the opinion of his wife.

I wanted, however, to discover whether the reply had not been given too 'mechanically'. Perhaps they had not realised to the full the sense of the question I had put, and had not weighed up properly the consequences of such a reply. Therefore I began to put questions to them in a somewhat provocative manner. How would Britain be able to continue the war? After all, her army was still only coming into being, and was far behind the German in its training; after all, her generals could not compare with those of Germany in their skill and experience; after all, her air force was numerically much behind the German . . . How then in such conditions would Britain go on fighting Germany?

'How shall we go on fighting?' Beatrice replied vivaciously. 'Just as we fought at the time of Napoleon. You know what took place then. At the beginning we created the first Coalition against Napoleon, and waged open war against him together with our allies, taking part mainly with our navy and our finance. Then the Coalition fell apart. For a time we retired to our islands, and being alone, waited for a change in the international situation, confining ourselves mainly to a naval war against France . . . The change in the international situation came, and we set up the second Coalition, as part of which we again waged open war against Napoleon in Europe. When the second Coalition fell apart, we again retired to our islands and again began waiting for a change for the better in the international situation . . . When that happened, we set up the third Coalition, and so on in the same way. You know that it was only the sixth Coalition that put an end to Napoleon: but it did put an end to him . . . That's the pattern we shall follow today as well.'

Sidney Webb, who had been listening to his wife's arguments in silence, only nodding with approval from time to time, now took up the thread:

'To all appearances, our first coalition in this war—the coalition with France—is coming to an end. I don't think that France under the leadership of Daladier will stand up to Hitler's attack . . . Well, we'll go back to our islands, defend them and wait for the day when a new coalition against Germany will become possible. That time will come. We must only display self-control and determination.'

And so the Webbs also considered that Britain would not accept peace with Germany even if France capitulated. They even anticipated the forms the war would take on England's part if she lost her Continental allies. Their forecast found complete confirmation in subsequent events.

Returning home in the evening, I began summing things up. Comparing my own views with the opinions of Eden, Lloyd

George and the Webbs, I felt that I could now with full responsibility tell my Government what should be expected in the immediate future. The same evening I sent a telegram to Moscow, the substance of which was that even in the event of the fall of France, Britain would remain at war with Germany.

And that is what actually happened.

2

The fall of France

THE German breakthrough at Sedan hung over the destinies of France like a dread shadow. We know now that France, as an independent Great Power, had only a little over a month more to live. At that time we did not know this precisely, but already from the middle of May a vast concern for the future of France spread in political circles in Britain. Many did not wish to speak of it openly, but in their heart of hearts they feared what the morrow might bring to their principal ally on the continent of Europe. The alarm spread beyond the ocean too. It is characteristic in the highest degree that on 15 May, the very next day after the breakthrough at Sedan, Roosevelt made an appeal to Mussolini to refrain from further extending the war. Mussolini, of course, remained deaf to this appeal—but it was quite clear that the American President would not have taken such a step if he did not fear the collapse of France in the most immediate future. During my 'inquiry' described earlier, people as competent as Lloyd George and the Webbs thought the early fall of France most probable.

Similar opinions were expressed by my other acquaintances among M.P.s, politicians and journalists. Naturally I followed all the events at the front with the greatest attention and no less alarm. For there things were taking a more and more sinister turn.

By the middle of May the question of Belgium and Holland had in essence been settled. The Dutch army had capitulated, but Queen Wilhelmina and her Government, evacuated to Britain, proclaimed that they would continue the war with Germany and join the Franco-British coalition. The Belgian army formally capitulated only on 28 May, but already by the middle of the month it had clearly been defeated, and Franco-British help could not save it. In addition, as was mentioned earlier, there had been a split between the Belgian King Leopold and his Government headed by Pierlot: the King had surrendered at discretion to the victor, while the Government decided to continue the war and established itself first in France and then in Britain.

Now Hitler was opposed on the Continent only by France—and on her he had succeeded, on 14 May, in inflicting a dangerous blow. This called forth a reaction in France both political and military. The Reynaud Government, which had replaced the Daladier Government after the Soviet-Finnish war, had fallen into a fever of re-organisation. On 10 May, immediately after the German attack on Holland and Belgium, the Premier decided to 'strengthen' his Government by extending it not to the Left (i.e. not closer to the people) but to the Right (i.e. closer to the '200 families'). Representatives of the Fascist elements in the country entered the Government. On 18 May, soon after the breakthrough at Sedan, Reynaud carried out a new reorganisation of his Government, introducing as Vice-Premier the sinister figure of Marshal Pétain, who in the future was to play the most treacherous part in the capitulation of France. On 19 May Weygand replaced Gamelin as commander-in-chief of the French armed forces. However all these reshufflings from one post to another well deserved the words of the poet Krylov: 'But however you change your places, friends, you're none the better musicians.' For both the old Ministers and generals, and the new, were recruited from one and the same *milieu* of the '200 families', rotten through and through, who considered that it was better to have Hitler than the Popular Front.

It is not surprising that such 'leaders' could not either inspire the masses of the people for the struggle or find the right way to save the country at the moment of deadly danger. This showed itself very speedily in practice.

Nominally, the numerical balance of the German and Franco-British forces in the battles of May 1940 in the West was almost equal. Churchill reports in his war memoirs[1] that the Germans began their offensive with 136 divisions (including 10 armoured and tank divisions with 3,000 vehicles), and were opposed by 135 French, British, Belgian and Dutch divisions. But in fact the

1. *The Second World War.*, Vol. II, pp. 27, 28.

Germans were considerably stronger than the Allies, for three main reasons.

In the first place, the German army surpassed its opponents in armament and methods of struggle. Its tanks, armoured cars, motorcycles and motorised infantry gave it a tremendous shock force and an impetuous speed of advance. This was supplemented by an as yet unprecedented power of its air force. On the other side, the Allied armies and their commanders, fossilised in the traditions of the past, lagged extremely behind the German army in the sphere of modern technique. It is sufficient to say that the 10 German armoured divisions were opposed by only one such French division, while the British had not a single one. In essence, the Allies in forming their armies between the two world wars had before their eyes the experience of the first, and had a poor idea of what the second would be like.

This was why even such a sagacious man as Lloyd George, in the conversation with me which I have quoted, was so astonished that in battle there could be seen on the side of the Germans only machines, hardly any men.

Secondly, the German army in this war for the first time in history applied quote new methods of struggle, which followed naturally from its high saturation with modern technique. The main method for breaking through the front and crushing the enemy became the combination of armoured operations on land and of dive bombers in the air. This had never yet been applied previously: the armies of the Allies were completely unprepared for this, either technically or psychologically: and therefore usually they did not withstand the enemy blow. A breach was immediately created in the line of the front, and tanks and armoured cars rushed into it with furious energy, wiping out everything in their path and emerging with incredible speed in the rear or in the flanks of the allied troops. Neither the French nor the British had either the technique or the habitude, nor had yet worked out methods, for parrying this kind of war, and therefore their armies fell into confusion, gave way to panic and began to retreat.

Thirdly, the German army was governed by a single will and a united command, and was full of the offensive spirit, whereas the armies of the Allies were broken up among several commands (Anglo-French, Belgian, Dutch) and—what was most important—were enfeebled by the corrupting spirit of defeatism emanating from the circle of the '200 families'. In his war memoirs Churchill makes an attempt to throw upon the USSR and the Communists the responsibility for the decomposition of the French army by the spring of 1940. He writes:

'The French Army, gnawed by Soviet-inspired Communism and chilled by the long, cheerless winter on the front, had actually deterioriated.'[1]

What a vivid example of the falsification of history! After all, Churchill could not but be aware that after the fall of France it was precisely from the circles inspired by 'Soviet Communist propaganda' that there emerged thousands of the most heroic fighters of the 'maquis' against the enslavement of their country by the German Nazis. No, the impotence of the French army in its struggle with the enemy was explained not at all by 'Soviet Communist propaganda', but by what amounted to the betrayal of their country by the '200 families' and the French generals closely connected with them. Churchill's argument just quoted is all the more strange because the chapters in his own memoirs which deal with the fall of France provide a lurid picture of the profound corruption of her political and military leadership. I will quote only one example out of many. In characterising such an important figure as Weygand, on whom was imposed the task of saving France from defeat, Churchill says:

'He had a profound, life-long dislike of the Parliamentary régime of the Third Republic. As an ardently religious Catholic, he saw in the ruin which had overwhelmed his country the chastisement of God for its abandonment of the Christian faith.'[2]

How could such a man lead an army to fight the enemy!

After all that has been said, can one be surprised that in the course of five days after the breakthrough at Sedan the Germans succeeding in crossing the whole of France from east to west and on 19 May in reaching Abbeville, on the shores of the Atlantic Ocean? In this way the Franco-British front was cut in two, the northern part of France was separated from the rest of the country, and all the Allied forces in the northern part found themselves in a trap, pressed against the shores of the North Sea and the English Channel. Among them was the British Expeditionary Corps commanded by General Gort.

These events aroused genuine panic in Paris. Churchill describes in his memoirs how on the morning of 15 May, i.e. the day

1. *Ibid.*, p. 26.
2. *Ibid.*, p. 176.

after the breakthrough, the French Premier Reynaud rang him up and exclaimed with despair in his voice that they had been defeated. Churchill vainly sought to calm him, and to prove to him that every breakthrough can be liquidated. In view of this, Churchill together with Generals Dill and Ismay on 16 May flew to Paris in order to strengthen the will to resist of the French leaders. He found a picture of depression and helplessness. General Gamelin, who was still in command, did not know what to do. And when Churchill asked: 'Where is the strategic reserve?' Gamelin shrugged his shoulders and replied: 'There is none.'[1] These reactionary generals proved entirely incapable even in the military sense!

At that time I did not know all the details of which Churchill writes, but the main and essential facts were clear already in May 1940. It was not by chance that precisely in these days I undertook my 'investigation' on the question of what Britain's attitude would be after France left the war.

After having cut off the northern part of France, the Germans began breaking up the Allied forces which had been caught there, seeking to capture separate groups. The capitulation of the Belgian army made their task much simpler. The French and British units resisted stubbornly, but still were obliged step by step to retreat to the coast. The question of evacuating them by ship from France became acute. It was essential to retain in the hands of the Allies a few ports where their troops could be taken on board, and it was also essential at 'lightning' speed to concentrate a sufficient number of ships in those ports. This proved very difficult.

At first it was expected that three ports—Boulogne, Calais and Dunkirk—would be used for the evacuation; but the Allies did not succeed in retaining the first two, so powerful was the German pressure. In the end there remained only Dunkirk with a small stretch of the coast. And now on this tiny space there were gathered over 300,000 men (mainly British), striving to get away to Britain.

The situation was exceptionally difficult. The German land army, disposing of a large number of tanks and armoured cars, was gripping the Dunkirk area in an iron ring. The German air force was bombing it without cease. A torrent of fire and destruction fell upon the troops of the Allies there, and on the vessels

1. *The Second World War*, Vol. II. p. 42.

which had arrived to evacuate them. It very soon became clear that, if the evacuation were not carried out within a few days, it would not take place at all, and the Anglo-French forces gathered there would inevitably be exterminated or captured by the Germans. For such a rapid evacuation of such a large number of troops, the port of Dunkirk was too small. It was necessary to organise the embarkation of the men direct from the seashore: but for this there was needed a vast number of small shallow-draught vessels, capable of coming close in-shore. Where could they be found?

And it was just at this moment that something took place which at the time created the greatest impression on the whole world. All over England there suddenly broke forth a kind of hurricane. Everyone wanted to do what he could to save 'our boys' there, on the Dunkirk shore. The owners of yachts, motor-boats, barges, fishing vessels, tugs, boats with outboard motors, even sailing boats, streamed into the Admiralty, offering their services to carry away the British soldiers from the French shore. It was a difficult and risky operation: the German planes and guns were doing all in their power to prevent the evacuation. But no one reckoned with the danger. The Admiralty succeeded in imposing a certain degree of organisation on this mighty national impetus. About 400 small vessels took part in Operation 'Dynamo' (the code name for the evacuation of the Allied troops), nearly half of them perished, but none the less they were of the greatest value. Coming right up to the shore, they took on men from boats or even straight out of the water, hurried over to Dover or some other British port, unloaded rapidly and again left for the French coast for a new group of evacuees. Many vessels made their journeys there and back dozens of times under bombs and shells, mostly under the shelter of darkness. And parallel with them large steamers and warships, defended by the British air force, withdrew entire units from the port of Dunkirk. This was a genuinely heroic evacuation, and the British were deservedly proud of it. It continued for ten days—from 26 May to 4 June—and was crowned with unquestionable success. True, all their armament and supplies had to be abandoned in France, but 338,000 men were saved and delivered to England, 100,000 of them taken off by small vessels direct from the shore. Among those saved were approximately 50,000 Frenchmen. Of 861 vessels which took part in Operation 'Dynamo'. 243 were sunk.

A deep sigh of relief could be heard over the whole country when the operation was completed. At every step one could see the usually calm and cool British congratulating each other, and their faces showing unwonted emotion.

One small but so characteristic recollection of those days remains with me. Not far from our Embassy there was a small but comfortable restaurant, where I liked to go in to have a cup of tea or drink a bottle of Guinness. Gradually I became fairly well acquainted with its owner, who was always at the counter. He seemed to me a typical English average man-in-the-street: socially you could place him somewhat on the boundary between petty bourgeois and middle class, politics did not interest him, but at the elections he always voted Conservative, if he voted at all. In the newspapers he read only the Stock Exchange reports and the sports pages, but most of all he talked about his restaurant and how to make money.

During the Dunkirk events I called at the restaurant. The owner was not in his usual place, and his wife was managing at the counter. Politely I inquired why I didn't see the master. His wife, all at once becoming serious and even solemn, replied significantly: 'He's over there'—and made an indefinite gesture in the air.

'Where, over there?' not understanding her at once, I asked.

'Well, there,' said the woman, looking at me in surprise, and then adding: 'At Dunkirk.'

'At Dunkirk?' My voice gave away my disbelief. 'What is he doing there?'

'What do you think he's doing?' exploded the lady. 'The same as everybody else: saving our boys from the Germans.'

And then, suddenly relaxing, in quite a different tone she continued:

'I am so worried, so afraid . . . It's terribly dangerous there. Anything may happen . . . We have a small motor-boat, and when my husband heard that small boats were needed to get our boys away, you couldn't hold him . . . I hope everything goes well.'

I was amazed. Least of all had I expected that a man like the owner of this restaurant would voluntarily take part in this Operation 'Dynamo'. But he did, and it was an eloquent sign. I remember thinking: 'It isn't easy to conquer such a people.'

On 4 June Churchill made a report to Parliament on the military situation and on Operation 'Dynamo'. After setting forth very frankly what had happened during the previous three weeks and describing in detail what was done at Dunkirk, the Premier admitted that in France and Belgium there had taken place 'a colossal military disaster' the consequences of which were hard to foresee. Churchill ended his speech with the following words:

'We shall go on to the end, we shall fight in France, we shall fight on the seas and oceans, we shall fight with growing confidence and growing strength in the air, we shall defend our island whatever the cost may be . . . And even if, which I do not for a moment believe, this island or a large part of it were subjugated and starving, then our Empire beyond the seas, armed and guarded by the British Fleet, would carry on the struggle until, in God's good time, the New World, with all its power and might, steps forth to the rescue and the liberation of the Old.'[1]

I was present at the meeting of the House of Commons, and could see the mood of the M.P.s. There was a severe and solemn silence in the Chamber. All parties without distinction were experiencing a double feeling of relief and satisfaction. Relief by the knowledge that 'our boys' had been saved. Satisfaction from the knowledge that at last the country had a Government which was willing and able to carry on a genuine struggle against Hitlerite Germany. After Dunkirk and the powerful upsurge of feeling among the broadest masses of the people to which it gave rise, Churchill's words about Britain's unbending will to fight sounded neither pompous nor romantic.

On my way home from Parliament I thought that the scene in the House of Commons which I had just witnessed vividly confirmed the opinions I had so recently heard expressed by the Webbs and by Lloyd George. It became clearer to me that even after the fall of France, of which there could be no longer any doubt, England would not make peace with Germany and would continue the war.

In connection with Dunkirk, great argument already arose during the war, and still more after the war, on the question of how the Germans could have permitted the successful evacuation of such large Allied forces which had been seemingly caught in a trap. In these arguments special emphasis was laid on the fact that in direct proximity to Dunkirk there were large armoured units of the German Wehrmacht, which were not, however, used against the British and French. Should the Germans have used them, Dunkirk too would have become a real disaster for the Allies.

1. *The Second World War*, Vol. II, pp. 103–4.

'Well informed' people, in military uniforms or without them, even built up various theories to explain such strange behaviour on the part of the Germans. Some asserted that Hitler had deliberately 'let out' the British, as he had counted very much after the fall of France on a rapid peace with Britain, and feared that the capture by the Germans of hundreds of thousands of British soldiers might make the agreement he so desired more difficult.

Others said that by the time of Dunkirk the German armoured units disposed near the place where evacuation was taking place were very exhausted: they had previously made a long journey and required repair and rehabilitation. These were essential as a preparation for the second phase of the 'battle for France', which was to open the road to Paris and made it possible to oblige France to capitulate. In the interests of the speediest possible completion of the French campaign, the Germans did not want to divert their mechanised forces from this main task for the sake of a comparatively secondary operation, the capture of the British Expeditionary Corps. A third group were convinced that some accidental error had overtaken the German military machine at the very time of Dunkirk: someone had misunderstood Hitler's instructions, someone had incorrectly passed on the orders of the higher military authorities to someone else, and when this was noticed it was already too late—the Anglo-French evacuation had been completed. Others again considered that the Germans, who as yet had not had great experience in air warfare, had overestimated the importance of the air-force and had decided that it alone, without the support of mechanised land forces, could upset the evacuation.

I must say that the literature published since the war (documents, memoirs and special studies) do not give any definite and convincing reply to the question. It seems to me therefore that the 'miracle of Dunkirk' is to be explained by a combination of the most varied circumstances—political, military and psychological—given one accidental, but very important factor: during all the critical days, the sea was absolutely calm. This made possible the large-scale use of a great number of small vessels for the evacuation, and the embarkation of hundreds of thousands of soldiers direct from the shore or even out of the water.

On 5 June 1940 the second phase of the 'battle for France' began. Having seized the northern part of the country, the Germans now turned to the south, with the object first of all of occupying Paris and, should this not lead to the capitulation of France, of continuing their advance in various directions up to the occupation of the whole of the country, if that proved necessary. However, there proved no need of this.

The Reynaud government and the military leadership headed by Weygand were least of all thinking of any serious resistance, although France still had large military forces at her disposal. On the contrary, their thoughts were now turned to the problem of how to bring about a cease-fire and conclude an armistice as soon as possible. A particularly sinister part in this respect was played by Pétain and Weygand. Rumours of this reached me even at that time. What I did not know then, and what became clear to me much later, was the attitude of Laval: he was not then in the government, but was very influential in government circles. It was not enough for him that France should leave the war and conclude peace with Germany: no, he wanted France to go over to the side of Germany and to support Hitler's policy of conquest.

The results of such moods among the ruling clique are comprehensible. The Germans broke through the French front without difficulty in several places, and began rapidly approaching Paris. Chaos, disorganisation and mass desertion began in the French Army. Panic seized on the population. Millions of Frenchmen of all ranks and classes left their dwellings and fled to the south to escape the Germans. All roads were choked with endless crowds of refugees, which made any movement of troops along them quite impossible. All the accustomed forms of life at once fell to pieces. Public discipline and order disappeared. A great country, with so many centuries of glorious history behind it, was seized with political, military and psychological paralysis. I need not dwell in any greater detail on the terrible June days of 1940 in France: they have been well described for Soviet readers in the book by G. M. Ratiani[1], and also in I. G. Ehrenburg's well-known novel *The Fall of Paris*.

On 10 June a new factor appeared in the bloody game: Italy declared war on Britain and France. Now, when the battle for France had in its essentials been decided by the strength of German arms, Mussolini in jackal fashion decided to snatch for himself a morsel of the attractive booty. Thirty-two Italian divisions were thrown against France. They were resisted by only three French divisions, and by fortress garrisons which added up to

1. *The End of the Third Republic* (in Russian). Moscow, 1964.

another three divisions. Thus the Italian Fascists were more than five times as numerous as the French. And nevertheless they proved impotent! Impotent, in spite even of the fact that the Germans were approaching the rear of the French troops fighting the Italians, in their advance from the north. The Italians were hopelessly stranded in the Alpine passes, stopped by the courageous resistance of the French, while their attempt to capture Nice was a failure: they could not manage to move beyond the outskirts of Mentone. This notable episode demonstrates once more that the fighting spirit of the French army was not broken by the German invasion, and that if it had had firm and courageous commanders, much would have turned out otherwise in the course of the second world war. But that is precisely what it lacked.

Churchill recounts in his memoirs how on 11 June, i.e. a week after the German advance southward had begun, he flew to France with Eden, accompanied also by Generals Dill and Ismay, to discuss with the Reynaud government the situation which had been created. In this discussion there took part on the French side, in addition to the Premier himself, Pétain, Weygand and Major-General de Gaulle, who had not long before been appointed Assistant Minister of Defence. Apart from the latter, all the French representatives were in a state of great depression and even despair.

Churchill suggested that they should defend Paris at all costs. This might have considerably delayed and hampered any further advance by the Germans. He was even naïve enough to refer to the example of Madrid, which in November 1936 had stopped the Franco offensive at the outskirts of the city, and had held the front line there brought into being, for the next two years and a half. How badly even such a man as Churchill understood the motive forces of contemporary history! Madrid held out because it was defended by a revolutionary people, with revolutionary leaders—and first of all Communists—at its head, men who believed in their future and were inspired by the slogan: 'Better to die on one's feet than to live on one's knees.' Could Reynaud, Pétain and Weygand do anything of the kind? Did they believe in their future? Could they inspire broad masses of the French people to battle in the name of the salvation of France?

The Reynaud Government rejected Churchill's proposal, and on 14 June the Germans occupied Paris without meeting any resistance.

At the same Anglo-French conference Churchill proposed the following plan: if France was not capable of carrying on a regular war with Germany, let the French Government transfer itself to North Africa, where there were large colonial possessions: let it make the utmost use of its powerful fleet: let it launch large-scale partisan warfare in France itself (particularly in the mountainous districts), for which purpose the French army units still in existence would be useful: let France continue the struggle against Hitler in this new form. Only de Gaulle was sympathetic to Churchill's plan; all the rest for various reasons declared it impracticable.

Instead, the French Ministers and generals insistently demanded that Churchill should immediately send over to their aid twenty-five squadrons of planes which had been made ready in Britain for defence against a German invasion. At that time such an invasion was expected immediately after the fall of France. Churchill did not agree to this, all the more that twenty-five squadrons would in any case have decided nothing: France at that time was in such a condition that it was already unthinkable that she could be saved from defeat.

The capitulation of France was preceded by one more final attempt of the British Government to retain her in the struggle against Hitlerite Germany. On 16 June it proposed the fusion of the two States, France and Britain, in a single Franco-British Union, with common departments of defence, foreign affairs, finance and economy. Every citizen of France would become a British citizen, and vice-versa. For the period of the war there would be set up a single War Cabinet, to which all the armed forces of both countries would be subordinated. The devastations brought about by the war would be covered by the resources of both countries, treated as a single fund.

However, the French Government categorically rejected the British proposal: Reynaud resigned, and Pétain became head of the government. The new Premier immediately went into action, and on 22 June an armistice was signed by France and Germany at Compiègne. Here in 1918 there had been concluded the armistice between defeated Germany and the victorious Allies—Britain, France and the USA. Now Hitler wanted to take his revenge: he demanded that in that very place there should be held the ceremony of signature of the armistice between vanquished France and victorious Germany. The conditions of the armistice were very onerous. Germany occupied about two-thirds of the whole of France, including Paris, while the rest of the country's territory was to be formally under the authority of the Pétain Government—which in effect meant the slightly-veiled authority of Germany. The French armed forces on land and sea were to be demobilised, and all their armament passed into the hands of the Germans. France undertook to cover the expenses of the German occupation troops, etc. For four whole years a gloomy night of Fascist reaction descended upon France, a night in which only the clanking of chains could be heard, and the ever more frequent bursts of fire from the heroic fighters of the Resistance...

Before concluding this chapter, I should mention one important episode which was played out already after the capitulation of France. Article eight of the armistice terms provided that the French navy should be 'concentrated in the ports which will be determined, and there demobilised and disarmed under German and Italian control'. This meant that the French fleet, as yet fully ready for war, would enter harbours which were in the hands of the Fascist Powers. What would happen then? Would it not then be seized by these Powers? Would they not make use of it for the war with Britain? To prevent anything similar happening was of decisive importance for the British Government. For the French fleet at that time ranked fourth in strength in the world, after the British, American and Japanese, and it represented a serious fighting force. The addition of the French fleet to the German and Italian would change the balance of forces at sea in a direction very unfavourable for Britain, and would make it easier for the Germans to invade the British Isles. In this way the fate of the French fleet became a question of life and death for Britain.

Churchill understood this perfectly, and therefore at his meetings with the French Ministers and generals in June, when the question of the capitulation of France was being faced in all its magnitude, he stubbornly insisted that the French fleet in any circumstances should not be handed over to the Germans. On 15 June the French Government decided to ask Hitler for the terms of an armistice, and at the same time requested the British Government to free it from the obligation not to enter into negotiations for an armistice or peace otherwise than by common agreement—an obligation undertaken in the Anglo-French Treaty of 28 March 1940. On 16 June the British Government replied that it would not raise objection to the proposed action of the French Government, but on the absolute condition that the French fleet would be immediately moved to British ports. Reynaud and Admiral Darlan, the naval Commander-in-Chief, avoided a pledge to fulfil this condition, but once again assured the British Government (as they had done more than once already) that in no event would they permit the French fleet to pass into the hands of the Germans. It was that same day that Reynaud resigned and Pétain became Premier. Darlan was appointed Minister for the Navy. The future of the French fleet was now doubtful.

The situation became even more threatening because the fleet was now entirely at Darlan's disposal.

This gallant Admiral represented an extremely sinister figure. Coming of an old naval family—one of his ancestors perished in 1805 at the famous battle of Trafalgar—Darlan was always extremely anti-British. He could never forgive the British the fact that, 135 years before, Nelson had defeated the Franco-Spanish fleet and thereby averted an invasion of Britain by Napoleon. Politically Darlan was an extreme reactionary, and the watchword: 'Better Hitler than the People's Front' found a sympathetic response in his heart. And it was now on him that to a great extent depended what would become of the French fleet.

In such circumstances the British Government decided to act immediately and sharply. The operation was fixed for 3 July.

At that time the French fleet was divided: part of it was at Toulon and other sections at Oran, Dakar and Alexandria.

On the morning of 3 July a British squadron approached Oran, commanded by Vice-Admiral Somerville. It was composed of the *Valiant* and *Resolution* battleships, the battle-cruiser *Hood*, the *Ark Royal* aircraft-carrier, two smaller cruisers and eleven destroyers. Somerville presented an ultimatum to Admiral Gensoul, commander of the French ships, in which he was requested: (a) to join the British fleet and together with it carry on the struggle against Germany and Italy, or (b) with reduced crews to leave under British control for one of the British ports, whence these reduced crews would be repatriated, or (c) proceed with reduced crews under British control to one of the French ports in America, for example, in Martinique, where the French warships could be demilitarised for the period of the war. If Admiral Gensoul found it impossible to accept any of these proposals, he must sink the French ships within six hours. Should he refuse to do so, Admiral Somerville would be obliged to use force.

During the whole day, negotiations between the two Admirals went on, but they brought no agreement. Thereupon, at about 6 p.m., Somerville opened fire on the French ships, to which they replied likewise. The battle continued no more than ten to fifteen minutes. As a result, the battleship *Bretagne* blew up, a second battleship *Provence* and the cruiser *Dunkerque* were seriously damaged, while the cruiser *Strasbourg* escaped from Oran and managed to reach Toulon; several other ships succeeded in doing the same.

At Alexandria things did not reach an open clash, and the French Admiral Godfroy, who was in command there, agreed to take a number of measures rendering the French ships incapable of battle.

On the same day, 3 July, the British took over control, almost without resistance, of the French warships at Plymouth and Portsmouth. On 8 July the British aircraft-carrier *Hermes* seriously damaged and put out of action the French battleship *Richelieu* at Dakar.

Sometime later, as a result of lengthy negotiations, two French light cruisers and one aircraft-carrier lying in France's American colonies, were demobilised.

On 5 July the Pétain government, which had chosen Vichy as its capital (and henceforth was called the 'Vichy Government') broke off diplomatic relations with Britain; and on 11 July Pétain became French President in place of Lebrun, who had resigned.

On 4 July, the day after the events at Oran, Churchill told Parliament of what had happened. I was present at the session. The Premier was visibly agitated. The members listened to him with bated breath. When Churchill finished, there took place a scene which, 'old hands' in Parliament told me, had never occurred before: all the Members with one accord, in a kind of spontaneous outburst, sprang up and gave the Premier a real ovation. It was obvious that, as it were, a mountain had fallen from their shoulders.

For me as Ambassador of the USSR the events of 3–4 July were also of great significance. They demonstrated convincingly that Britain really would continue to fight on.

3

Awaiting the Invasion

THE thought of a German invasion of the British Isles or, at least, of a serious attempt at such an invasion after the fall of France, penetrated the whole atmosphere in Britain, and coloured all the feelings and actions of the population like some poisonous admixture. Churchill somewhat obscures this element in his war memoirs. He strives to show that Hitler never had any chance of a successful fulfilment of 'Operation Sea-Lion', the code name for the invasion operations, and that leading circles in Britain were allegedly quite convinced of this already in the summer of 1940. It seems to me that Churchill here falls into an error characteristic of many writers of reminiscences—to depict themselves and their immediate colleagues, retrospectively, as cleverer than they were at the moment the events themselves took place. In fact, matters stood somewhat differently.

Many facts bore witness to this. First of all, it was evidenced by the sharp struggle over the fate of the French fleet which I have described earlier. Extremely indicative, too, was my conversation with Churchill on 3 July 1940 at his official residence in 10 Downing Street. The Premier was full of life and energy, and seemed very cheerful and fresh. It appeared to me that he was in a very exhilarated mood. It was only next day that I realised the explanation.

Our conversation was brief, but most significant. I asked Churchill how he conceived of the further fate of the French navy. Sitting face to face with the Premier, I did not yet know that it was just on that day, 3 July, that that fate was being decided. The tremendous importance of this question was clear to me, and therefore I wanted to hear what the Prime Minister himself thought on this subject.

Churchill puffed at his cigar, which was as always between his teeth, and, with a sly flash of his eyes through the bluish smoke, replied in the formal bureaucratic phrase which I knew so well from my correspondence with the Foreign Office: 'This question is receiving attention.'

It was just at that moment that the broadsides of the British warships were thundering at Oran.

I continued: 'May I ask what will be your general strategy now, after the fall of France?'

Churchill once again drew at his cigar, and replied with a smile: 'My general strategy at present is to last out the next three months.'

This had to be understood in this way: Churchill feared a German invasion of the British Isles, but from the end of September (i.e. in approximately three months), equinoctial storms begin in the Channel, and then the landing of an enemy army on the British coast becomes impossible.

On 12 July I went to see Eden, now War Minister. After a brief exchange on the situation created, Eden said *inter alia*:

'Immediately after Dunkirk, the situation was terrible: over three hundred thousand men brought away from France represented simply a mass of patriotically inclined, but completely disorganised and unarmed lads . . . Now things have become a little easier: divisions have appeared, we have some arms, but nevertheless the situation is exceptionally difficult. We are awaiting invasion . . . Of course we will fight to the last . . . But if we had more arms! We have so little! . . .'

'But have you no possibility of increasing the quantity of your arms?' I asked. 'You yourselves have a large war industry, and you could get quite a lot from the USA.'

'We are taking steps! The most energetic steps!' cried Eden. 'But all this takes time, and will Hitler give us the time?'

I did not think it convenient to dwell in greater detail on the question of armament in my conversation with Eden, but I knew from other sources in just those days that negotiations were proceeding between Churchill and Roosevelt about the urgent supply to Britain from the USA of a large number of rifles and guns, and also of several dozen destroyers. At the time of my conversation with Eden the negotiations were not yet completed, but it will be probably suitable to mention at this point what was their final outcome.

The Americans gave the British half a million rifles, several hundred guns and fifty destroyers—all equipment which was left over from the first world war. No new models were received from the USA. In the extremities to which Britain was reduced after the fall of France, even this armament was of great value, and I well remember with what agitation and worry the Ministers awaited the convoys which were bringing the American 'gift' across the ocean. The rifles were at once distributed to members of the 'Home Guard', which had been formed specially to defend the country in the event of invasion: in many cases they replaced the sports guns, pikes and clubs with which many had been armed earlier, for lack of anything better. The artillery as it arrived was distributed partly to the regular army, and partly to the same Home Guards. The destroyers, which reached the British Government rather later, played their part in the naval war which was extending and intensifying.

It was not by accident that I have put the word gift in quotation marks. I admit that Roosevelt was personally ready to hand over the American equipment without any compensation, because as a man of far-seeing views, he well understood that Britain was the first line of defence for the USA against the threat of Hitler's world domination, and that therefore the basic strategic interest of the USA dictated the strengthening of that front line in every possible way. But Roosevelt had to reckon with the predominance of short-sighted and greedy businessmen in the leading circles of his country, who wanted to sell even their own safety for dollars. As a result, the Anglo-American transaction of 1940 assumed a much less generous character. On one occasion, much later, Lloyd George said to me:

'Uncle Sam has remained Uncle Sam . . . He hasn't been very generous . . . For this old iron we have had to pay with several very important bases on our territory . . . But what could we do? There was no other way out.'

Lloyd George had in mind the Anglo-American agreement announced by Churchill in Parliament on 5 September 1940: in exchange for the 'old iron', the British Government was leasing to the USA for ninety-nine years territory lying along the eastern shores of the American continent (in Newfoundland, the Bermudas and Bahamas, in Jamaica, Antigua, St. Lucia, Trinidad and

British Guiana) for the establishment of naval and air bases.

Eden expected a German invasion. It was expected at the other end of the social ladder, too. One day in July I drove with an English acquaintance out of town and on the road we stopped to change a tyre. Near by was the house of a small farmer. The owner, a man of about sixty with muscular arms and a sunburned face, came up to us and began helping in fitting the spare wheel. Then we began talking, and he invited us into his house. He showed us his barns, his pigs, his chickens and finally his fields. But the strange thing was that the fields were littered with roots of trees, logs, broken ploughs, harrows and other agricultural machinery. I asked him without thinking:

'What's all this for?'

The farmer smiled slyly and replied;

'So that the German planes will not be able to land in this field... Many people have done this in our district.'

At that time a German invasion was thought of in two main forms—by sea and from the air. It was anticipated that the main invasion area would be the south-eastern corner of England nearest of all to the Continent. The Germans would come by sea across the Channel, particularly in the most narrow part, Calais-Dover and on the east coast, between Dover and the Wash. This was less dangerous, because the British fleet far surpassed in numbers and power anything that Hitler could oppose to it at sea. Much more serious was the danger from the air, because the German air force was stronger than the British, and could in certain conditions drop parachutists and even carry out landings in the rear of the troops defending the coasts, and deeper inland at the most important key points. It was just because of this that all aerodromes were made ready for action, and put under special guard against all possible attempts by the Germans to use them for landing their own planes: and all lawns, fields and sports grounds at all suitable for landing were disfigured by the most fanciful pits, ditches, mounds and other obstacles. The beauty of the English landscape suffered from this, of course, but in return security against air invasion by the enemy was increased. At the same time the Government was hastily forming 'mobile reserves', which could at any moment be sent to any part of the country to fight German parachutists or German landings from the air.

Parallel with this there went on feverish preparation of the country and the people for a life-and-death struggle. Along the south and eastern coasts a 'defence zone' was brought into being, twenty miles deep, strongly fortified and equipped with a large number of reliable shelters. The majority of the people in this zone were evacuated. Their place was taken by troops and Home Guard detachments. Heavy batteries were established at Dover capable of covering the Straits. Large naval forces were concentrated at the near approaches to possible invasion areas. The Air Force was on duty day and night, ready to go into battle at the first signal. Minefields were sown in the Channel at the approaches to Britain. School-children were evacuated to the North from the towns of southern England. Everywhere volunteers were called upon to build fortifications. Housewives sacrificed their aluminium saucepans, frying-pans and cups for the aircraft industry. Builders stopped using iron and steel in order to increase the output of arms. Thousands of public and private bomb shelters were hurriedly built in London and the provinces. Hundreds of barrage balloons hung in the sky over the towns. In every small place the defence was entrusted to the Home Guards. Armaments and aircraft works operated all round the clock. The newspapers, the BBC, the Church, the cinema called on all and sundry to help in beating off the danger, and recalled the patriotic feats of past generations. So-called silence columns were organised to combat defeatism. A struggle went on a broad front with the British Fascist groups, and most of their leaders (Mosley, Admiral Domville and others) were arrested. All this taken together, and much else, gave rise among the general mass of the people to a feeling of determination, tenseness, concentration and purposefulness such as is not often encountered in history. Everyone was deeply penetrated with one thought, one feeling and one striving—to give a heavy rebuff to the terrible enemy, and to stand fast at all costs.

From the second half of July the Germans began concentrating ships, self-propelled barges and fast motor-boats in the Belgian and French ports across the Channel. At the same time they established heavy batteries in the neighbourhood of Calais, capable of bombarding the British coast. Large German forces began to be concentrated in various towns of northern France. The peril of invasion was clearly increasing. The strain upon the country grew higher. The British Government took steps to reduce the German peril: almost daily the British Air Force was bombing the ships which the Germans were concentrating, the Home Guards, now numbering more than a million, were training energetically, and as far as possible the Government was perfecting the armament of the regular army. It paid particular attention to speeding up the output of aircraft, sanctioning all the resolute measures for this purpose which Lord Beaverbrook was taking as Minister of Aircraft Production.

And still there was not complete confidence that an invasion was impossible. It did not exist either among members of the Government or among rank-and-file British people.

It was in those days that, being on one occasion in Parliament and meeting Arthur Greenwood in the Lobby—he was Minister without portfolio in Churchill's Cabinet, on behalf of the Labour Party—I asked him what he thought of the probability of invasion. His reply was very characteristic:

'Probability? No! Possibility? Yes! But in any case we shall fight to the bitter end.'

A few minutes later I encountered Walter Elliot, several times a Minister in former Conservative governments and my old acquaintance. I put the same question to him.

'An invasion is possible,' Elliot replied, 'but unquestionably it will fail.'

My opinion at that time coincided to a large extent with Elliot's. I thought it possible that the Germans would make an attempt on Britain by sea and from the air, and that for a certain time they might succeed in occupying this or that piece of territory: but I thought it out of the question that they could firmly establish themselves there, and still less could they conquer the whole island. In particular, I reckoned with the possibility of a temporary appearance of the Germans in London, or at any rate in some parts of London. Just because of this, at that time, I even inquired of Moscow how I should conduct myself if the Germans were to occupy the district in London in which our Embassy is situated, and received the necessary instructions from the People's Commissariat for Foreign Affairs.

Britain spent three months—July, August and September—in the greatest possible tension, in an extreme state of alarm, in daily expectation of invasion by the enemy; and it was only after the autumn equinox, when the usual storms began in the Channel, that both the Government and the mass of the people began gradually to return to calm. It became clear to everyone that the peril of a German invasion was over, at least for that year.

Today, many years later, one involuntarily seeks a convincing reply to the question, why did this happen? Why did the Germans not risk attacking the British Isles?

The historians, politicians and publicists who have studied this question since the war have not been able to arrive at a common opinion as to the reasons which forced Hitler to renounce this alluring objective. Partly this is explained by political and national differences among them. However, summing up all the opinions and considerations, conceptions and theories, expressed on this subject, and also recalling everything I myself saw and heard in 1940, I am inclined to come to the following conclusion.

Undoubtedly, Hitler after the fall of France at once began preparing in every possible way for the most rapid ending of the war with Britain. If he had succeeded in this, he would have had a free hand in action in other directions, first of all against the USSR. Moreover, if Britain left the war when the balance of forces was such as existed in the summer of 1940, it would mean the final hegemony of Germany on the European continent (not reckoning the Soviet Union), with all its human, industrial and natural resources, which could have been harnessed in the service of German might. It would have been a decisive step on the road to building up the world domination of Hitlerism. Temporarily left in peace, Britain would soon have felt the heavy hand of the Führer.

But how was the war with Britain to be ended?

Hitler naturally preferred to do this by signing a peace advantageous for Germany. There is much evidence that he expected Britain to express her submission not later than three weeks after the capitulation of France, i.e. approximately by the middle of July. When this did not happen, he informed his Chiefs of Staff on 21 July that, since England did not wish to recognise her defeat, reckoning on the help of the USA and hoping for a future change in German-Soviet relations, the carrying out of the plan for 'Sea-Lion' on which the German Staffs had been working since the very beginning of the war, was now on the agenda. The fulfilment of this plan required the landing of forty divisions on the British Isles, and assuring their regular reinforcement and supplies.

When in this way the plan for 'Sea-Lion' was transformed from studies in an office into an urgent operational task, there gradually began to be revealed the vast difficulties of its realisation. Britain unquestionably dominated the seas, while the German navy, always far weaker than the British, had in addition been seriously weakened during the Norwegian operation, losing about one-third of its ships. The German Air Force was more numerous than the British, but the latter all the same was strong enough to offer serious resistance to its adversary. Britain was ruled by a Government which did not admit even the thought of capitulation, while the great mass of the people were filled with resolution and were preparing for an obstinate defence. All this made an attack on Britain a very dangerous operation, and the memory of the unsuccessful attempts by Napoleon and other would-be conquerors to step down on to the shores of Britain had a chilling effect on Hitler, and particularly on his military advisers. For long they went on arguing, wavering, changing their plans; and meanwhile the days ran by, and the convenient time for invasion was passing. In the end Hitler appointed 15 September as the day of invasion—which for climatic reasons was in reality already late—but the Germans were unable to maintain even this date. Raids by the British Air Force constantly put out of action the vessels assembled by the Germans for transporting their troops across the Straits, and this caused inevitable postponements and delays in realising the plan for 'Sea-Lion'. And when the autumn storms began in the Channel, the whole plan had to be indefinitely postponed; while later, owing to the changed course of events, the Germans had to forget about it altogether.

It seems to me that a very great part in winding up the plan for 'Sea-Lion' was played by the German Admiral Raeder, who was ceaselessly emphasising the whole time that he could ensure the transporting of German troops to Britain only if there were complete domination of the Dover-Calais area by the German Air Force. Goering could not meet such a condition, and as a result the attempt at an invasion of Britain did not take place.

4

The 'Big Blitz'

It began on 7 September 1940.

There had been German air raids on London earlier, in July and August. But these were individual raids. They did not last long—two to three hours, and there were considerable intervals between them. But now something quite different fell upon the giant city.

I well remember the first raid on 7 September. Exactly at 9 p.m. there began high in the darkened sky a kind of strange and unaccustomed roar. It seemed as though a multitude of enormous birds was circling in the sky, each of them giving out a protracted, howling and piercing sound. At once it was frightening and revolting. Then dull blows could be heard. Now here, now there, now nearer, now further off.

We went up to the top floor of the Embassy building, and saw from there how there were shooting up in various places, slightly dimmed by the London darkness, high tongues of flame. We awaited answering fire from the earth, frequent and numerous—but it did not take place. Only here and there, in the thick darkness of the night, a feeble crack could be heard. We expected that, after hurling down their deadly cargo, the German planes would leave, and there would once again be stillness in the sky. But no! After a half-hour's break there was again in the air that protracted howling and heart-freezing sound, again the dull blows, again the long tongues of flame. Evidently this was the second wave . . .

Then followed a third, then a fourth, and so continuously until 6 a.m. Exactly at six everything ended, and the sky became the usual London sky.

But on the earth everything was upside down. At 7 a.m. my wife and I took our car and drove through the city. The district which had been attacked by night was comparatively far from the Embassy, and we could see nothing in particular in the neighbouring streets. But the more we approached the zone of German bombardment the more terrible the picture became.

Wrecked houses . . . Fallen walls . . . Heaps of ruins, broken furniture, smashed cars . . . The still smoking remains of timber-yards, coal stores, oil tanks . . . Crowds of frightened people, trying to salvage something from their broken property . . . Terrible cries coming from somewhere below, from the foundations of houses collapsed into heaps of stones and earth . . . Mothers sobbing over the mutilated bodies of their children . . . Men cursing with furious glances at the sky . . . And everywhere the sharp smell of burning and the particular odour left by an exploded bomb.

In one place I saw the inside wall of a three-storey house: all the rest, as though cut off by a ruler, lay in heaps below. In the wall was an alcove. A child's cot was hanging by some miracle in the air, suspended by its corner from the wall of the alcove. On the cot lay a large doll with a red ribbon in its hair . . . One's heart momentarily froze with the thought: 'And where is the mistress of that doll? Probably under a heap of ruins with a broken skull.' For long I could not forget this scene, so simple and so pathetic.

Civil Defence detachments were everywhere busy around the ruins, digging out those buried in them, putting out still burning pyres, carrying away the wounded and other victims, allocating those who had remained homeless to their temporary refuges. As this was the first case of such a raid, however, the work of the rescuers did not go very smoothly, and there was friction and inconsistency. There was a good deal of noise, with many complaints and protests. Later, when the 'big blitz' became something usual, everything changed. The Civil Defence detachments acquired skill, aptitude, experience, organisation, and displayed themselves magnificently able to combat the consequences of the German raids.

The following day, 8 September, once again exactly at 9 p.m., the now familiar and disgusting sound was heard in the sky: it almost made one sick. We understood at once what a night again lay before us. The previous day, out of curiosity and a kind of half-boyish defiance, the Embassy staff did not go into the bomb-proof shelter provided in the Embassy. Now one had to take a more serious attitude to the danger revealed, and I instructed everyone, except two duty officers, immediately to descend into our underground premises. From that day there was a firm regulation in the Embassy that in the event of German raids the staff were to go down into the bomb shelter.

The 'big blitz' over London continued for fifty-seven nights in succession. With truly German punctiliousness, the German bombers appeared in the air every day at a particular hour, and after doing their foul work left the next morning upon the completion of their nine-hour 'working day', which they strictly observed. The number of planes taking part in these raids varied from night to night, but was never less than 200. Sometimes it rose to 300 or 400, and there was an occasion when the number of planes reached 500. London is too great (about 35 miles in diameter) to be bombed as a whole in one night, and therefore the Germans usually selected for each attack some particular district, and concentrated the whole force of their blow there. The following night they fell upon some other district, then a third and so on, until the whole territory of the British capital had been covered. The death-dealing 'presents' falling from the sky were not all identical. At the beginning there were simply high-explosive bombs, then—approximately from the middle of September—they were supplemented with delayed-action bombs, and in October there appeared incendiary bombs and huge mines sent down on parachutes. Whether there was any system in all this, I don't know, but one could not doubt the variety of devilish playthings at Hitler's disposal.

What purpose did he pursue in developing the 'big blitz' over London?

Churchill expressed the view in his war memoirs that Hitler in doing so had two objectives: to destroy the British Air Force, and to break the spirit of the British people and force it to capitulate.[1] I think Churchill's assessment is not quite accurate. Of course, Hitler was striving both to destroy the British Air Force and to terrify the British people, but more than this was in question. In beginning the 'big blitz', Hitler cherished much more serious plans: he wanted to *conquer* Britain. The thought of subjugating 'proud Albion' always lived in his consciousness. It was fed by the

1. *The Second World War*, Vol. II, p. 302.

false information about Britain supplied to him by Ribbentrop, who represented that country as a stagnant marsh. Ribbentrop, who as German Ambassador in London mixed almost exclusively with 'Cliveden' circles, and had no knowledge at all of the British people, assured Hitler that Britain was corrupted beyond recall and was incapable of serious resistance. It had only to be given a smashing blow at the head, and then everything would follow of itself.

Hitler willingly swallowed the sweet pills offered him by Ribbentrop, and his hopes of becoming master of Britain grew stronger and stronger. The plan for 'Sea-Lion' was to have brought this about. For various technical military reasons it had had for the time to be postponed—but if Goering was promising with the help of the air arm to bring Britain to her knees, why not try? If the same end could be achieved by other means, where was the difference? And finally, even if the air force alone could not conquer Britain, the damage inflicted by intensive air bombardment would be so great that it would put her out of action as an active factor in the war for a long time. Therefore it was worth while giving Goering complete freedom to show what the air forces of Nazism were capable of. Such in my view was the calculation of Hitler when he gave the order to develop the 'big blitz' over London. All the more because at that time exaggerated ideas of the power of the Luftwaffe were widely circulating in European military quarters.

What could Britain put up against the German 'blitz' at that time?

Very little, so far as arms and planes were concerned. Churchill says in his memoirs that at the beginning of the 'blitz' there were only ninety-two anti-aircraft guns for the whole of London! This was nothing over such a vast territory. I did not know then the figures given by Churchill, but I well saw and felt the complete defencelessness of the capital against the German raids. One would sit at the Embassy and hear the repulsive 'ugh-ugh-ugh' in the night sky, and then the frequent and loud: 'Bang! . . . Bang! . . . Bang!'

This was the bombs falling. And in reply—nothing! Only very rarely somewhere there would chatter a solitary weapon, and suddenly stop. Then for half an hour you would hear: 'Bang! . . . Bang! . . . Bang!'

Once again somewhere the solitary weapon would rattle, and stop suddenly again.

At moments like that I was seized by a kind of fury, and cursed Chamberlain, Baldwin and many other Conservative leaders who on account of their political stupidity had not prepared Britain to repel the Nazi 'blitz'.

The British Air Force offered resistance to the German attacks. Qualitatively it was superior to the Germans, but quantitatively there could not even be any comparison! Moreover it was still only training in night operations, and naturally made many mistakes. But the main thing was that the British at that time had so few fighter planes and pilots!

I remember one occasion. At the very height of the 'big blitz' my wife and I were dining one evening with Beaverbrook. As the dessert was being served the sirens began to howl: a raid was beginning. Everyone remained at table, only Beaverbrook's private telephone began ringing almost continuously. He would listen, give some abrupt reply, but we could not catch the sense of the mysterious conversation. I could only see that Beaverbrook was extremely disturbed and sitting on pins and needles. We wanted to leave for home as soon as possible, but our host would not let us go, and insisted that we should wait until there was at least a temporary break in the German bombing (there were small intervals in these nightly representations). Two hours went by in this way. Finally Beaverbrook put down the receiver and said with profound relief:

'Well, thank God, we have beaten off that attack!'

A few minutes later my wife and I left. After many months, when Germany had attacked the USSR and we had become allies of Britain, Beaverbrook told me that on that memorable evening the outcome of the air battle hung by a thread.

'Do you realise that the Germans were attacking and attacking,' said Beaverbrook, 'and we had only five fighter planes left in reserve? Only five!'

But if matters did not stand well as regards armaments, the spirit of the people was above all praise. Ribbentrop understood nothing in this respect. The spirit of the people, the spirit of the working masses as a whole, was firm and inflexible. This could be seen at every step, in many facts and actions.

The 'big blitz' completely reversed the normal life of London and its people. One-and-a-half million of the inhabitants, children first and foremost, had been evacuated from the capital to the provinces and distributed in the main in the agricultural areas.

Those who remained were faced with the problem of sleep in all its acuteness. In case of extremity, one could manage two or three nights without normal rest, but when it was a question of fifty-seven nights, it was quite a different situation. The Londoners solved this problem in different ways, each in the way he could.

Those better off worked as usual, on the days when there were no big raids, in their institutions, offices and shops, and in the evening, before the raids began, drove into the country and there passed the night in peace. All hotels, boarding-houses, furnished apartments and private houses in a zone 20–25 miles from the capital, were instantly filled with temporary guests, who willingly paid the most fantastic prices.

The less well-off, who could not allow themselves such a luxury, spent their nights in the shelters and the 'Tube'. There were still too few shelters, but in the 'Tube' every night hundreds of thousands of Londoners settled down to rest. At six or seven in the evening all over the vast city one could see the same picture: endless lines of people moving through the streets in the growing shadows of advancing evening, with suitcases and sacks in their hands or rucksacks on their back; men, women and children, infants in their prams, old men leaning on sticks: workmen, shopkeepers, clerks, intellectuals, actresses, dockers, caretakers—everyone loaded with bedding and a small supply of food: all moving in an irresistible torrent to the 'Tube', for shelter against the next night's raid. Underground, on the platforms and station premises, variegated and noisy temporary settlements were formed. People arranged themselves for the night in families and groups, eating, drinking, talking, reading the newspapers, denouncing the Nazis and saying what they would like to do to Hitler. At six in the morning, when the German raid was over, they would all get up off the floor, go home (if their home still existed), have a hasty breakfast and then hurry to work. And so day by day, for two months.

However, those who left London and those who passed their nights in the shelters and in the 'Tube' still represented taken together only a minority of the London population . . . What of the rest? The rest, all these five or six millions, spent the night at home, under the noise of the planes, the thunder of the bombs and the flashes of flame, relying on chance or good luck. The result can be understood: during the period of the 'big blitz' about 50,000 people perished, and many times more that number were injured. Over a million houses and cottages were destroyed or suffered serious damage.

In addition, many important and well-known buildings suffered—the British Museum, the Tate Gallery, the Tower, the Bank of England, Buckingham Palace, the American and Japanese Embassies, the Treasury, the buildings of the *Times*, *Daily Express*, *Daily Herald* and *Daily Worker*, Westminster Abbey, St. Paul's Cathedral, the Carlton Club (citadel of the Conservatives) and many others.

And still the people did not waver! Firmly, stubbornly, in businesslike fashion, without any affectation or theatricality, it resisted the German attack. One occasion left a particularly deep impression on me.

Just by the BBC there was then the large Queen's Hall, devoted to concerts. The German bombers sought at all costs to destroy the radio station, but somehow they failed in this. In revenge, the buildings surrounding the BBC experienced the fury of the 'blitz' in full measure. The concerts at Queen's Hall, however, continued, and there was no lack of an audience. One evening my wife and I went to such a concert. Not less than two thousand people were present. At the very height of the concert the wailing of the sirens began. The concert was interrupted, the manager came out on the platform, and he stated that the nearest shelter was in such-and-such a place: those wishing to leave could do so. I waited with interest to see what would happen. Ten people—I counted them carefully—got up and went out, the remaining two thousand remained silently in their seats. The manager withdrew, and the concert continued as though nothing were occurring, even though the horrible sound of the planes was continuous, and now to the right, now to the left, the crash of the falling bombs could be heard. The orchestra played astonishingly well: probably the dread peril itself inspired its members in a special sort of way . . .

Yes, the people stood firm in this cruel trial, and Hitler's hopes to conquer Britain were defeated once again.

On 3 November the 'big blitz' ended. However, this did not mean at all that the air war ceased. The main trick had been lost, but Goering wanted at least to do the greatest possible harm to Britain. On 14 November there was a terrible blow inflicted on Coventry. 500 planes fell with unusual ferocity on this industrially important, but comparatively small city, in which there were about 200,000 inhabitants. The whole central quarter of Coventry was destroyed and a vast number of people killed and wounded. Then followed big raids on Birmingham, Liverpool, Bristol, Glasgow and other leading cities. But all these were really rearguard actions in the air. They caused serious damage to Britain, but they could not hide the collapse of the 'big blitz', on which Hitler had pinned such high hopes.

A very important stage in the war was over.

The last big raid on London, of which there remains with me a vivid but somewhat peculiar impression, took place on the night of 10 to 11 May 1941. The raid was prolonged and intensive, a large number of German bombers taking part. That night the House of Commons was destroyed. On the morning of 11 May, when we learned what had happened, my wife and I immediately drove to the Parliament building. It was surrounded by a ring of policemen: but one of them, who worked regularly at the House, recognised me at once as a frequent visitor at Westminster, let us through and even willingly undertook to be our guide through the ruins. The damage done by the bombs was enormous. The Chamber I knew so well was smashed, disfigured, covered with heaps of stone and wood. In many places fires were still burning. The gallant policeman described to us in detail all the events of that terrible night, the bombs, the great pillars of flame, the roof crashing down, the people who perished and the blood everywhere. It was a gloomy picture that built itself up before our eyes. My wife involuntarily asked:

'Were you very frightened?'

'Yes, of course, it was not like a walk through the park,' replied the policeman.

What I noticed was that his voice, when he uttered these words, scarcely registered any emotion. As always, he was calm and matter-of-fact.

Suddenly, as though he had remembered something, he became excited and even grew red in the face. Striking the palm of his left hand with the back of the right, he said:

'The most terrible thing was that all through the night we couldn't even get a cup of tea: the gas and water were cut off, because the pipes were broken.'

I couldn't help laughing. Yes, I had before me a real 'pure-blooded' Englishman.

The blitz caused not a little difficulty and worry to the Soviet

Embassy and the Soviet colony. True, the bomb shelter which had been built at the Embassy made our position somewhat easier, but only somewhat.

In the first place, it did not relieve us of the danger that the building of the Embassy might be destroyed. So far as I could then judge, the Germans were directing their heaviest blows against the richest and the poorest districts of London. The quarters where the middle sort of people lived suffered considerably less.

I gave myself the following explanation of this strategy on the part of the Germans. Hitler wanted, on the one hand, to terrorise the ruling circles of the country and, on the other hand, to rouse the masses against them—they were suffering, so to speak, because Churchill's Government didn't want to make peace with Germany: this was the idea. Whether my explanation was right or wrong, I don't know: but there could be no doubt that the wealthy districts caught it badly. And as our Embassy was situated in the 'millionaires' quarter', the bombs did not spare our street either.

The Embassy is at No. 13. During the blitz bombs fell on No. 11 and No. 15. One bomb hit a house diagonally across the street from the Embassy. It was a good thing that all these bombs were comparatively small, and did not cause too much damage. In the Embassy building all the windows were twice broken by blast, but the walls stood up well. In Kensington Gardens, about two hundred yards from the Embassy, a delayed-action bomb fell. It was not defused in time, and when the explosion took place our whole building rocked so that it seemed ready to fall asunder. However, the old brickwork proved sufficiently solid: the house did not suffer, only here and there stones fell away from the outer wall.

On another occasion the Germans strewed our whole district with thousands of incendiary bombs. From the windows of the Embassy there suddenly was revealed an amazingly beautiful and terrible picture—a fiery rain falling on Kensington Gardens. About a dozen 'fire lighters' fell on the roof of our Embassy and the garden behind it. From the very beginning of the 'blitz' we had organised at the Embassy a self-defence detachment, which included everybody, from the Ambassador to the cleaners. The detachment now went into action and rapidly liquidated any danger.

However, the struggle against the Nazi 'presents' from the sky was only one side of our worries at that time. There was another and very important one. The Embassy shelter was planned only for such a number of people as were strictly necessary for the functioning of the Embassy as an institution. The shelter at the Trade Delegation was built on the same principle. But what was to be done with the families of the Soviet staff? What was to be done with the school for their children then existing in London? How could they be assured of at least a minimum of peace and safety?

We decided to evacuate the families and the school to some quiet country locality. The search for a suitable district and suitable premises began. It proved a far from easy task. As I have already said, from the beginning of the 'blitz' about one-and-a-half million people were evacuated from London. Everything in the zones neighbouring on the capital, and even in more remote areas, was filled with adults and children. But an unexpected occasion came to our aid.

One day during the 'blitz' we were invited to lunch at the Chinese Embassy. Among the guests was also Butler. When lunch was over, Butler came up to my wife and began a social conversation with her. At that moment my wife had a flash of inspiration: warmly and sharply she began to complain to the Under-Secretary for Foreign Affairs of the difficulties we were experiencing in evacuating the families of the Soviet personnel. This made a powerful impression on Butler. He apologised for his compatriots, and said: 'I will help you to settle that problem.'

Butler kept his word. The machinery began to work quickly, and at the beginning of October 1940 we were able at last to send our school, in which there were at the time twenty-five children, together with the teaching staff, to the quiet village of Withington, not far from the small town of Cheltenham, approximately 100 miles from London, where it stayed two years. At the end of 1942, when most of the German Air Force had been transferred to the Soviet front and raids on Britain had almost ceased, the school returned to London. At Withington it was established in a fairly large and comfortable house, where both children and teachers lived. The surroundings were healthy and pleasant, and there were no bombs.

I would like to record the kindness shown by the local people and the local authorities to our school. Our children became very good friends with the children of the English school at Withington. They played together and went on excursions together: the English children would come to the Soviet school celebrations and parties, and the Soviet school children to the English; the parents of the English children gladly met and talked with our teachers. On one occasion the Soviet school was visited by the Mayor of Cheltenham, who asked whether his help was needed in overcoming any difficulties. All this took place at a time when in London political wiseacres were treating the Soviet Embassy almost as though it were an agency of the enemy! Simple rank and file British were both more humane and more far-sighted than those who at that time were acting as their official leaders.

After the question of the evacuation of the school[1] (to a considerable extent also of the women-folk, many of whom went with their children to Cheltenham) had been satisfactorily settled, my wife and I began thinking about the best possible organisation of our own 'everyday life'. My wife categorically refused to leave London, and I did not insist on it. Her presence by my side in the circumstances of the blitz was a serious support for me. And for political reasons it was more to our advantage that the British should see the wife of the Soviet Ambassador 'in the front line', not in the rear. We spent the night in the Embassy shelter. But still such a night did not provide a real rest. Then we had the idea of going out of London for the week-end, at least, and to sleep normally outside the city, if only for one night or two a week. But where could we go? I could not travel far from London, because in the event of any extremity I must have the possibility of getting back quickly. On the other hand all the neighbouring areas around the capital, as I have said, were crowded with the wealthier Londoners who came there to spend the night. My attempts to find in those districts some residence at all suitable were fruitless. But the difficult problem was solved unexpectedly.

A few days after the women and children had been evacuated, my wife and I went down to visit them, to see how they had settled down. On our way back we called on the former Premier of the Spanish Republican Government, Juan Negrin, who was then living in emigration in Britain. He had taken a very pleasant English country house at Bovingdon, not far from London, with

1. One of the teachers at the school, A. P. Manyukova, gave me these details of its life in evacuation, and I take this opportunity of expressing my sincere thanks to her.

its own garden, vegetable allotment, outhouses and even an English manservant, who had been left there by the owner of the house. During the conversation I happened to mention my difficulty in finding a place for our proposed week-ends. Negrin replied instantly:

'But come to us! You will be our welcome guests! We shall find a room in our house for you and your wife.'

My wife and I exchanged glances, and I said a little cautiously: 'Thank you, we shall try.'

We did, in fact, try at the following week-end, and were most satisfied. Thereafter Bovingdon became our regular resting-place at week-ends.

In connection with the blitz, I retain the memory of one characteristic incident which I wish now to recount. In conversation with Halifax one day, I expressed the opinion that the shelters which were then being intensively constructed by the Government were mainly disposed in the more prosperous parts of the city, but that in the poorer quarters there were too few shelters. Halifax was offended, and began arguing with me. Then he said:

'If you wish, I will ask Admiral Evans, who is now in charge of the organisation of bomb shelters in London, to show you what the Government is doing . . . Then you will see yourself how wrong you are.'

I willingly accepted the Foreign Secretary's offer, and next day Admiral E. R. Evans came to see me at the Embassy. He was a very brave and resolute man, who in his youth had accompanied the famous Captain Scott in his expedition to the South Pole: then had had a long career in the British Navy, receiving many orders and decorations: had won a high position in society: and now, in the circumstances of the 'big blitz', was doing everything he possibly could to ensure shelter against the bombing for the inhabitants of the capital. Admiral Evans was a cheerful and witty person, who liked to tell and could tell funny stories, and made an extremely pleasant impression: but . . . he understood very little about politics.

My wife and I drove with Evans to look at the London shelters. Most of them were of a single type, but fairly light and capable of defending people only against blast and splinters, but not against a direct hit. When I drew Evans' attention to this aspect, he shrugged his shoulders and replied:

'That's for the politicians to say. There I can't interfere. They say there's not enough money for anything better.'

After making a fairly wide tour of London, we arrived finally at the East End, where the poor live. With a triumphant expression, Evans led us up to a kind of vast tunnel, descending at an angle underground. We got out of the car, and Evans said significantly:

'Now you will see how the Government cares about the security of the humblest people in London.'

We moved off down the tunnel. It widened rapidly, and turned out to be a vast underground warehouse, built some time or other by one of the British railways. Now there were no goods there, but the whole store was filled with people of all ages and condition. There were many women and children. They not only were sheltered against the German bombs at night, but also spent much time during the day, cooked their meals, played cards, read books and papers.

'In this shelter there are at this moment 4,000 people,' said Evans.

I was rapidly recognised: my portraits often used to appear in the press. People began to say in the crowd: 'Maisky's come! Maisky's here!' Hundreds of people began to gather around. Suddenly there was a loud shout: 'Speech! Speech! . . . Let Maisky speak!'

This didn't suit me at all. If I was to speak to these people at all, I had to say something sympathetic to them, something likely to raise their spirits in their heavy struggle. But to say something of that nature meant for me, as Ambassador of the USSR which was then in 'friendly relations' with Germany, to put not only myself but the Soviet Government as well in a difficult situation. After all, the USSR was maintaining an attitude of neutrality. I tried to avoid speaking, asking Evans to finish the visit to this shelter as soon as possible. Nothing of the kind! Evans wouldn't even think of it. We must look at some other corner. We must go and see such and such a corridor . . . He did not understand the delicacy of my position at all!

Meanwhile, the crowd around us was growing ever larger and the demand for me to speak became ever louder. Evans yielding to the prevailing mood said to me: 'Why shouldn't you say a few words to these good people?'

Those standing nearest to us heard Evans say these words, and broke from their places at once. I felt someone's strong hands picking me up and putting me on to a lorry standing close by. Then Evans was picked up and put by my side. Then my wife somehow appeared on the lorry. A roar of many voices suddenly echoed under the arches of the store:

'Speech! Speech!'

To retreat was impossible, and I began speaking. I did not speak long, for about five minutes, and spoke in general terms, phrased in such a way that the Germans could not accuse the Soviet Government of infringing its obligations. The crowd, however, felt that a representative of the Soviet working-class stood before it, that he was a friend of the British proletariat, and that he could be trusted.

When I ended, there was loud applause. Then someone began singing the 'International'. Others picked it up. The words of the famous hymn resounded under the arches of the vast shelter. Evans listened, and then naïvely asked, turning to me: 'What are they singing? Is it the "Red Flag"?'

I did not want to enlighten Evans, and grunted something not very distinguishable. We got off the lorry and, surrounded by an enthusiastic crowd, slowly moved towards the exit. When we took our seats in the car, Evans said with great satisfaction: 'That's turned out very well! I am very pleased . . . Now you see yourself that our Government looks after the people.'

I thought to myself: 'There's a man who doesn't understand anything about politics.'

5

Military affairs

THE 'big blitz' and the subsequent raids on Britain were only a part, though truly the most dramatic one, of the war which Britain had to wage during the year which elapsed between Churchill's coming to power and Germany's attack on the Soviet Union. There were other important 'theatres of war' as well, on which operations were proceeding: probably the most dangerous of them for Britain was the war at sea.

On the eve of the second world war the economic structure of Britain was of a very special character. She was an industrial country in which about 80 per cent of the population lived in towns, and about 60 per cent of all the food she required was imported. The degree of dependence of Britain on the import of foodstuffs could be well illustrated by the two following curious incidents.

During the first war winter of 1939–40 the best present you could make to any lady in society was . . . an onion. For that winter Britain all at once found herself without any. Why? Simply because onions were usually imported from Egypt, and now maritime connections with Egypt were a great difficulties. To grow the onions in Britain was now too late, because the war had started on 1 September. Only the following year was the 'onion crisis' solved.

The other curious event was in connection with eggs. There was a famine in this respect too, because usually they were imported from other countries, including the Baltic States. I very well remember how pleased my wife was when Aras, the then Turkish Ambassador in London and a well-known friend of the USSR, sent her a present of ten eggs.

In addition to foodstuffs, Britain imported a very large quantity of raw materials—timber, cotton, wool, oil, iron ore, non-ferrous metals, etc. These were the 'bread' for her factories.

In such conditions the maintenance of her supremacy on the seas, and thereby of the possibility freely to bring in the products she required, was for Britain a basic problem. Without its satisfactory solution, the country could not only not carry on a war, but might simply die of hunger.

The Germans understood this perfectly, and even in the first world war made tremendous efforts to isolate the British Isles and cut the lines of their food and raw materials supplies. The main forms of weapon which the Germans used in naval warfare at that time were submarines, surface 'raiders' (among which most fame was gained by the *Goeben* and *Breslau*), and the minefields sown on the approaches to British commercial harbours. In 1914–18 the war at sea proceeded with varying success, yet nevertheless there were moments in the life of Britain when she felt herself severely injured. In the second world war aviation was added to all the previous forms of German armament used against British shipping, and this considerably complicated the problems faced by the British Government in the war at sea. And this all the more because Hitler reckoned even less than did the Kaiser with 'world public opinion'.

As a result, the Germans made full use of past experience in conducting an attack on the British fleet, naval and commercial, from the very beginning of the second world war. I have already told of their successes in this sphere at the end of 1939. But these were only beginnings. Full development came later, particularly after mid-1940, when the 'phoney war' had come to an end. Churchill in his war memoirs gives some very eloquent figures: in May 1940, when Chamberlain was forced to resign, the losses of the British merchantile marine amounted to 82,000 tons, but in the following month of June they suddenly rose to 283,000 tons, and remained approximately at that level up to the end of the year:[1] while over the year (from April 1940 until April 1941), according to Admiralty figures, a total of about 3·5 million tons were sunk, or approximately 270,000 tons a month. The Germans did not confine themselves to British vessels, however. They also sank the ships of Britain's allies, and even of neutral Powers, if those ships were making for her ports. According to the same

1. *The Second World War*, Vol. II, p. 639.

Admiralty figures, there were lost during that year in addition more than 1,500,000 tons of ships of other countries. It is not surprising that Churchill should write in his memoirs: 'Towards the end of 1940 I became increasingly concerned about the ominous fall in imports.'[1]

About that time, as I remember, I had a conversation with Gwilym Lloyd George, who then held an important post in the Board of Trade. He complained a great deal of the difficulties created by the Germans in the sphere of supplies, quoted the figures of British losses at sea (already being published in the papers) and told me of outrageous cases of cruelty of the German submarines when sinking merchant ships. Gwilym was visibly shaken by the events of the war at sea, and I even had the impression that he was not quite confident that the British would be able to win it.

I heard him out, and then said to Lloyd George's son:

'I don't doubt that in the long run you will be victorious at sea.'

'What is your confidence based on?' asked Gwilym.

I replied:

'You British have the sea in your blood . . . Such a nation cannot perish from war at sea . . . You will think of something.'

Gwilym looked at me with surprise, and then said with a air of some relief:

'Your optimism is very encouraging . . . We shall certainly fight to the bitter end!'

My optimism proved quite justified. Of course the merciless sea war which Hitler developed caused Britain not a few difficulties and complications, but nevertheless she stood the test, and in the long run overcame the stern peril.

Another theatre of war to which the Churchill Government had at the same time to devote much attention was that established by Fascist Italy.

After the fall of France, Mussolini decided to inflict a blow on Britain in Africa. He set himself the task of conquering Egypt. It seemed as if he had sufficient forces for this. Abyssinia, Eritrea, Somaliland were in Italian hands, and there were large Italian garrisons there. They were also masters of Tripoli and Libya. Even before the war they had built an excellent motor-road along

1. *Ibid.*, p. 532.

the whole coast of North Africa, about 900 miles long. In June 1940 there were along that road, from the borders of Tunis to the frontier of Egypt, more than 200,000 Italian Fascist troops (approximately fifteen divisions). Mussolini considered that this was more than sufficient to overcome the resistance of the 50,000 men whom Britain at that time had in Egypt. True, among the Italian Fascist leaders there was not an identity of views on the question of conquering Egypt. Even at that time information reached me (and was fully confirmed after the end of the war) that Marshal Graziani, commander-in-chief of the Italian forces in North Africa, thought that insufficient preparations had been made for a serious attempt to conquer Egypt, and therefore was pressing for postponement. Mussolini and all his entourage in Rome, on the contrary, considered that the time for a blow against Britain in North Africa was exceptionally favourable. I did not know then the details of all these arguments, and did not know that in the end Mussolini faced Graziani with the alternative: either . . . or else . . . Graziani gave way. All this was of secondary importance. What was really important was that on 13 September 1940 the Italian armies commanded by Graziani began a general offensive against the British forces in Egypt.

The position of the British was difficult. They were not only numerically much weaker than the Italians, but they were considerably inferior to them also in the sphere of armament, and had a very uncertain rear to reckon with. King Farouk, who was then on the throne, visibly sympathised with Fascism and therefore did not wish to support the British. Farouk was conducting a very suspect policy, and there were not a few spies and agents of the Fascist Powers, particularly Italy, among his entourage. In these conditions General Wavell, commander of the British forces, began a slow fighting retreat before the troops of Marshal Graziani. But the latter was not disposed to conduct operations rapidly and energetically. On 17 September, four days after the offensive had begun, the Italian troops reached Sidi Barrani, and stopped there for three whole months.

During that period the British Government succeeded in reinforcing Wavell with troops and arms (all of which had now to be sent for security reasons round the Cape of Good Hope) and thereby noticeably strengthening its positions in Egypt. On 6–9 December 1940 the British began a big counter-offensive, and although numerically they were still far behind the Italians,

Graziani was unable to withstand their blow. The Italian troops not only left Egyptian territory, but began rapidly rolling back further and further to the west, along that splendid motor road which Mussolini had recently built. On 12 December they left the Sidi Barrani area, on 3–5 January 1941 they evacuated Bardia, on 21–22 January Tobruk and on 8 February Benghazi. In two months the British had advanced nearly 200 miles and had taken prisoner more than 113,000 men. The Italian troops proved quite incapable of battle, and were surrendering to their adversary in whole divisions and garrisons, headed by their generals. The quantity of equipment taken by the British was enormous.[1]

At the same time Italy was suffering defeats on another African front. In December 1940 a rising began in Abyssinia. The Emperor Haile Selassie returned to the country from emigration. The British armed forces sfforded him serious support, particularly the troops of the Union of South Africa. The struggle extended to Somaliland and Eritrea. The whole 'East African Empire' of which Mussolini was so proud was collapsing and falling apart before our eyes. At the beginning of April 1941 the British occupied Addis Ababa, Massawa and other most important points in the country. The rule of Italian Fascism in this part of Africa was liquidated.

Reverses overtook Italy at sea also. On 30 March 1941 there was a battle at Cape Matapan between the Italian and the British fleets, in which Italy lost three large cruisers (*Pola, Fiume* and *Zara*) and two destroyers, while several other Italian warships were seriously damaged. On the British side there were no substantial losses.

Quite naturally these successes, coming at such difficult times for Britain herself, raised her spirits and strengthened confidence in the future.

Mussolini on the contrary was raging and cursing, but could do nothing about it. Then the Germans came to his assistance. They landed their troops in Northern Africa, and in March 1941 the united Italo-German forces went over to the offensive towards Benghazi. At the beginning of April the British evacuated that place and retreated to Tobruk. The Fascist troops pursuing them, however, did not display any particularly aggressive spirit. In the Tobruk district operations died down, and the line of the front was stabilised at that point for many months.

1. *The Second World War*, Vol. II, p. 554.

I well remember meeting Walter Elliot in the middle of April in Parliament, and him saying to me with satisfaction:

'Things are going well for us in Africa! . . . Frankly speaking, when the Italians last autumn began their advance on Egypt, we were very worried. But events proved kinder to us than we expected.'

Elliot was only expressing the general feeling which prevailed at that time in Britain. Both people and Government seemed encouraged, and were looking more hopefully at the prospects—even though at that very time Britain had to submit to a severe trial in yet another theatre of war.

On 28 October 1940, while the Italian forces were still pressing back the British in the district of Sidi Barrani, Mussolini suddenly attacked Greece. Contrary to his expectations, he encountered serious resistance. The Greek people wanted neither alien rule nor Fascism. It displayed great heroism in the struggle with the Italian aggressors. In such circumstances the Metaxas Government then in power took a firm attitude, and the Greek army received a good commander in the person of General Papagos. As Britain on 13 April 1939 had given a guarantee to Greece, it was now bound at the request of the Greek Government to come to the aid of her ally. But what could she do? Britain herself just at that moment was straining every effort in the fight against the 'big blitz', and her armies, comparatively small as yet, were engaged in the battles in Africa. There remained only the Mediterranean Fleet which, as mentioned earlier, sank several Italian warships at Cape Matapan This, however, could not exert any special influence on the course of land operations. With the consent of the Greek Government, Britain occupied Crete, making it an important base for itself in the Aegean, and also arranged to supply the Greek army with arms and munitions. Generally speaking, Britain's help to her Greek ally, particularly at first, was very modest; and this only confirmed how right was the judgment of more far-sighted people, such as for example Lloyd George, who were in vain pointing out to Chamberlain in April 1939 that without a military and political agreement with the USSR the guarantee to Greece (and also to Poland and Rumania, then also being discussed) was of little practical value.

Yet nevertheless Greece proved able to offer Italy strong and stubborn resistance. More than that, the Greek army in November

1940 went over to a counter-offensive, expelled the Italian troops from its territory and forced them to retreat into Albania. Here they settled down at a distance of about thirty miles to the north of the Greek frontier and, in spite of repeated attempts, were unable to break through the Greek lines. Mussolini had never yet been so disgraced!

It was to be expected that the Germans would soon appear on the scene in order to 'help' the Italians, and still more in order to consolidate their own hold on the Balkans. At that time nothing was yet known about 'Plan Barbarossa' (for the attack on the USSR) which had been signed by Hitler on 18 December 1940; but even without this Germany had sufficient grounds for seizing a region so strategically important and so rich in raw materials and foodstuffs. The British Government cherished the idea of opposing to Hitler's probable offensive a united front of Yugoslavia, Greece and Turkey, which thanks to its topographical conditions and the existence, at least on paper, of sixty to seventy divisions might successfully beat off a German-Italian attack. In order to organise such a front Eden, as Foreign Secretary and member of the War Cabinet, was sent to the Balkans and the Near East in the middle of February 1941. He was away for about two months, visited Cairo, Ankara, Athens and wanted to visit Belgrade, but . . . It would be best for me to quote what Eden himself said, in describing his journey in much detail, when I visited him in the middle of April, on his return to London.

'The position in North Africa', said Eden, 'does not worry me much. Possibly we may make a tactical withdrawal from Sollum to Mersa Matruh, but that is not important: no danger threatens Egypt from the Western Desert. Turkey and the Balkans are a different affair.'

At this point Eden told me that, according to his impression, the Turks were loyal friends of Britain, but at present their attitude was that if the Germans attacked Turkey, they would resist, but they did not want to intervene in Balkan affairs. As regards the Balkans, the Greeks were conducting themselves heroically, and at the beginning of March the British had sent them help, withdrawing troops from the Nile Army.

'Of course, not so many as we should have liked,' added Eden somewhat apologetically, 'but we have done what we could . . . But Yugoslavia has proved the weakest spot in our calculations, and now I don't know what may happen.'

In reality, events in Yugoslavia could only arouse the greatest concern for the future. After the murder of the Yugoslav King Alexander in France in 1934,[1] his young son Peter II came to the throne. The Regency Council was headed by Prince Paul, a man of feeble character, easily falling under external influence. Since February 1938 the post of Premier had been occupied by Stoyadinovich, who had pursued a policy of co-operation with the Powers of the Fascist 'Axis'. This aroused a strong opposition among a large section of the people, and at the beginning of 1941 Stoyadinovich had had to resign. Tsvetkovich had been appointed Premier, and Markovich Minister for Foreign Affairs. Both were inclined towards a more independent policy; but when in the middle of February they had been 'invited' by Hitler to visit him at Berchtesgaden, they were incapable of resisting the pressure exercised on them, and verbally promised that Yugoslavia would join the 'Axis'. However, at home they encountered strong resistance not only from the masses, but also from certain army circles, headed by General Simovich. Desiring to exercise 'psychological pressure' on Yugoslavia, Hitler began flirting with Bulgaria. The Bulgarian King Boris willingly went . . . or rather ran to meet him, and on 1 March 1941 Bulgaria became a member of the 'Axis'. Then Hitler 'invited' Prince Paul to see him, worked on him for five hours and thoroughly terrified him. On 25 March Tsvetkovich and Markovich signed in Vienna a pact bringing Yugoslavia into the 'Axis'. When the news of this reached Belgrade, there was a *coup d'état* on 27 March in the Yugoslav capital, Prince Paul and his Government were overthrown, and power passed to a new Government headed by General Simovich.

The events in Yugoslavia aroused Hitler to fury, and he decided to act immediately—and not only against Yugoslavia but also against Greece.

'When in February,' Eden said, 'on my way to Cairo I arrived in Athens with General Dill, I had intended to visit Belgrade from there. But Prince Paul categorically opposed this. He was terribly afraid that my visit would compromose him in the eyes of the Germans . . . When on my way back from the Near East Dill and I were again in Athens, I once more wanted to visit Belgrade; but

1. Alexander was murdered at Marseilles on 9 October 1934 during an official visit to France. With him was killed the French Foreign Minister Barthou who had come to meet him. The assassination was the work of Croat terrorists, behind whom stood Mussolini.

the newly formed Government of Simovich also asked me not to do it, out of fear of "provoking" Hitler. After long negotiations Simovich agreed that General Dill might come to Belgrade, but in conditions of secrecy and in civilian attire. Dill urged Simovich that a common military plan for the Yugoslav and Anglo-Greek forces should be immediately worked out, for a German attack might be expected in the very immediate future. But Simovich considered that the Germans were not yet ready for an offensive against Yugoslavia and Greece, and that he had at least a month to make his preparations. As a result, nothing definite was decided. They only agreed that Simovich should enter into direct contact with General Papagos and the British commander, General Wilson. However, Simovich was in no hurry to establish this contact. On 5 April Papagos and Wilson urged Belgrade immediately to send a responsible representative of the Yugoslav army for negotiations; but it was already too late...'

Yes, of course, it was already too late, for on 6 April 1941 Hitler fell upon Yugoslavia. Belgrade was subjected to a most savage bombardment from the air, and German armies began an attack on Yugoslavia from different directions. At the same time the Germans attacked Greece as well. If the Yugoslav, Greek and British forces had been acting jointly on a previously elaborated plan, they could have made use of the mountainous territory of the Balkans to make a stand, or at any rate to delay the advance of the Germans and Italians for a long time. But nothing of the kind took place. The Yugoslavs fought alone, the Greeks and British did the same. In addition the Yugoslavs, who potentially represented the most serious of these forces, had neither a strictly unified command not a well-thought-out plan of resistance. In such conditions the Germans, whose numbers, training and armament far surpassed those of the Yugoslavs, developed a real 'blitzkrieg'. On 13 April, one week after the beginning of the offensive, they occupied Belgrade, and by the end of the same month became masters of all Yugoslavia.

In Greece matters went no better. The main Greek forces, fifteen divisions, were tied down in Albania by the Italians. Three or four divisions were defending Macedonia. Here, on the 'Aliakmon Line', the Greeks were supported by the British. The total number of British troops in Greece (not only on that line) was about 50,000 men. The German attack, made principally from the territory of Bulgaria, was so powerful that the Anglo-Greek front could not withstand it and began rapidly rolling back southward. An attempt was made to make a stand at the famous Thermopylae, but it was unsuccessful. The result is comprehensible: at the end of April the Greek armies in Epirus and Macedonia surrendered, and the British forces, after losing about 20 per cent of their personnel, were hastily evacuated to Crete. Thither also went the Greek King and the Greek Government.

However, the Germans were not satisfied with the occupation of mainland Greece. At the very end of May 1941, using their air force and air landings, supported by a comparatively small landing from the sea, they seized Crete and forced the British—or rather the New Zealanders, commanded by General Freyberg—out of the island. True, the Germans lost about 15,000 men in this operation, but the British losses likewise, in the defence and evacuation of Crete, were not much smaller.

So ended the tragic Greek campaign.

At that time many details were unknown to me, such as names, facts and figures which were published only at the end of the war, but the general sense of developing events was quite clear. In my diary for 2 June 1941 I described the situation as follows:

'The drama of the Balkan Peninsula is at end. Hitler has won a decisive victory. The British as always have acted according to the rule of "too little and too late". I am not even inclined to blame them. In their present condition they probably could not do more. But why have they proved to be in such a condition? Here before me there rises unasked the image of Chamberlain. It is he and all his Cliveden set who are guilty. If in 1939 there had been concluded and honestly carried out the Triple Pact of Mutual Assistance on which the USSR was insisting, there would have been no Balkan drama, and probably no war. And now the fire which began two years go is extending more and more, and beginning to approach quite close to our frontiers. I don't like the fact that Rumania, Hungary, Bulgaria and now also Yugoslavia and Greece have joined the "Axis" or have been turned into German provinces. What can we expect of the coming day?'

At the same time as the Germans invaded the Balkans Hitler made an attempt to seize Iraq. In March 1941, Rashid Ali, who was in close contact with the Nazis, became Premier at Bagdad. The Regent, Emir Abdul-Ila, who was ruling the country until the King reached his majority and who supported a British orientation, was obliged to flee, and Rashid Ali became master of the situation. His first step was an attack on the British air base at Habbaniya, which was approximately thirty miles from Bagdad. Military operations began on 2 May. Rashad Ali concentrated there about 9,000 Iraqi troops with fifty guns. Habbaniya was defended by approximately 2,000 British, mostly training at the School of Aviation there. Small reinforcements were sent to support them from Basra and some other places. The fighting went on for five days, and ended in a reverse for Rashid Ali: the Iraqi troops were unable to stand up to Briish air attacks, and retreated to Bagdad. Then Germans appeared on the scene. Beginning with 13 May, German warplanes came to the help of Rashid Ali, and were followed by Italian air units. They tried to put matters right for their agent, but were unsuccessful.

On 27 May Rashid Ali fled with his associates to Persia, and on 31 May Abdul-Ila was restored to his rights as Regent: a new Government came to power which was friendly to Britain.

In this way Hitler suffered a defeat in Iraq. This, of course, was a poor compensation for the defeat which Britain had suffered in the Balkans: but in those difficult days there was a lot of noise in the press and in political circles about the military and political success of the British Government in Iraq.

In the first half of 1941 there also took place an event which was really a very serious victory for Britain, even though it was not on the battlefield (though the event was of the greatest importance for the conduct of the war). I have in mind the adoption of the Lend-Lease Law in the USA.

In 1939–40 the USA was giving help to Britain in all kinds of ways, guided by the principle: 'Everything but war.' The USA built ships and planes for Britain, supplied guns and machine tools, energetically supported her in the press and on the radio. How was Britain to settle with the Americans for all the help it was getting? In the capitalist world very tough rules and customs prevail in this respect. I have already described how, in the summer of 1940, the British had to pay for fifty old destroyers and half-a-million rifles of first world war vintage by handing over to their trans-Atlantic cousins a number of extremely valuable naval bases within the British Empire. Now, when the question arose in all its magnitude of providing military supplies for Britain on a much bigger scale, the chief American magnates argued quite simply:

let London pay for everything in cash and securities, so long as it has any, and then we shall see. The meaning of this demand was clear: to weaken the British competitor economically, take possession of his most important enterprises and squeeze him out of his most profitable positions. It was an illustration to the saying that friendship is friendship, but business is business. The American behaviour did not please the British, but what was to be done? I remember the Labour leader Morrison saying to me at the time:

'It's hard to fall to the position of a junior partner after you've owned an independent business so long. Sometimes your blood boils and you clench your fists. But now there is no other way out!'

Towards the end of 1940 the gold and securities owned by the British began to be exhausted. And that was not surprising. By 1 November 1940 the value of all the orders placed by Britain in the USA had risen to 2,500 million dollars. A decision had to be taken: what was to be done now?

At that moment Roosevelt came forward to show himself once more a statesman of great stature and courage—of course, bourgeois through and through, but with a broad understanding and undoubted far-sightedness (qualities which he had already displayed at the time of the 'New Deal'). He rejected the proposals which were being made from different quarters: to grant Britain a large private loan, or open a Government credit for her, or (as Eleanor Roosevelt was proposing) simply to grant her the necessary resources for carrying on the war as a gift. Instead of all such forms of financial aid, redolent of the traditions of the past, Roosevelt put forward a new and original plan, never yet tried in history, namely Lend-Lease. The essence of the plan was that the USA would provide Britain with all it needed for the war (armaments, raw materials, foodstuffs, etc.) 'on loan and on lease,' without requiring payment at the time: while later, after the war, Britain would pay her debt to the USA either by returning the property received on loan if it was still of value, or by paying off the debt with new products and goods, or in some other form of compensation acceptable to the USA (lowering its customs tariffs for American manufacturers, facilitating their entry into the Empire market and the like).

On 18 December 1940 Roosevelt made public the principles of Lend-Lease at his press conference. It was a thrilling sensation not only for the USA but also for the whole of the rest of the capitalist world. Hitlerite Germany made an official protest. In America itself an acute internal struggle began between the supporters and opponents of the plan proposed by the President. In a message to Congress on 6 January 1941 Roosevelt declared that the USA must be 'the arsenal of democracy'. War Secretary Stimson in a speech on 16 January supported Roosevelt's plan, underlining that Britain was 'the first line of American's defence' against world conquest by the totalitarian Powers. Roosevelt was energetically supported—and this was very important—by the Republican candidate for President, Wendell Wilkie.

Opposed were the leaders of the 'isolationists', Senators Nye, La-Follette, Vandenberg, Johnson and others, the notorious Colonel Lindberg, who extolled the might of Germany and prophesied the inevitable defeat of Britain, the president of the National Economic Council in New York, Mervin Hart, and others.

Joseph Kennedy, the former American Ambassador in London in 1938–40 and father of the future President John Kennedy, took up an ambiguous attitude. I have described elsewhere his panic mood after the fall of France, and how insistently he then 'advised' Britain at all costs to make peace with Germany. Now, in a broadcast on 18 January 1941, Joseph Kennedy thought it possible to allege that he had never been a pessimist as regards Britain being able to win the war, and that he had never defended the idea of Britain signing a peace of capitulation with Germany. He then went on to support the granting of aid to Britain by the USA, but declared that the war now being carried on by Britain was 'not our war and Britain is not fighting our battle'. From this Kennedy drew the conclusion that great care should be exercised in granting help to Britain. It was quite clear that Kennedy still believed in Germany's might and did not believe in Great Britain's capacity to survive.

After fierce arguments in various stages of the US parliamentary machine, the Lend-Lease Bill was finally adopted and on 11 March 1941 signed by the President.

A few days later Lloyd George said to me:

'This is a big victory for us! Now all the financial difficulties and worries involved in carrying on the war have been solved for us . . . Winston has been luckier than I was . . . My God, what a terrible problem the financing of the last war was for me! But Winston can now concentrate his attention entirely on the purely military side.'

On 10 June 1941 I made the following entry:

'Summing up everything that has happened during the 21 months of war, it has to be recognised that things have turned out much better for Britain than many expected. Of course there were not a few defeats and difficulties, but there were also quite a number of successes and achievements. The overall balance is undoubtedly a positive one. Britain lives, fights and even hopes in the long run to win, or at any rate to arrive at an acceptable peace. My confidence in Britain's ability to resist Germany strongly, which I expressed in conversation with US Ambassador Kennedy after the fall of France, is justified in practice, and I feel much satisfaction. Not because I have turned out a good prophet, but because the preservation of an independent Britain I consider exceptionally important from the point of view of the interests of the USSR and the whole world.

'But if the total balance of these 21 months is positive for Britain, this does not yet mean that the main difficulties have been left behind. Far from that! Summing up my impressions over the whole period, I can note that the "general strategy" of the British Government has during the period changed at least three times.

'In the winter of 1939–40, in the days of Chamberlain, it was considered that the "Maginot Line" and the blockade plus a little aerial warfare would do what was necessary, and would oblige Germany to seek for a peace that was "reasonable" from the Anglo-French point of view.

'This pleasant conception (for the British) was rudely overthrown by the Germans in the spring and summer of 1940, when they seized Denmark, Norway, Holland and Belgium and forced France to capitulate.

'With the coming to power of the Churchill Government, there was a sharp change. It was not by accident that the Premier, talking to me on 3 July 1940, said frankly that his "general strategy" at that moment amounted to one thing: "to survive the next three months", i.e. not to permit a German invasion of Britain before October, when after the autumn equinox the storms begin in the Channel, and the landing of an enemy army on the British shores would become impossible.

'When these anxious three months were over, and Britain remained uninvaded, the Government's "general strategy" changed once more. Now the Government argued as follows. The British Empire is carrying on the war against Germany and Italy alone.

Potentially she has sufficient resources to win the war and remain a Great Power, but approximately eight to ten months are required in order to mobilise the resources of the Empire. For that time Britain must withdraw to its islands, turn them into an impregnable fortress and, behind its "Maginot Line" of sea, build up a powerful army and a powerful air force and then take the offensive. First, in the spring or summer of 1941, a "small offensive" against Italy in Africa, and later on—say in the spring or summer of 1941—develop a "big offensive" in Europe, against Germany. In this great hopes were pinned, on the one hand, on the sympathy of the peoples enslaved by Germany and, on the other hand, on growing help in arms, finances, etc, from the USA.

'Such in the main has been the third stage of "general strategy" pursued by the British Government up to the present day. How the events of the last three months, and particularly the seizure of the Balkan Peninsula by Germany and Italy, will affect this third stage is not yet clear. So far one feels only considerable confusion and division in Government circles on the question of "general strategy". The future will show what all this will lead to. All kinds of surprises are possible in war.'

6

London and Moscow

WHAT were Anglo-Soviet relations like during those thirteen months which separated Churchill's coming to power from Germany's attack on the USSR, i.e. from 10 May 1940 until 22 June 1941?

As early as 27 March 1940, i.e. before the formation of the Churchill Government, I had on instructions of the Soviet Government proposed to Halifax that negotiations on trade relations should begin between our countries. During the following six weeks London and Moscow exchanged diplomatic documents, which, however, did not move affairs forward at all. The reason was simple. The Chamberlain Government required that the Soviet side should 'reassure' it in respect of the quantities of Soviet products supplied to Germany, and the final destination of commodities imported by the Soviet Union from abroad (principally from the USA). In practice this meant that Britain sought in one form or another to establish its own control of Soviet foreign trade. Naturally the USSR could not permit such intervention in its internal affairs by a foreign Power, and as a result no agreement on questions of trade between London and Moscow could be arrived at.

One of the first acts of the Churchill Government was to state its desire to improve Anglo-Soviet relations. On 20 May Halifax unexpectedly invited me to come and see him in the evening, which was unusual. I could not help wondering what this might mean.

When I entered the Foreign Secretary's room, he informed me with visible agitation that there had just been a meeting of the

Government, at which it had been recognised as undesirable that discussions should go on any further between the two countries about trade relations by means of memoranda and counter-memoranda, and that the British Government had decided to send Stafford Cripps to Moscow in the capacity of 'Ambassador on special mission', to settle this question by direct talks with the Soviet Government. Halifax asked me most urgently to make the arrangements for Cripps's journey to the USSR

Secretly I was delighted with the selection of Cripps for this purpose, because I knew his striving to promote Anglo-Soviet co-operation; but I gave no sign of this, and maintained an expression of complete diplomatic calm. Returning to the Embassy, I immediately telegraphed to Moscow about Halifax's *démarche*.

The reply from Moscow came six days later. Meanwhile events in the West advanced at breathtaking speed. The Germans, having broken through the French front at Sedan on 14 May, were rushing ahead on their tanks and armoured cars towards the Atlantic. Confusion reigned in Paris, and the collapse of the Reynaud Government became ever more certain. France was clearly moving towards catastrophe. Connections between London and Paris were becoming more and more unreliable. In these circumstances, Butler rang me up on the evening of 24 May to tell me that the Foreign Office had decided, while air communications through London, Paris and Rome were still open, to send Cripps to Athens the next day, in order that he should await there the completion of negotiations between the British and Soviet Governments about his visit to Moscow. If the next few days were lost, it might happen that Cripps would not manage to get to the USSR quickly at all. The Foreign Office plan was immediately put into effect, and Cripps settled down for some time in the Greek capital.

On 26 May the reply came from Moscow. The Soviet Government said it was ready to accept Cripps, but not as 'Ambassador on special mission' to discuss problems of Anglo-Soviet trade, but as a regular 'Ambassador of His Majesty' (Sir William Seeds, the British Ambassador in Moscow, had demonstratively gone home 'on leave' at the beginning of January 1940, and whether he would return to the USSR at all was not known). Halifax did not like our attitude at all, and began to suggest various other compromises, but in the end had to give way.

At the beginning of June the status of Cripps as the regular

Ambassador of the British Government was agreed, but now another question arose: how could Cripps have delivered to him the credentials which were now necessary? For by this time the Germans had already begun their advance on Paris, and the airline which Cripps had used ten days before had ceased to operate. There still remained the road to Athens through America, the USSR and the Balkans: but this was very complicated, and the occasion could not wait: Cripps needed to become the British Ambassador in Moscow immediately. What was to be done?

Butler long racked his brains over this problem, and in the end confided his difficulties to me 'Nothing could be easier,' I assured him. 'Send the credentials by cable.'

'But will your Government accept cabled credentials?' asked Butler anxiously.

I burst out laughing, and replied: 'Of course it will! You need have no worry about that.'

An expression of hesitation appeared on Butler's face. Something was continuing to worry him, but what precisely he did not say. Then he cautiously said: 'I must consult with my experts.'

From the depths of the Foreign Office there appeared a grey-haired sage of very respectable appearance, and Butler told him the problem.

'No, that is impossible!' categorically declared the expert.

'But why?' I asked uncomprehendingly.

'During all the nearly 200 years of history of the Foreign Office', explained the expert in tones which did not permit question, 'there has never been a precedent for the King's signature being sent by cable' (the credentials of British Ambassadors are signed by the King).

'There you are,' said Butler profoundly.

'Your argument does not convince me one little bit,' I said to the expert. 'It may be that there has never been such a case in the history of the Foreign Office, but then in the history of mankind there has never been a war like the present one. One must keep pace with the times, and you British are sometimes able to do this . . . Here is an example: in former years the Houses of Parliament were lit with candles, while now they have electric lighting . . . Follow the example of Parliament, and send Cripps his credentials by telegraph.'

The expert, however, proved to be very obstinate, while Butler was silent, looking at him in all reverence. It was one more illustration of the relationship between British Parliamentarians and the machinery of officialdom. Internally I was laughing, but all the same it was necessary to find some practical way out of the situation. So I proposed:

'Prepare Cripps's credentials, send them officially to me at the Soviet Embassy, I will just as officially inform you that I have received them, and then I will myself transmit the contents of the credentials to Moscow by cable. And I will dispatch the original to the People's Commissariat for Foreign Affairs when an occasion presents itself.'

The faces of the two men suddenly brightened, and Butler cried: 'That's splendid! That's what we'll do!'

As a result, Cripps a few days later became British Ambassador in Moscow, and on 1 July was received by Stalin, to whom he handed a personal letter from Churchill. In his letter the British Premier said (how up-to-date it still sounds!) that, in spite of all the differences between the systems prevailing in Britain and the USSR, relations between them in the sphere of international problems could be 'harmonious and mutually profitable', and that Britain was firmly resolved to fight against the hegemony of Germany, which was menacing Europe.

In spite, however, of these encouraging words, 'harmonious and mutually profitable' relations never seemed to come about, because the world situation, and particularly that in Europe, was so filled with complexities and contradictions, at the time, that not merely the serious improvement but even the simple normalisation of political and economic contacts between the two countries were made very difficult. In order to give some idea of the character of the difficulties, I will quote only one example.

As the reader is aware, Estonia, Latvia and Lithuania in the summer of 1940 entered the USSR. On 15 August of that year I visited Halifax and, in the name of the Soviet Government, asked him to take steps to wind up the British missions and consulates which had hitherto existed in the Baltic States, and also the former Baltic diplomatic missions in Britain. Halifax avoided giving a direct answer to my *démarche*, and instead entered upon a long discourse on the subject of how the actions of the USSR in relation to the Baltic States should be described—as aggression or not aggression? In the end, Halifax came to the conclusion that the actions of the USSR should be regarded as aggression, with all the consequences that follow.

Listening to the British Foreign Secretary, I thought how best could I react to his arguments. Naturally, I could easily clothe my reply in the reasonable Marxist-Leninist formulas to which we are accustomed: but from long experience I knew that for people like Halifax they were completely incomprehensible. These formulas rebound from their consciousness like peas from a wall. Yet it was important for me to say something to Halifax which could influence his intelligence and his feelings, and push him into some practical steps for winding up the British diplomatic missions in the Baltic and the Baltic diplomatic missions in Britain. It was necessary therefore to find a language which Halifax would understand, and clothe my arguments in such concrete shape as would convey something to his mind and his fantasy.

'You know, Lord Halifax, that I am a Siberian,' I began. 'So let me tell you a story about a Siberian peasant . . . In a certain village there lived a peasant by the name of Ivan. He fell seriously ill, and his neighbours decided that he was doomed to die . . . So then, without waiting for the sick man's demise, one of the neighbours went and led away his horse. A second led away his cow. A third went and stole his plough . . . But then the unexpected happened: the sick peasant recovered, and saw what his neighbours had done during his illness. Then he went to the first neighbour and said: "Give me back my horse." The neighbour began resisting. The peasant punched him hard, and took back his horse. Then the peasant went to the second neighbour and said: "Give me back my cow." The second neighbour, seeing what had happened to the first, made a fuss, used bad language, but in the end gave up the cow without a fight. Then the peasant went to the third neighbour and said: "Give me back my plough." After the experience of the first two, the third neighbour did not even risk a row, and simply handed over the plough to its former owner . . . So now, Lord Halifax, who was the aggressor in your opinion, the peasant Ivan or his neighbours?'

Halifax was silent for a long time after my 'story', then looked at the ceiling, then rubbed the bridge of his nose and finally pronounced: 'Yes, that's an interesting point of view.'

Of course I understood that the story about the Siberian peasant was not the last word in Marxist-Leninist theory, but it had practical results: Halifax never again called us 'aggressors', and, moreover, talk about my 'story' leaked out into Parliamentary and journalistic circles, where many said: 'You know, perhaps he's right.' Such an attitude was undoubtedly valuable for us. It ate away the anti-Soviet tension which prevailed in Britain after the entry of the Baltic States into the Soviet Union.

Here I want to make a small digression, and show by one vivid example with what caution one should treat official British historiography of the second world war.

In 1962 there appeared in London a stout work (about 600 pages of large size) entitled *British Foreign Policy in the Second World War*, from the pen of Sir Llewellyn Woodward. It is part of the series of books on the history of the second world war published by the Stationery Office, the official publishing house of the British Government. On pages 29–30 of this book the author gives the content of a conversation which I had with Butler on 30 January 1940. The conversation touched upon various questions, including German-Soviet relations, which at that time were of particular interest to the British Government. And Woodward writes:

'He (that is, I—*I.M.*) explained that there was "nothing sentimental" about the Russo-German *rapprochement*. The Soviet Government intended to follow only their own interests. "We lived in a period of change, when anything might happen, and in the jungle the strangest of animals got together if they felt that their joint interests made this advisable."'

The expressions I have quoted are intended to be the reproduction of my own words, allegedly used in conversation with Butler.

I willingly confirm that on 30 January 1940 I really did have a long conversation with Butler on various themes (mainly about the Soviet-Finnish war which was then taking place), but that not one word was said either about 'jungles' or about the 'strangest of animals'.

But was there ever any mention of 'jungles' in my conversations with Butler? Yes, there was, and in the following circumstances. I quote the record I made on 27 November 1940 (i.e. nearly ten months after the talk of 30 January):

'I visited Butler today. We had a long conversation, in which among other things we touched on the question of the British proposals for improving Soviet-British relations presented by Cripps in Moscow on 22 October. The essence of these proposals is that (a) the USSR maintains in relations with Britain as favourable neutrality as in relations with Germany; (b) the British

Government will consult with the Soviet Government on questions of post-war organisation, and will ensure its participation in the future peace conference; (c) Britain will not set up or take part in anti-Soviet alliances, if the USSR does not set up or take part in anti-British alliances; (d) Britain and the USSR develop their trade to the widest possible extent, and Britain is ready to supply the USSR with all that it requires for its defence; (e) the British Government gives *de facto* recognition to the sovereignty of the USSR in the Baltic States, Bessarabia, Western Ukraine and Western Belorussia; (f) Britain and the USSR conclude a pact of non-aggression similar to that between that of Germany and the Soviet Union.

'Butler asked me what I thought of these propositions. I replied that they aroused in me two feelings: surprise and irritation. Surprise, because the British proposals had no realistic foundation. An example was that the British Government was promising us *de facto* recognition of Soviet sovereignty in the Baltic States—but then we already had such recognition: the British diplomatic representatives had not so long ago left the territory of the Baltic Republics at our request. So what did the present proposal of the British Government add to the situation?

'"And what is it that arouses your irritation?" asked Butler with a certain anxiety.

'"What arouses irritation in me", I answered, "is the section of the British proposals where the British Government promises to assure the participation of the USSR in the future peace conference. Does the British Government imagine itself to be something like the Apostle Peter who, as legend tells us, holds in his hands the keys to Paradise?"

'Butler was somewhat confused, and began saying that perhaps the formulation of this point of the proposals was not a very happy one. In any case, any feeling of haughtiness and arrogance was foreign to the British Government.

'"You see, Mr. Butler," I said, "what we now see in Europe, and perhaps throughout the world, is a jungle" (Butler nodded his head in agreement). "But in jungles they reckon only with hard and severe reality. Where is the reality of the British proposals? I don't see it."'

That is what took place in fact. It is quite unlike what is put down in Woodward's book: both the date of the conversation and its content are wrong. I don't know what this implies but one thing is clear: the statements contained in Woodward's book require a careful and very critical approach.

I return, however, to the substance of the question. The negative attitude of the British Government to the entry of the Baltic Republics into the USSR gave rise to a number of disputes between London and Moscow, which poisoned the atmosphere of Anglo-Soviet relations and interfered with their normalisation. In this connection I well recall a conversation with Halifax on 17 October 1940. The conditions in which it took place were very characteristic. It was cold and draughty in Halifax's room: all the glass in the windows had been blown out by a big mine which the Germans had dropped the night before in St. James's Park. The mine had fallen into a lake, and the effect of the explosion was considerably reduced. Nevertheless, not a single whole window had been left in the Foreign Office and in Buckingham Palace, which are on opposite sides of the lake. It was a cold day, and there was a drizzle of rain. Halifax resembled a cock with ruffled feathers, and was sitting by a brightly burning fire. He sat me down by his side and began talking about an improvement in Anglo-Soviet relations.

'Is that possible?' Halifax asked me.

'Of course it is possible', I answered, 'but only on one absolute condition, that London does not wreck what is done in Moscow. Here is an example. Hardly had Cripps succeeded in beginning more serious trade negotiations in Moscow than on 14 October, in London, the Ministry of Shipping requisitioned the Baltic steamers . . . Of course all the effect of Cripps's efforts at once evaporated.'

Halifax began demonstrating to me that now, in war-time, Britain was in great need of tonnage. I asked with a smile:

'I hope the fate of the British Empire does not depend on thirty Baltic ships?'

'Of course not,' replied Halifax, somewhat nettled at my sarcasm.

'Then why the affair?' I asked again. 'Believe me, Lord Halifax, we are tired of your good intentions, we can be convinced only by your good deeds.'

But there were no deeds—and as a result Anglo-Soviet relations remained unsatisfactory right up to 22 June 1941.

7

Before the German Attack on USSR

AT the beginning of May 1941 there came to see me one day the Swedish Minister Prytz. Prytz was closely connected with the well-known Swedish ball-bearings firm of 'SKF', was interested in politics, and was a great admirer of the diplomatic activities of Alexandra Kollontay. He had been in the Soviet Union several times, was a supporter of good Swedish-Soviet relations and extremely disliked the German Nazis. We had established good relations, and frequently met to exchange opinions and talk about current political affairs.

On that occasion Prytz told me that he had recently been with some other diplomats at a luncheon given by Churchill, and had heard much that was interesting. Most of all he had been struck by the fable of 'the two frogs' which the Premier had told. I looked at the Swedish Minister with some surprise, and he understood my silent question.

'You know', Prytz began, 'that the affairs of the British are not brilliant just now: Hitler has seized the Balkans, Greece has had to be evacuated, Crete is next and they will hardly be able to retain it; the losses at sea are enormous . . . It's all not very cheerful . . . After lunch, over the coffee, someone asked Churchill about the further prospects. In reply the Premier told us the fable of "The Two Frogs" . . . "Once upon a time", he said, "there were two frogs, one an optimist the other a pessimist. One evening the frogs were jumping about the grass near a dairy. The scent of the milk from the open window of the dairy attracted the attention of the frogs. They jumped into the window to have a taste of the milk. The frogs, however, had calculated badly, and leapt straight into the bowl of milk. They looked round and they saw that the sides of the bowl were high and slippery. The pessimist frog at once lost heart, decided that salvation was impossible, folded her little paws and went to the bottom. The optimist frog decided to fight for her life, and began floundering in the milk, hoping to keep alive that way. She didn't know exactly how this could happen, and whether it was possible at all, but she didn't want to die without a struggle. Throughout the night the optimist frog struggled in the bowl of milk, swam, beat the milk with her paws and, to her happiness, by the morning she was floating on a thick slab of butter which had been churned by her efforts during the night . . ." Having told this story, Churchill concluded: "Now I am an optimist frog too!"'

Prytz smiled and added: 'As you see, Churchill is not losing heart... Who knows, maybe he is right.'

On 1 June 1941 I put down the following:

'In spite of the painful military reverses (evacuation of Greece, loss of Crete) all Britain during the last three weeks has been living under the impression of the flight here of Hitler's deputy, Rudolf Hess. When one tries to separate out what seems the most probable from the mass of tales, reports, guesses, suppositions, rumours, etc., surrounding this strange, almost romantic story, approximately the following picture emerges.

'Hess piloted the plane himself. He landed, or more precisely came down by parachute, in Scotland near the estate of the Duke of Hamilton, whom apparently he met once in Germany. Kirkpatrick, who before the war was Counsellor at the British Embassy in Berlin, identified Hess. Kirkpatrick and Simon, on the instructions of the British Government, questioned Hess and tried to find out why he had flown to Britain, and on whose instructions. Hess stated that he had received no instructions from anybody in Germany, that Hitler had not the least idea of his intentions and that he had come on his own initiative and moved by his own considerations.

'Hess considers that Germany is invincible and that the continuation of the war threatens Britain with terrible bloodshed, starvation through the blockade and complete defeat. On the other hand, the war is inflicting painful wounds on Germany as well. He has been in Hamburg, and has seen the devastation caused there by British air raids. Hess does not understand why two very great "Nordic" Powers, bulwarks of civilisation, should destroy each other. Churchill is a war incendiary, it's all the same to him, but Hess does not doubt that there are more sensible people in Britain whom the British people would follow if they were told the truth. Among such sensible people Hess classes the Duke of Hamilton: that is why he came down where he did. Hess named several more persons who, in his opinion, can be classed as sensible, but I have not been able to find out who they were.

'What does Hess want? In his own words, he wants most of all a reconciliation between Germany and Britain. On what basis? Approximately the following: Britain retains her Empire, while Germany is given freedom of action on the European continent. A treaty to such a division of the world could be concluded for a period of twenty-five years. Naturally, the preliminary for an Anglo-German agreement should be the elimination of the Churchill Government and the creation of a "truly British" Government.

'The attitude of the British newspapers to Hess has gone through a number of phases. At first, in the articles and reports printed on 13 May, he was represented as a "sincere" and "honest" man, a kind family man, almost an "idealist" of a Nazi kind. Allegedly he hates the USSR by profound conviction, and therefore condemns Hitler for his "appeasement" of the Bolsheviks. Hack-writers have been found to begin extolling Hess as a "great convert", something like a modern Buddha or St. Francis (Ward Price in the *Daily Mail*). During the next days the press began to sound the retreat, but still continued to put a high value on Hess and his mission. Then, by the end of May, Hess's shares fell heavily, and they began to write and talk of him as of a prominent representative of "that same band of gangsters" who plunged the world into disaster. It has also been stated that Hess has been interned as a prisoner of war and will remain in confinement up to the end of the war.

'What has gone on? So far as I know, a struggle began behind the scenes in British politics directly Hess arrived. Churchill, Eden, Bevin and all the Labour Ministers generally at once declared definitely against any negotiation for peace with Germany with him or through him. But among the Ministers there have been found men like Simon who, supported by the former "Clivedenites", have considered that the Government should make use of such an unexpected opportunity for establishing contact with Hitler, or at any rate for soundings about possible peace terms. In the long run Churchill was victorious. No small part was played by anxiety among the masses aroused by Hess's arrival. The struggle behind the scenes has found its reflection in the press as well.

'Churchill's success can only be welcomed; but the question is not yet cleared up as to who is Hess? A camouflaged emissary from Hitler or a solitary psychopath? Or is he the representative of some grouping within the Nazi top leadership, disturbed at the prospect that the war may drag out too long?'

Since the above lines were written, nearly a quarter of a century has passed. During that period there have been published many documents, memoirs, monographs and researches on the subject of the second world war, but up to this day there is still no precise reply to the question of who Hess was, after all.

Churchill in his war memoirs expresses the opinion that Hess came of 'his own free will', and that he was 'a medical, not a criminal case, and should be so regarded'.[1] Schellenberg, the Gestapo's chief of counter-espionage, asserts in his reminiscences that Hitler gave Hess no instructions and did not even know of his plans.[2] Kirkpatrick is roughly of the same opinion.[3] However, A. M. Nekrich, the Soviet historian, writes:

'At the Nuremberg trial there was a curious episode, to which sufficient attention has not been paid. On 31 August 1946 Hess stated at a session of the Tribunal that he wished to state on oath what happened to him during his stay in Britain. "In the spring of 1941 . . ." Hess began. But at this point he was interrupted by the British President of the Tribunal, Lord Lawrence. Perhaps history has not yet said its last word about the "Hess mission"'.[4]

However that may be, one thing is beyond doubt: all that was basic and essential about Hess's flight was known to the Soviet Embassy already at the time, in the spring of 1941. The twenty odd years that have passed since then have added only various precisions and secondary details.

I want to describe three occasions which bear witness to J. V.

1. *The Second World War*, Vol. III, p. 49.
2. *The Labyrinth. Memoirs of Walter Schellenberg.* New York, 1956, p. 187.
3. *The Inner Circle.*
4. *International Affairs* (Russian edition), 1960, No. 9.

Stalin's disbelief in the imminence of a German attack on the eve of 22 June.

At the beginning of June 1941 the Foreign Office passed over to me a letter from the British Consul at Barcelona which deeply moved me. In the Tarragona prison, near Barcelona, there was a Soviet citizen, Makh-Borzhetskaya, who had worked as an interpreter with the Soviet officers who had been fighting on the side of the Spanish Republic. Makh-Borzhetskaya was captured by the Francoists and sentenced to thirty years' imprisonment. In some way or other she had managed to establish contact with the British Consul in Barcelona, and through him she asked that her husband and children in Moscow should be informed that she was alive, but in prison in Spain.

Naturally, I cabled immediately to the People's Commissariat for Foreign Affairs the information I had received, and asked that the unfortunate woman's request be acted upon. I did not, however, confine myself to this, and put to the Soviet Government the question of whether the return of Makh-Borzhetskaya to the USSR could not be secured by way of exchange or in some other way. I expected the Soviet Government either to make use of the Red Cross for this purpose, or to instruct me to come to an agreement with the Foreign Office about British mediation. What was my surprise when a few days later I received a communication from Moscow to the effect that the Soviet Government had applied for assistance to Berlin. Moreover, from the tone of the message it was clear that Moscow expected that the application would be successful. I unconsciously shrugged my shoulders, thinking: 'What? Now, when a number of signs make one expect an attack on the Soviet Union by Hitler almost any day, to hope at such a moment for the liberation of Makh-Borzhetskaya through German mediation? . . . Incomprehensible!'

On 10 June Sir Alexander Cadogan, the Permanent Under-Secretary for Foreign Affairs, asked me to come and see him. When I entered his room, he said:

'On the instructions of His Majesty's Government, I have to make an important communication to you. Please take a sheet of paper and put down what I tell you.'

I acted as he asked, and Cadogan began to dictate from documents lying before him:

'On such-and-such a date two German motorised divisions passed through such-and-such a point in the direction of your frontier . . . On such-and-such a date six German divisions were concentrated at such-and-such a point near your frontier . . . During the whole of May there passed through such-and-such a point in the direction of your frontier from 25 to 30 military trains a day . . . On such-and-such a date in such-and-such a district bordering on your frontier there were discovered such-and-such a number of German troops and German planes . . . By such-and-such a date from such-and-such a district bordering on your territory the evacuation of the whole of the local population was completed . . .'

Cadogan was speaking in a monotonous voice, naming more and more places and ever new military units. I was writing down under his dictation almost mechanically. In my imagination there arose the image of the Nazi troops, vast masses of Nazi troops—infantry, artillery, tanks, armoured cars, aeroplanes—which were irresistibly streaming to the east, ever further to the east . . . And all this avalanche, breathing fire and death, was at any moment to descend upon our country!

Finally the dictation ended. Cadogan rose to show that he had performed the task imposed on him, and then added:

'The Prime Minister asks you urgently to communicate all these data to the Soviet Government.'

Immediately I had returned to the Embassy, I sent an urgent cypher cable to Moscow with all the information received from Cadogan, and began awaiting results. Of course, I did not accept Cadogan's communication as 100 per cent true. Information from military intelligence is not always accurate; the British were interested in war being let loose in the east, and might deliberately heighten the colours in order to have a bigger effect on the Soviet Government. For these reasons I made a considerable discount in my mind from what Cadogan had told me. Nevertheless, the Under-Secretary's information was so serious, and the reports he had communicated were so precise and concrete, that (it seemed to me) they should give Stalin serious food for thought, and lead him urgently to check them and, in any case, give strict instructions to our Western frontier to be on guard!

It is easy therefore to understand my extreme amazement when on 14 June TASS published a communiqué stating:

'Even before the arrival of Sir Stafford Cripps, British Ambassador in the USSR, in London, and particularly after his arrival, there began to appear in the British and foreign press generally rumours about "the imminence of war between the USSR and Germany" . . . In spite of the evident senselessness of the rumours, responsible circles in Moscow have nevertheless thought it necessary, in view of the stubborn circulation of these rumours, to authorise TASS to state that such rumours are clumsily cooked-up propaganda by forces hostile to the USSR and to Germany . . . TASS states that . . . Germany is just as unswervingly observing the conditions of the Soviet-German Pact of Non-Aggression as is the Soviet Union; in view of which, in the opinion of Soviet circles, the rumours about Germany's intention to tear up the Pact and undertake an attack on the USSR are devoid of any foundation, while the movement in the recent period of German troops, set free from operations in the Balkans, to the northern and north-eastern districts of Germany is due, it should be supposed, to other reasons, not connected with Soviet-German relations".[1]

I simply did not know what to think and what to do. The shaft in the direction of Britain with which the TASS communiqué began left no room for doubt that it was the reply to the warning given by Cadogan.

And nevertheless, I confess, even at that dread moment there was still a warming hope in my heart: 'Perhaps Stalin is right after all?'[2]

Finally, one last fact. By 20 June 1941 preparations were completed for dispatching to the USSR the steamer *Yelna*, carrying sailors from the Baltic States who had got stuck in Britain on account of war-time conditions. The same day I asked Moscow by what route it was most convenient to dispatch her. Reckoning with the peril of a German attack on the USSR, I suggested that the *Yelna* might be sent not to Murmansk (as would have been natural in more tranquil conditions), but to Vladivostok, through the Panama Canal. The reply came on the evening of 22 June, when

1. *Izvestia*, 14 June 1941.

2. At a conference of historians held in Moscow on 14–16 April, 1965, on the occasion of the twentieth anniversary of the victory over Nazi Germany, Army General P. A. Kurochkin discussed the initial Soviet reverses in his report on cardinal problems of the war. After dealing with the overwhelming superiority of the Wehrmacht at the outset in training, experienced cadres, equipment and degree of mobilisation, he went on to 'the big blunder made before the war by Stalin in the evaluation of the military situation, its military and political aspects, and also of the designs and potentialities of Fascist Germany. It led to delay in the fulfilment of the entire complex of Government measures to prepare the country for defence. This miscalculation was primarily responsible for the unpreparedness of the Soviet armed forces to beat off the aggressor's attack'.

war had already begun, but it was dated the 21st. The reply was: 'Dispatch the *Yelna* to Murmansk.' Of course, in the situation now existing I did not fulfil this instruction, but detained the vessel in Britain. Later the *Yelna*, in the changed situation, did not go to the USSR at all, but entered the British merchantile marine, as Britain was now the ally of the Soviet Union.

Part Three

*

Germany's Attack on the USSR

I

22 June 1941

SATURDAY, 21 June, was a hot sunny day. Such days do not often occur in London. Therefore immediately after work had ended at the Embassy, at 1 p.m., my wife and I left for Bovingdon, where we had been staying at week-ends in Negrin's house for nearly a year.

'What news?' asked Negrin as he shook hands.

I made a gesture of doubt: 'So far nothing special, but the atmosphere seems thundery . . . There may be a storm at any moment.'

I had in mind the reports, the prophecies, the rumours of a coming 'leap' by Hitler to the East, against the USSR, on which the West had been living for the preceding months.

Changing into a light summer suit, I went wandering through the park surrounding Negrin's house. I sat on the benches and lay on the vivid green grass under the rays of the warm sun. The earth and the air were full of the intoxicating perfumes of high summer, and I absorbed them greedily and joyfully, enjoying them and trying not to think of the dread perils of the moment.

Reason told me—as I had more than once already let Moscow know—that an attack by Hitlerite Germany was close, almost round the corner, but the heart somehow did not wish to believe it. Lying on the grass on that memorable day, I was thinking:

'Can it really be war tomorrow or the day after? . . . Will the Hitlerite hordes burst through our frontier? Will the Fascist bombs really fall on our cities? . . . Are tens and hundreds of thousands of Soviet people really doomed to a cruel death under the blows of the enemy? . . . If only all this could be avoided!'

Suddenly I was called to the telephone. It was a secretary of the Embassy ringing from London: Stafford Cripps wanted to see me immediately. Cripps, then British Ambassador in the USSR, had returned to Britain at the beginning of June for consultations with his Government. He had been twice to see me and had said that his work in Moscow didn't seem to advance at all and that he intended to resign. Why did he now so urgently need me? That at once put me on my guard.

An hour later I was in the Embassy. Cripps came into my room very excited.

'You remember,' he began, 'that I have already warned the Soviet Government more than once that a German attack was imminent . . . Well, we have reliable information that this attack will take place tomorrow 22 June, or at the very latest 29 June . . . You know that Hitler always attacks on Sundays . . . I wanted to inform you of this.'

After we had exchanged brief remarks about his information, Cripps added: 'Of course, if war against you begins, I return to Moscow immediately.'

When Cripps left, I at once sent off to the People's Commissariat for Foreign Affairs an urgent cypher message about his communication. Then I returned once more to Bovingdon—to its rural peace, shaded garden, the perfumes of summer: but in my thoughts there rose even more acutely than before the insistent question: 'Can it really be war tomorrow?'

I passed an uneasy night, and at eight in the morning on 22 June there was once again a call from the Embassy. The Counsellor, K. V. Novikov, terribly excited, said rapidly:

'Have you heard the British radio? . . . Hitler attacked the Soviet Union early today! . . . The Germans have crossed the frontier and are bombing our towns . . . There are battles and casualties . . .'

'So it's begun! . . .' there flashed through my mind. 'What is to happen now?'

Negrin and all his household were already on their feet, half-dressed and extremely disturbed. By the telephone itself there was an excited exchange of opinions on the sensational news and the prospects ahead. Then my wife and I hurriedly changed and took our seats in the car. On the way from Bovingdon to London I was thinking over the immediate practical steps to be taken, and when we arrived at the Embassy, was told by the secretary that there had just been a call from Eden: the Foreign Secretary wanted to see me in his office at midday. At about 11 a.m. the Soviet radio announced that the People's Commissar for Foreign Affairs would broadcast at midday. I rang up Eden and, referring to this, asked him to receive me after the speech by V. M. Molotov. Eden willingly agreed and, in fact, my meeting with the British Foreign Secretary took place at about 1 p.m.

When I heard of the forthcoming speech, the first thought in my mind was: 'Why Molotov? Why not Stalin? On such an occasion a speech by the head of the State was necessary.' However, I did not attribute particular importance to this circumstance, but concentrated my main attention on the content of the speech by the People's Commissar for Foreign Affairs. It was brief, not longer than a quarter of an hour. It underlined the perfidy of Hitler and his responsibility for letting loose war: it drew a distinction between the band of Fascist leaders and the German people: and it expressed confidence that the Soviet armed forces would be able to expel the German invaders from our country, as our forefathers had done in the Napoleonic era. The speech ended with the words: 'Our cause is just. The enemy will be defeated. Victory will be ours.'

The speech of the People's Commissar for Foreign Affairs made a good impression on me. It answered completely to my feelings and my firm conviction that we would defeat Germany. But at that moment—I frankly admit it—I did not imagine what a terrible price we should have to pay for victory. But this was due to the fact that in the summer of 1941, like very many others, I did not clearly understand either the cult of Stalin's personality or all the tragic consequences of that cult.

Eden received me with great warmth, and spoke at length of the fellow feeling and sympathy of Britain and her people with the Soviet Union at this dread hour. I thanked the Foreign Secretary for his good words, but was more interested in what would now be the actions of the British Government. I was very worried by the thought that, having acquired by the will of fate a powerful ally in the East, the rulers of Britain as had more than once happened in the past would let the main burdens of the war fall on his shoulders, and would themselves seek to step aside to some extent. Therefore I put to Eden the direct question: what would be the policy of the British Government in relation to the USSR, and would it not begin somewhat reducing its 'war effort' for the defeat of the enemy? What would likewise be Britain's attitude to

Hitler's 'peace offensive' in the West, which evidently should be expected at this moment, when he had thrown all his main forces to the East against our country?

Eden replied firmly that it would be less possible to talk of peace now with Hitler than ever, that Britain's war effort would continue to develop at full speed, and that the policy of the British Government in relation to the USSR would be friendly and responsive.

'This evening the Prime Minister will make a big speech on the radio,' continued Eden. 'You will be able to hear all this from his own lips.'

I expressed my satisfaction, and promised immediately to inform the Soviet Government. Then I added: 'May I make a request?' When Eden said that he was quite ready to do whatever I wanted, I continued: 'Please tell the Prime Minister that it would be exceptionally important in his speech today to be as definite as possible on two points: that Britain will firmly support the USSR in this war, and that Britain would not in any case make peace with Germany.' Britain and the USSR had before them no small historic period in which to go forward together. To avoid unnecessary friction and differences, it was essential to prevent the possibility of any misunderstandings between the two sides.

Eden heard me out and said:

'I will gladly do what you ask. I don't doubt that the Prime Minister will treat it with great consideration. There must be complete clarity in the relations between us.'

Later developments, alas, showed that precisely this 'complete clarity of relations' between London and Moscow did not exist throughout the whole war: but that was still in the bosom of the future, and therefore I went away very encouraged.

At 9 p.m. Churchill made his broadcast. I listened to him carefully. The Prime Minister did not conceal that he was and remained a consistent opponent of Communism and that he would 'unsay no word' spoken against Communism during the preceding quarter of a century. But, continued Churchill, 'all this fades away before the spectacle which is now unfolding . . . I see the Russian soldiers standing on the threshold of their native land, guarding the fields which their fathers have tilled from time immemorial. I see them guarding their homes where mothers and wives pray—ah yes, for there are times when all pray—for the safety of their loved ones, the return of the bread-winner, of their champion, of their protector. I see the 10,000 villages of Russia, where the means of existence was wrung so hardly from the soil, but where there are still primordial human joys, where maidens laugh and children play. I see advancing upon all this in hideous onslaught the Nazi war machine . . .'

Further touching on Britain's policy in the war, Churchill said:

'We are resolved to destroy Hitler and every vestige of the Nazi régime . . . We will never parley, we will never negotiate with Hitler or any of his gang . . . Any man or State who fights on against Nazidom will have our aid . . . It follows therefore that we shall give whatever help we can to Russia and the Russian people.'

Churchill based his attitude to the USSR and its struggle on the genuine interests of Britain. Hitler, he said, 'wishes to destroy the Russian power because he hopes that if he succeeds in this, he will be able to bring back the main strength of his army and air force from the East and hurl it upon this Island . . . His invasion of Russia is no more than a prelude to an attempted invasion of the British Isles . . . The Russian danger is therefore our danger and the danger of the United States, just as the cause of any Russian fighting for his hearth and home is the cause of free men and free peoples in every quarter of the globe.'[1]

After hearing Churchill I thought: 'For today I may be content: my wishes have been fulfilled: the Premier has quite clearly declared that Britain would not now make any deal with Hitler, and that it would give help to the Soviet Union" . . . But what help? In what forms? To what extent? The formula "whatever help we can" permits of various interpretations. And we know from history what fierce disputes and differences there have often arisen within military coalitions even when their participants were States with one and the same social system. But in this particular case there is a military coalition of two socially different Powers—capitalist and Socialist. What will be their mutual relations? Will they be able to live together within the framework of a single military alliance?'

I meditated long on this subject; but then remembered the saying in the New Testament which I had first heard in my schoolboy days, 'Sufficient unto the day is the evil thereof', and decided: 'Let's rejoice at today's success, and later on we shall see.'

And then there arose before me of itself, as it were, the image of Beatrice Webb, with whom I had talked a year before about

1. *The Second World War*, Vol. III, pp. 331–3.

Britain's path in this war, and I could not help drawing the conclusion: 'So Beatrice has been proved right. The course of events confirms her anticipation. Britain has acquired her second Coalition.' The first, which had ended in the summer of 1940, was with France.

The second day of the war came, but there was not a sound from Moscow. The third and fourth days of the war followed, but Moscow continued its silence. I waited with impatience for any directions from the Soviet Government, and first of all for instructions as to whether I should prepare the ground in London for the conclusion of a formal Anglo-Soviet military alliance—but neither Molotov nor Stalin gave any signs of life.

I did not know what the situation was in the Kremlin in the first days after the German attack, and explained Moscow's silence to myself by the Government, being overwhelmed with super-urgent military affairs, simply not having the opportunity to deal with diplomatic questions.

However, I did not think I had the right to sit with hands folded only because I had received no 'tasks' from Moscow. Certainly not! A vast misfortune had descended on my country, thousands of people were perishing, rivers of blood were running, our people were faced with the question of freedom or slavery, and I, a Soviet citizen, and moreover a Soviet Ambassador in Britain, must remain passive awaiting directives from the Government? My conscience could not put up with this, and I decided to act, to act independently, arising out of my own understanding of the situation and the most pressing needs of the Soviet Union.

It was clear to me that without Moscow's sanction I could not undertake negotiations for the conclusion of an Anglo-Soviet military alliance. Well, but what about creating a second front in France? That was quite another affair. The Germans were always afraid of a second front. A second front in any conditions would be useful for the USSR: why should I not raise this question with the British? I saw no obstacles to this, and decided to make the appropriate *démarche*.

But with whom should I speak on such a subject? It would have been most logical to raise it with the Premier, but a number of symptoms led me to think that Churchill would be unfavourable to such an idea (and so it turned out later on). With Eden? This would have been most correct of all from the standpoint of diplomatic etiquette: after all he was Foreign Secretary. But even admitting the possibility that he would feel sympathy for the proposal of a second front, Eden was under too strong an influence of the Premier, and would hardly venture to oppose him. For these considerations I renounced the idea of turning on this question to Churchill and Eden.

Then to whom? After careful consideration I came to the conclusion that probably it would be most expedient to make the first approach to Lord Beaverbrook. He was a bold and independent personality. He easily accepted new ideas and original methods of action. Beaverbrook was at that time a member of Churchill's War Cabinet and, as such, was concerned with general questions of strategy and conduct of the war. In addition I had established good personal relations with him during the previous six years. He used to visit me at the Embassy, I had visited him in his town apartment and in his country house at Cherkley. During the last years before the war Beaverbrook had done a good deal in the way of propaganda for an Anglo-Soviet *rapprochement*. All this gave me some grounds for supposing that Beaverbrook might accept the idea of a second front with greater sympathy than Churchill or Eden. Of course, such outflanking of the Prime Minister and the Foreign Secretary represented a certain departure from the normal rules of diplomacy, but could one reckon with this at a moment of such terrible danger? An unusual situation naturally demanded unusual methods. And I made up my mind: on the fifth day after the beginning of the German-Soviet war, I travelled to Cherkley and asked Beaverbrook to raise in the War Cabinet the question of opening a second front in France.

At that moment information about the situation on the German-Soviet front was very confused and contradictory. The Germans of course were shouting about their 'shattering successes', and representing matters as though the Red Army was collapsing before their eyes. British sources were more cautious, but they too recorded the victories of the Wehrmacht and the defeats of the Soviet troops. In the British Ministry of Defence people said at the time that the Germans would 'go through Russia as a knife goes through butter', the pessimists asserting that Hitler would become 'master of Russia' in six weeks and the optimists that it would take him three months. The Soviet military communiqués represented the state of affairs in a more favourable sense. But all the same they made clear too that the Wehrmacht was advancing and the Red Army retreating.

In raising before Beaverbrook the question of a second front, I based my arguments in the main on the realistic interests of Britain herself. She alone, even with her Empire, I said, could never win victory over the Third Reich and maintain her position in the world. For this she required a strong ally on land. Such an ally she now had. True, for the moment he was suffering certain reverses, but this was only temporary. Sooner or later there would be a turn of the tide, and then the Germans would begin to suffer reverses.

To demonstrate this I drew upon some historical examples out of Russia's part. It was to Britain's advantage that such a turn should take place as soon as possible, and that the defeat of Hitlerite Germany should occur in the nearest possible future. For this a second front was necessary, and the quicker the better.

Beaverbrook listened to me attentively, and then said:

'All you say is very good, but...'

He stopped for a moment and then, looking at me searchingly, added:

'Let me be quite frank with you . . . Will you really fight? Won't the same thing happen with you that happened in France?'

I was so thunderstruck by his question that at first I almost lost the power of speech. Pulling myself together, I cried indignantly:

'We will fight like devils.'

Beaverbrook looked at me attentively, then patted me on the shoulder and said, in a rather more friendly voice that usual:

'I believe you . . . Very well, I will try raising the question of a second front with the Government. I think a second front now is essential.'

Later, when the Soviet Union was carrying on its heroic struggle against the Hitlerite hordes, Beaverbrook said to me more than once:

'I am glad I believed you then . . . Your people are really fighting the Nazis like devils.'

Beaverbrook himself from that time became a hot supporter of the second front, and later on did not a little to bring it about. Eloquent testimony of this is contained in a number of documents published after the war. He also rendered us many services in respect of war supplies, but I will return to this question later.

I immediately sent a cable to Moscow about my conversation

with Beaverbrook. No objections to my initiative followed. On the contrary the People's Commissar for Foreign Affairs called in Cripps (who had returned to Moscow immediately after 22 June) and, referring to Beaverbrook's sympathy for the idea of a second front, requested the British Ambassador to raise this question with the British Government. Cripps informed London about the request, and then a curious diplomatic incident occurred. Eden asked me to come and see him and, pointing to a cypher message from Cripps lying on his desk, began asking me whom I had seen about a second front: the cypher clerk had muddled something up and the name of my collocutor was distorted in the telegram, which was incomprehensible.

I replied: 'I talked with Lord Beaverbrook.'

A shadow of irritation and dissatisfaction passed over Eden's face. 'Oh, Lord Beaverbrook . . .', Eden drawled.

And he rapidly began to reproach me for not having come directly to him with my question about a second front: such a problem was directly within his competence, as a member of the Cabinet and Foreign Secretary.

Beaverbrook's attempt to interest the Cabinet in the question of a second front was unsuccessful. Churchill, as I had supposed, was unfavourable to this idea. He was supported by a majority of members of the Cabinet. Three years of stubborn struggle by the Soviet Union were required before the second front in France was at last opened, and then only because the Western Powers were afraid that the Red Army might come to Berlin before they did.

Possibly Anglo-American historians, politicians and military writers may wish to challenge this statement. Nevertheless it is true. When today, many years later, one sums up all the material on the question of the second front, it becomes quite clear that the motive of aid to the USSR played a second- or third-rate part in organising the invasion of France in the summer of 1944. And throughout the three years during which the struggle for the second front lasted, its main opponent invariably proved to be Winston Churchill, the Prime Minister of Great Britain. That was how in practice his formula that the British would give to the USSR in this war 'whatever help we can' was deciphered.

2

First Weeks of War

ON 3 July, the twelfth day after Germany's attack on the USSR, J. V. Stalin spoke on the radio for the first time. I listened to him with bated breath, and strove to find in his words some hope of a decisive turning point in military events, and in the most immediate future: but had little success.

'The Hitlerite troops', said Stalin, 'have succeeded in occupying Lithuania, a considerable part of Latvia, the Western part of Belorussia, part of Western Ukraine. The Fascist air force is extending the fields of operations of its bombers, subjecting to bombardments Murmansk, Orsha, Mogilev, Smolensk, Kiev, Odessa, Sevastopol.' Thus it was now indubitable that the Germans had occupied extensive areas of Soviet territory, and that the Red Army had withdrawn from the frontiers deep into the country. And the call by Stalin 'to create partisan detachments in the districts occupied by the enemy' and to destroy 'all valuable property' in the places evacuated by the Red Army, inevitably led to the thought that a speedy turn for the better could not apparently be expected—all the more because further on Stalin said plainly: 'It is a question of the life and death of the Soviet State, the life and death of the peoples of the USSR.'

Against my will the fatal question rose in my mind, how could this happen? Had the experience of the Finnish war really taught us nothing? Had the Red Army really proved unprepared for the German attack? Were measures really not taken in time for a massive counter-blow, should the Fascist hordes hurl themselves against us? Here I remembered my telegram about the concentration of German troops on the Soviet frontier, sent to Moscow on

10 June, and the publication after it, on 14 June, of the TASS statement with its assurance that Germany was loyally observing the Pact of Non-Aggression.

A week passed after Stalin's speech, and a second week, but as before there was no turn in the tide. True, battles went on over the whole expanse from the Baltic to the Black Sea: true, the Germans were suffering great losses: true, at individual points and districts our soldiers were holding up the German invaders for a considerable time: but all the same, as a whole, the Red Army was continuing to retreat, and even now hundreds of thousands of square kilometres were falling under the yoke of the Hitlerite bandits.

I could not understand. But the dread real fact had to be faced: the Hitlerite hordes were advancing at speed towards Moscow and Leningrad, while the Red Army was retreating further and further. And in my mind there arose the question, ever more sharply and insistently: who bore the blame for the terrible tragedy which had befallen the Soviet Union?

I had at that time no clear answer to this question, but I well remember that it was precisely in the first weeks of the German-Soviet war that my doubts about the statesmanship of Stalin, which had first appeared in the days of the Soviet-Finnish war, began to grow stronger.

From the beginning of July Soviet-British diplomatic activity was resumed. In Moscow the question was raised of clothing the new relationships between the two countries in appropriate form. On the same subject, by the instruction of the People's Commissariat for Foreign Affairs, I talked with Eden in London. Churchill was somewhat put out by the fact that Stalin did not in any way respond to his broadcast of 22 June, but decided all the same to take the first step towards establishing more friendly relations with the head of the Soviet State. On 7 July he sent Stalin a letter giving him to understand that Britain's help to the Soviet Union would take the form principally of air bombardments of Germany. Cripps personally handed this letter to Stalin, and had a conversation with him lasting about an hour. During the conversation, Stalin expressed the view that Britain and the USSR should conclude an agreement containing two points: mutual aid during the war, and the obligation not to sign a separate peace with Germany. Churchill agreed with this, and on 12 July 1941 Molotov and

Cripps signed in Moscow an agreement for mutual military assistance, which provided:

'1. The two Governments mutually undertake to render each other assistance and support of all kinds in the present war against Hitlerite Germany.

'2. They further undertake that during this war they will neither negotiate nor conclude an armistice or treaty of peace except by mutual agreement.'[1]

This was a foundation stone in the system of Anglo-Soviet relations during the second world war.

About the same time (or more precisely on 8 July 1941) a Soviet military and naval Mission arrived in London. Its head was General F. I. Golikov, and his deputy was Admiral N. M. Kharlamov. I presented the Mission to Churchill and some other members of the Government, and our Soviet colony at once surrounded its members with a warm atmosphere of friendship and comradeship. Our military also rapidly and easily found their place in the colony as its worthy members. All underwent wartime difficulties together, all sought to relieve the difficult situation together by evenings of amateur art in the Embassy and the club. During two years of relationship with the military and naval Mission (right up to my final departure for Moscow) I cannot recall a single case of any serious dispute involving the Mission. And today I want to say my word of thanks to its members for their conduct in those painful times.

General F. I. Golikov stayed in Britain only a short time, and soon flew to the United States on business. He did not come back to work in London. The *de facto* chief (and from the middle of 1943 the formal chief) of the Mission was Admiral N. M. Kharlamov, who remained in London until the end of 1944, when he returned to work in the USSR. He directed the work of the Mission with wisdom and tact, knowing how to protect the interests of the USSR and at the same time not to make relations with the British too difficult, which would have been extremely disadvantageous for us. Naturally it was not always possible to avoid individual disputes with the British authorities—I shall say more about this later—but, looking back over the work of the Mission during the two years in which I was closely acquainted with it, I must record that it succeeded in grappling with its tasks successfully. And those tasks were not at all easy.

1. *Soviet Foreign Policy during the Patriotic War* (London), Vol. I, p. 77.

For in addition to the necessity of maintaining connections usual in such cases, between the armed forces of two allied States carrying on a great and painful war, our Mission was also concerned with the taking over from Britain of the arms and military equipment intended for the USSR, and had also to concern itself with the rapid and as far as possible safe transporting of these supplies to our country. As will be seen later, such transport represented in the conditions then prevailing an extremely complex operation, and its carrying out in practice more than once gave rise to mutual friction and dissatisfaction. However, these awkward moments were successfully overcome in the long run, and our Mission made its valuable contribution to this end.

Unlike the swollen personnel of the military missions of other Powers, our military and naval Mission was distinguished by an almost Spartan 'leanness': it numbered only about fifty naval and military men, but most of them were people with high professional and personal qualities.

In that connection I would like to mention some members of the Mission, and of the staffs of the different Attachés, who played a particularly important part at that time—A. E. Brykin, N. G. Morozovsky, K. S. Stukalov, I. A. Sklyarov, S. D. Kremer, M. N. Sharapov, N. N. Pugachov. The name of the latter is bound up with painful recollections: he died in Britain in an air disaster, and all our Soviet colony in London was deeply moved by this quite unexpected tragedy.

In the first weeks of the war there was one strange episode which I should like to describe here. The Spitzbergen Archipelago belongs to Norway, which exploits the coalfields there. The USSR has a concession to do the same. As it was extremely probable that, following the German attack on the USSR, they would try to capture Spitzbergen and turn it into their northern base, while it would be very difficult for the Allies to defend it, the Governments of the USSR, Britain and Norway came to an agreement for the evacuation of the Soviet and Norwegian miners. The British Government undertook to effect this operation, for which a large passenger liner, the *Empress of Canada* was selected, together with several warships to protect it. I received an urgent directive from Moscow to send one of the diplomatic staff of the Embassy with the expedition as a representative of the USSR, since about 2,000 Soviet citizens—the miners and their families—had to be evacuated from Spitzbergen. The telegram came on the eve of the departure of the expedition. The matter was extremely urgent and important. My choice fell on a young attaché, P. D. Yerzin, who had recently arrived in London. I called him in and said:

'Pavel Dmitrievich, tomorrow you will have to leave for the Arctic to carry out a difficult but honourable job.'

It is easy to realise Yerzin's amazement. In a few words I explained to him what was involved. Pavel Dmitrievich replied:

'I will try to carry out your instructions as well as possible.'

The following day, equipped with the necessary documents by the Embassy, Yerzin sailed from Britain.

Ten days later the British flotilla reached the shores of Spitzbergen. The Soviet miners, warned beforehand from Moscow of the coming evacuation, were ready for departure, and in the course of the next two days embarked together with their baggage on the *Empress of Canada*. The affair did not pass, however, without 'unforeseen circumstances'—which nevertheless had no sad consequences. During those two days of embarkation there appeared in the world two new Soviet citizens, whose reception was facilitated by British naval surgeons. Some excitement was also caused by a dog—an extremely sensible and noble animal—which the Captain of the liner for some reason did not want to embark. It ran about anxiously on the shore while the miners were being brought to the liner, and when the last motor-boats with personnel set off, the dog swam after them and reached the steamer. There it began to howl so pitifully that in the end it was brought on board.

The British flotilla delivered the Soviet miners to Murmansk and then returned to Spitzbergen, took on board all the Norwegians there, numbering between 700 and 800, and left for Britain with them, since Norway was occupied by the Hitlerites.

On the return journey there awaited Yerzin a quite fantastic surprise, possible only in wartime. When the flotilla arrived at Spitzbergen from Murmansk, two Soviet citizens presented themselves to Yerzin. They had not been able to leave with their fellow countrymen, because during the two days of the embarkation they were far from the harbour in the mountains, and knew nothing about the forthcoming evacuation. What was to be done? Yerzin found the only possible way out of the situation: he took both miners away with him to London.

In the middle of July I received an instruction from Moscow

immediately to conclude pacts of mutual assistance, modelled on the Anglo-Soviet Pact, with the emigrant governments of Czechoslovakia and Poland, then resident in London. I set about this at once.

The negotiations with Czechoslovakia did not present any difficulty. After Hitler had seized the country in mid-March 1939, the majority of the leaders of the country who emigrated gradually gathered in France, whither Benes also travelled from the USA, where he had gone after Munich. In November 1939 a Czechoslovak National Committee was set up in Paris, under the presidency of Benes. The French and British Governments recognised it, and gave it a certain support. After the fall of France the Committee migrated to London, and after a little while set up a Czechoslovak Government in exile, with Benes as Premier and Masaryk, Czechoslovak Minister in Britain before Munich, as Minister for Foreign Affairs. The British Government, however, for reasons not quite comprehensible delayed official recognition for several months.

The instruction to conclude a pact of mutual assistance with Czechoslovakia greatly delighted me. After the signature of the German-Soviet Pact of Non-Aggression in August 1939, diplomatic relations between the USSR and Czechoslovakia were in a state of temporary lethargy, and the Czechoslovak Ambassador in Moscow, Zdenek Fierlinger, soon afterwards went to Paris and then, together with the Czechoslovak National Committee, to London. Although from the end of 1939 there were no diplomatic relations between the Soviet and Czechoslovak Governments, I, nevertheless, continued 'unofficially' to meet Benes, Masaryk and Fierlinger. This seemed to me desirable in view of the possible changes in the relations between the USSR and Germany in the course of the war; moreover Benes disposed of very valuable information about the situation in Germany and Central Europe, which he willingly shared with us. Most frequently of all I used to meet Fierlinger, and had many opportunities of realising his high qualities as a person and as a politician. We established most friendly relations, which we still maintain today.

On receipt of the telegram from Moscow, I at once told Masaryk, as Foreign Minister, of its contents. He was very glad, and replied: 'Let's sign such a pact at once!'

The following day, 18 July, Masaryk arrived at the Soviet Embassy, and after reading through the draft pact I had prepared said he had no objections. Fierlinger, who accompanied him, was of the same opinion. Then followed the official signature: Masaryk signed the Pact on behalf of Czechoslovakia and I on behalf of the USSR. The Pact in the main followed the Anglo-Soviet model, but had two special additional points. In the first place, Article 1 provided that the two Governments would immediately exchange Ministers. Secondly, Article 3 provided for the formation of Czechoslovak military units in the territory of the USSR, composed of Czechoslovak citizens living within its territory. In fact such units were organised later, and played a glorious part in battles for the liberation of their native country.

After the ceremony of signature, we rounded off this act by the clinking of glasses of champagne, and Masaryk, usually sparkling with humour, said with a solemnity not customary for him: 'After today I can say with confidence that I have not lived in vain.'

Some time later Fierlinger left for Moscow as Czechoslovak Minister.[1]

Much more complicated and difficult were the negotiations with the Polish *émigré* Government. The latter arose in Paris in October 1939, immediately after the defeat of Poland. It was headed by General Sikorski—a good military man, but a bad politician, an honest patriot of the old Polish type and a convinced supporter of the French orientation. Sikorski's outlook, so far as I could ascertain from what I saw myself and heard from others, lay somewhere between moderate liberalism and moderate conservatism of the bourgeois type. Sikorski's misfortune was that he was always surrounded by too many ultra-reactionary figures, who used his name as a cover and whom he was unable through weakness of character to put in their place. This is why the 'Sikorski Government', which existed in Paris and in London in 1939–43 left behind so many melancholy recollections. This Government-in-exile was recognised by Britain and France, and gradually around it there grew up various auxiliary organisations of a political, military and cultural nature. Its residence at first was in the French city of Angers and, after the fall of France, London.

Ruling circles in Britain were very favourably disposed towards Sikorski, and I more than once heard the wish expressed by British Ministers and politicians that he should take his place at the head

1. Simultaneously with the signature of the Soviet-Czechoslovak Pact the British Government at last gave formal recognition to the Czechoslovak Government.

of the new Poland which would rise from its ruins at the end of the war.

To begin negotiations with the Czechoslovak Government I had required no intermediaries, because I had known its leading people well before. With the Poles things were otherwise. Personally I had never met either Sikorski or any other members of his Government. In addition, relations between Poland and the USSR in pre-war years, unlike Soviet-Czechoslovak relations, had little that was friendly about them, and at times were simply hostile. I was not certain how the Sikorski Government would receive the Soviet proposal for a pact of mutual assistance. It was therefore desirable (this was Moscow's opinion as well) to carry out preliminary soundings with the aid of some sufficiently authoritative intermediary. Out of such considerations I visited Eden and asked him to clear up the question. Eden warmly welcomed the Soviet Government's intention and willingly agreed to be an intermediary between myself and Sikorski.

The following day, Sir Alexander Cadogan rang me up and told me that Eden had had a talk with Sikorski, and that Sikorski was ready to begin the negotiations we proposed. Now it was only a question of how to organise them.

'General Sikorski', Cadogan continued, 'would be glad if you came to see him and agreed with him all the details for the procedure of the negotiations.'

I laughed and replied: 'For the first meeting I would prefer a more neutral territory.'

Cadogan understood me and, laughing also, said: 'If my room at the Foreign Office is in your opinion sufficiently neutral territory, I am ready to give it up to you and General Sikorski. I will even leave it in order not to embarrass you.'

'Well, I do think your room is a suitable place for our first meeting', I replied.

Cadogan expressed his satisfaction, and promised to get in touch with the Polish Premier on this question. Half an hour later Cadogan again rang me up to say that Sikorski had no objection to a meeting in the Foreign Office and had suggested that it should take place at 4 p.m. next day. Cadogan asked if the time was convenient: I replied that it was, and asked him to inform Sikorski. I imagined that now all the preliminary conversations were over, and at once set about working out the formulation of the proposals which I was to make to the Poles the next day. However, I was mistaken. After another half hour, Cadogan rang me up for the third time and said:

'General Sikorski asked me to let you know that he would come to the meeting tomorrow not at 4 p.m., but three minutes later.'

Mentally I burst out laughing. Evidently these sacramental three minutes were to symbolise the difference in our ranks, Sikorski was a Premier, while I was only an Ambassador. But aloud I said: 'If General Sikorski considers it a virtue to be unpunctual in arriving at a meeting we have agreed, I don't object.'

I heard Cadogan laughing at the other end of the line, and then he added: 'You will pardon me for having had to pass on this somewhat strange message, but that is the fate of an intermediary . . . The main thing after all is that negotiations should begin as soon as possible.'

The next day, exactly at 4 p.m., I was in Cadogan's room. The weather was warm and sunny, and I naturally appeared in the Foreign Office in a light summer suit of light grey. After shaking hands with Cadogan, I said with a smile: 'Three minutes, then,' and began attentively looking at the minute hand of my wrist watch.

Exactly three minutes later the door of Cadogan's room opened, and there appeared on the threshold Sikorski in full General's parade uniform, with all his orders and decorations. From behind his back there peeped the figure of Zaleski, the Polish Minister for Foreign Affairs. His fairly bulky body seemed to be bursting out of his black jacket and striped trousers. A high white collar buttressed his bulky cheeks. Sikorski glanced at me, and a slight grimace of surprise, almost of indignation, passed over his face the General was clearly shocked by the light-heartedness of my everyday summer suit. But there was nothing to be done: reality had to be taken as it was.

Sikorski's appearance in Cadogan's room was preceded (as eye-witnesses described to me) by an even stranger scene. The General arrived at the Foreign Office with two vast cars. In the first he sat together with Zaleski, in the second were his adjutants in military uniform. The adjutants rushed headlong into the Foreign Office building and along its corridors, pushing aside those whom they met and shouting loudly:

'The General is coming! The General is coming!'

And in the wake of the adjutants there majestically followed Sikorski accompanied by Zaleski.

Cadogan presented us to one another and left. The three of us sat down at the table and began our conversation. On behalf of the Soviet Government I proposed to Sikorski and Zaleski that we should sign a pact of mutual assistance against Hitlerite Germany, and added that the USSR undertook in the future to facilitate the re-establishment of the Polish State in its national frontiers.

Sikorski and Zaleski met my words without great enthusiasm, and Zaleski immediately asked how they were to understand the formula 'the Polish State in its national frontiers.'

I explained that as we saw it the future Polish State should only consist of Poles, and should cover those territories which were inhabited by Poles.

A gloomy expression appeared on the faces of my partners. Zaleski began speaking, and read a long lecture on the theme that in Poland before the Hitlerite attack there were only Poles, and therefore that the future Polish State must coincide with the Polish State in its 1939 frontiers. To confirm his thesis, Zaleski began monotonously and tediously quoting figures from the censuses taken in pre-war Poland, and the purport of his argument was that somehow there were scarcely any Ukrainians or Belorussians in that Poland, and that the only national minority ('if that may even be considered a national minority!', Zaleski added, raising his finger) within the Polish Republic were the half-million Jews.

The Minister for Foreign Affairs wanted to continue his arguments on the same subject, but I broke in and said:

'Mr. Minister for Foreign Affairs, in my youth I was a statistician myself, and am well acquainted with all the statistical tricks which the Tsarist Government often used in order to prove the unproveable . . . Therefore don't let's talk any more about statistics . . . The Soviet Government has its own, sufficiently justified, conceptions of the national composition of the population of pre-war Poland, and in its name I want to repeat once more that it is ready to promote the restoration of the Polish State in its *national frontiers*'—I specially underlined these last two words —'and this is its basic principle. If you are unwilling to accept such a principle, then . . . In that case, I think it's hardly worth while beginning negotiations'.

My hint evidently had its effect, because Sikorski now intervened, and in a more conciliatory tone began speaking of the necessity of thinking out carefully all the questions connected with the conclusion of a pact of mutual assistance.

There is no necessity here to set forth in detail the course of the further negotiations, which took up a great deal of time and required much expenditure of nervous energy. I will only say that they were very difficult negotiations, and that several times they were on the verge of rupture. However, the insistence and flexibility of the Soviet Government in the long run overcame all the obstacles, and on 30 July 1941 the Pact was signed by myself and Sikorski.

The most complex question turned out to be that of the frontiers of the future Polish State. Although Sikorski, it seemed, represented a somewhat different variety of the Polish military clique from the notorious 'Colonels' who had led pre-war Poland into destruction, there was still sufficiently strong in him and his entourage the spirit of aggressive imperialism. He had insufficient political realism, and 'romantic' ancient traditions of the Polish nobility kept him firmly in their grip. After long arguments and acute polemics, it was finally decided not to mention the question of the future frontiers of the Polish State in the Pact at all, and to confine it to the statement of the Soviet Government that the Soviet-German treaties of 1939 regarding territorial changes in Poland were considered to have lost their validity. Such a formula was introduced into Article 1 of the Pact.

Furthermore, the Pact defined that diplomatic relations were re-established between the USSR and Poland, that both side would afford each other every kind of aid and support in the course of war, and that the Soviet Government gave its consent to the formation of a Polish army in the territory of the USSR. In addition, it was provided in a special protocol that the Soviet Government would 'grant an amnesty to all Polish citizens now detained on the territory of the Union of Soviet Socialist Republic, either as prisoners of war or on other sufficient grounds'.[1]

The signature of the Pact took place in very ceremonious circumstances, which the British saw to. Eden had from the outset attributed great importance to a reconciliation between the USSR and Poland, closely followed the course of negotiations, at critical moments gave his assistance behind the scenes, and now that this diplomatic enterprise had been crowned with success wanted to bring about as much noise as possible around it, which would be favourable for the Allies. The explanation was, on the one hand,

1. *Soviet Foreign Policy during the Patriotic War* (London), Vol. I, pp. 81–2.

the importance of strengthening internal unity among the Allies and, on the other hand, the desire to advertise Sikorski as widely as possible, because as I have already said the British Government had far-reaching plans bound up with his personality.

The procedure of signature itself took place in the Foreign Office, in Eden's room. In addition to the Secretary of State, Churchill was present. There were many journalists, photographers and film reporters. On all sides we were blinded by the floodlights. Sikorski and I exchanged speeches. Then the leaders of the British State shook hands with us. Then we thanked them for their assistance. And then—the following day—the British press made the conclusion of a Soviet-Polish Pact the main 'sensation' of the moment. I did not object to the actions of the British: in the summer of 1941 the Soviet-Polish Pact was of great positive importance, and it was important to bring this fact to the knowledge of the widest possible circles, both among the Allies and in the ranks of the enemy.

3

Harry Hopkins flies to Moscow

THE first message from Stalin to Churchill came from Moscow on 19 July 1941. The second world war brought an important innovation into traditional diplomatic practice. Up till then heads of governments had communicated with one another, as the usual expression was, 'through the normal diplomatic channels', i.e. through the Ministers of Foreign Affairs and Ambassadors. Direct messages from heads of governments to one another were extremely rare, and for the most part bore the character of ceremonial etiquette—in connection with some congratulation, condolence, or the like. Now the situation had changed. Heads of governments began avoiding the usual diplomatic procedures and exchanging direct messages on the most important and vital questions. Churchill said to me one one occasion:

'In our feverish age the "normal diplomatic channels" are too tardy and too gradual . . . The essential tempo is too easily lost . . . That's why I prefer to correspond with Roosevelt direct.'

Churchill attempted to establish the same method of communication with Stalin even before the German attack on the USSR, but unsuccessfully. Stalin simply did not reply. After 22 June 1941 the British Premier now considered he had the right to approach the head of the Soviet Government directly. On 8 and 10 July he sent Stalin two messages assuring him of Britain's readiness to help the Soviet Union, and proposing the publication of a joint Anglo-Soviet declaration (it was from this that there sprang the Pact of Mutual Assistance between the two mentioned earlier). Stalin's message received on 19 July was a reply to these two messages from the British Premier.

In this message Stalin wrote:

'It seems to me . . . that the military position of the Soviet Union, and by the same token that of Great Britain, would improve substantially if a front were established against Hitler in the West (Northern France) and the North (the Arctic). A front in the North of France, besides diverting Hitler's forces from the East, would make impossible the invasion of Britain by Hitler . . .

'It would be easier still to open a front in the North. This would call for action only by British naval and air forces, without landing troops or artillery. Soviet land, naval and air forces could take part in the operation.'[1]

As we see this was the first official *démarche* of the Soviet Government with the demand for a second front in Northern France . . . How many of them followed, before such a natural and reasonable Soviet demand was finally put into effect—only in 1944!

The message was deciphered, I personally translated it into English for the sake of secrecy, and myself typed it out. Then the question arose of how to deliver it to Churchill. It could have been sent in a sealed envelope with the secretary of our Embassy. It could be handed to the Premier personally. I chose the second method, because I wanted to see Churchill's direct reaction to the message, and also to have the opportunity of replying at once if the message aroused any questions from the addressee. I adopted this method of passing on Stalin's messages on every occasion thereafter, and had no reason to regret it. I shall describe later how useful the procedure I adopted for passing on the messages of the head of the Soviet Government proved to be.

19 July was a Saturday. Churchill was on that day at Chequers, the country residence of British Prime Ministers, where they pass the traditional week-end, receiving their guests and discussing State affairs in an easier atmosphere. I decided to go to Chequers and there to hand Premier Stalin's message personally.

Chequers was full of ladies and gentlemen, only some of whom I knew. Churchill received me in his study, and at once quickly read through the message I had brought. Then he shrugged his shoulders and said:

'I quite understand Mr. Stalin, and sympathise with him deeply, but unfortunately what he asks is at present impracticable.'

1. *Correspondence between the Chairman of the Council of Ministers of Ministers of the USSR and the Presidents of the U.S.A. and Prime Ministers of Great Britain during the Great Patriotic War of 1941–1945*, Vol. I, (English edition), Moscow 1957, p. 13.

And then Churchill began a detailed justification of his statement. In his words, the Germans had forty divisions in France and a well-fortified coast along the Channel, in Belgium and in Holland. The forces of Britain, which had for more than a year been fighting alone, were under extreme strain and scattered far afield in the home country, in Africa and in the Middle East. The sea battle for the Atlantic, on which the very life of the country depended, was absorbing a vast amount of energy. In such conditions the British Government was not in a position to provide a sufficient number of troops, planes and vessels for a serious invasion of France, all the more because the night at present lasted no more than five or six hours. And to attempt an invasion with insufficient forces meant facing certain defeat, which would be of benefit neither to the USSR nor to Britain. All that the British Government could do at present to ease the burden on the Soviet Union was to increase its air bombardments of Germany and to organise some naval operations in the region of Northern Norway and Spitzbergen. He, Churchill, was very sorry that in present conditions Britain was incapable of doing more—but one had to take account of realities.

I began objecting, demonstrating to the Premier at considerable length that the massive concentration of German forces in the East made it impossible for the Germans to maintain forty divisions in France, and that there were times in history when peoples and governments for their own salvation should undertake super-human tasks. It was a moment of that kind that had now arrived, not only for the USSR but for Britain too.

Churchill, however, could not be shaken. Then we went out of his study into the drawing room, where there were many guests of both sexes. The Premier led me up to a tall, very thin, frail-looking man with a long face and lively eyes, who was standing with his back to the fire, and presented me to him:

'Let me introduce you: this is Mr. Hopkins.'

Hopkins' name was well known to me. I knew that he was Roosevelt's closest adviser, and was playing a big part in determining the foreign policy of the United States. I knew that Hopkins was a man who had retained his loyalty to the democratic traditions of President Lincoln. I knew, likewise, that he had been sent by the President to negotiate with the British Government, and that Churchill treated him with great respect. Therefore I looked at Hopkins with particular attention, trying from his expression and his gestures to understand as well as I could what he represented.

'Here is Stalin asking for the creation of a second front in France', said Churchill rapidly to Hopkins. Then, shrugging his shoulders, he went on: 'We can't do it at present . . . We are not strong enough . . .'

Then the Premier moved away to the other guests, while Hopkins and I remained by the fire. I briefly told Hopkins the substance of the conversation I had just had with Churchill. He put a few questions to me, I replied, and then we were approached by Mrs. Churchill with the offer of tea. The occasion for a more serious talk with Hopkins was clearly unsuitable, and I soon left for home, carrying away the impression that Hopkins's attitude to the question of aid for the USSR was much more sympathetic than Churchill's. This gave rise to the wish to meet Roosevelt's emissary again, and to have a detailed discussion with him on the subjects which interested me. I thought: 'Perhaps it's just here that lies the key to a real solution of the question of aid?'

On Monday, 21 July, I telephoned to John Winant, the American Ambassador in London, and asked him where Hopkins was staying, and could I see him for a frank talk about events on the Soviet-German front? Winant, who previously had for many years been Director of the International Labour Office at Geneva, had not very long before been appointed United States Ambassador in London, and even before the German attack on the USSR had displayed a strong desire to maintain close contact with me.

In reply, Winant said on the telephone:

'Nothing can be simpler: come to lunch with me tomorrow, I will invite Hopkins, and the three of us will talk.'

In fact, on 22 July my meeting with Hopkins took place at Winant's table. I described in detail the situation created on the Eastern front, explained the reasons for our reverses and underlined the exceptional importance of a second front. Hopkins listened to me very attentively, and with obvious sympathy for the Soviet Union. Winant openly declared for a second front.

'We in the USA', Hopkins began at length, 'are a non-belligerent country now, and cannot do anything to help you in regard to a second front. But as regards supplies things are different . . . We are providing Britain with much in the way of armaments, raw materials, ships and so on. We could give you too quite a lot . . . But what do you require? Couldn't you tell me?'

I was now in a difficult position. For, although in general terms I had an idea of our difficulties, I could not take upon myself precisely to enumerate what we needed and in what quantities. Then an idea flashed through my mind:

'Mr. Hopkins', I said, 'couldn't you yourself visit Moscow and there, on the spot, receive from the Soviet Government all the information you require?'

Winant energetically supported me, but Hopkins avoided any definite reply. Instead he began urgently pointing out how important it would be to make Roosevelt and Stalin more closely acquainted with each other. This would be of great importance.

'You understand,' said Hopkins, 'for Roosevelt, Stalin is at present just a name. He's never seen the head of your Government, never talked to him, and in general has no idea of what sort of a man he is. Probably Roosevelt for Stalin too is also a very dim image. We ought to change this situation—but how?'

I replied that to bring the heads of the two Governments together there might be three ways: a personal meeting, anexchange of persons in whom they had confidence, an exchange of personal messages. The first way in present conditions was clearly impracticable, and consequently the other two remained. In this connection I returned to the idea of Hopkins going to Moscow.

He meditated a little and cautiously replied: 'Yes, all that has to be thought over.'

Then we said good-bye to one another.

Five days passed. On Sunday, 27 July, when I was as usual at Negrin's house in Bovingdon, I was suddenly rung up from the Embassy and told that Winant wanted particularly to come and see me today, not later than 10 p.m. Naturally I returned to London at once. About 10 in the evening Winant did, in fact, appear in my study, and put down three American passports on my desk.

'Be so kind as to visa these passports right away,' he said to me without explanation.

They were the passports of Hopkins and two persons accompanying him. I looked at him with surprise. He understood, and began to explain:

'After our meeting last Tuesday Hopkins began thinking what he ought to do. In the end he came to the conclusion that your proposition for him to go to Moscow personally was very wise.

Of course, physically Hopkins doesn't feel quite well, but that's the sort of man he is: if he thinks anything important he will certainly do it in spite of everything. He realised that a visit to Moscow is exceptionally important . . . Well, of course, he asked the President's opinion: the President replied that he was in agreement . . . And now today, or more exactly at this very moment, Hopkins is leaving for Moscow . . . When I left to go and see you, Hopkins set out for the station . . . The train for Scotland is leaving in half an hour, and tomorrow morning he will leave Scotland by air for Russia.'

'By what route?' I quickly asked.

'He is going on a "Catalina" flying boat, round Norway, direct to Archangel . . . About twenty-four hours' flying, if everything goes well . . . A dangerous and difficult journey, especially for such a sick man as Hopkins, but he doesn't reckon with anything.'

And then Winant, nodding at the passports, added:

'Please rush this . . . When I leave you, I shall go straight to the station, and hand over the passports to Hopkins and his companions.'

I was in a considerable difficulty. All the visa seals were at the Consulate. The Consulate was not in the Embassy building but in quite a different place, which it would take ten minutes by car to reach. It was Sunday, and one might suppose that neither the Consul nor his deputy, who had flats at the Consulate, would be at home, and they had the keys of the safes where the seals were kept. But I had no more than five minutes at my disposal, otherwise Winant might not be in time to catch the train before it left . . . What was to be done?

I took Hopkins' passport and wrote on it by hand: 'Harry Hopkins to be permitted to cross any frontier station of the USSR without examination of luggage, as a diplomatic person. I. Maisky, Ambassador of the USSR in Great Britain.' At the side I added the date, and stamped it with the Embassy seal. I did the same for the other two passports.

Winant thanked me, and hurried off to the station. Later he told me that he had arrived at the very last moment: the train was already moving, and he thrust the passports at Hopkins through the open window of his carriage.

While I, directly Winant had left me, sent an urgent cipher cable to Moscow, reporting Hopkins' departure and requesting that all the necessary steps be taken for a friendly welcome on his arrival at Archangel or Murmansk.[1]

Everything went off well, and on 30 July Stalin received Hopkins in Moscow and had a long talk with him. The next day, 31 July, there was a second conversation. Hopkins received authoritative replies to all the questions in which he was interested. By the same route, on the 'Catalina' flying boat, Hopkins returned to Britain, and from there at once flew home to the USA. The report which Hopkins made to the President on the results of his visit to the USSR made a deep impression on Roosevelt and had important consequences.

On 15 August 1941 Roosevelt and Churchill held their so-called Atlantic Conference. The two leaders from there sent a message to Stalin which began as follows:

'We have taken the opportunity afforded by the consideration of the report of Mr. Harry Hopkins on his return from Moscow to consult together as to how best our two countries can help your country.'[2]

And the two leaders went on to report that shiploads of all kinds of supplies had been dispatched to the USSR, and proposed that there should be held in Moscow in the immediate future a meeting of 'high representatives' to work out a long-term plan for supplies to the USSR by the USA and Britain during the war. Such a conference did, in fact, take place in the capital of the USSR from 29 September to 2 October, 1941: but I will deal with it later.

In this way from practical experience I first realised in the course of the war the significance of a 'chain reaction' in the political sphere (though that term was not yet in general use at the time). Later on I shall give several examples of how the same 'chain reaction' helped us more than once.

Here I want to say a few words about my last meeting with Hopkins, which took place in Moscow four years later. The war was only just over, and it had ended in victory: but many problems

1. In his well-known book, *The White House Papers of Harry L. Hopkins*, Vol. I, 1948, p. 318, Robert E. Sherwood considers the question of how Hopkins got the idea of going to Moscow. He writes: 'It is remotely possible, though unlikely, that Roosevelt had discussed the possibility of a trip to Moscow before Hopkins left Washington. If so, there is no mention of it in any of the notes that Hopkins took with him to London, and it was the recollection of Churchill, Winant and Harriman that Hopkins himself conceived the idea for the trip very suddenly, and acted on it immediately.' It will be clear from what has been set forth above how the idea of going to Moscow came to Hopkins.

2. *Correspondence, etc.*, Vol. I, p. 17.

linked with the war still required their solution. Among these problems one of the most painful was the future of Poland. On this point there were big differences between the USSR on one side and the USA and Britain on the other. At the end of May 1945 President Truman (Roosevelt had died on 12 April) sent Hopkins to Moscow for talks with J. V. Stalin. It did not prove possible to settle this acute problem at that time, but during the negotiations Stalin, as was customary, gave a big dinner at the Kremlin in honour of Hopkins. I was among the guests invited to the dinner, and as Hopkins had come to Moscow with his wife, my wife also was present. As always, many toasts were proposed. One of the toasts in English to Mrs Hopkins was given by my wife. After dinner there was dancing, in which Hopkins took part, to my extreme amazement: he seemed to be so exhausted, so emaciated, so ill. He partnered my wife for one dance. After returning her to her seat, Hopkins for a long time could not get his breath. Drops of perspiration were shining on his forehead. He touched my hand with his: it was limp and cold. I was suddenly very anxious. But Hopkins, as though understanding my feeling, with a smile to which he tried to attribute a somewhat audacious expression, said to me under his breath:

'You know, I've got leave of absence from death.'

The next day he left. A year later, I read in the newspapers the report of his death.

In my memory, Harry Hopkins has remained as one of the most advanced people among the leading personalities in the bourgeois world during the second world war.

4

British Arms for the USSR

Two months had gone by since the day of Germany's attack on the USSR. The war was proceeding with unrelenting ferocity. The 'pessimists' who had expected that in six weeks Hitler would become 'master of Russia' were at a loss: their anticipations had not been justified. The Soviet people would not fall on its knees, and the Red Army was offering resistance to the enemy. A revision of ideas began in many British heads, and many British politicians, soldiers, journalists and ordinary men in the street could not help beginning to ask themselves: 'Maybe our previous ideas as to the relative strength of the Germans and the Russians were not quite right? Maybe the resistance of the Soviets will turn out longer and more stubborn than we thought? Maybe Hitler will be hopelessly tied up in those vast expanses, among those countless millions of strange and incomprehensible people?' At one and the same time the British wanted to believe that such would be the turn of events, and were afraid to believe it lest disappointment overtake them. Echoes of these moods I could clearly notice in British people of the most various walks of life with whom I had so often to meet after 22 June.

Personally I was also at a loss, but for quite a different reason. I quite realised that during the first two or three weeks the Hitlerites might have superiority over us: they were the attacking side, they had mobilised completely before us, they had the initiative, and were choosing the points and directions for striking which were most advantageous for them and disadvantageous for us. In view of this we might have surprises at first, misadventures, moments of confusion and loss of control. But only at first. Further on, it seemed to me, the High Command of the Red Army was bound to regain control of the situation, throw fresh units into battle and to halt, or at any rate strongly to delay, the German advance.

But day followed day without any change. Now here, now there the Germans broke through our front with their tank columns, impetuously rushed forward, seizing ever new territory, surrounded and destroyed our military units and were approaching ever closer to Moscow and Leningrad. Every day the Soviet commiqués reported that we were retreating.

Ever and again there arose before me the same terrible question: how could all this have happened?

I repeat that at that time I had no reply to this question. But the practical conclusion from the situation created was for me quite clear; if such a terrible disaster had overtaken my country, then—irrespective of its causes—I was bound as Ambassador of the USSR in Britain to do all that was humanly possible to relieve its trials. I intently watched the international situation, seeking any symptom containing the promise of something favourable for our country.

Naturally, I warmly welcomed the message which Roosevelt and Churchill had sent on 15 August from the Atlantic Conference to the head of the Soviet Government. But it was clear that the practical results of the decision to help the USSR would not be forthcoming at once. Yet help, serious and rapid, was needed. And when I heard on the radio, on 20 August, the appeal of K. E. Voroshilov, A. A. Zhdanov and P. S. Popkov to the people regarding the mortal danger threatening Leningrad, I decided to act immediately, although I had had no instructions from Moscow.

I asked for a meeting with Eden, and on 26 August had a long conversation with him. To be precise, it was not so much a conversation as an ardent attack on the Foreign Secretary, and even more on the whole British Government.

I began with a brief but strongly-worded description of the situation on the Soviet-German front. I underlined the exceptional difficulty and even dangerous nature of our position, dwelling particularly on the great losses in men and arms which the Red Army had suffered in the latest battle. Then I continued:

'In this terrible war the USSR and Britain are Allies, but what help is our British Ally giving us at present? In fact, none! All these ten weeks we have been fighting alone! . . . We asked you to open a second front, but you replied with a refusal. At the Atlantic

Conference you promised us economic and military help on a large scale, but so far those remain only good words . . . Just think, our Air Ministry asked yours to let it have urgently sixty big bombs—but what has happened? There has been a long exchange of correspondence, as a result of which we have been promised six bombs!'

Eden was clearly upset: he tried to explain to me the reasons for refusing a second front, and underlined the importance of the ever-strengthening British raids on Germany.

'Of course air bombardments of Germany', I said, 'are a certain form of help to the Soviet Union, but . . . It's not enough to pinch a wild beast by its tail, it ought to be beaten over the head with a club!'

Eden began speaking of the profound sympathy of the British people for the peoples of the USSR and the universal admiration of their heroism and fortitude now burning in any British heart: but I interrupted him not quite politely and said:

'You know, Mr. Eden, when I hear such frequent words of praise addressed to us, I think with irritation: "If only there were less praise and more aircraft for our front" . . . Yet now you are not even supplying us with arms, in anticipation of the time when the Moscow conference which you have proposed will have discussed and settled all supply questions . . . Things can't go on like this! If you decided with the Americans at the Atlantic Conference to help us in principle, then don't delay! Begin to give us help immediately, even bit by bit, even as an advance, before this whole question has been settled at the future Moscow conference. If that is not done, Soviet people may lose faith in their British ally.'

My words made their impression on Eden. He became very worried, and said:

'I shall have a talk about all this with the Prime Minister this very day, and then we shall meet again.'

Some days later, Eden asked me to come and see him, and with evident satisfaction told me that, since we were particularly suffering losses of aircraft, Churchill had decided immediately to send, as a 'present to the Red Army', 200 Hurricane fighters. I knew that the Hurricanes were at that time considered one of the best types of British fighter plane (though not the very best like the Spitfire) and, thanking Churchill for his action, expressed the hope that things would not stop at this point. Churchill's gift was, in fact, urgently dispatched to the USSR and passed duly into the hands of Soviet pilots.

In my conversation with Eden I was struck by one trait which I had never noticed before: the Foreign Secretary felt embarrassed at the refusal of the British Government to organise a second front in France, and strove to soften our disappointment at this by underlining British readiness to give us help on a large scale in the form of military supplies and otherwise. I felt the same note of apology in the statements of other highly-placed British people with whom I had to deal in the days that followed. It showed itself most clearly, perhaps, in the conversation I had with Brendan Bracken, formerly editor of the *Financial News*, now one of the closest advisers of the Prime Minister and later on Minister of Information. This tall, gaunt, red-haired man spent a long time assuring me that both Churchill and members of his Government would very much like to launch large-scale military operations in France, but that they simply were unable to do this at the moment, and this was causing them grief and melancholy. I 'made a record' in my head that such was the frame of mind in Government circles, and began thinking how best I could make use of them in the interests of my country. A fortunate accident gave me the opportunity.

When I reported to Moscow my *démarche* to Eden, and Churchill's 'gift' to the Red Army, I did not expect any response. Moscow at that time was not spoiling me with a particular abundance of communications, instructions or opinions. I explained this by the extreme preoccupation of the Government with military questions, and was not offended. I was doing my work in London in the light of my own understanding of the situation, and feeling satisfied with the knowledge that I was doing my duty as citizen and Ambassador to the utmost extent of my capacities.

And suddenly, quite unexpectedly, in reply to my report on the talk with Eden, I received a telegram signed by J. V. Stalin. Such things happened very rarely. Usually there corresponded with me either People's Commissar V. M. Molotov, or one of his deputies, most frequently A. Y. Vyshinsky. The telegram itself was quite unusual.

Stalin wrote in it that he approved my *démarche* to Eden. He was particularly glad that in my conversation with the British Foreign Secretary I had managed so well to convey the moods now predominant among Soviet people as a result of the behaviour of the

British Government. The Soviet country was going through a most painful time, and immediate active help by its ally was extraordinarily important and necessary.

I remember how I long held Stalin's telegram in my hand, thinking and thinking again what else I could do to help my country. In the end I formed a definite plan.

I addressed to Stalin a request that he should send Churchill a second message, raising two points: one on the opening of a second front in France, the other on supplying the Red Army with arms and war materials. I warned Stalin that on the first question there would be no practical results, but it was important constantly to remind the British of the need for a second front But on the second question, I wrote, judging from mood prevalent in London, there were chances to get something real.

On 4 September a second message from Stalin to Churchill arrived from Moscow. It was dated the previous day. While it was being deciphered and then translated by myself into English, and while I was typing out the translation, evening fell. Nevertheless I at once rang Churchill's secretary and asked for an immediate meeting with the Premier on an extremely important and urgent question. Churchill made the appointment for 10 p.m.: he usually worked very late. It was a bright moonlight night. Clouds fantastic in shape were speeding from west to east. Whenever they covered the face of the moon, their edges began to be tinged with a reddish-black tone, and then the whole picture seemed gloomy and sinister as though the world were on the eve of destruction. As I drove through the familiar streets, I was thinking: 'a few more minutes, and an important moment will arrive, pregnant with important consequences. Representatives of two opposite worlds, which by the wheel of history have found themselves in the same camp, will meet, and I shall give Churchill two sheets of typescript. He will read them, and then give me his reply. I don't know what the reply will be: but I know that very much will depend on its sense—maybe even the whole future development of history . . . Have I enough strength, energy, flexibility, resourcefulness to play my part worthily, with the maximum of success for the USSR and for all mankind?'

Churchill received me in his official room, where usually meetings of the Government were held. He was in evening dress, with the inevitable cigar between his teeth. By the Premier, at a long table covered with green cloth, sat Eden in a dark grey suit. Churchill looked at me from under his eyebrows, puffed at his cigar, and grunted in bulldog fashion:

'Do you bring good news?'

'I am afraid not,' I replied, and gave the Premier J. V. Stalin's message.

Churchill took the message out of the envelope and, putting on his spectacles, began rapidly reading it. He read now in silence, now muttering, sometimes stopping at individual words and phrases, as though thinking over them. I sat at the other side of the table, attentively following his reactions. Churchill read in an undertone:

'Please accept my thanks for the promise to sell to the Soviet Union another 200 fighter aeroplanes in addition to the 200 fighters promised earlier...'

As Churchill uttered the word 'sell', his right eyebrow rose in surprise. I made a mental note of this, but drew no conclusions from it as yet.

Then Churchill read several more lines in silence, and again in an undertone read the following:

'The relative stabilisation of the front, achieved some three weeks ago, has been upset in recent weeks by the arrival of 30–34 fresh German infantry divisions and enormous numbers of tanks and aircraft at the Eastern Front, and also by the activisation of 20 Finnish and 26 Rumanian divisions. The Germans look on the threat in the West as a bluff, so they are moving all their forces from the West to the East with impunity... As a result we have lost more than half the Ukraine and, what is more, the enemy is now at the gates of Leningrad... This has resulted in a lessening of our defence capacity and has confronted the Soviet Union with mortal danger. Here it is pertinent to ask—what is the way out of this more than unfavourable situation?'

Churchill stopped, thought for a moment and then continued in his undertone:

'I think the only way is to open a second front this year somewhere in the Balkans or in France, one that would divert 30–40 German divisions from the Eastern Front, and simultaneously to supply the Soviet Union with 30,000 tons of aluminium by the beginning of October and a minimum *monthly* aid of 400 aeroplanes and 500 tanks (of small or medium size). Without these two kinds of aid the Soviet Union will be either defeated or weakened to the extent that it will lose for a long time the ability to help its Allies by active operations at the front against Hitlerism.'[1]

When he had finished reading, Churchill passed the message over to Eden, who at once rapidly read through it. Then Churchill took the cigar out of his mouth, and turning to me, began saying that he was grateful to the head of the Soviet Government for frankly depicting the situation in which the Soviet Union at present found itself: that he, Churchill, wanted with all his heart to come to our aid: but that unfortunately the question of a second front in France or in the Balkans at the present time was unreal. Britain was not in a condition to undertake it.

I began objecting. I said that up to the present the Soviet Union in substance had had no real aid from Britain, and that never yet in the history of our country had we had to stand up against an invasion of such strength as at that moment. I did not wish to have recourse to unnecessarily dramatic language, yet nevertheless, calmly regarding the situation existing, I was inclined to think that the world had reached one of the turning points in its development. Either Hitler would be stopped in the East, and later on the backbone of Fascism would be broken: in that case there would open before humanity wide opportunities of progress and civilisation. Or else Hitler would be victorious in the East, and then there would descend on humanity a black night of the most monstrous reaction, and who could know how long it might continue? And if Hitler were victorious, what would be the fate of Britain? It was not difficult to imagine . . . Therefore the duty of every individual, every Government, every country which wanted to see the progressive development of mankind, was just at this moment to strain all its forces and afford the maximum of assistance to the USSR, in order to facilitate and accelerate the crushing of the German aggressor. In concrete terms this meant that Britain ought in the nearest possible future to open a second front in France, Belgium, Holland, such as would divert from the Eastern front at least 30–40 German divisions.

I said all this heatedly, excitedly, almost with inspiration, because my words only expressed the profound feeling which filled me at the time.

Churchill heard me out very attentively, but suddenly blew up and cried:

'Don't forget that only four months ago we stood alone against

1. *Correspondence, etc.*, Vol. I, pp. 20–1.

Germany, and didn't know whose side you would be on.'

'Thank Chamberlain for that', I parried, hinting at the sabotage by Chamberlain and Daladier of the 1939 negotiations for a triple pact of mutual assistance between the USSR, Britain and France against Hitlerite aggression. 'You yourself were then against Chamberlain'.

Churchill obviously found this reminder unpleasant. He grew heated, and in vigorous terms began demonstrating that we had no right to demand that Britain should renounce her own interests, or still more demand that she should do the impossible. The opening of a second front in northern France was for the time being a task quite beyond Britain's abilities. The Channel, which was preventing Germany making a leap into Britain, was also preventing Britain making a leap into occupied France.

Knowing the temperament of the Premier, I began to fear that in the height of his irritation he might say a good deal that was unnecessary, and thereby render our further relations more difficult. Therefore I interrupted him at the first opportunity, and said with a smile:

'Less warmth, dear Mr. Churchill, more calm! After all, we must come to some practical result.'

My remark had a calming effect, and Churchill lowered his tone. Then, in his usual voice, he repeated that there could be no question of immediately opening a second front in France, but that things were otherwise as regards questions of supply. Here the British Government would do the maximum to meet the needs of the USSR, and without the slightest delay. He, Churchill, would this very night call together the Chiefs of Staff (of the Army, Navy and Air force) and would discuss with them to what extent Britain could meet Stalin's wishes. Next morning Eden would communicate to me the decisions adopted at that consultation.[1]

1. Describing our meeting of 4 September 1941 in his memoirs, Churchill writes that he became indignant when it seemed to him that some hidden threat to Britain could be read into my words. This impression evidently was so deep that he thought it necessary to inform Roosevelt. In his telegram of 5 September the day after our conversation, Churchill wrote: 'Although nothing in his language warranted the assumption, we could not exclude the impression that they might be thinking of separate terms. . . I feel that the moment may be decisive' (*The Second World War*, Vol. III, pp. 406–9). Of course in the conversation of 4 September I had no idea whatever of the possibility of a separate peace with Germany. This was an obvious illusion on Churchill's part, because his conscience on the question of a second front was not quite clear. Looking back on the events of those days, I think that the impression which Churchill formed of my words at the time was perhaps almost useful for us. It obliged the wheels of the British political and military machine to begin turning more rapidly, and in particular to the granting to us of Lend-Lease.

I shook hands with Churchill and Eden, and set off for home. It was already midnight, the moon was hidden, and profound darkness reigned in the blacked-out streets. Sitting in my car, I turned over in my mind the details of the meeting we had had, and returned again and again to the Premier's raised eyebrow. What did it mean? Evidently the Premier was surprised that Stalin had used the word 'sell'. In other words, he had expected that Stalin would ask for supplies of arms on some other basis? On what? On credit, as usually happened in previous wars? Or by Lend-Lease, as the British were now receiving their war supplies from America?

I could not arrive at an end of my guesses, but felt there was that here some possibility, or at any rate some chance, of doing something useful for our country. Of course it would be senseless to communicate with Moscow on such intangibles as guesses based on Churchill's raised eyebrow, and there was no time in any case. Therefore, when going up the Embassy steps that night, I firmly decided to try and get Lend-Lease the following day.

At 11 a.m. on 5 September I was already in Eden's office. He was not alone. All three Chiefs of Staff, accompanied by experts, were sitting in the same room at the long table.

'The Prime Minister,' Eden explained, 'has decided that it would be better if our reply to Mr. Stalin's message of yesterday were given not by myself alone, but also by our military leaders.'

Then Eden called on the Chiefs of Staff, and each in turn gave a very circumstantial report on the aspect for which he was responsible. The consensus was that Britain at the present time was unable to open a second front in France or in the Balkans. I listened to their statements attentively, and said I would transmit their content to my Government. What else could I do? I had no means of checking the words of the Chiefs of Staff in any way, and I could not justify my doubts as to the correctness of their conclusions by any concrete data and facts.

But on questions of supply all of them—both Eden and the Chiefs of Staff—were much more optimistic. They thought they could satisfy all the demands of the Soviet Government, but on the basis that approximately half would be covered by Britain and the other half by the USA. However, the British would undertake themselves all the negotiations with Washington. They promised to begin making their deliveries immediately, without waiting for the Three-Power Conference in Moscow. This seemed much more encouraging.

Then the Chiefs of Staff left, and Eden and I remained alone. I asked the Foreign Secretary to express my gratitude to Churchill for the speed and energy with which he had solved the problem of supply. And then, after deliberately keeping silence for a moment, I asked: 'And on what conditions will you supply us armaments and war materials?'

'Eden seemed somewhat surprised, and replied: 'Mr. Stalin in his message refers to sale...'

Again I was silent for a moment, as though gathering my thoughts, and then, looking expressively at Eden, said: 'Don't you think that buying and selling is a somewhat out-of-date form for transactions of such a kind? There are more modern ones.'

Eden, also looking at me with understanding, asked: 'What you are thinking of is Lend-Lease?'

'Yes, I have in view Lend-Lease', I replied.

Eden thought for a moment, and continued: 'I cannot decide that question myself... I will report your wishes to the Cabinet, and will have a talk with the Prime Minister.'

'Looking at it from the long-term point of view', I explained, 'the use of Lend-Lease in this case is in the interests of Britain herself.'

And I developed the idea that if the USSR were restricted in its acquisition of armaments from Britain by its existing resources for payment, this might lead to reverses at the front, and the victory of the Germans in Eastern Europe would have the most disastrous consequences for Great Britain. Eden agreed with my considerations, and once again promised to give his reply about Lend-Lease as soon as possible. He kept his word. The day after our conversation, on 6 September, Eden again invited me to come and see him, and said to me:

'All war supplies by Britain to the Soviet Union will be made on a Lend-Lease basis.'

Only then did I cable to Moscow about my conversations with Eden and their result.

I will not conceal that I was happy and proud that at such a difficult moment for the USSR I had succeeded in rendering it an important and serious service.

In addition to everything else, British Lend-Lease greatly facilitated our receipt of American Lend-Lease. At the beginning of September 1941, when I was making my *démarche* to Eden, there was still an internal struggle going in the USA on the subject of whether Lend-Lease should be granted to the Soviet Union at all. Very powerful groups in the ranks of the American ruling class were strongly objecting, and demanding that the USSR should pay for American supplies in gold, foreign currency and natural resources, or in extreme necessity should make economic concessions, particularly by abolishing the State monopoly of foreign trade. The granting to us of British Lend-Lease was a most significant precedent which enabled Roosevelt to extend the Lend-Lease Act to the USSR.

In this way one more chain reaction begun by my conversation with Eden on 26 August facilitated a satisfactory solution of the problem of military supplies to the USSR from Britain and the USA.

On the subject of Lend-Lease there took place an interesting exchange of opinions between Churchill and Stalin. In his message of 6 September, i.e. after the problem had been solved, the British Premier wrote to Stalin:

'In your first paragraph you used the word "sell". We had not viewed the matter in such terms and have never thought of payment. Any assistance we can give you would better be upon the same basis of comradeship as the American Lend-Lease Bill, of which no formal account is kept in money.'

To this, J. V. Stalin in a message on 13 September replied:

'Please accept my thanks for the promise of monthly British aid in aluminium, aircraft and tanks. I can but be glad that the British Government contemplates this aid, not as a transaction of selling and buying aircraft, aluminium and tanks, but in the shape of comradely co-operation.'[1]

1. *Correspondence, etc.*, Vol. I, pp. 23–4.

5

The conflict between Stalin and Churchill

HOWEVER, events at the Soviet-German front were becoming more and more menacing. On 2 October Hitler proclaimed the beginning of the 'decisive offensive against Moscow', and two German armies commanded by General Bock, reinforced on their flanks by large tank formations, delivered a heavy blow at the western front. By the middle of the month the situation in the west had grown so much worse that the evacuation of Moscow was announced, and the seat of government was temporarily transferred to Kuibyshev. On 16 October *Pravda* wrote that 'the maddened Fascist beast is threatening Moscow', and appealed: 'Stop the enemy, at all costs bar the road to the merciless German invaders.' On 20 October battles were already proceeding in the districts of Mozhaisk and Maloyaroslavetz, and a state of siege was declared in Moscow. On 25 October *Pravda* wrote: 'The Hitlerite pack continues to thrust at Moscow', and on 29 October battles were already beginning in the area of Volokolamsk. On 3 November it was announced that battles were going on in the Kalinin direction. The Germans were making tremendous efforts to encircle Moscow. At the same time their armies were rapidly advancing on the southern front. On 21 September they occupied Kiev, on 17 October Odessa, on 22 October Taganrog, on 29 October Kharkov, and in November battles began in the area of Rostov-on-Don.

In the course of November the Germans suffered vast losses, but continued slowly to approach the capital. In some places they could even see its highest points through field-glasses. However the mood of the people of Moscow, of the whole people, of the army and the Government was unwavering, that Moscow should be defended to the end. The city was turned into a military camp, the streets blocked with barricades and anti-tank obstacles, and the best divisions of the Red Army (among them many from Siberia) were concentrated at the approaches to the capital...

The turning-point at the western front came at the beginning of December. On 6 December the Soviet counter-offensive began. It went forward at a rapid pace. The Germans by that time had clearly lost all their impetus, and were proving incapable of resisting a heavy blow by the Red Army. Their hopes of capturing Moscow by the end of the year collapsed. They retreated, clinging to every position that could be conveniently defended. This did not prevent the Red Army from liberating Tikhvin and Yeletz on 9 December, Klin and Yasnaya Polyana on 15 December, Kalinin on 16 December, Volokolamsk on 20 December and Kaluga on 30 December. The German retreat continued until the front line was re-stabilised for a certain time at Rzhev. Germany had suffered an undoubted defeat: the first defeat in the course of the second world war. The myth of her invincibility began to fade—but only began. *Pravda* wrote not without foundation on 13 December: 'The enemy has been wounded but not killed'. However, at that time this was of tremendous political and psychological significance, not only for our country, but for the whole world.

As distinct from the Soviet-German front, military events on other fronts in the second half of 1941 were modest in their scale, and not very influential as regards the general situation. The British on 18 November began an offensive in Northern Africa: on 9 December they occupied Tobruk, on 19 December Derna and on 24 December Benghazi. This made no essential changes even in the situation existing in Africa. The war at sea continued in its previous forms and on its previous scale: Britain's enemies with the help of submarines and planes were sinking about 200,000 tons every month of the ships supplying her needs. There was a considerable improvement of Britain's position in the air war: after 22 June 1941 the mass attacks of the German air force on British towns stopped for more than two years. They were renewed, in the form of V-1 rockets, only in 1944, when I was no longer in London.[1]

1. From the end of 1943 I was working in Moscow as Deputy People's Commissar for Foreign Affairs.

On 7 December 1941 Japan treacherously attacked Pearl Harbour in the Pacific. This at once dragged into the maelstrom of war two more Great Powers—Japan and the USA—and had incalculable military, political and economic consequences. However, these began to tell only in 1942, and revealed themselves completely still later.

Such was the situation in which there began the political and diplomatic events to the description of which I now proceed.

I have already mentioned that Roosevelt and Churchill at their Atlantic Conference decided to organise a consultation in Moscow between the representatives of the three Powers, to discuss matters relating to military supplies for the Soviet Union. Initially, neither the Americans nor the British displayed any particular energy in this respect, and there was a danger that the putting of the decision into effect would drag out for a long time. Only our démarche of 4 September in London introduced an element of urgency, and as a result there arrived in London by 17 September a mission headed by Averell Harriman, which was to represent the USA at the forthcoming meeting. The British Government, on its part, also appointed a mission, which was headed by Lord Beaverbrook, Minister of Supply. Both these appointments seemed to me most appropriate. On 22 September they left on the British cruiser *London* from Scapa Flow for Archangel, and on 28 September they arrived in Moscow. Harriman and Beaverbrook were twice received by Stalin, Molotov and Litvinov being present. Then for three days the conference of the three proceeded (Harriman, Beaverbrook and Molotov), and worked out and adopted 'Protocol No. 1', covering a period of nine months (from 1 October 1941 to 1 July 1942). This 'Protocol' enumerated in detail what the USA and Britain were undertaking to deliver to the USSR on the basis of Lend-Lease, and in what quantities. It was provided that during the second half of 1942 the conference of the three would be resumed, and would adopt a similar 'Protocol No. 2', determining the volume of supplies to the USSR for a year ahead, up to 1 July 1943. Churchill in a message to Stalin on 6 October promised that the transporting of the supplies provided for under 'Protocol No. 1' would take place by an unbroken chain of convoys, protected by warships, at intervals of 10 days.

Churchill in his war memoirs complains that in Moscow 'the reception was bleak, and discussions not at all friendly . . . The

Soviet General and Admirals gave no information of any kind to their British and American colleagues. They did not even inform them of the basis on which Russian needs of our precious war materials had been estimated. The Mission was given no formal entertainment until almost the last night, when they were invited to dinner at the Kremlin'.[1]

It seems to me that Churchill somewhat exaggerates here. I was not in Moscow myself during the Three-Power Conference, and therefore cannot assess Churchill's complaints at their proper value on the basis of my own impressions. But I must record that neither Beaverbrook nor Harriman, even in a hint, ever expressed any dissatisfaction to me with regard to their reception in Moscow. Nor should it be forgotten that the meeting was taking place at the time when the Germans were approaching Moscow. The reserve of Soviet official representatives in supplying information to the British and Americans was quite comprehensible: until that time they had not done much to win our confidence.

However that might be, the success of the Moscow Three-Power Conference was a big step forward in bringing the USSR, the USA and Britain closer together, and I welcomed this with all my heart. Now all my attention was turned to the speediest possible practical application of the decisions of the Conference, which in London depended principally on two men, Churchill and Beaverbrook. Fortunately I had had good personal relations with them even in the pre-war years, and made the maximum possible use of this in the interests of the USSR.

It seemed as though relations between the three countries had entered upon the path of gradual but strengthening improvement, which in the difficult circumstances of those days was of exceptional importance for us. And then suddenly . . .

On 7 November 1941 Churchill sent Stalin a message which began with the words:

'In order to clear things up and to plan for the future, I am ready to send General Wavell, the Commander-in-Chief in India, Persia and Iraq, to meet you in Moscow, Kuibyshev, Tiflis or wherever you will be. Besides this, General Paget, our new Commander-in-Chief designate for the Far East, will come with General Wavell . . . They can reach you in about a fortnight. Do you want them?'

1. *The Second World War*, Vol. III, p. 415.

Further, the message went on to say that in addition to the supplies agreed upon through Archangel, its transporting through Iran was also beginning, and that the British and the Americans were straining and would strain every effort to help the USSR. Then, in a somewhat veiled form, there followed complaints. Churchill wrote: 'Please make sure that our technicians who are going with the tanks and aircraft have full opportunity to hand these weapons over to your men under the best conditions. At present our Mission at Kuibyshev is out of touch with all these affairs. They only want to help. These weapons are sent at our peril, and we are anxious that they shall have the best chance . . . I cannot tell you about our immediate military plans, any more than you can tell me about yours, but rest assured that we are not going to be idle.'

In his message Churchill touched upon one more point which in the future was fated to play no small part in the Soviet Union's relations with Britain and the USA. Finland, Rumania and Hungary, as allies of Germany, were waging war on the USSR, but Britain and the USA continued to preserve normal diplomatic relations with them. If the conduct of the USA could be understood, since formally it was not taking part in the war against Germany, we had every right to expect from Britain that, as our ally, she would declare war on these three countries. And we were demanding this. But the British Government on various pretexts was avoiding such a step. In his message of 7 November Churchill set forth to Stalin the reasons why the British Government was delaying the performance of its allied duty.[1]

Churchill's message arrived in Moscow when heavy battles with the Germans were still taking place a few tens of miles away. The German forces were no longer able to break through the defence of the capital, but the Red Army likewise was not yet able to throw them back. The mood in Moscow was exceptionally tense and anxious. The absence of a second front in the West was felt with particular acuteness. Before the November holidays, the Central Committee of the Communist Party and the Government seriously discussed the question of whether a military parade should or should not be held, in the existing situation, on the Red Square on 7 November? In the end it was decided to hold the parade. It took place under the menace that at any moment it might be assailed by a death-dealing hail from German bombers. I

1. *Correspondence, etc.*, Vol. I, pp. 31–2.

well remember what an inspiration this parade was for all the Soviet people in London.

Shortly before the Novenber anniversary there had been an unpleasant incident, which had aroused much irritation in Moscow. The discussions about Britain declaring war on Finland, Hungary and Rumania were being carried on by strictly confidential diplomatic channels. Churchill of course was taking Roosevelt's advice on this question. And suddenly news of the negotiations leaked into the press from American quarters!

All these circumstances should be born in mind when reading J. V. Stalin's reply to the British Premier's message quoted above. Stalin's reply is dated 8 November. This means that the head of the Soviet Government sent it immediately after receiving Churchill's message, and under the direct impression of the words he had just read.

'I agree with you,' wrote Stalin, 'that we need clarity which at the moment is lacking in relations between the USSR and Great Britain. The unclarity is due to two circumstances: first, there is no definite understanding between our two countries concerning war aims and plans for the post-war peace settlement; secondly, there is no treaty between the USSR and Great Britain on mutual military aid in Europe against Hitler. Until understanding is reached on these two main points, not only will there be no clarity in Anglo-Soviet relations but, if we are to speak frankly, there will be no mutual trust . . . If General Wavell and General Paget, whom you mentioned in your message, come to Moscow to conclude agreements on the main points stated above, I shall be willing, naturally, to meet them and consider these points. If however the mission of the two Generals is to be restricted to information and examination of secondary issues, then I see no need for keeping them from their duties, nor can I myself go out of my way to engage in talks of that nature.'

In the second part of his message Stalin gave free rein to his indignation about the leakage in the press of information about the talks concerning a British declaration of war on Finland, Hungary and Rumania.[1]

On receiving this message, I sat for a long time thinking over its contents. The *substance* of the ideas it expressed aroused no doubt in my mind. Of course there was not complete clarity in relations between the USSR and Britain. Of course there was no under-

1. *Correspondence, etc.*, Vol. I, pp. 33–4.

standing about war aims and the post-war peace settlement. Of course the pact of mutual war-time assistance between the two countries signed on 12 July bore too narrow and temporary a character, and it would be a good thing to replace it by a more general treaty and for a more prolonged period, determining the relations of the two sides on all the European questions. All this was a fact. But it was hardly timely to raise such big and complex problems just at that moment, when the German hordes were still hanging over Moscow and it was particularly important for us to strengthen co-operation with Britain in every possible way—a co-operation which might not completely satisfy us, but all the same was essential. Surely one could not doubt that both the war aims and the plans for post-war reconstruction, of the Soviet Union and Britain respectively, were different, and that at best the achievement of any compromise acceptable to the two sides was impossible without a great deal of time being lost and, what was still more important, without serious arguments, differences and disputes? Why was it necessary at such a dangerous moment to evoke a spirit of dissension between us? Would it not be better to have waited with this until a more favourable moment? It seemed to me that for the moment it was more profitable to advance into the foreground what united us with Britain, and to push into the background everything that divided us.

Such were my meditations when I was sitting in my study with the text of Stalin's message. And nevertheless, even at that critical moment, there again and again came to my mind the thought: 'But perhaps he understands the situation and the play of world forces better than I do? Perhaps, in spite of everything, he is right?'

The next day I set off to see Churchill with the message from the head of the Soviet Government. Foreseeing the possibility of a sharp reaction on the part of the Premier, I asked Eden to be present at our conversation. Churchill received me in his room at the House of Commons. Handing him Stalin's message, I said:

'I very much ask you, Mr. Churchill, to treat this with the greatest possible calm.'

Churchill looked at me suspiciously, and taking the message out of the envelope, he began to read it. His face immediately went red, and then his left hand began agitatedly closing and opening. When Churchill reached the passage in which Stalin spoke of the conditions on which he was ready to receive Wavell and Paget, the Premier seemed to explode. He jumped up from his chair and began hurrying from corner to corner of the room in a state of extreme excitement.

'What'? he shouted in indignation. 'I send Stalin my best men, and he doesn't want to receive them! . . . I try to meet him in every possible way, and he replies by letters like that!'

The Premier made an irritated gesture at the letter lying on the table. Then in terrible agitation he continued:

'I can't understand what Stalin wants? Bad relations? A rupture? . . . Whom will that benefit? . . . Now, when the Germans are at the gates of Moscow, and Leningrad is ringed with blockade!'

Here I interrupted Churchill and seized on his last phrase to try and calm him at least a little.

'You are right', I observed. 'The Germans are at the gate of Moscow, and Leningrad is ringed with blockade . . . But just these facts should suggest to you in what a difficult position my country is, and what a painful atmosphere now predominates in Moscow . . . We should be able to rise above petty everyday misunderstanding, frictions and causes for offence, and be guided only by the big fundamental interests of our countries. Those big fundamental interests today coincide: both you and we have to smash Hitler . . . Consequently, we must go forward together.'

My words, and perhaps still more my calm and balanced tone, evidently, somewhat cooled down Churchill. To this was added Eden's influence. He advised the Premier not to decide anything just now, but carefully to consider with other members of the Cabinet how to act in this case. Churchill, however, still could not calm down and continued to pace the room, though more quietly. Finally, he sat down at the table and, giving me to understand that the audience was over, said in his usual tones:

'We shall think over all this.'

The next day Beaverbrook asked me urgently to come and see him. He sat me down in an armchair in his study, himself took the armchair opposite and began in a friendly and confidential tone:

'An unpleasant thing has happened . . . There's been a misunderstanding between Winston and Uncle Joe . . . That's no good at all . . . They should be reconciled . . .'

Then Beaverbrook said that at present the most important thing was to postpone as long as possible Churchill's reply to Stalin's last message. At present Churchill was breathing fire and brimstone. In such a condition he might easily say a lot of things to Stalin which would only make matters worse. The best thing would be for Churchill to keep quiet, recover his balance and calm down. He, Beaverbrook, together with Eden would undertake to bring this about. But it was important that in the immediate future from the Soviet side as well there should be nothing done which might once again anger the Premier: and Beaverbrook asked me to give my assistance in this respect.

I agreed with Beaverbrook's plan and promised him my help, although, frankly speaking, I had a very hazy idea at the moment of what form that help could take.

On the British side the plan indicated was put into effect: day followed day without any message from Churchill to the head of the Soviet Government. Churchill maintained silence and waited. Possibly he was doing this demonstratively, because until then he had usually replied to Stalin's messages without delay.

I don't know whether Stalin was at all influenced by any information about the impression made in London by his last letter; but on 19 November, i.e. ten days after he had sent the message of 8 November, a cipher message suddenly came from Moscow in which I was instructed immediately to inform Eden that, in sending his last letter, Stalin was very far from any intention of insulting any member of the Government, least of all the Prime Minister. He was endlessly burdened with questions connected with the conduct of the war, and could not think of anything else. The problems he had raised in his message—about military mutual assistance against Hitler and the post-war organisation of peace—were too important to complicate them with personal feelings and misunderstandings. Stalin was very offended by the revealing of the negotiations about Finland, but he was only seeking to reach agreement with Britain on the questions he had raised.

Eden was very pleased with my communication, and thought it a good bridge for the restoration of 'peace' between Churchill and Stalin. In fact, on 21 November the British Premier sent to Moscow his first message since the conflict, in which he assured Stalin that he wanted to work with him on just as friendly terms as he was working with Roosevelt. Furthermore Churchill told him that in order to discuss both wartime and post-war questions he intended to send Eden to Moscow, accompanied by high military and other experts. In this connection, Churchill made a very valuable admission.

'The fact that Russia is a Communist State and that Britain and the USA are not, and do not intend to be, is not any obstacle to our making a good plan for our mutual safety and rightful interests.'

How timely this sounds for the present day!

Finally Churchill promised that if Finland did not within the next fortnight cease from its military operations against the USSR, Britain would officially declare war on her.[1]

On 23 November Stalin sent Churchill his reply. He wrote that he sincerely welcomed 'the desire to co-operate with me through personal correspondence on a basis of collaboration and trust', and expressed his satisfaction at the British Government's decision on the question of Finland. Further, Stalin said that he 'fully supported' Eden's visit to the USSR in the immediate future, adding:

'I also agree that difference of political system in the USSR on the one hand and Great Britain and the USA on the other, should not and cannot be an obstacle to a favourable solution of the fundamental problems of safeguarding our mutual security and rightful interests.'[2]

The conflict between Stalin and Churchill was settled. The next thing was to be Eden's visit to Moscow.

By chance I have preserved a note I made on 22 July 1941 i.e. exactly one month after the beginning of the Soviet-German war (I liked, in addition to my regular diary, sometimes to put down separately on paper the ideas which came into my head).

'A month of war on the Soviet-German front has passed . . . A terrible month! The Red Army is constantly retreating, retreating, retreating . . . The Germans are plunging deeper and deeper into our country, seizing cities, fortresses, villages, whole territories . . . And so far no signs of any change . . . I simply cannot understand why this has happened . . . Our defeats are so unexpected, so inexplicable, so unnatural . . . But in my heart of hearts I still cherish the hope—no, not the hope but the confidence, some kind of spontaneous internal confidence—that our present defeats are only temporary. I recall Napoleon's campaign against Russia. Then too the Russian army at first retreated and retreated, even gave up Moscow, and then . . . But I don't want even to think of the possibility of Moscow being surrendered now to the accursed Fascists! . . . Somewhere, at some time, even before Moscow, we

1. *Correspondence, etc.*, Vol. I, pp. 34–5.
2. *Correspondence, etc.*, Vol. I, pp. 35–6.

shall stop the German hordes and then drive them back . . . But where and when? May the moment come rapidly! . . . But meanwhile—courage, courage and again courage! How often in the past they have tried to conquer Russia, subjugate her, enslave her: but without success! We survived in the past, we shall survive today. Such a people as ours cannot perish!

'All that is so, but it is difficult to persuade the British of our ultimate invincibility. Yesterday I saw David Low. We have long been on good terms, and he often talks with me quite frankly. At present he is terribly worried and upset by what is happening on the Soviet-German front. I tried to dissipate his gloomy thoughts, arguing from history and from the present. He listened to me carefully and said:

'"I very much want to believe that you are right, but do you know what is being said at present in Fleet Street, and in Parliament too? People say that Russia will not hold out very long . . . The pessimists give her six or seven weeks, and the optimists three months . . . At all events, all will be over by the autumn . . . There is a particularly bad atmosphere in the War Office: there they are saying all the time that the Germans will go through Russia as a knife goes through butter."

"I could not help laughing, and said that the British War Office was never distinguished by a high degree of sagacity. Low gave a wry smile, and added slowly:

'"One Colonel I know was assuring me today that there's nothing to hope for from the Russians. During the Finnish war they messed about for three whole months before they overcame their little adversary . . . How can they stand up against the Germans? So he is against sending large quantities of arms to Russia from Britain and the USA: what would be the point? All the same it would fall into the hands of the Germans. Better keep it for ourselves.'

'"Your Colonel", I remarked, "probably comes from the Blimp family?"

'"Yes, of course he is a Blimp", Low replied. "But many people in the newspapers and in politics trust him, and that is dangerous."'

What Low was telling me gave a good picture of wide-spread feelings in Britain during the first weeks after 22 June. I noticed expressions of them every day and everywhere, in all circles—from Ministers to taxi drivers. And there arose before me as

Soviet Ambassador in Britain ever more sharply the problem of how to combat these defeatist attitudes? How could one promote stronger faith among the British in our capacity to wage war to the end? How could one create in them the conviction that in the long run we would win?

This problem was of first-class importance in the summer of 1941 (and later too), and to solve it required the greatest effort and ingenuity on our part. We Soviet workers in London thoroughly discussed the problem, consulted Moscow on it, and little by little from all our discussions, projects and proposals there crystallised out definite measures which justified themselves in the further course of the war.

The first of such measures was the creation of a daily bulletin of *Soviet War News* published by the Embassy. At first it contained almost exclusively war news: communiqués from the Soviet front, orders by army commanders, reports by war correspondents, and so forth. Its purpose was to oppose Soviet information about events in Eastern Europe to the information from British, American and particularly German sources. Gradually, however, the framework of the bulletin began to expand, and there began to appear in it more and more frequently reports of civilian life in the USSR, of the heroic efforts of the Soviet people in the sphere of the national economy, science, culture, music, literature and art. Finally we came to the conclusion that the pages of the bulletin were too narrow for our needs, and founded a journal, *Soviet War News Weekly*, which could illustrate the whole of Soviet life in all its aspects in war time more fully and broadly. *Soviet War News* was sent gratis to prominent political, public, military, trade union and party personalities, at first in about 2,000 copies (by the end of the war it had reached 11,000). *Soviet War News Weekly* (later *Soviet Weekly*) was sold through ordinary commercial channels, in about 50,000 copies.

This undertaking was undoubtedly successful, a result in no small measure due to the successful choice of editor in the person of S. N. Rostovsky. Rostovsky was a politically very knowledgeable and cultivated man, with an excellent knowledge of international relations, a capable journalist and a master of several languages. In pre-war years he had published abroad, under the pen name of Ernst Henri, two books—*Hitler Over Europe* and *Hitler Over Russia*—which were very popular at that time. In addition he was a real newspaper man, with a very high working capacity. And this was particularly important, because from the very beginning we realised that the materials which were being sent to us from Moscow for the bulletin and the weekly could not be published in Britain without far-reaching amendment.

Different nations have different customs and traditions in the intellectual sphere, including the sphere of newspaper and magazine material. Here the tastes and habits of the Russians and the British are far from identical. Thus Russians easily swallow long articles, the British on the contrary will read only short articles, and simply throw aside lengthy ones (I have in view, of course, the average reader). The Russians don't object if in an article, say, on an economic subject there are many figures: the British on the contrary have an extreme distaste for a large number of figures, and if figures are unavoidable they demand that they should be presented in some vivid form. Tell an Englishman that Works X produces 400,000 cars a year, and it slips past his consciousness and is not recorded in his memory. But tell an Englishman that at that works a completed car leaves the conveyor every minute, and it will make an impression on him and remain in his head as an interesting fact.

Our Moscow comrades, of course, had the best intentions, and often sent *Soviet War News* extremely valuable materials, but nearly always, with rare exceptions, they were written 'in Russian' not in the philological sense but in the sense of style and manner. All had to be remade in London and brought into a form acceptable to the British reader. In practice, the editorial office of *Soviet War News* (i.e. Rostovsky himself first and foremost) usually took the facts and events from the material received, and rewrote them into articles suitable for British consumption. It was very complicated, delicate and hurried work, with which Rostovsky coped excellently.

Both Soviet organs from day to day and from week to week bombarded British minds—particularly the minds of leading people in the country—with the truth about Russia—and in this way waged a stubborn battle against the defeatist moods regarding the USSR which at that time were widespread in the British Isles. This struggle produced its results even in the most difficult first period of the war, and had still greater successes later, when the optimism of the Soviet publications began to be reinforced more and more frequently by the concrete facts of events at the front.

When this most important undertaking had been set on foot, I began to think over whether anything else could be done to encourage and strengthen the faith of British people in the unbreakable will of the Soviet people to be and remain a great people with a great future? Could not anything be done which would demonstrate to them with conviction that Hitler's efforts to crush and enslave our country were vain?

Finally I came to the conclusion that it would be important just now to put into the hands of the British reader two books: Tolstoy's *War and Peace* and *Napoleon's Invasion of Russia*, by Acadamician E. V. Tarle.

Tolstoy's great novel (I always considered it the greatest novel of all times and peoples) had of course been published previously in Britain more than once, but at that time it was not of such topical importance as now. It would be most valuable urgently to bring it out in a new edition and with as great a print as possible. I had fairly good connections with the publishing world, and in a short time I was able to report with satisfaction that one of the biggest London publishing firms—the house of Macmillan[1]—had taken on this proposition, which apart from anything else promised to bring good profits (as in fact happened). In 1942 a solid volume in red binding appeared in the bookshops. It contained 1,352 pages, but as it was printed on india paper it did not weigh heavy in the hand. This was the full text of Tolstoy's novel, with maps and appendices. At once it became what the British call a 'best seller'. It was read everywhere: in palaces and huts, among M.P.s and workmen, in the houses of farmers and clerks, on board ship and in the carriages of the London Underground. I myself saw Foreign Office typists reading it. The famous work passed through the country like a hurricane, arousing profound and strong reactions. Of course those who read it did not all become convinced that the USSR was invincible, but very many understood and felt that the Russians were a great people, who could not perish so easily.

Soon after the appearance of this new edition of *War and Peace*, my wife gave Mrs. Churchill a copy, with the following inscription:

1. Harold Macmillan, the future British Prime Minister, was at that time the head of this publishing firm and at the same time an M.P. He was inclined to Churchill's group, defended the idea of Anglo-Soviet co-operation, and not infrequently was a guest at our Embassy. We were on good terms, all the more that Macmillan knew and admired Russian classical literature.

'1812–1942. We destroyed our enemy then, we shall destroy our enemy also today.'

Much later, in February 1943, Mrs. Churchill presented my wife with the same book. In it was written:

'Here is a book for those who would penetrate the vastness and mystery of Russia. Clementine S. Churchill.'

Evidently Tolstoy's novel made a great impression on Mrs. Churchill, leading her to see our people in a new way and to feel its tremendous vital force . . .

Almost simultaneously with *War and Peace*, E. V. Tarle's book on Napoleon was published. Of course it had not as wide an audience as Tolstoy's novel. It was read mainly in intellectual circles, particularly by politicians, journalists, historians and the military. They read it attentively, making inevitable comparisons with the days of the second world war. And as that class of reader played a great part in Parliament, in the press, in the army and the navy and in various State institutions, the psychological effect of the work of Tarle was probably no less than the effect of Tolstoy's great epic.

Both these books represented heavy artillery in the struggle against British disbelief in the unconquerability of the Soviet Union. But there were also smaller shots fired with the same target. I recall that a noticeable impression was made by the booklet *Notes of a Partisan* by Polyakov, which appeared soon after the beginning of the war. We translated it into English, brought it out in a large print and widely circulated it among the population. I recall another characteristic occasion. One of our British well-wishers brought to the Embassy a remarkable collection of caricatures of the year 1812, from the pencil of the British artist Cruikshank and the Russian artist Terebenyev. They depicted in the main Napoleon's fiasco in Russia. Beaverbrook published an album of these caricatures, and I wrote a small preface.

Somewhat later, at the beginning of 1943, we managed to arrange for the London Old Vic to present Konstantin Simonov's *The Russians*: at that time it was not only of literary but also of great political importance. Very useful, though in a somewhat different context, was the appearance on the British book market of Ilya Ehrenburg's well known novel *The Fall of Paris*, which showed so vividly how and why France had fallen in 1940.

The result of all the above-mentioned efforts on our part, and of many others (later I will dwell in particular on the work of the Red Cross in this sphere) was that the defeatist moods of the British in regard to military prospects on the Eastern front, so widespread in the first months after 22 June, gradually began to grow weaker. When six weeks, and then three months, of the bloody struggle in the east had passed, and the Soviet Union had still not collapsed, had still not bowed the knee to Hitler, was still continuing to fight and to inflict heavy and exhausting blows on the enemy, there began to shine in the mind of the British the star of hope of victory, as yet distant and unclear, a star which pierced with its rays the darkness which had fallen heavily over Europe. Somewhat later, the operations of the Red Army began to transform that hope more and more into confidence that sooner or later there would be a fundamental turning point in the Soviet-German war, and that the road to victory would open before the Soviet Union—and with it before the entire anti-Hitler coalition...

One more form of struggle against defeatist moods about my country among the British were my speeches and statements as Ambassador of the USSR.

In countries of bourgeois democracy, like Britain, the USA, Scandinavia and some others, an Ambassador must know how to speak. To speak not only tête-à-tête in the study of the Foreign Minister, not only with some group of visitors who have come to see the Ambassador to clear up some complicated question of current politics, but also publicly—at a crowded dinner arranged by some large organisation, at the meeting of a learned corporation interested in the Ambassador's views on some subject with which it is concerned, at a lecture in a university where the students want to learn something about the country which the Ambassador represents, at a meeting of workers organised on some appropriate occasion by the trade unions or the Labour Party. In countries of bourgeois democracy that is accepted: and an Ambassador who avoided such speeches would at once lose his prestige, and begin to be regarded only as a postman for transmitting Notes from one Government to the other. And the reputation of a postman greatly reduces the possibility of the Ambassador's influencing, in the sense he desires, public opinion in the country where he is accredited, and in the long run injures the interests of the State which sent him there.

Very soon after my arrival in London I had realised how this operates, and strove to make the maximum use of the opportunity of public statements in order to spread the truth about the Soviet Union. In Moscow, at that time, far from all the leading comrades realised the value of such speeches, and looked somewhat askance at my activity in this sphere. But so long as M. M. Litvinov remained People's Commissar for Foreign Affairs, no obstacles were put in my way: Maxim Maximovich himself knew perfectly the procedures of bourgeois democracy, and encouraged in every possible way my efforts to use this method as well, to break through the wall of hostility surrounding us in Britain at the beginning of the 30s. With his departure from office in May 1939 the situation somewhat changed: but just in this period—right up to 22 June 1941—the worsening of Anglo-Soviet relations considerably reduced my opportunities for influencing a British audience by the spoken word. But now, after Hitler's attack on the USSR, I began to be invited on all sides to speak in public at luncheons, dinners, meetings, sessions and other occasions. I willingly accepted these invitations, because every such speech was an excellent opportunity for telling the truth about the USSR or dealing a blow at defeatist moods regarding its strength among the British. My difficulty now often consisted in the fact that there were too many invitations, and I had to make a choice between them.

What did I speak about in these first most terrible months of the war on the Soviet-German front? I will give a few extracts from my speeches at that time, the texts of which have been preserved (I usually spoke in English without notes, but prepared a text beforehand).

On 29 July 1941 the L.C.C. gave a reception in honour of the Soviet Ambassador and his wife. We were welcomed by the Chairman of the Council in a short speech in which he emphasised the admiration of the British at the heroic struggle of the Red Army and the exceptional importance of close co-operation between Britain and the USSR. The members of the Council applauded warmly and expressed in every possible way their sympathy for us as representatives of a great people and a friendly Government. Then it was my turn to reply. I expressed my pleasure and gratitude at the warm reception given by the Council to us as emissaries of the land of Soviets, and continued:

'At this stage of the war it would be premature to make any prophecies about the future. In every great war the tide ebbs and flows, there are changes and surprises: but already two things are beyond doubt: first of all, the peoples of my country, closely united around the Soviet Government, will fight stubbornly against Hitlerite Germany, and secondly, in the long run we shall conquer. But victory will come the more quickly, and will require the fewer sacrifices, the closer is the friendship between our peoples and the more equally are the difficulties and dangers of the war divided between them.'

Bound up with the speech of 29 July in my mind is one amusing and at the same time instructive recollection. The reception at the L.C.C. was fixed for 3 p.m. On the same day, at 1 p.m., in one of the biggest London hotels there was to be a luncheon of the Foreign Press Association, at which Eden had promised to speak at length. Among the guests of honour at this luncheon were the American Ambassador Winant and myself. I had calculated that in 1½–2 hours all would be over, and I would have time to reach the Council. But there was some unexpected delay in the serving of the luncheon, the Foreign Secretary's speech proved somewhat longer than usual, and as a result I found myself, as the chess players say, in "time trouble.' It was approaching three o'clock, and Eden's speech was still continuing. I could not leave before it was over. What was to be done? I sent a telephone message to the L.C.C. that I would be fifteen minutes late, and explained the reason for my delay. My communication was received there without the slightest enthusiasm, but they were obliged to put up with what they could not avert. As soon as Eden finished speaking, I sent him a note in which I expressed my satisfaction at his speech, and asked his pardon for having to leave the luncheon before it ended. Then my wife and I rose and withdrew. This did not pass unnoticed. The next day there was a rumour in political and journalistic circles that Maisky had been so indignant at Eden's speech that, without waiting for the luncheon to end, he had demonstratively left. Then this story appeared in the press. So lightly are various political legends born! And so well founded are the 'reliable source' to which in such cases journalists usually refer! Hence the conclusion that often events in international affairs in which newspaper men or amateur diplomats see 'a profound significance' and 'sinister calculations' are in reality the result of chance or the most ordinary human reasons . . .

On 31 August 1941 there was a mass demonstration at Feltham, one of the London suburbs, in the open air on a big common.

There were people of all sorts and conditions there, but most of all workmen from local factories. There were also present civil defence and anti-aircraft detachments. At 3 p.m. I arrived at the demonstration, where there was a vast and noisy crowd already. I was met with a guard of honour. Then a religious service began. Hymns were sung, and the Rev. P. D. Godfrey delivered a sermon. Then there were speeches: I was called on first. I spoke from a little mound and, I confess, was very moved by all this majestic picture, which reminded me of the far-off Chartist meetings which I had often seen depicted in books on the history of the British Labour movement.

'The Soviet people and the Red Army', I said, 'are heroically fighting not only for their own country, but also for the freedom and independence of all the peoples in the world who are threatened by German Fascism . . . We shall not stop half-way, we shall fight to the bitter end, until Hitlerite Germany is completely defeated . . . How can that be achieved? The reply is perfectly clear: it can be achieved only by means of the closest military, economic and political co-operation between the British and the Soviet peoples. The closer is that co-operation, the fewer will be the sacrifices and the nearer final victory.'

My words were received with great enthusiasm. One felt that they had reached the hearts of these thousands of ordinary British people, who understood, and still more felt, what a terrible menace hung over the world and how important it was to avert it by the joint struggle of the two peoples.

I was followed by a number of other speakers. All of them denounced Nazi Germany, swore to carry on the war to the bitter end and to strengthen in every possible way co-operation with the Soviet Union.

Then a resolution was moved which contained, among other things, the following:

'We are firmly resolved to strain every effort for victory over Fascism . . . to work in the factories as we have never worked before . . . We call on His Majesty's Government urgently to afford immediate mutual aid to the Soviet Union . . . We are convinced that our people together with the people of the Soviet Union and all freedom loving people throughout the world will be victorious in the end.'

The resolution was adopted unanimously, amid great applause.

In conclusion, the 'International' and 'God Save the King' were sung. Listening to the singing, I thought: 'What strange mixtures there are in life—yet in this particular mixture is the guarantee for victory over Fascism, and consequently it serves the cause of freedom for mankind . . .'

22 September 1941 at Birmingham. In connection with the decision of the British Government to supply the USSR with arms (about which we had talked with Churchill on 4 September) there was a 'Tanks for Russia Week' all over Britain. I was asked to be present at one of the big works making tanks.

The smoke-blackened factory buildings. Thousands of workers who had come out to welcome the Soviet Ambassador. Subdued voices, close attention, friendly handshakes and occasional shouts: 'Long live the Soviet Union!' Somebody's strong hands lift me up and put me on the tank.

I cast a glance over the sea of heads surrounding me, and begin with the profound gratitude of the Red Army and the Soviet people for the tanks which my audience make, and which help our soldiers in their battles with the Germans. Then I explain why we need tanks from Britain and the USA even though we have our own tank industry.

'In a battle on such a scale', I say, 'as that which we have been carrying on for the last three months, our losses in tanks are very great. They cannot be replaced in the course of normal production. I must add moreover that some of our important industrial areas have fallen into the hands of the enemy, and many factories and works have been evacuated. Before they begin to work in their new places, a certain period of time will be needed. That is why we so need the help of Britain and the USA at the present time in supplies of arms. Our watchword at the present time is simple and understandable: "More tanks, more planes, more guns!". And with all my heart I beg you to put it into practice.'

A storm of applause. Curses on the Nazis. Shouts of 'Hurrah for the Red Army!'

27 September 1941 in London. The third session of the British Association for the Advancement of Science. Its inspirer was the famous British writer H. G. Wells. The greatest luminaries of the British scientific world were present. Some foreigners were in attendance, including Juan Negrin, the former Premier of Republican Spain (before the war he was a professor of physiology). The conference worked in a number of sections. In the section 'Science and human needs', U.S. Ambassador Winant presided; in

the section 'Science and technological progress' Eduard Benes, Premier of the Czechoslovak Government in exile, was in the chair; in the section 'Science and post-war aid' the president was the Chinese Ambassador, Wellington Koo; and in the section 'Science and world intellect' H. G. Wells was in the chair. I was charged with presiding in the section 'Science and world planning'. I opened it with a short speech in which I first of all read greetings from the Academy of Sciences of the USSR, signed by its President V.L. Komarov, its Vice-Presidents O.Y. Schmidt and I. A. Chudakov, and a number of its members—A. N. Bach, A. A. Bogomoletz, N. N. Burdenko, A. E. Fersman, A. F. Yoffe, P. L. Kapitsa, L. S. Stern, E. V. Tarle and others. The Soviet scientists called on their British colleagues to bend all their efforts to victory over Nazism which would be 'the victory of liberty, culture, science, civilisation over barbarism, tyranny, obscurantism, the victory of a bright future over the gloomy past'.

Then it was my turn, and in a cautious and tactful form I spoke of it being hardly timely at present to go deeply into the problem of world planning, and gradually moved the burden of my speech to the tasks of the present day:

'We have always considered that science must help mankind in its needs. But what is most needful to mankind at the present time? It is most of all to destroy the system of German Nazism, which wishes to dominate the whole world and terrorise the whole world . . . Scientists must help in solving that basic problem of our day.'

Universal agreement, applause, warm handshakes . . .

21 November 1941. In order to strengthen Anglo-Soviet unity, an Anglo-Soviet Public Relations Association had been set up, including prominent representatives of Parliament, the Government and leading circles in the City. This Association organised a big luncheon at which a well-known surgeon, Lord Horder, presided. Churchill sent greetings in which he wished the Association every success in its work, and promised it all kinds of help. The main speaker was Eden, who said that the British Government wanted most of all to create a healthy and firm basis for British-Soviet relations. In this war, said Eden there was one aim and one cause, and they must give each other mutual help. British resources must be also Russia's resources, and the resources of Russia must also be Britain's resources. The same ships which

were now carrying munitions to Russia were bringing back valuable raw materials from Russia for the British war effort. This interconnection and this mutual interest must continue to develop and grow stronger during the war and after it was over. There should be the closest co-operation with the USSR in the post-war organisation of peace.

In my reply I first of all drew some conclusions from the first five months of the war in the East, and placed on record the complete failure of all Hitler's plans and calculations. Then I went over to the question of the struggle against Hitlerite Germany which, wherever it was taking place, should be regarded as the one common front of the Allies, and that all their resources and energies should be shifted from one part of the front to another as the military situation demanded. While recognising to the full the importance of the struggle against Germany at sea and in the air, I said that nevertheless Germany had always been in the main a land Power, and that in reality it could be finally beaten on land. I called also for a spirit of urgency, speed and tirelessness to be introduced into the whole war effort of the Allies, and quoted with sympathy Beaverbrook's remark, a little while before: 'We must raise the head of steam!' In conclusion I warned against the danger of winning the war and losing the peace, and suggested that preparations should already begin to work out plans for the postwar organisation of the world, basing them on the principle of self-determination of nations.

I could tell at great length of the ways and means with which we strove to overcome defeatist moods about the Soviet Union among the British in those difficult days, but I think this is unnecessary, after the examples I have given. I wish to say only one thing in addition. With the most rigorous examination of our efforts, we could record with satisfaction that they were a useful contribution to the stabilisation of British opinion. Although it was still a very long way to Stalingrad, the British nevertheless were gradually abandoning their first apprehensions, and little by little were beginning to concede (come even to believe) that 'the Russians' would after all be victorious—of course not at once, not now, but later, in some indefinite future. At that time such a conclusion was of great and positive significance.

6

With Eden to Moscow

EDEN'S departure for Moscow, of which Churchill had spoken in his message to Stalin on 22 November, was fixed for 7 December 1941. The world situation in which this visit was to take place was of a very threatening character.

At the Soviet-German front heavy battles were continuing. The Germans were driving towards Moscow, and although our resistance had stiffened in November, they were nevertheless continuing slowly to advance, seeking to surround the capital of the USSR from the north and the south. At some points the Hitlerites were only about twenty miles from Moscow, and no one could foretell what would be the end. The war at sea went on as before, and Britain continued to strain every nerve to overcome the vast losses it was suffering at the hands of German submarines and planes. The sinister spectre of war was rising more and more clearly in the Pacific. Japan was obviously preparing to attack: she was increasing her war budget, concentrating her navy in strategically important points and carrying on a furious press and radio campaign against the USA and Britain.

At the same time the Japanese Government, striving to make the blow it was preparing as unexpected as possible, was hypocritically negotiating in Washington for the settlement of all questions in dispute between itself and the United States. Nomuta and Kurusu, the official representatives of the Japanese Government in these negotiations, were not stingy in lavishing their most conciliatory gestures and their most friendly words in the talks. The extent to which the double-faced Japanese behaviour went is evident by this fact: on 6 December (i.e. the eve of the

Japanese attack at Pearl Harbour) the spokesman of the Government Information Bureau in Tokyo made an official statement that, in spite of all rumours and inventions, the Japanese-American negotiations would continue, that the Japanese press was wrong in accusing the USA of 'insufficient sincerity and deliberate dragging-out of the negotiations', and that 'both sides would with complete sincerity strive to work out a formula acceptable to the two sides'. In spite of such assurances, however, everyone felt that a storm was gathering in the Far East, and that the thunder would roll and lightning flash tomorrow, if not today.

In these conditions the closest possible co-operation between the USSR and Britain, and the significance of a visit by Eden to Moscow, were all the more important. Wishing to bring about as favourable an atmosphere as possible for the forthcoming visit, I had a talk with Eden at the beginning of December in which I underlined that it was extremely desirable immediately to satisfy the request of the Soviet Government (set forth in Stalin's message to Churchill on 8 November) that Britain should declare war on Finland, Hungary and Rumania. I pointed out that the time-limit of fifteen days given by Churchill to Finland for her leaving the war, about which he had written to Stalin on 22 November, was now expiring, but Finland was not even dreaming of putting an end to military operations. I did not know at the time that, as Churchill says in his memoirs,[1] Mannerheim had on 2 December rejected the British Premier's request; but the behaviour of Finland left no doubt as to her intention to continue the war. Eden agreed entirely with my considerations, and in fact on 6 December 1941 Britain declared war on Finland, Hungary and Rumania. Thus the way was cleared for the Moscow conversations in the military and diplomatic sphere.

It seemed to me necessary, as is usual in diplomatic practice, that I should accompany Eden in his journey to the USSR. I had asked permission for this from Moscow in good time. What was my dissatisfaction and disappointment when a negative reply came from the People's Commissariat for Foreign Affairs! I could not understand what was wrong, but did not leave it at that, and began objecting. Then it turned out that the PCFA had not refused my request at all, but that the cipher clerks had simply made a mistake in the first cable, and the text I had received was the opposite of what in reality had been sent. Such may be

1. *The Second World War*, Vol. III, p. 474.

occasionally the result of carelessness in the cipher department! After the misunderstanding had been cleared up I breathed more freely and began urgent preparations for departure.

In war conditions, Eden's journey to Moscow was naturally surrounded with the greatest secrecy. The plan drawn up was as follows. Eden would travel by sea from Britain to Murmansk, and the British Government took responsibility for that part of the journey. From Murmansk he would travel to Moscow, and there, naturally, the Soviet Government assumed responsibility. The departure from London was appointed for 1 p.m. on 7 December, a Sunday. A special train was to deliver Eden and the persons accompanying him to the well-known naval base of Invergordon in Scotland, and from there a specially selected destroyer was to carry them to the still better-known naval base of Scapa Flow in the Orkneys, where the whole delegation was to embark on the large cruiser *Kent* and proceed to Murmansk. The *Kent* belonged to the type of so-called Washington cruisers, the displacement of which, under the Washington Treaty of 1922, was officially fixed at 10,000 tons. In reality, the *Kent's* tonnage was about 15,000. It was a very powerful and speedy warship with four propellers, developing a speed of 27 knots. There were long discussions in the Admiralty about whether the *Kent* should be given an escort of three or four destroyers, and in the end it was decided not to do this. It was difficult for the destroyers to keep pace with such a fast cruiser, especially in stormy weather; moreover, such a considerable group of ships could be more easily discovered and traced by the Germans. It was thought safer to send the *Kent* alone, since its high speed made it almost invulnerable for submarines, while the darkness predominant in northern latitudes at that time of the year protected it against attacks by German bombers.

At our Embassy no one, except my wife, our Counsellor K. V. Novikov and the cipher clerks, knew of my forthcoming journey. On 7 December, about midday, my wife and I went out together as though for our usual walk in the neighbouring Kensington Gardens, proceeded to the nearest Underground station, and in that way reached the terminus where the delegation's special train stood in a siding. The British were already there, and also K. V. Novikov who was seeing me off. My simple baggage consisted chiefly of warm clothes for the journey.

There had been a lot of trouble over these warm clothes. I had neither fur coat nor felt boots in London: they were not needed there. My wife had sought out, with great difficulty, and bought for me an imitation fur coat of knitwear. It was light and warm, but coloured yellow. At first glance I even doubted whether I could venture to put it on. Later, in Murmansk, the frost made me overcome these doubts. I walked about the streets of Moscow in my yellow 'fur coat' almost as an apparition; people meeting me in the street stopped dead, looking at me in amazement. When in 1943 I returned to the USSR for good, I dyed the coat black, and since then have been wearing it with great satisfaction: it keeps me warm, is not heavy and in addition reminds me of the historic event in which I had to take part. Of course it was impossible to buy felt boots in London, and I was procured fur-lined boots, such as pilots wear, from the Air Ministry. I also had my fur cap with earpieces, remaining with me by chance from the days when I was plenipotentiary representative in Finland. With such an outfit I felt myself completely prepared for the journey through the Polar regions, and was not mistaken: there was no beauty, but in return there was warmth.

After saying goodbye to my wife and shaking hands with Novikov, I went up into the carriage. Eden and his colleagues were already there. The train rapidly went off, and everyone began settling down in their place as comfortably as possible. Looking out of the window I mechanically followed the stations, towns, villages, woodlands and green fields rushing by, and meditated. I meditated on what awaited us on the journey, and how we would be met in Moscow? I meditated on what the forthcoming negotiations might lead to, and what influence they would have on the further course of the war. I also remembered my conversation the day before with Churchill. I called on him to say goodbye. The Premier, as always, a cigar between his teeth, was very amiable, and expressed his wishes for complete success in the meeting between Eden and the Soviet leaders. I thanked him, and remarked in passing that I would be glad to see Moscow again. Churchill gave a puff at his cigar and then, looking at me sideways through the blue cloud of smoke, asked:

'Are you sure that the meeting will take place in Moscow?'

The Premier was clearly reflecting the fears then predominant in Britain that in the long run we would not succeed in preserving the capital. Why otherwise had Moscow been evacuated? Why had Kuibyshev become the new official seat of government?

I was angry, and replied energetically:

'What a question! Of course the negotiations will take place in Moscow.'

Churchill looked at me somewhat ironically, and then said in a conciliatory tone:

'Well, wherever the negotiations take place—in Moscow or' (he stumbled for a moment and pronounced the word with difficulty) 'in that Ku . . . Kuibyshev of yours, I wish them complete success all the same.'

Now, sitting in the carriage, I unwillingly put myself the question: where would the negotiations after all take place? In Moscow or in Kuibyshev? Somehow spontaneously and beyond my control, intuitively, the reply formed itself strongly: Of course in Moscow! Only in Moscow! . . . No, we would not give up Moscow to the Germans at any price!

At five o'clock we all gathered in Eden's carriage for the traditional British 'tea'. The Foreign Secretary was accompanied by his Permanent Under-Secretary, Cadogan, the Deputy Chief of the General Staff, General Nye and two Foreign Office officials, Oliver Harvey and Frank Roberts. The conversation was of a general social nature, not very interesting, and I was making ready to go back to my compartment, when something strange and incomprehensible suddenly happened. The train was moving fast, stopping nowhere. At about 6 p.m. we hurtled through some small station, and noticed there was great excitement on the platform: there was an unusually large number of people there, hurrying, gesticulating and apparently hotly arguing. At the next small station, through which the train likewise passed without stopping, we saw the same picture. This interested us, but we could not understand what was the matter?

One thing only was clear, that something important had happened. Thereupon, on Eden's instructions, a short halt was made at the following station. One of Eden's staff jumped out, and came back with a shattering piece of news a few minutes later: Japan had attacked the USA. The station-master at this small place had heard the news on the radio, but could not tell us of any details, and in particular did not know where and how the attack had taken place: but there was no doubt about the fact of the attack.

Eden was very agitated, and immediately put the question to me: 'What do you think of this?'

I replied that Japan's action could have been expected at any moment, and that now the war in essence had engulfed the whole world: but the relationship of forces between the two camps had clearly changed to our advantage.

'What do you think?' Eden continued, 'Should I now go on with the journey to Moscow? Perhaps it would be better to return to London?'

'Not on any account,' I objected. 'On the contrary, your journey to Moscow has now become even more necessary.'

Late at night, at a larger station, we learned all the details of the Japanese attack on Pearl Harbour, and early in the morning we arrived at Invergordon. Eden in my presence at once rang up Churchill and put to him the same question that he had put to me the night before, namely, was it worth while him continuing the journey to Moscow. Then he broke away from the mouthpiece and said:

'The Prime Minister thinks as you do, that my journey to Moscow is now more necessary than ever.'

Then Eden continued the conversation, and I heard him say:

'You ask what my companion thinks? He is of the same opinion as you.'

Eden put down the receiver, and added with evident relief:

'That's all clear. So let us go on with our journey!'

The destroyer on which we embarked rocked considerably, and Eden, who in addition had a slight cold, did not feel well. The doctor came and began taking the necessary measures. About 5 p.m. we arrived at last at Scapa Flow, passing through a long chain of all kinds of barriers, and tied up by the *Kent*. In the depth of night, the cruiser left for the open sea.

The whole way from Scapa Flow to Murmansk took four-and-a-half days. We travelled north along the western shores of the Scandinavian peninsula, but at a long distance from the coast from Norway. This was shorter and safer, since the Germans at that time were in occupation. Then we rounded the North Cape, and with great precautions passed through the dangerous zone between the North Cape and Bear Island, where the Germans most frequently launched air or submarine attacks against ships travelling to the USSR, and finally turned south to Kola Bay. We did not encounter great storms, but what the seamen call 'fresh weather' prevailed the whole way. Our ship rocked, but not uncontrollably, and I withstood the play of the capricious elements comparatively undisturbed. In general everything went off satisfactorily, but there were some discomforts.

Principal among them was the strong vibration of the warship—or, more precisely, of that part where I was accommodated. There were two so-called Admiral's state-rooms on the *Kent*'s stern: they were given to Eden and myself, as the two most 'distinguished passengers'. Eden had the state-room on the left in the direction the ship was moving, and I the one on the right, with only a narrow corridor between us. Each state-room consisted of a drawing-room, a bedroom and a washroom. They were furnished magnificently, of course, in naval style. All would have been excellent, if the four shafts of the four powerful propellers of the cruiser had not passed under the floor of the corridor between the state-rooms. When the *Kent* was developing high speed, as was its task, when all its propellers were furiously thrashing in the cold black water, the whole of the stern began to shudder so violently that I felt myself quite broken-up. On account of the vibration I slept badly, ate badly and even thought with difficulty. At one moment I wanted to ask the commander of the cruiser to change my 'dwelling-place' and to transfer me to some other cabin—less 'distinguished' but more tranquil—but thought better of it, knowing the devotion of the British to traditionally established forms and procedures.

I made the acquaintance of the *Kent*'s commander and his immediate assistants on several occasions when I sat at his table during luncheon and dinner: but I spent the greater part of my time in my 'Admiral's state-room' plunged in re-reading Herzen's *My Past and Thoughts*, which I had taken with me. I had first read these greatest memoirs in Russian literature while I was still a schoolboy, at Omsk, and they had left me with an ineffaceable impression. In after years I had more than once, at moments free from urgent business, found myself turning over the familiar pages, dwelling on those which echoed particularly the thoughts and feelings of the moment. Such contact with the world of *My Past and Thoughts* always aroused in me a kind of revival of the spirit, a burst of inspiration as it were, as though I had only just met and talked personally with that great revolutionary democrat. Now, on board the *Kent*, I was most of all carried away by those chapters in Herzen's memoirs where he described London in the middle of last century and the people whom he met there. As I read, I thought: 'How simple the world was in Herzen's time, compared with ours! How uncomplex were the problems which agitated him! How modest was the scale of events at that time! . . .

How different in our day! And I began turning over and over again in my mind what was happening on our planet. And particularly I thought about what was to happen in Moscow in a few days' time.

For various small services I had attached to me one of the sailors. He was a tall, young and good-natured lad, very sociable and cheerful. Every morning he brought my breakfast, and told me the latest news received by radio or of events among the 800 of the warship's crew. I was always glad of his coming, and every time we talked on various current topics. The sailor was very interested in our country, and I had to reply to dozens of his questions, some of which astonished me by their naïveté and even stupidity. But such was his crying ignorance of everything concerning the Soviet Union—an ignorance in which the ruling circles of Britain had striven for a quarter of a century to keep the masses of the people in their country, and particularly its armed forces. Early in the morning on 11 December my attendant arrived worried and downcast. Handing me my breakfast he said gloomily:

'There's been a great misfortune.'

'What has happened?' I cried, fearing to hear of something unpleasant from the Moscow front.

'The Japanese in Malaya have sunk two of our big warships, the *Prince of Wales* and the *Repulse*. It's a great loss for Britain.'

And then the sailor told me some of the details: the two warships had attacked Japanese transports carrying troops and armaments; Japanese planes had attacked the British ships with many aerial torpedoes; the vessels were badly damaged, overturned and sank; the British had lost many men, among them also Admiral Phillips, in command of the squadron.

Admiral Phillips? . . . I could not help remembering how four years ago I had negotiated with him in London about the limitation of naval armaments. He had made on me the impression of an intelligent, businesslike and politically well-read person. And now he had perished.

At times, when I was very tired of sitting in my state room I went out on deck, clothed in my yellow coat and flying boots. I found a place to sit down sheltered from the wind, and became all ears and eyes. It was a dark and demonic picture: black sea, black sky, stormy waves, a pillar of ice which had grown up on the forepart of the ship, and somewhere below that unceasing steady sound of the engines, monotonously shaking the vessel. Often it seemed as though in the profound darkness of the Polar night, between the darkling sky and the darkling sea, an enchanted darkened ship was hurrying into the unknown...

And then I could not help rembering that exactly twenty-five years ago, in 1916, on this same journey Lord Kitchener, the British War Minister had been lost without trace. It is thought that the warship on which he was travelling struck a mine and sank with all on board. But in reality one cannot be sure of this, since no one was saved. I turned over in my mind the imaginary details of this mysterious drama of the sea and thought:

'Such things don't happen twice in history . . . We are threatened with quite other dangers.'

On 12 December we arrived at last at Murmansk. A thick covering of fog hung over the sea, at which we rejoiced: it concealed the *Kent* from the German air force, which was disposed hard by, not far from Murmansk, on the other side of the front. A tug came out to sea to meet us, and the Soviet pilot went up on board the cruiser. Then the tug turned and moved ahead slowly, clearing a path for entry into Kola Bay. The *Kent* carefully followed the tug. Three hours later the cruiser dropped anchor in the roadstead opposite Murmansk. Eden was welcomed in friendly fashion by the local authorities, civil and military. There were also representatives of the People's Commissariat for Foreign Affairs who had flown in specially from Moscow: F. F. Molochkov, head of the Protocol Department, and F. T. Gusev, head of the Second European Department (in whose competence Britain fell).

It was decided at once that Eden's whole group should remain for the moment on the cruiser, while I would go on shore to take part in the discussion of all the details of the next stage of the journey. Then there took place a 'council of war', in which there took part comrade Starostin, secretary of the Murmansk Regional Committee of the Party, General Panin who commanded the Murmansk front, Admiral Golovko, commander of the Murmansk flotilla, and several other responsible people. The question was, whether Eden should proceed to Moscow by air or by rail? Both means were at our service (I had asked while still in London that by the time we arrived at Murmansk both means of transport should be ready) but each of these means had its plusses and its minusses.

By air the journey was very much shorter. But in the first place, the planes sent from Moscow were not heated (which in the conditions of the bitter winter of 1941–2 was of great importance), and secondly—which had even greater weight—the planes would have to travel for several hundred kilometres without any cover from fighters. The air line from Murmansk went through Archangel. Murmansk could give cover for the first part of the journey, Archangel might send out cover for its latter part (the radius of operation of fighter planes at that time was comparatively limited): but between these two zones of comparative safety there lay a fairly wide stretch over which planes had to travel without any protection. After weighing up all these circumstances, our 'council of war' rejected the air route.

And so our orientation necessarily was on the railway. This would take longer, but it was more reliable. However, here too there was one complication. Somewhat to the south of Kandalaksha there is a small station with the Finnish name of Louhi, which means 'witch'. The front at this point ran only twelve to fifteen miles from the railway line, and Louhi station itself was fairly often subjected to German air raids. After a lively discussion we came to the conclusion that we should pass through this area by night, and that for this one night the maximum of armed forces should be concentrated there to meet any eventuality. The departure from Murmansk was fixed for the following day, 13 December.

After the 'council of war' I returned to the cruiser and, without going into detail (in particular, saying nothing about Louhi), I told Eden about the decisions we had taken. Eden replied:

'Let it be as you say: you know local conditions best.'

I spent the night of 12–13 December on shore, and late in the evening had a long and interesting talk with the local comrades. I questioned them about the front, the rear, the mood of the people, while they asked me about the situation in Britain, the purpose of Eden's visit, Churchill's views, and most of all about when would the second front be opened at last?

The next morning there came a communiqué which aroused tremendous excitement in everybody. It announced the defeat of the Germans near Moscow. All went about as though they had had a birthday, and were shaking hands with each other and crying in delight: 'Now that's something!' I went on board the cruiser and told Eden of the pleasant news. He already knew something about it from the British broadcasts, but the details I brought had a powerful effect on him too.

'That's marvellous!' he said. 'For the first time the Germans have suffered a reverse!'

Then we went on shore, and together with Eden drove round the whole city, which was sprinkled with snow and slightly wrapped in mist. Eden stood for a long time on one hillock from which there was a broad view of the whole of Murmansk, of Kola Bay, of a chain of hills covered with snow, and said:

'Nature is severe here! But it has its beauty.'

During the day there was a parade of troops of the local garrison. The Red soldiers, in their warm caps and substantial greatcoats, looked very well and made a favourable impression on Eden. He said with a smile:

'Now I can see for myself what an important weapon the greatcoat is at the Soviet front. Luckily the Germans have very few of them.'

And then, pointing to the Soviet and British flags, which were being held high by two tall Red soldiers—they were so sharply defined against the background of dazzling white snow—Eden added:

'That is a symbol. In it lies the hope of final victory over Hitler.'

Our train, seen off by all the local authorities, moved off from the platform at about 5 p.m. It was a very imposing armada. In the middle was an armoured saloon car, accommodating Eden and his suite. Next to it was an international sleeping car, in which I, Molochkov, Gusev and some other Soviet comrades were travelling. Immediately after the engine came, in two carriages, an armed guard with rifles and machine guns. At the back of the train were two large goods platforms, on which anti-aircraft guns had been placed, with several gunners in enormous fur coats. In front of the train, a certain distance away, there went a railway engine testing the security of the line.

It was already twilight when we set off. In addition snow was falling—not very thickly, but sufficiently to make it 'non-flying' weather. This we sincerely welcomed. Our only desire was that the snow should continue all night, particularly in the hours when we should be passing Louhi. Of course I did not tell Eden anything of our worries and alarms, but was very disturbed myself. The British were pleased with the comfortable accommodation and good supper, felt themselves at ease and went to bed early. I could not sleep and decided to sit up until Louhi. The train went on at a smooth pace, snow was falling, there was profound darkness. We passed by Olenya station without incident, passed Kandalaksha, passed a few more small stations: everything was peaceful and the weather continued to favour us. At about 1 a.m. we arrived at last at Louhi. I went out on to the platform and . . . was horror-struck: the snow had stopped, the sky was clear, and a glorious Aurora Borealis was glittering and playing in fire. It was light as day. Nature seemed to be laughing at us. The train commandant told me that according to plan we were to stay twenty minutes at Louhi. I demanded that the train should set off immediately. The station master came running up and began demonstrating that for technical reasons this was impossible. I remained inflexible, however. Seven minutes later the train moved off. I went into my compartment and began tensely waiting: until Louhi, bathed in light, was left behind us, until the danger zone was passed, until the train was a sufficient distance from the front. Only at three o'clock, when nothing threatened our precious 'cargo' any longer, I calmed down at last and fell asleep.

The rest of the journey to Moscow passed without any complications. From Belomorsk we turned into a recently built branch line connecting the Murmansk railway with the Archangel-Vologda-Moscow line. Then we turned southward along the latter and began rapidly approaching the capital. Somewhere near Vologda we met a special train in which the British Ambassador in the USSR was travelling to meet Eden. Cripps transferred to the Foreign Secretary's carriage and travelled back with us to Moscow. The frosts throughout our journey were terrible: the sky was blue and the sun vivid, but on the earth everything was gripped in a cruel cold. Eden several times went out at the stopping-places, and learned about the Russian winter in practice. Strolling along the train with me, he said, pointing to the gunners accompanying the anti-aircraft installations on open platforms:

'How can your people stand such cold?'

'Our people are accustomed to severe winters,' I said. 'Besides these artillery men are suitably dressed.'

Eden shrugged his shoulders, and added a moment later:

'Well, the Germans are not used to such frosts.'

On 15 December, late in the evening, our train arrived in Moscow at last. It was powdered with snow, and long icicles hung down from the roofs of the carriages. At that time there was a strict black-out in the capital because of the danger of German raids. It was plunged in darkness. But as an exception, on the occasion of Eden's arrival, the terminus was lit up for 15 minutes. People's Commissar for Foreign Affairs Molotov met Eden, and told his guest immediately that just today the Red Army had driven the Germans out of Klin. Other official persons were also present.

When the members of the British delegation, in their fur caps and coats, left their carriages and, mixing with the Soviet reception party, walked along the platform in the light of the suddenly lit-up lamps, when clouds of steam and smoke from the engine were cloaking both the people and the arches of the station high above them, it seemed to me for a moment that all this was not the harsh reality of the second world war, but a spectral picture out of some sinister fairy tale . . .

A moment later, the lights suddenly went out. We came out on to the square in front of the station and, now in complete darkness, began to take our places in the cars which were waiting. The British went to the 'National', which had been allotted to them as their residence, while I went off to the 'Moskva' hotel.

7

Moscow Negotiations

THE negotiations began the day after Eden's arrival in Moscow, on 16 December. They took place in the Kremlin. Thus Churchill's doubts about the place where they would be held were dissipated by the facts. The USSR was represented by Stalin and Molotov, and I was also present, with the obligations in addition of an interpreter. Britain was represented by Eden and Cadogan, and Cripps was also present, taking notes. From time to time General Nye appeared.

Before the meeting opened, Stalin took out of his pocket our draft proposals and asked me:

'What do you think, will the British accept this?'

I ran rapidly through a few typed pages. They contained the drafts of two treaties which the USSR would like to conclude with Britain. The first treaty provided for mutual assistance of the two States, both during the war and after its conclusion; it was to replace the Pact of Mutual Assistance of 12 July 1941, the validity of which extended only to the period of the war. The second treaty indicated the post-war organisation of peace. In the main, it provided for the restoration of Yugoslavia, Austria, Czechoslovakia and Greece in their pre-war frontiers, and also the transfer to Poland of East Prussia and the separation of the Rhineland from Prussia. The treaty furthermore recognised the 1941 frontiers of the USSR (i.e. including in it Estonia, Latvia, Lithuania, Western Ukraine and Western Byelorussia), and the right of Britain to have bases necessary for her security in France, Belgium, Holland, Denmark and Norway.

Having read through the documents, I replied to Stalin:

'I think these drafts can serve as a basis for negotiations with the British. Probably, there will be objections and amendments on their part to some of the clauses, but it will not be particularly difficult to come to an agreement.'

My forecast was justified at the very first session. After hearing our proposals, Eden said that on the whole they seemed to him acceptable, but that he reserved the right to make certain changes and modifications in them.

At the same session there was a general exchange of opinion on the question of reparations, and of the possibility of creating after the war something like a pact of military mutual assistance between all the Powers standing for peace: and it was clear that here too agreement between the USSR and Britain was quite possible.

I noted with satisfaction that there seemed to be no serious differences between the two sides, and that consequently the signature, or at least the initialling, of both treaties was possible. However, somewhere in the depths of my consciousness there was worrying doubt: could everything really pass so smoothly and satisfactorily?

My doubts were very soon confirmed. When after an interval the second session began, Stalin suddenly took a small sheet of paper from his pocket and, turning to Eden, said:

'I suppose you will not object if we add a small protocol to our agreement on post-war reconstruction.'

For me this was a complete surprise. Stalin had not shown me the draft protocol before the session, and did not even warn me that such a document was possible. I rapidly ran through the paper lying before me. It was brief, and provided for the immediate recognition by Britain of the Soviet frontiers of 1941.

I knew that the British were not inclined to adopt any decision on future frontiers until the end of the war. If it had been a question only of the British, there might still have been some hope of persuading them somehow. What was worse was that Roosevelt had secured from the British a firm promise not to do anything of the kind without a preliminary agreement with the USA. But the Americans at that time did not recognise the Soviet frontiers of 1941, and particularly did not recognise the entry of the Baltic States into the USSR. In such conditions the whole affair of the protocol was quite hopeless. Six months later Stalin himself was convinced of this, and the twenty-year Treaty between the USSR and Britain for alliance, collaboration, etc., signed on 26 May 1942 in London, did not contain recognition of the Soviet frontiers of 1941. The protocol presented by Stalin in the December negotiations could serve only as an apple of discord between Britain and the USSR. Yet we were extremely interested in the closest possible collaboration with Great Britain. After all, at that moment vast Soviet territories were occupied by the enemy, Leningrad was blockaded and the Germans were close to Moscow; although the Soviet troops had just hurled them back from the capital, it was still a very long way to victory over Hitlerite Germany. What was the point of creating friction between the two Governments, moreover on questions which had no immediate practical importance?

As soon as Eden had read the text of the protocol, he replied at once that the British Government could not at present sign it, and explained the reasons in detail, specially underlining the position of the USA on the question of frontiers.

Stalin began objecting, and tried to convince the British Foreign Secretary, but in vain. This badly spoiled the atmosphere of the negotiations, and both sides left the meeting in low spirits.

On 18 December there was a third session, at which the discussion continued on the question of the treaties and the protocol. The British gave us to understand that they were ready to carry on the negotiations, and hoped that an agreement would be possible on the draft treaties, but on the question of the protocol no change in their attitude could be seen. In his turn, Stalin declared that without the protocol the treaties could not be signed. It was a blind alley from which no direct issue could be seen. The only thing in which Stalin succeeded was to secure a promise from Eden that the disputed questions would be laid before the British Cabinet for examination, and also before the Governments of the British Dominions. He did not exclude either the possibility of consultation with the Government of the USA.

After the third meeting it became clear that there could be no agreement of the two sides in Moscow: but neither the USSR nor Britain were interested in revealing to Hitler and Mussolini the differences existing between them. It was therefore decided to publish such a communiqué on Eden's visit as could provide no satisfaction to the enemy. The drafting of the communiqué was assigned to me. When I had finished the work, I showed my draft to Stalin. He approved it.

Then I showed the draft to Eden, and it received his approval. He even added: 'The communiqué is better than I hoped.'

In this way both sides were agreed on the text. But its publication, naturally, had to be postponed until the British delegation had got home. In wartime conditions it was impossible to do otherwise. In fact, the communiqué appeared in the Soviet and British press on 29 December 1941, the very day that, as I shall describe later, the *Kent* cast anchor at Greenock, on the Scottish coast.

The following are the most essential passages in the communiqué.

At the very beginning, after enumerating the persons who had taken part in the Moscow negotiations, it stated that between the two sides there had taken place 'an exhaustive exchange of views on questions relating to the conduct of the war and the post-war organisation of peace and security in Europe'; after which there followed:

'The conversations, which took place in a friendly atmosphere, established the identity of views of both parties on questions relating to the conduct of the war, and especially with regard to the necessity for the utter defeat of Hitlerite Germany and the adoption thereafter of measures to render completely impossible any repetition of German aggression in future. The exchange of views on questions relating to post-war organisation of peace and security provided much important and useful material, which will facilitate a future elaboration of concrete proposals on this subject. Both parties are convinced that the Moscow conversations constitute a new and important forward step towards the further rapprochement of the USSR and Great Britain.'

As we see, the communiqué provided no ammunition for the Hitlerites, and at the same time fully corresponded to the truth: there could after all be not the slightest doubt that the exchange of opinions between the two sides on questions of the post-war organisation of peace and security, in spite of the differences which had been revealed, really did provide much important and useful material, which would in the future facilitate the elaboration of proposals acceptable to the two sides.

At one of the sessions Eden asked Stalin for the opportunity to visit the front. Stalin agreed, and recommended Eden to visit the Klin district, where battles were still going on with the retreating German troops. On 19 December this visit took place. Eden and the persons accompanying him took part, while on the Soviet side there were the Head of the Protocol Department of the People's Commissariat for Foreign Affairs, F. F. Molochkov whom I have already mentioned, and myself.

When our cars, accompanied by the necessary escort, left Moscow in the morning, a bright but cold winter sun stood high in the sky. There was a sharp frost. Towards the end of the short December day, the weather grew worse, and there was a slight ground wind. However, we had enough time to see the harsh picture of the front by daylight, at a distance of some fifty miles from the capital.

First of all it was signalised by the villages burned by the Germans in their retreat. It was a frightening spectacle. Not a single house, not a shed or a fence! A plain covered with snow, and strung out along it, as though on a death parade, long rows of village stoves and chimneys which had escaped the fire. One could not help wondering what had happened to those who had quite lately been living in these houses which had ceased to exist? Had they perished, or fled? And if they had fled, what were they doing now? Where had they found refuge and food? . . .

We saw many bodies lying on the road, in ditches, in the fields powdered with snow, to the right and to the left. Most were Germans in their greenish-blue uniform, but there were also Red Army men in their long grey greatcoats. The corpses were already frozen stiff, often in the most strange and incomprehensible poses: some with arms flung apart, some on all fours, some standing up to their waist in snow.

Here too, on the road and aside from it, lay a vast number of overturned lorries, smashed tanks, broken guns, scattered automatic weapons, loops of telephone wire and every other kind of remains of the most varied forms of equipment. I thought: 'It is as though the devil had been playing here with his infernal toys . . .'

Finally we reached Klin. The town had suffered comparatively little, as the Germans had had to evacuate it too hastily, without having time for arson and destruction. But the house where the great composer Peter Tchaikovsky had lived—a sacred place for any Soviet person—was in a terrible condition. The house itself had survived, but inside everything had been turned upside down, broken and befouled. One of the rooms on the first floor had been turned into a toilet. In other rooms there were scattered on the floor heaps of half-burned books, pieces of wood, sheets of torn up music-paper. The German fascists had evidently paid tribute in their own way to one of the greatest geniuses in the musical history of mankind. Eden and I slowly walked from room to room, noticing at every step the traces of the animal barbarism of the Hitlerite bandits. Finally, Eden could not restrain himself and said, with an expression of disgust on his face:

'This is what we could have expected if the Germans had landed in our islands . . . They are the real dregs of humanity.'

Then we drove round the whole town and wanted to move on further towards the front line: but General Zakhvatayev, chief of staff of the Klin front, who was accompanying us, now intervened and protested vigorously against our intention. He said that remnants of the broken German units were hiding in the neighbouring woods, and from time to time were making unexpected sallies. The General did not think it possible to subject the British Foreign Secretary to such a risk. Willy-nilly we had to submit and turn back. Here there suddenly appeared F. F. Molochkov, and rapidly led us to a fairly large but much damaged village house, in which he hospitably offered everyone a 'campaign lunch'. The freezing air was blowing through the broken windows, but the lunch proved very appetising. Eden, on behalf of all his British colleagues, heartily thanked F. F. Molochkov for his 'magic carpet' and, at the same time, gave his meed of praise to the renowned 'Russian hospitality'.

Then Eden expressed a wish to see some German prisoners. From some neighbouring half-shattered hut six of them, just captured in battle, were brought in. Their appearance was very pitiable: in crumpled greenish-blue greatcoats without lining, with women's kerchiefs on their heads and feet bound up in rags of some kind, they were shivering with cold and fear. Eden put several questions to them through his interpreter: where did they come from, had they been fighting long, in what battles they had taken part and so forth. But he was most interested in watching them and observing their behaviour. The prisoners did not resemble at all the 'heroes' which the Hitlerites often represented themselves to be when falling into the hands of the Red Army in the summer of 1941. Now, in December, they had lost all their glitter. The six of them stood, shifting from foot to foot, and intensively assured us that they, as a matter of fact, were not responsible for anything, that they had all been made to fight. One even cried:

'Hitler kaput!'

While we were returning to Moscow in the evening, Eden said:

'Now I have seen with my own eyes how the German army can suffer defeat, retreat and flee . . . The myth about the invincibility of the Germans has been exploded . . . This will be of tremendous importance for the psychology of all the peoples of Europe and for the whole future of the war.'

He was silent a little and then added:

'And as for those poor devils whom we saw'—Eden had in mind not only the prisoners but the German soldiers generally—'I don't envy them: in such light clothing in the Russian frost . . . brr! . . . Yes, I can see very well now, that a warm coat on the Eastern front is a serious weapon of war.'

Next day Stalin gave a big dinner at the Kremlin Palace in honour of Eden. At the long table, in addition to the British delegation, there sat members of the Political Bureau, People's Commissars and generals. Stalin was in the chairman's seat, with Eden on his right: I sat next to Eden, and interpreted for them both. Stalin gave the main toast in honour of the British Foreign Secretary. At the end of the dinner Eden replied with a toast to his hosts.

At the very beginning of the dinner there was a strange incident. On the table before Eden, among the wines, stood a large bottle of pepper-brandy. The yellowish colour of the liquid somewhat recalled Scotch whisky. Eden was interested in the bottle, and asked Stalin: 'What is that? I haven't seen such a Russian drink before.'

Stalin smiled, and with a sly glance replied:

'This is our Russian whisky.'

'Oh, I should like to try it,' Eden said.

'Please.'

Stalin took the bottle and poured Eden a large glass.

Suspecting nothing, Eden raised the glass and took a large mouthful. Good heavens, what happened to him! The pepper-brandy at once burned his mouth, he grew terribly red, choked with his eyes nearly bursting from their orbits. When Eden had caught his breath again a little and was restored, Stalin moralisingly remarked:

'Only a strong people can take such a drink. Hitler is beginning to feel this.'

After dinner, as was usual at Stalin's banquets, there was a film show with intervals in the neighbouring room, and it continued until late in the night.

In spite of the incident with the pepper-brandy, Eden was very pleased with the evening with Stalin. He thought it a symptom that the differences which had made their appearance during the negotiations would not spoil the friendly atmosphere between the two countries. And the next day we were able to raise the spirits of the British Foreign Secretary still higher.

The ever-tireless F. F. Molochkov invited the British delegation to the ballet, which was then appearing at the subsidiary of the Bolshoi. Neither Semyonova nor Ulanova was there, as they had been evacuated; but nevertheless the ballet, at which Eden was present, was a very good one, and made a deep impression on the British. Sitting by my side, Eden even said.

'Such a ballet, in Moscow now, when the front is only some sixty miles away, simply inspires one. It creates the hope—no, more, the confidence—that you will be able to withstand this terrible trial.'

These words of Eden's are well echoed in the lines of Churchill's war memoirs which relate precisely to the period of the Moscow negotiations:

'In the six months' campaign the Germans had achieved formidable results and had inflicted losses on their enemy which no other nation could have survived. But the three main objectives which they had sought, Moscow, Leningrad, the lower Don, were still firmly in Russian hands. The Caucasus, the Volga and Archangel were still far away. The Russian Army, far from being beaten, was fighting better than ever, and would certainly grow in strength in the coming year. The winter had fallen. The long war was certain. All the anti-Nazi nations, great and small, rejoiced to see the first failure of a German Blitzkrieg.'[1]

During those few hours which I had free from the negotiations and from various diplomatic functions, I sought to look more closely at the stern face of wartime Moscow, and to meet comrades and friends.

Moscow in December 1941 was very different from that variegated, noisy, overcrowded and somewhat careless Moscow which I had known in the pre-war years. Everything now looked

1. *The Second World War*, Vol. III, p. 476.

otherwise. There were few people in the streets, and those who showed themselves hurried along, obviously preoccupied. You could not hear the laughter so usual in the city—all faces were serious, even grim, with tightly closed lips. Every now and then there passed by military units, or columns of mobilised civilians, shouldering spades. On many squares and cross-roads there were dark and sinister looking anti-tank barriers and barricades. Huge accumulations of snow lay both on roadways and pavements. Windows of houses were often blown out, and temporarily covered with planks or plywood. At night there was utter-darkness: the universal blackout was very strictly applied. All the talk turned on the war, the heavy battles, the air raids, the food difficulties, the cold apartments, the interruptions in city transport. But nowhere was there panic or defeatism. Moscow in December resembled a man who had lost his fat, who had grown thin, but had preserved his steel muscles and unbending will.

I saw some old friends working in various spheres of Soviet life—economic, party, diplomatic or cultural—and everywhere felt the resolution to defend Moscow to the end, and some profound internal confidence that in the long run, however great the losses and sufferings, we should be victorious. This greatly inspired me.

I had interesting conversations also with leading personalities of the Soviet State. I talked long with K. E. Voroshilov on the course and prospects of the war and with A. I. Mikoyan on war-time economic relations between the USSR and Britain, and on how to adapt the Soviet Trade Delegation in London to the new conditions.

I had a very interesting meeting with N. G. Kuznetsov, People's Commissar for the Navy. I mentioned earlier that at the beginning of July 1941 a military and naval Mission of the USSR had arrived in Britain. At that time it was difficult to say how events would develop; in particular it was not clear how long the Mission would have to stay in London. In such circumstances it was natural that the members of the Mission had come without their families. But by December 1941 much had become clearer. It was now obvious that the war would be a very long one, that our military and naval Mission would work in London for a long time and that all its members would have to stay there for long. Thereupon there arose quite legitimately the question of bringing their families over. The attempts of the members to settle this question themselves through departmental channels were unsuccessful. In view of this I decided, when leaving for Moscow with Eden, personally to raise the question in the appropriate quarters, and particularly with N. G. Kuznetsov, on whom the transport of the families to England depended in the first instance. At the People's Commissariat for Foreign Affairs they tried to dissuade me from such a step, prophesying that it would be fruitless. And about N. G. Kuznetsov they said frankly: 'He's a harsh man, reckons very little with the feelings of his subordinates, won't give his agreement to the families leaving or to their being transported by sea—why ask for a direct refusal?' However, I did not listen to them, had a talk on the question at the Central Committee of the Party and then went to see Kuznetsov. I set forth the essence of the question and energetically supported the request of the members of the Mission, using various arguments, both human and practical. What was my surprise and pleasant disillusionment when he immediately agreed with me, and promised at once to take steps for the dispatch of the families to London! He carried out his promise, and in 1942 a long chain of wives and children began to travel from the USSR to Britain, overcoming many difficulties, dangerous adventures and even really risking their lives. And for me personally this first meeting with N. G. Kuznetsov was the beginning of a friendship which grew stronger in the subsequent years.

On one occasion, when preparations were being made for the next meeting of the two delegations, I was in Molotov's study, together with Stalin. Molotov was sitting at his desk, while Stalin paced from one end of the study to the other, expressing his views and giving instructions. When all the preparatory work was complete, I asked Stalin:

'Can one consider that the main lines of strategy in our war and in the war of 1812 have been approximately identical, at least if one takes the events of this war during the first half-year?'

Stalin walked from end to end of the study once more, and then replied:

'Not quite. Kutuzov's retreat was a passive retreat, up to Borodino he nowhere offered any serious resistance to Napoleon. Our retreat is an active defence, we are trying to hold up the enemy at every possible barrier, inflict a blow on him and by a large number of such blows to exhaust him. What was common to the two retreats was that they were not planned beforehand, but forced retreats.'

Encouraged by Stalin's readiness to talk on more general themes, I continued:

'If you will allow me, I would like to put one further question. In your speech in October you said that not later than a year from now Hitlerite Germany must suffer collapse. What was that prognosis based on?'

My question evidently did not please Stalin, and he tried to wave it aside: 'Well, I said that, what of it?'

'You're not the kind of man to throw away your words lightly,' I objected. 'Probably you had sufficient grounds—military, political, economic—for such a statement.'

Stalin said with an irritated gesture: 'Well, I had to raise the spirits of our people somehow, to cheer them up: so I said that not later than in twelve months the enemy would be defeated.'

Then Stalin turned and went out of the room.

However, the most interesting meeting which left a vivid mark on my memory was with M. I. Kalinin. I was very fond of Mikhail Ivanovich. The relations between us were good, and I took advantage of a free moment to visit him, all the more because he lived close by in the Kremlin. When I called at Kalinin's apartment, it was evening, and he was sitting alone drinking tea. He was very glad of my coming, poured me out a glass of tea and began asking me in detail about the progress of the war in the West, opinion in Britain, Churchill and the prospects of a second front. I willingly told Mikhail Ivanovich all I knew about the questions which interested him, but told him only what was really the case. I never permitted myself any deliberately favourable colouring of events. Therefore I could say nothing encouraging about the early prospects of a second front. Mikhail Ivanovich listened attentively, at times put supplementary questions, but went on listening.

Then it was my turn to ask Kalinin about our internal and military affairs. He also replied willingly to my questions, but that evening was very depressed by news just received that, in the battles near Moscow, General Dovator, one of our best cavalry commanders, had been killed.

I listened to him, looked at him and a particular kind of deep feeling of pride and affection rose in me. Here before me was this man, no longer young, greying considerably, in a simple Russian shirt, unbuttoned at the neck . . . A wise and noble person, with a great store of sagacity born of experience in life and statesmanship . . . In his hand he held the cigarette he had just rolled himself, and was about to light it with a match . . . All his appearance showed him the most ordinary Russian workman who had come from the peasantry . . . And here was this man the President of a vast State, the official head of one of the greatest Powers in the world . . . Where, in what other country was anything like this possible? Nowhere, nowhere else!

And once again the conclusion arose in my mind: no, no one will be able to conquer such a country. Such a country will withstand every trial, and will defeat German Fascism!

I went away from Kalinin with a tremendous charge of inspiration, encouragement, enthusiasm, which was so valuable to me in the further course of the war.

The British delegation left Moscow on the evening of 22 December, after staying exactly a week in our capital. The return journey from Moscow to Murmansk went off quite smoothly. Even Louhi did not cause us any trouble: when we arrived at that unfortunate station this time, the sky was not lit up with the Aurora Borealis. On 24 December our train arrived at Murmansk, and the British delegation immediately embarked on the cruiser *Kent* which had been waiting for it: I followed the delegation's example. At depth of night on 25 December the British warship weighed anchor and went out into open sea. The whole way from the shores of the USSR to those of Scotland took up a little longer than four days, just as on the first occasion. But this time we were moving from north to south, and gradually the Arctic darkness gave way more and more to light or, more exactly, half-light, because in December the sun does not rise very high in these latitudes. This was pleasant. But what was quite unpleasant was that there was a raging storm, which tossed about our heavy cruiser like a chip of wood. I am only an average 'seaman'. 'Fresh' weather does not upset me, but I can't easily bear a storm. I lay almost the whole of the return journey in my 'Admiral's cabin', with a heavy head and an unpleasant taste in my mouth. Only when the *Kent* was already in Scottish waters did the storm subside, and I began to come out on deck. On the night of 29 December we arrived at Greenock, near Glasgow, and at once boarded the special train which was waiting. On 30 December we were in London.

On the way from Greenock to the capital Eden and I talked a great deal, summing up the results of the Moscow visit. Both of us came to the conclusion that, in spite of the differences which had shown themselves, its significance was positive. First of all, each side now better knew the position of the other on a number of important questions, which might facilitate for the future an agreed strategy and policy. Secondly—and this was not less important—Eden and his British colleagues, after visiting the USSR and making direct contact with Soviet reality, better understood the roots of our vitality and were more firmly convinced of our readiness and capacity to carry on the war against Hitlerite Germany to the very end.

On New Year's Eve, at the request of the BBC, I made a small speech on the radio, in which I said, amongst other things, the following:

'The future is wrapped in mist. Any prophecy is guesswork. And yet the events of the year ending today give some indication of the way things will go in the coming year 1942. The war has really become a world war. All continents have been dragged into it. Much more definite has become the watershed between the two camps—the camp of freedom, uniting the democratic and freedom-loving countries, and the camp of oppression and slavery, which concentrates the blackest forces of reaction which have ever existed in the history of mankind. The main enemy of the nations is Hitlerite Germany. The main sector of the world front of struggle is my country. The fundamental embodiment of the malignant forces which are now torturing the whole of the human race is the German army; its most important weapon, by the side of its tanks and planes, up till now has been the myth of its invincibility. But now, at the very end of 1941, this myth has been exposed on the fields of battle near Moscow and Leningrad, near Rostov and in the Crimea, and also in Libya.'

After briefly recounting my impressions of what I had seen at the front near Klin, I ended my speech with these words:

'What has happened in recent months on our front is a turning-point in the course of the German-Soviet war and even in the course of the whole war in its entirety. We should not give way to excessive optimism. We must look the truth straight in the eyes. Ahead we have still many difficulties. The road to victory will still be long and painful . . . And nevertheless, on the threshold of the New Year, a firm hope is rising in the hearts of all freedom-loving peoples that the hour is approaching when Hitlerite Germany will lie in ruins.'

Part Four

*

The Struggle for The Second Front

I

The Military and Political Situation

ALTHOUGH, as can be seen from the foregoing, the problem of a second front arose from the very first day of the attack by Hitlerite Germany on the USSR, and although this problem was already the subject of serious conversations between Moscow and London in 1941, it became specially acute in 1942. There were two main reasons for this.

The first reason was that, on 22 June 1941 and during the next five-and-a-half months, Britain was fighting alone against Germany in the West. In these circumstances Churchill's assurances that it was beyond the power of the British Government to open a second front in France immediately, assurances with which he replied more than once to the *démarches* made by Moscow, aroused a mixed reaction on the Soviet side: we both believed it and did not believe it. Such a mood on the Soviet side naturally did not create favourable conditions for putting the question of a second front unconditionally. But when in December 1941 Japan attacked Pearl Harbour and the USA were drawn into the war, the position changed sharply. Now there were two Great Powers fighting Germany in the West, and it became quite clear that they now had sufficient strength and resources to create a second front in France. All the pretexts about the physical impossibility of such an operation could be discounted.

The second reason was that the latter half of 1941 was occupied with large-scale and complex negotiations between the USSR and the Anglo-Americans on the question of war supplies and war policy. On 12 July 1941 there had been signed in Moscow the Pact of Mutual Military Assistance between Britain and the

Soviet Union. At the very end of July Harry Hopkins had paid his visit to Moscow, one fraught with great political and military-economic consequences. In the middle of August, at the Atlantic Conference, Roosevelt and Churchill decided to afford to the Soviet Union the maximum aid in war supplies. On 5 September the British Government made it possible for the Soviet Government to acquire such supplies by means of Lend-Lease. On 29 December there opened in Moscow the conference of representatives of the USSR, USA and Britain, at which the question of supplies to the USSR for the whole period of the war was settled, with not only Britain but the USA as well undertaking to do this by means of Lend-Lease. Then began the organisation of the transport of the supplies from the western countries to the USSR, which was no mean task in those conditions. Churchill, refusing the request of the Soviet side to organise a second front, sought to soften the blow by his readiness to meet it on a large scale in the sphere of supplies. He was supported by Roosevelt, who moreover, as the head of a still 'neutral' Power, evaded discussion of the problem of a second front.

All these circumstances had as their result that the attention of the Soviet Government in 1941 was concentrated mainly on questions of supplies for its war economy, all the more because as yet no way was visible for solving the problem of a second front in practice.

Only when the USA had entered the war, and the questions of supplies had been settled in the main, were conditions created for putting problems of a second front as the main point *on the agenda* (I emphasise, putting it on the agenda, because for its solution a very much longer period was still needed). This is why the next year and a half—1942 and the first half of 1943—during which I was still working in Britain as Ambassador of the USSR, were passed in acute struggle around this problem.

That does not mean, of course, that in the period mentioned relations between the USSR on one side and Britain and the USA on the other reduced themselves exclusively to negotiations about a second front. No, life is complex and does not permit such monism. Throughout 1942–3 there were in British-Soviet relations many other events, many other conversations on other themes, as I will describe later on. Nevertheless, *the main problem, dominating all other diplomatic questions in those days, was that of a second front.*

The December counter-offensive of the Soviet troops before Moscow played a most important part in the development of the second world war. It not only saved the Soviet capital from capture by the Hitlerites, which the Führer had confidently reckoned upon, but also was the first serious reverse of the German army. The 'blitzkrieg' was clearly not coming off. The Soviet Union, which for fully six months had been retreating and suffering defeats at the front, and which many Western 'experts' had already sentenced to death, suddenly revived quite unexpectedly for them, rose up and inflicted the first heavy blow which the enemy had suffered. At first the 'experts' lost their bearings, and tried to explain the German defeat by accidents: according to them, 'General Winter' had interfered (the winter really was very severe that year) and the Hitlerites had had to retreat temporarily in order to prepare better for a new offensive in the summer. They even put forward a 'theory' of their own: the winter was Russian, the summer German, i.e. the Russians had the military advantage in winter, and the Germans in summer. From this these immensely wise 'experts' drew the authoritative conclusion and prophecy that the Soviet successes before Moscow were a chance affair, and impermanent: and that with the coming of spring the Germans would take a cruel revenge and capture Moscow and Leningrad. After that, what would remain of Soviet resistance?...

However, all these bourgeois Cassandras were fated to endure a great disappointment. The battle before Moscow did not prove by any means a single or isolated operation. It was followed by the opening of a general counter-offensive of the Red Army, along an enormous front from Lake Ladoga to the Black Sea. The German High Command clearly was setting itself the task of retaining during the winter the positions it had seized before the Red Army's offensive, in order to make ready a new and, it thought, decisive blow in the spring. But its calculations were mistaken. Of course, the Soviet counter-offensive was not equally powerful and successful everywhere; of course, it had both successes and failures; of course, serious losses in men and arms befell not only the Germans but also the Red Army . . . Yet all the same, the Soviet command tore the initiative out of the hands of the Hitlerites and threw back the enemy lines from 100 to 350 kilometres westward. Unfortunately, the Red Army at that moment did not yet possess the necessary superiority in numbers, experience and technical equipment over the German. And therefore the winter counter-offensive of 1941–2 could not bring about the defeat of the enemy. The whole operation remained incomplete.

Nevertheless, the events I have described were of vast importance, not only purely military but also moral and political. They demonstrated for the first time the vulnerability of the Hitlerite army and the possibility of defeating it. They revealed for the first time before the whole of mankind that there was a country in the world, there was a Power in the world, which was capable of effectively resisting Fascism and even inflicting heavy blows upon it. This raised the spirit of all the peoples, both those already bearing the Hitlerite fetters and those who feared a similar fate. It was at the time the sole ray of light which had broken through the leaden clouds that covered the sky: for the situation on other fronts of the second world war in the winter of 1941–2 was still very little favourable for the anti-Fascist coalition.[1]

For in effect, British operations in North Africa during that period very much at first resembled marking time, and from the spring of 1942 were transformed into a systematic withdrawal under the pressure of the German and Italian troops headed by Rommel. The Fascist forces penetrated into the territory of Egypt and reached Mersa Matruh. The Anglo-German war at sea continued with unfailing intensity.[2] In February 1942 there was a big scandal: two large German warships, the *Scharnhorst* and the *Gneisenau*, which had been under repair at Brest, broke through the English Channel and the Straits of Dover and reached Germany. The British were amazed both at the uncommon audacity of the Germans and at the astounding impotence of their own defences, which had shouted so loudly about special vigilance along the southern shores of the country. The incident had serious political consequences, of which more later. Churchill had

1. I should, however, add here that in Britain, and particularly in the British working class, a deep impression of confidence and strength was left by the visit of a delegation of the Soviet trade unions, led by their secretary N. M. Shvernik (29 December 1941—4 February 1942). By arrangement with the General Council of the Trades Union Congress, the delegation divided into three groups, each of which went out to a series of industrial undertakings in the course of its stay. In all, some sixty large establishments of importance for Britain's war effort were visited in this way. At each, the Soviet trade unionists inspected production, chatted with workers and management, and spoke at mass meetings in the factories, shipyards, etc., describing what Soviet working men and women were doing in similar industries. Everywhere they were received with sympathy and real enthusiasm.

2. A table in Churchill's war memoirs shows that the losses of Britain and her Allies during the first half of 1942 were on the average about 700,000 tons a month (*The Second World War*, Vol. IV, p. 860).

to console himself only by the organisation of big air raids on Germany, and that only when weather permitted. In his message to Stalin on 12 March 1942 he wrote *inter alia*:

'Now that the season is improving we are resuming heavy air offensive both by day and night upon Germany.'[1] However, the records show that another six weeks were still required before Britain could send some really powerful air armadas (with a thousand bombers in each) over the Ruhr and the Rhineland.

Even worse were affairs in the Far East. Japan was advancing headlong, occupying country after country, island after island, city after city, without meeting any serious resistance anywhere. In January 1942 the Japanese occupied the Philippines and Malaya, in February Singapore, parts of Borneo and the island of Timor, in March the island of Java and Rangoon, capital of Burma, in April made an air raid on Ceylon and sank two British heavy cruisers and the aircraft carrier *Hermes*, in June landed on the Aleutian islands of Kiska and Attu. In brief, during the first five months after her entry into the war Japan became mistress of the situation in South-East Asia and in the waters of the Indian Ocean. The wave of Japanese aggression came close to the frontiers of India.

The USA, on whose shoulders fell the main struggle against Japan, could make at that time only the first steps in gathering its forces. In February American troops appeared in Australia and New Zealand. In March the American General Stilwell became Chief of Staff to Chiang Kai-Shek. In April General MacArthur was appointed Commander-in-Chief of all the armed forces of the Allies in the South-Western part of the Pacific. At the same time American troops arrived in India, and American aircraft for the first time bombed Tokyo, Kyoto, Nagoia, and other Japanese cities. Of course, the resources of the USA were enormous, and in good time, when they were mobilised, Japan might await heavy blows. But the road to such a moment still seemed endless, and many asked themselves, would that moment ever come?...

Yes, the military situation in the first half of 1942 seemed sufficiently gloomy for the Allies. Only on the Soviet front it seemed as though dawn was appearing: but people who had been so accustomed in the previous three years to the unbroken successes of the Fascists were afraid to believe in the approach of day before it actually appeared.

1. *Correspondence, etc.*, Vol. I, p. 40.

In my diary, for 15 February 1942, there is an entry which describes the political reflection in Britain of the military situation. I will quote some extracts from it.

'What is the reaction of Britain to the military successes of the USSR during the last ten weeks?

'In general, all are pleased, especially against the background of the reverses in Libya, Malaya and elsewhere. It is so pleasant to have good news, even if only from one front—the front of fronts! All are beginning to understand here more and more that it is on our front that the fate of the war is being decided, and from there salvation will come. The prestige of the Red Army has grown to a colossal extent. All speak of it with delight. The legend of German 'invincibility' has been broken. They hope that we shall soon break the ribs of the German army. Half-jokingly, half-seriously, some of my acquaintances here are asking: "Couldn't we get a couple of your generals on loan?" Cripps has raised the prestige of the "young" Soviet commanders very much. All are very grateful to us that during the last nine months there have been no German raids on Britain, and that the threat of a Hitlerite invasion has disappeared. Yes, the USSR at present is very popular here. This rebounds on my person too: during January I received 100 invitations to various social, diplomatic and Government receptions. I must look out not to be crushed in friendly embraces!

'Such is the picture: but what about its analysis?

'The masses of the people are very glad of our successes without any reservations. It is otherwise with the ruling class. In its breast there are now two souls, which one may call for the sake of brevity "Churchillite" and "Chamberlainite" (although Chamberlain himself is dead).

'The "Churchillite" soul argues approximately as follows. Germany has raised her hand against the British Empire and the world positions of Britain: consequently, she must be defeated. The Russians are beating the Germans, and maybe will defeat them. Very good. The Russians are doing the dirty work for the British. The British then, without great losses, will enter Berlin in a ceremonial parade. At the future peace conference Britain and the USA will constitute "a healthy counterpoise" to the Bolsheviks. Everything is turning out very well: we shall win victory at a cheap price. Let the Russians go on with their work.

'The "Chamberlainite" soul is already trembling with fear. What if the Russians get to Berlin first? What if they become too strong? What if the Red Army becomes master of the Continent? What if under the influence of Soviet successes Europe is Bolshevised? What if Moscow imposes a "Soviet peace" upon us? Who will be strong enough to prevent her?

'The Churchill group (Eden, Beaverbrook, Brendan Bracken, Cranborne and others) hate Germany too much not to be ready to go along with the Bolsheviks for the sake of defeating her. The group of Chamberlainites (Margesson, Kingsley Wood, Anderson and others) hate "Communism" too much not to be ready for a compromise with Germany, particularly Germany of the generals and landowners, for the sake of avoiding the "bolshevisation of Europe". The Labour leaders' attitude is indefinite: their spinelessness and enmity to the Communists are an influence here.

'So long as our successes are still not very large, the "Chamberlainites" are silent, while the "Churchillites" even praise us. But what will happen if the Red Army begins to approach Berlin, and moreover alone? . . . A nightmare! At the very thought, many representatives of the British ruling class (and not only the "Chamberlainites") break out in a cold sweat . . . I think that the moment may come when the British themselves, without any urging on our part, will rush to open a second front in order to prevent the occupation of Berlin by the Red Army alone.'

As will be seen from this quotation, even at that early period of the great Patriotic War I had no illusions as to the true inclinations and calculations of the British Government. What followed only confirmed the accuracy of my assessment of the situation. In particular, the Second Front in France was opened only when the British and the Americans found themselves faced with the real 'threat' that the Soviet armed forces would get to Berlin before they did.

The prevailing moods in Britain after our victory before Moscow made possible the successful completion of one admirable initiative of the British Communists. In 1939, even before the second world war, they had raised before the London County Council, in which there was a Labour majority, the question of putting up a memorial plaque on the house where Lenin lived in 1902–3 (30 Holford Square, Finsbury). At first, while negotiations were still going on for a pact of mutual assistance between the USSR, Britain and France against Hitlerite aggression, the Council displayed a certain willingness to satisfy the request of the

Communists. But when as a result of the stubborn sabotage by Chamberlain and Daladier the negotiations broke down, the Council hastened to put the question into cold storage. Now, at the beginning of 1942, the situation had changed completely, and the Communists managed to get a decision adopted that a memorial plaque should be put on the house in Holford Square. Unfortunately, by that time the house itself had been greatly damaged by German bombs: but half of its front façade still remained. It was to this fragment of a wall that the memorial plaque was fixed in the middle of March 1942. There were present at the opening representatives of the Municipal authorities as well as guests, among them Harry Pollitt, the leader of the British Communist Party. Speeches were made on both the British and Soviet sides. Opposite the house where Lenin had lived, there was put up in a small square a bust of Vladimir Ilyich, the work of a local sculptor. Fascist hooligans several times attempted to damage the bust and the plaque, but unsuccessfully. We Soviet people in London experienced a feeling of deep satisfaction that here too, in the very heart of capitalist Britain, there was a monument to our great leader. It was still a modest one, too modest for such a giant in human history, but its importance in principle was enormous.

I received on 14 March 1942 a message from Stalin to Churchill which quite unexpectedly had very important consequences. The message itself was brief, and contained nothing very special. Stalin thanked the British Prime Minister for the measures taken to ensure the deliveries of war material to the USSR and for reinforcement of the air bombardments of Germany, advised him of the necessity to exchange opinions as to the formulation regarding the frontiers of the USSR in the Anglo-Soviet treaty for the post-war organisation of the world which was being prepared (its discussion as we have seen was not completed during Eden's visit to Moscow in December 1941), and wrote:

'I feel entirely confident that the combined efforts of our troops, occasional setbacks notwithstanding, will culminate in crushing the common enemy, and that the year 1942 will see a decisive turn on the anti-Hitler front.'[1]

This was one more slightly veiled reminder of the necessity to open a second front in France. On this question, as we know, there had been going on for several months already between the

1. *Correspondence, etc.*, Vol. I, p. 41.

Soviet and British sides a prolonged and not quite friendly argument, which up till that time had not produced any practical results.

On receiving Stalin's message, I rang up Churchill at once. It turned out that he was not well, and was at Chequers, the out-of-town residence of British Prime Ministers. The secretary got in touch with Churchill, and half an hour later passed on to me the invitation to come and lunch with Churchill at Chequers on 16 March.

When at the appointed hour I arrived at Chequers, I was met by Eden who took me to the Prime Minister. The latter was in his usual 'siren suit' and at once sat me down at table on his right. Eden sat on the left. The three of us did our duty by the products of the British cuisine, and then I at once passed over Stalin's telegram. Churchill rapidly ran through it and then, shrugging his shoulders, said with a slight note of irritation:

'I don't see how 1942 can become a decisive year.'

Then followed a long lecture on Britain's incapacity in that year to fulfil our demands. I had heard the Premier's arguments already more than once, and from frqeuent repetition they had become a kind of hackneyed common-place, which sounded tedious and inconvincing. I began objecting, even with heat and some eloquence. Churchill clearly felt embarrassed, but still firmly defended his old position. Then I thought: 'These arguments about a second front lead nowhere. Would it not be better to try now, taking advantage of the Premier's embarrassment, to secure some real step on his part? Let it be much less than a second front, providing it eases our position in practice. But what step?' For an instant I was undecided, but then had a flash . . .

When leaving for Chequers, I had run through the Soviet communiqué just received, in which among other things it was stated that the Germans somewhere in the neighbourhood of Borisov had made use of gas . . . 'That's it!' I said to myself. And turning to Churchill I remarked:

'You say, Mr. Churchill, that you're not strong enough to create a second front in France, even in spite of America's entry into the war . . . Don't let's go on arguing about that . . . But if you can't help us by creating a second front, give us immediate and practical help in another way . . .'

'What way?' asked Churchill with a certain suspiciousness.

'This way,' I continued. 'Information has just been received that the Germans have used gas on our Western front. There are grounds for supposing that in the spring offensive which they are now preparing, the Germans will develop gas warfare on a large scale . . . Help us to avert at any rate this new misfortune!'

My words clearly made an impression on Churchill. It was as though he had blown up. He cried:

'What, gas warfare? That as well?'

'There you are,' I said. 'Gas warfare at the Soviet front is inevitable if you British don't take the necessary steps in good time.'

'What can we do?' asked Churchill in some doubt.

'You can do a great deal, and very easily too,' I answered. 'Let the British Government publicly state now that, in the event of the Germans using gas on the Soviet front, British aircraft will cover German towns with gas bombs. That will be sufficient to restrain Hitler from this savage act.'

My idea evidently pleased Churchill. With a sudden gleam in his eyes, he began to tell me with satisfaction that Britain had at her disposal very powerful means of chemical warfare, and that if matters came to a showdown, the Germans would not get off lightly from the British gas retaliation. Then the Premier, turning to Eden, asked him:

'What do you think about that?'

Eden replied that in his opinion the statement which I had suggested could be made.

This fired Churchill's imagination still further, and with blazing eyes he began to draw a picture of the horrors which would descend on the Germans if Hitler did not stop in time.

Wishing to strike the iron while it was hot, I put the question to Churchill: 'When will the British Government make its statement?'

A sudden shadow seemed to pass over the Prime Minister's face, and he answered in a somewhat different, more matter-of-fact and usual tone: 'Oh, I shall try not to delay it. I only have to consult with my experts on all the practical steps.'

We said goodbye, and I began to await the fulfilment of Churchill's promise.

In a message to Stalin on 21 March, Churchill wrote:

'Ambassador Maisky lunched with me last week and mentioned some evidences that Germans may use gas upon you in their attempted spring offensive. After consulting my colleagues and the Chiefs of Staff I wish to assure you that His Majesty's Government will treat any use of this weapon of poison gas against Russia exactly as if it was directed against ourselves. I have been building up an immense store of gas bombs for discharge from aircraft, and we shall not hesitate to use these over all suitable objectives in Western Germany from the moment that your armies and people are assaulted in this way. It is a question to be considered whether at the right time we should not give a public warning that such is our resolve, as a warning might deter the Germans from adding this new horror to the many they have loosed upon the world. Please let me know what you think about this.'[1]

In a reply on 29 March Stalin wrote:

'I convey to you the Soviet Government's gratitude for the assurance that the British Government will treat any use of poison gas upon the USSR by the Germans as if that weapon were directed against Great Britain, and that the British Air Force will not hesitate to use the large store of gas bombs available in Britain for dropping on suitable targets in Germany.'

Stalin further asked that the British warning should be extended to Finland as well, since there were signs that poison gases might be used also by the Finns, and added that the USSR in its turn was ready to issue a similar warning to Germany in the event of a gas attack upon Britain. Stalin expressed the wish that the British warning should come not later than the end of April or the beginning of May.[2]

From the middle of April I began inquiring when precisely the warning would be published. I put this question several times to Eden, and twice I asked Churchill about it when meeting him by chance in Parliament. Both assured me that the question had been decided in principle, that the warning would certainly be given, it was only necessary still to inform someone and to consult with someone . . . And at last, on 10 May, the Premier broadcast his regular survey of military operations. It included the following passage:

'The Soviet Government have expressed to us the view that the Germans in the desperation of their assault may make use of poison gas against the armies and people of Russia. We are ourselves firmly resolved not to use this odious weapon unless it is

1. *Correspondence, etc.*, Vol. I, pp. 41–2.
2. *Ibid.*, pp. 42–3.

used first by the Germans. Knowing our Hun, however, we have not neglected to make preparations on a formidable scale. I wish now to make it plain that we shall treat the unprovoked use of poison gas against our Russian ally exactly as if it were used against ourselves; and if we are satisfied that this new outrage has been committed by Hitler, we shall use our great and growing air superiority in the West to carry gas warfare on the largest possible scale far and wide against military objectives in Germany. It is thus for Hitler to choose whether he wishes to add this additional horror to aerial warfare.'[1]

About a month later, on 5 June, Roosevelt made the announcement that the United States Government was receiving reliable information that the Japanese armed forces in various localities of China were using poison gases. He wished to make it quite clear that, if Japan persists in using this inhuman form of warfare against China or any other of the United Nations, its action would be considered by the United States Government as directed against itself, and would arouse on its part full retribution in the same coin. The responsibility for this would fall on Japan.

These two warnings, made in good time and openly, proved a cold douche for the reckless aggressors: poison gas was not used on any large scale in the course of the second world war. Thus, by means of yet another chain reaction, my conversation with Churchill on 16 March 1942 gave an impulse to a number of events which saved mankind from the additional horror of gas warfare.

1. *Times*, 11 May 1942.

2

The Anglo-Soviet Treaty

THE Moscow negotiations regarding two treaties (for mutual assistance between the USSR and Britain and regarding the post-war peace settlement), which took place during Eden's visit to the USSR in December 1941, had not been completed because of the differences about the second treaty which had revealed themselves. The negotiations were to continue in London. As a result, Eden and I had a number of meetings between January and March 1942, in which we tried to come to some agreement. However, the tempo of negotiations proved to be fairly slow, owing to two main reasons: a Government crisis in Britain and the difficulty of overcoming the above-mentioned differences.

The Government crisis arose in connection with those same military reverses which Britain suffered at the beginning of 1942, and which were mentioned earlier. Particular agitation was aroused in the country by the escape of the *Scharnhorst* and *Gneisenau* through the Straits of Dover (12 February) and the fall of Singapore (15 February). In my diary there is the following entry, dated 18 February 1942:

'On the 17th I was in Parliament. Churchill spoke about the fall of Singapore. He did not look well, and was irritable, ready to take offence and stubborn. The members were critical and wrought-up. They received Churchill badly, and reacted badly to his statement. I have never seen anything like it before . . . After the Premier's statement it became clear that a general debate in Parliament was inevitable. There was an argument about the date. Churchill again was stubborn. It was decided to hold it next week. My general impression is that a crisis is rapidly advancing . . .

'Churchill is making it increasingly harder for even his friends to support the Government. At every step he insists: "I answer for it all." This means that no one must criticise Ministers, generals, etc., even though under his defensive umbrella there have gathered quite a number of fools, mediocrities and potential representatives of the "Fifth Column" . . . As a result criticism is rising in Parliament, in the press and among the masses. A big part is being played by the military reverses. Yesterday's session showed that the wave of discontent is high. If Churchill continues to be stubborn, it may topple over his head. I think Churchill will yield, and accept a compromise.

'Who are the possible successors of Churchill, should he resign? Two names are widely quoted: Eden and Cripps. Eden has long ago been favoured. Cripps's star has made a fairy-like ascent now (after his return from Moscow, where he had been Ambassador, I. M.). The reasons are that the man in the street is convinced that Cripps "brings luck" (it was no accident that Russia, where he had been Ambassador, had entered the war!), moreover he was progressive, intelligent, a good speaker and, above all, he has always played a winning card—the USSR. On top of all this, he is outside any party, and party manoeuvres have sickened everybody . . .[1] But is Cripps's popularity stable, however? I doubt it. But I don't doubt that if there were a reconstruction of the Government today he might become Premier or at least a member of the War Cabinet.

'I personally am in favour of Churchill as Prime Minister. He is reliable, as an enemy of Germany; he is a man with a will of his own, and takes decisions himself. Neither Cripps nor Eden are strong enough to govern the country at such a stormy time.'

Some days after these lines had been written, there really was a reconstruction of the Government. Some of the Chamberlainite Ministers were dropped, and some new Ministers were appointed from among the Churchillites. Churchill remained Prime Minister, Cripps became a member of the War Cabinet and Leader of the House of Commons (an important post in the British parliamentary hierarchy). As a result, the Government crisis was overcome and Churchill's position grew stronger again. But not completely. I will give two characteristic signs.

1. Cripps had been expelled from the Labour Party for advocating a united front in the working-class movement. During his work as Ambassador in Moscow, and then in London as a member of the Government, Cripps officially was considered non-party.

On 20 March I was visited by a delegation from the majority of the Labour Party in the House of Commons. It consisted of the following M.P.s: Seymour Cocks, Milner, Bellenger, Ridley and Beaumont, and declared (I quote here from my diary, dated 20 March 1942):

'Things are going badly. Britain is suffering defeats. The strategy of the British Government is bankrupt. On the horizon is the spectre of a lost war. The country must wake up, re-organise, mobilise, go over to the offensive and above all, build up close friendship with the USSR . . . But the Government is delaying, wavering, displaying no fighting spirit, energy and resolution. The Labour M.P.s put questions to their Ministers in the Cabinet, but the latter (particularly Attlee) evade direct answers. The majority of the Parliamentary Party have sent the delegation to me in order to know the truth.

'I satisfied the interest of the delegation, and gave a detailed justification for the importance we attach to the second front. My guests fully agreed with me, and promised immediately to attack their Ministers.

'When we were saying goodbye, one of the members of the delegation said:

'"Oh, if only your generals could come to Britain to teach our army the methods of modern war!"'

And here is one more entry in my diary, dated the same 20 March 1942:

'Lord Mottistone came to see me—a Conservative die-hard, a retired general, who has in the past held high posts, including that of Secretary for War. He is 74. Up to now he has always been a vicious enemy of Soviet Russia. Mottistone's visit has the following purpose. He is indignant at the instruction issued by the British Home Office, which in the event of a German invasion advises the people to "stay put" and "preserve calm" (only people in uniform should fight). Mottistone calls the authors of this instruction Quislings, and is raising the matter in the House of Lords. He wants to know what are the instructions of the Soviet Government to the people in such a case. I gave Mottistone Stalin's speeches. He promised to quote them. Mottistone is in complete agreement with our view on the role of 1942 in the war, and is in favour of a second front. In conclusion Mottistone said: "No, the Bolsheviks are splendid! You fight very well! You have saved us and civilisation. And I used to attack you!"

'I asked with a smile: "Perhaps you now recognise that there is something healthy in our system?"

'"Of course, I do," Mottistone responded. "I am a soldier. Since you have been able to create such an army, it means there is something healthy in your system."'

Yes, Churchill's position even after the reconstruction of his Government in February could not as yet be considered finally stabilised. If he had survived the crisis and remained Prime Minister, this was chiefly because no other or better leader could be seen on the horizon at that time. The people felt this, and the political circles of the country, without distinction of party, understood it too.

However that might be, the beginning of March 1942 saw the elimination of the first reason for the delay in negotiations for a treaty—the Government crisis. But there remained the second and more serious reason—the difference between the two sides about the contents of the treaty itself.

Stalin required that Britain should now recognise the Soviet frontiers of 1941 (i.e. including the Baltic Republics, Bessarabia, Western Ukraine and Western Belorussia). The British side, on the contrary, wanted to postpone the question of frontiers until the end of the war. Cripps on one occasion spoke to me about the reasons for this (I quote the entry in my diary on 4 March 1942):

'Cripps dined with me. He is making every effort to get the Cabinet to agree to recognise the Soviet frontiers of 1941 . . . But to his regret, about a year ago—at the time still when Britain was fighting alone and wanted to draw the USA into the war—the British Government gave the American Government the promise not to recognise changes in European frontiers without consultation. In this way the British have fallen into dependence on the Americans. It is inconvenient, but what can they do?'

Cripps was telling the truth, but not the whole truth. Of course the promise given to the Americans tied the hands of the British Government to a certain extent: but apart from that the British Government itself—as could be seen from many symptoms—preferred to postpone all frontier questions until the post-war peace conference. Nevertheless, taking account of the war situation then existing, the London Government displayed a certain willingness to meet our point of view.

Today, from the materials published by the British Government, it can be seen that already, at the end of January 1942, the

Foreign Office had presented a memorandum to the Government in which it insisted on the necessity in one form or another of satisfying the desire of the USSR to assure its security after the war. The Cabinet was of the same opinion, and did not exclude the possibility in view of this of recognising the 1941 frontier. But the USA strongly objected. As, however, the military situation dictated to Britain the necessity of close co-operation with the USSR, and as Britain, being a European Power, needed good relations with the USSR after the termination of the war, Churchill finally decided that they would have to recognise the 1941 frontier (except for Poland) at once, in the Anglo-Soviet Treaty.[1]

At that time I did not know all these details, but in my negotiations with Eden could see that from meeting to meeting his resistance to our requirement was weakening: and in Churchill's message to Stalin on 12 March I read the following words: 'I have sent a message to President Roosevelt urging him to approve our signing agreement with you about the frontiers of Russia at the end of the war.' Replying to Churchill on 14 March, Stalin said on the question of the USSR frontiers that 'we still shall have to exchange views on the text of an appropriate treaty, if it is approved for signing by both parties'.[2]

On 8 April Eden proposed that in order to complete the negotiations and sign the Treaty, the Soviet People's Commissar for Foreign Affairs, V. M. Molotov, should come to London. The People's Commissar, however, replied that at the moment he could not leave Moscow, and I was being empowered to finalise the question of the treaty. Eden received Molotov's refusal rather sensitively, but the negotiations continued, although without much enthusiasm. At the end of April Molotov suddenly and quite unexpectedly cabled that he accepted the invitation of the British Government, and would be in London in the course of May. I did not know the reasons for this change in the People's Commissar's plans, and only during his stay in Britain did it become clear that it was Roosevelt who had played the decisive part in this respect.

The thing was that, in connection with the differences arising on the question of a treaty, the American President had entered into direct contact with Stalin. The President was interested also in

1. Sir Llewellyn Woodward, *British Foreign Policy in the Second World War*, H. M. Stationery Office, 1962, pp. 192–3.

2. *Correspondence, etc.*, Vol. I, pp. 40–1.

many other problems connected with the war. His idea was to meet Stalin personally, and by a friendly discussion settle all matters in dispute between the two sides. Subsequently M. M. Litvinov, who was then Soviet Ambassador in Washington, told me that, according to his impression, Roosevelt wanted to talk with Stalin *tête-à-tête*, without Churchill being present.

This impression of M. M. Litvinov's is confirmed by my own experience too. On 2 February 1942 one of Roosevelt's intimate advisors, Averell Harriman, had flown to London and invited me to lunch. We met on 5 February, and were alone. Harriman put me the direct question, would it not be possible to arrange a meeting between Roosevelt and Stalin? Harriman knew that Roosevelt wanted such a meeting, but did Stalin want it? As a possible meeting-place, Harriman suggested either Iceland or the region of the Behring Straits.

I asked first of all whether there had been any conversations with Litvinov about this in Washington, since the question was entirely within his competence. Harriman said he did not know, but he allowed that there may have been no such conversations with Litvinov. By way of explanation, he remarked that this question was still in too 'unfinished' a form for the American Government to think it possible to make even unofficial soundings on such a subject through the Soviet Ambassador accredited to the President. It was more convenient to do it through London.

I informed Moscow of the conversation with Harriman, and received the reply that Stalin thought a meeting with Roosevelt desirable, but on account of the tense position at the front he could not leave the USSR, and suggested a meeting at Archangel or Astrakhan. I passed on Moscow's reply to Harriman. By that time the *Scharnhorst* and the *Gneisenau* had already broken through into the North Sea, and Harriman said that in such conditions Iceland and Archangel were ruled out, it was too far for Roosevelt to go to Astrakhan, and there was only one possibility left, the region of the Behring Straits. But the reply came from Moscow that the Behring Straits were too far for Stalin to go. As a result, the meeting did not take place.[1]

From all that I have described, the impression was left with me that Roosevelt really did want to meet Stalin alone, without Churchill, but that Stalin for some reason did not want this at all. Somewhat later, in January 1943, Stalin also refused to go to

1. I informed M. M. Litvinov of all this affair in my letter of 27 February 1942.

Casablanca, where he had been invited for a conference with Roosevelt and Churchill. Encountering Stalin's unwillingness in the spring of 1942 to leave Moscow, Roosevelt wrote in a message of 12 April:

'Perhaps if things go as well as we hope, you and I could spend a few days together next summer near our common border off Alaska. But, in the meantime, I regard it as of the utmost military importance that we have the nearest possible approach to an exchange of views. I have in mind a very important military proposal involving the utilisation of our armed forces in a manner to relieve your critical Western front. This objective carries great weight with me. Therefore I wish you would consider sending Mr. Molotov and a General upon whom you rely to Washington in the immediate future.'[1]

Such was the pre-history of Molotov's visit to the USA. But since he was going to Washington, it was natural that he should stop in London on the way. Hence followed the unexpected change in plans of the People's Commissar.

Meanwhile, as part of the preparations for the forthcoming negotiations between Molotov and Eden, about 1 May I presented to the Foreign Office our counter-proposals in relation to the treaty, from which it followed that the Soviet side considered the question of the Soviet-Polish frontier as falling within the competence only of the USSR and Poland. They contained also a new proposal—that the British Government should in a protocol sanction the conclusion by the Soviet Union of pacts of mutual assistance with Finland and Rumania. After reading our counter-draft, I thought: 'This alternative has no chance of being approved by the British.'

And so I began awaiting the arrival of the People's Commissar for Foreign Affairs in London. In wartime conditions this was a far from simple operation. We were warned that the People's Commissar would fly direct from Moscow to Scotland, where he would land at an aerodrome in Dundee. A fairly numerous company travelled there in a special train to meet the Soviet People's Commissar. The British side was headed by Sir Alexander Cadogan, the Permanent Under-Secretary for Foreign Affairs, accompanied by several civil and military representatives. On the Soviet side, apart from myself, there were the Trade Representatives Borisenko, the head of the Military Mission Admiral

1. *Correspondence, etc.*, Vol. II, pp. 22–3.

Kharlamov, and also the Soviet Ambassador to the Governments in exile in Britain, A. E. Bogomolov.

Here I want to make a digression. When Hitler occupied nearly the whole of capitalist Europe, Britain became the residence of a number of Governments in exile, evacuated from the countries seized by the Nazis, or formed later beyond the reach of the Nazis. Such were the Governments of Norway, Holland, Belgium, Poland, Czechoslovakia, Yugoslavia, and also the 'Free French' movement headed by De Gaulle. After Germany had attacked the USSR, the Soviet Government had established diplomatic relations with all these Governments, and had then been faced with the question of how to maintain the necessary diplomatic contacts with them. The question was settled in an original and very successful way. The Soviet Government sent A. E. Bogomolov to London as Ambassador Extraordinary and Plenipotentiary to all the Governments in exile there. He arrived in London in October 1941. His work was very complex and delicate, but presented considerable political interest. Thus, in virtue of the exceptional circumstances brought about by the second world war, there arose a peculiar diplomatic precedent, when in one and the same country, Britain, there existed two parallel Ambassadors Extraordinary and Plenipotentiary from one and the same country, the USSR, but with different addresses for their accreditation.

Our train arrived in Dundee and was put on a siding. We supposed that the Soviet plane would arrive the following morning (the flight itself was to take place at night), but by the evening news had come from Moscow that in view of bad flying weather at that end the flight was postponed until the next day. The following day there again by the evening arrived a communication that there was bad flying weather in Moscow. On the third day the weather in Moscow improved, but in return, as though to spite us, the weather at the British end turned out to be unsuitable. The same happened on the fourth day as well: such a game of hide-and-seek by the weather continued for about a week. The reception party was bored, did not know what to do with itself, cursed, went out into the surrounding country as a distraction, but did not leave Dundee.

However, the special train from London standing on the sidings, and inhabited by unusual personages including foreigners, could not but attract the attention of the railwaymen. Soon they came to know why the train was there. This aroused universal curiosity even more. The town of Dundee is not a very large one, everybody knows one another there, and every kind of 'news' spreads among the inhabitants with unusual speed. It was not surprising that on the fifth or sixth day after our arrival in Dundee there appeared before the carriages of the special train the Town Provost, in his official garb and chain, in order to welcome 'His Excellency the Ambassador of an Allied Power' on behalf of the population. The Mayor was accompanied by several town councillors. I invited the deputation from the town into my carriage and, thanking them for their attention, entertained them to tea and biscuits. But when the deputation had departed, we held a 'council of war' and decided that things could not continue in this way. Obviously the purpose for which the train had arrived had become an open secret, and this might create a menace to the security of Molotov's flight from the USSR to Britain. The conclusion which we drew led to this, that the following morning the whole train with its inhabitants returned to London. Before its departure the rumour was spread that the visit of the Soviet People's Commissar had been cancelled. Only two persons were left on the spot to meet Molotov: V. N. Pavlov, his interpreter, who had arrived in Britain earlier, and one Foreign Office official, who did not as yet hold a particularly high post.

Molotov arrived in Britain on 20 May. I travelled out to meet him on the road from Dundee to London. Somewhere half way I transferred from a train going north to the train going south, in which were travelling the Soviet People's Commissar and those accompanying him, including the 'general on whom you rely' about whom Roosevelt had asked Stalin. On the way, in the carriage, I briefly informed Molotov of the state of affairs in Britain, and among other things warned him that our draft treaty stood little chance of being approved by the British side. The People's Commissar was obviously displeased by my information, but aloud said only: 'We shall see.'

Shortly before reaching London, the Soviet guests were met by Eden and Cadogan, who took them off to Chequers, where an official residence had been prepared for the People's Commissar. This was a symbol of respect. Only the highest visitors from other countries stay in the Prime Minister's country dwelling.

That same evening Churchill gave a big dinner at Chequers in honour of the Soviet delegation, many members of the Government attending, and after dinner he led Molotov, Eden and myself to his study and began the conversations. There were only four of us. I acted as interpreter. We spent two hours in the Prime Minister's study. I well remember Churchill standing at a large globe, describing in detail, with passion and heat, how Britain had carried on the war up to the present and what were her calculations for the future. Illustrating his words on the globe, he specially underlined the courage and resolution of Britain—these small islands representing an almost microscopic fragment of land amid vast continents and boundless oceans—in resisting the alliance of three Great Powers which had adopted the way of world aggression.

'And now', exclaimed Churchill, 'two years have passed, we have held out, and we have not only held but are gathering our forces, growing stronger, reckoning on victory! It is like a real miracle!'

The Premier preferred not to mention that the British Isles were supported by a giant Empire; and he said little about help from the USA.

As regards the forthcoming negotiations for a treaty, Churchill remarked somewhat mysteriously that, if agreement could not be reached on the existing texts (British and Soviet), he possibly would make some alternative proposals.

The following day formal negotiations with Eden began at the Foreign Office. Molotov had in addition to myself Sobolev and his interpreter Pavlov. Eden was accompanied by a group of Foreign Office officials headed by Cadogan.

As could have been expected, big differences arose between the two sides, especially on the question of Poland. We insisted on the immediate recognition of the Soviet-Polish frontier as it stood before 22 June 1941, while the British insisted on leaving the settlement of this question until the peace conference after the end of the war. They also objected to the Anglo-Soviet protocol sanctioning the conclusion by the Soviet Union of pacts of mutual assistance with Finland and Rumania. There were also other points of difference.

Two more sessions passed in fruitless argument without bringing any agreement. At the fourth session Eden, recording the fact that, on the existing draft treaties, it would evidently be difficult to reach unanimity, presented quite a new document. This contained the alternative proposals which Churchill had mentioned during our first evening's conversation.

The reaction of the Soviet side was sharply negative, because the alternative proposals completely avoided the question of the frontiers of the USSR. A cable in this sense, with the text of the proposals, was sent to Moscow.

And suddenly from Moscow there came an unexpected reply: the Soviet delegation was instructed to withdraw all its previous proposals and conduct the further negotiations on the basis of the new British draft.

I don't know what obliged Stalin so sharply to change his attitude, but, however that might be, the change had been made. On the basis of the alternative proposals it was now easy to reach agreement on the final text of the treaty. On 26 May, in ceremonial circumstances, the Treaty was signed by Molotov and Eden in the latter's study, in the presence of Churchill, Attlee and Sinclair (as leaders of the three parties composing the Government coalition), and amidst a vast concourse of photographers and film cameramen. It bore the official title of: 'Treaty for an Alliance in the War Against Hitlerite Germany and her associates in Europe and for Collaboration and Mutual Assistance after the War.'

The contents of the Treaty amounted to the following. In Part I, which replaced the agreement for mutual military assistance of 12 July 1941, it was stated that both sides undertook during the war to afford each other military and other assistance of all kinds in the struggle against Hitlerite Germany and her European associates, and also undertook not to enter into any negotiations with them except by mutual consent.

In Part II, which was to remain in force for twenty years, there were laid down the basic principles of post-war collaboration between the USSR and Britain. In Article III both sides declared their desire to unite with other like-minded States in taking common action to preserve peace and resist aggression. In Article IV they guaranteed mutual assistance in the event of one of the sides being again involved in hostilities with Germany or her allies. In Articles V–VII the parties undertook not to take part in any coalition directed against the other, and not to seek territorial aggrandisement for themselves or to interfere in the internal affairs of other States.

As will be seen, this Treaty completely left aside the question of frontiers. Nevertheless, in the circumstances then prevailing it was of very great value, both military and political. It was ratified by the Soviet Union on 18 June, and by Great Britain on the 24th, and entered into force after the exchange of ratifications on 4 July 1942.

3

Churchill and a Second Front

At the beginning of March 1942 I met the American Ambassador Winant at a diplomatic reception. As I have already said, his attitude to the USSR was friendly. He led me away into a secluded corner, and said confidentially:

'I can give you a pleasant piece of news: President Roosevelt and General Marshall, the Chief of our General Staff, consider Germany, not Japan, enemy No. 1, and think the immediate action by the USA and Britain should be an invasion of northern France. Our British friends do not fully agree with this, but I hope in the end our point of view will get the upper hand.'

I attempted to question Winant about details of the American plans, but he replied that as yet he himself did not know them. I don't knew whether that was really the case—perhaps Winant simply thought it inconvenient as yet to go too deeply into the subject—but from all he said it was clear that personally he very much sympathised with Washington's intentions.

Winant's information gave me the idea of making a public statement in favour of a second front. This might have a certain effect on British public opinion, and indirectly on the Government. It was essential, however, to observe great care not to irritate Churchill and not to bring about some unnecessary conflict. A favourable occasion helped me to effect my purpose.

At the end of 1941 the British Government had already sent several squadrons of its planes to Murmansk, to combat together with the Soviet pilots the German armed forces in the North Cape region. These were greatly hindering the passage to Murmansk and Archangel of the Anglo-American convoys with war supplies for the Red Army (of which I write more later). The British fought well, and some of them were decorated with Soviet Orders. Four of the British pilots had returned home before the Soviet Government's decision to decorate them, and I was instructed to invest them with their Orders in London. The act of investiture took place on 25 March. It was arranged on a fairly impressive scale. We invited to the Embassy a number of people prominent in public life, political and military, representatives of the press, the radio and the cinema. Mrs. Churchill was also present. The white salon of the Embassy was packed, and there was a certain intentness in the gathering, as always on some important occasion.

At the investiture I made a speech in which I said a good deal complimenting the four British pilots, though no more than they deserved, and then proceeded to questions of a more general character. I expressed the hope that '1942 is destined to become a turning point' in the development of the war, and that military collaboration between Britain and the USSR in that year would be as close and comradely as had been the collaboration between British and Soviet pilots at Murmansk. Then I went on to develop the idea that for such collaboration to be successful it was necessary always to keep in mind four most important things.

First, that 'we are now waging a *modern* war, not a war of the nineteenth century, not even the war of 1914–18, but a war of 1939–42'. The present war was a war of engines, and therefore 'speed becomes the watchword of the day'.

Secondly, that 'the simple arithmetical superiority of one side over the other in population, territory, natural wealth, industrial capacities does not in itself guarantee victory . . . In the struggle there must be reckoned with first of all not the potential, but the actually mobilised resources . . . *The secret of victory consists in having a decisive superiority over the enemy at the decisive moment and in the decisive sector*'.

The third is to *keep the initiative at the front in one's own hands*. 'At the Soviet front the initiative has been torn from Hitler's hands . . . But on some other fronts the initiative is still in the hands of the enemy . . . The Allies must put an end to such a situation.'

Lastly, '*the principle that supposedly "time is on our side"*, is by no means an axiom'. On the contrary, 'there is a race to gain time between the two camps . . . The enemy is betting on 1942. It is just in the spring and summer of this year that he intends to make a 'super-human" effort to conquer. The task of the Allies is obvious: they too must put their money on 1942, and in the spring and summer of this very year make their own "super-human" effort to defeat the enemy'. I ended my remarks with the following words:

'Often one can hear that the Allies have not yet completed their preparations. I don't know whether in history there has ever been a commander-in-chief who said on the eve of battle that he was quite prepared for it . . . All the Allies taken together have already all that is necessary for victory: troops, tanks, planes, arms. One cannot wait until the last button has been sewn on the tunic of the last soldier. The times are too perilous. Moreover, history is not the pavement of Piccadilly . . . This is the decisive moment—1942: the decisive sector of the world front is the USSR. From this all should follow. If the Allies really want victory (and that I do not doubt), then . . . all the work of the Staffs must be penetrated by one thought and one watchword—1942, not 1943!'

My speech appeared in the British and Soviet press. In London it did not please everybody—in Government circles it was met without the slightest enthusiasm—but all the same it aroused no diplomatic complications. And in return, in the broadest circles of the British people, the speech made a very favourable impression. I remember one trade union leader of the second rank visiting me in the Embassy, shaking me long by the hand and repeating several times:

'You said what Churchill ought to have said, and the Labour leaders in the Government.'

My speech met with a wide response in the Soviet Union. Particularly fortunate proved my phrase that 'one cannot wait until the last button has been sewn on the tunic of the last soldier'. I was more than once reminded of it when later I returned home and began working in Moscow.

In speaking of the second front, I ought to dwell with particular attention on the attitude of Winston Churchill, since there can be no doubt that, apart from reasons of a more general character, he personally played a tremendous part in the fate of this whole problem.

Recalling now all that I saw and heard in the war years, all that I knew of Churchill from my numerous meetings and talks with him both before and during the war, all that I have read about him and been told about him, I can draw sufficiently accurately a picture of his attitude to the question of a second front in Northern France.

When in 1934 we first made each other's acquaintance, he said to me quite frankly that his God was the British Empire, and that all his political activity was determined by the interests of preserving the Empire. It was just because of this that, after Hitler had seized power in Germany, Churchill came to the conclusion that at that moment Hitler represented the greatest danger to the Empire, and that to defend it Britain should rebuild the Entente of the first world war, i.e. bring about a bloc with Soviet Russia, against which in 1918–20 he had as is known organised the crusade of fourteen States.

Now, after 22 June 1941, the interests of the British Empire as before dominated the consciousness of Churchill: but in the circumstances of the second world war he considered that those interests were bound up first of all with the Atlantic and the Pacific, the Mediterranean and the Near East. The question of Russia (as Churchill preferred to call the USSR) was of secondary importance, and, moreover, was fraught with an internal contradiction. Russia was needed as an ally against Germany, but at the same time Russia was dangerous; for if she emerged very much strengthened from the war, she might put the British Empire in a difficult position—not as a conqueror of her territory, but as a powerful moral and political factor facilitating its internal disintegration. Churchill did not wish for a defeat of the USSR, for in that event victorious Germany would with redoubled strength fall upon Britain and, probably, in the long run would occupy the British Isles. But Churchill also did not want the complete defeat of Germany, for in that event the USSR would become too powerful, and the influence emanating from it would threaten to undermine the colonial foundations of the British Empire, and in general to arouse in the world great convulsions of an anti-capitalist nature. From Churchill's point of view, it would be ideal if both Germany and the USSR emerged from the war greatly battered, bled white and, for at any rate a whole generation, would be struggling along on crutches, while Britain arrived at the finish with a minimum of losses and in good form as a European boxer. Hence naturally followed the striving to display the utmost economy in spending her own resources for winning the war and, on the contrary, to transfer the maximum of effort, suffering and losses in the attainment of this objective to the Soviet Union.

Such a striving was all the more irresistible because it was buttressed in the age-old traditions of British policy. It is well known that in past centuries Britain had more than once taken part in general European wars, but in doing so had usually—up to the first world war—participated with her money, her political influence and her navy. Land operations always devolved on Britain's continental allies, to support whom she would send only a 'symbolic' expedition of her army of very modest size. This expedition had as its purpose not so much to afford real aid to the allied troops as, by its presence, to raise their spirits and increase their readiness to make sacrifices in the defence of British interests.

The first world war demonstrated that in the circumstances of the twentieth century such a strategy was no longer possible: Britain in its course was obliged to send a vast army to the Continent. The second world war displayed still more vividly that Britain needed such an army. However, Churchill strove to salvage from the old strategy what still could be salvaged, and not unsuccessfully. The proof of this can be the astounding fact that, during the six years of the greatest war in history, Britain lost not more than 400,000 dead.

Of course, concern to carry on the war with 'the least possible bloodshed' deserves all approval, but on one essential condition, that it is not bought by exaggeratedly 'large bloodshed' on the part of an ally or allies. In this particular case that basic condition was violently infringed: the losses borne by the Soviet Union in the war reached 20 million dead. Even taking account of the difference in the size of population, the length of front, the numbers of the armies engaged, etc., it is quite obvious that disproportionately vast burdens fell on the shoulders of the Soviet Union. And this was by no means in a small degree explained by the attitude taken up by Britain and the USA on the question of a second front.

Throughout 1941–3 I had many conversations with Churchill on military strategy in general, and on a second front in particular: and I was always amazed by his one-sided stubborness in defending views which he had once formed. He resembled a woodpecker who is able to strike only one note. How did Churchill conceive of the picture, the course and outcome of the war?

Approximately as follows:

Enemy No. 1 was Germany. Japan was in the second place. The war against Germany should have the character not of assault by storm (of course, adequately prepared assault), but of a prolonged siege. Germany should be blockaded as strictly as possible in the economic sense, and also exhausted and weakened by secondary military operations on the periphery of her European 'Empire'. Gradually these operations should penetrate deeply into the 'Empire', tightening the ring around Berlin more and more. The pressure of the Allies from without would inevitably be supplemented by growing disintegration from within under its influence, and also under the influence of ever-stronger air raids. Sooner or later the moment must come when the combined effect of both factors would undermine the power of Hitlerite Germany, and it would begin to collapse. That is when it would be the moment to open a second front in Northern France. It would not require great sacrifices, and probably would be transformed into something like a triumphal march of the British and American troops to Berlin. Churchill calculated at this point that the Western Powers would be in the German capital earlier than the USSR, and this would very much strengthen their position when solving all the post-war problems.

Such was the general conception of the British Prime Minister. I don't wish to say that he frankly set it forth to me in such a completed form: of course not! But from the numerous conversations with him, from his remarks, assessments, judgments and expressions of opinion which I had occasion to hear at various times, I could catch more and more the essence of his internal 'credo'. This helped me to calculate my own practical steps better.

Of all my talks with Churchill on the subject of a second front, two have particularly remained in my mind. One was in the middle of March 1942, on the same day that I received from the Premier the promise to make a public statement that Britain would take gas reprisals in the event of Germany launching gas warfare in the USSR. In the message from Stalin which I had handed over, it was said that 1942 should become the decisive year of the war. Churchill objected to this, and postponed the opening of a second front in Northern France to 1943. In my polemics with the Premier, I said (and I quote from the entry in my diary on 16 March 1942):

'I don't know how you see it, but I consider we are now face to face with a threatening situation. A really decisive moment has come in the course of the war. Either—or. What is the situation? Germany is preparing a huge spring offensive this year. It is putting its money on this year. If we are able to defeat Germany's spring offensive, the war in essence has been won. The backbone of the German military machine will have been broken, and there will remain only to finish off the wild beast. And with the defeat of Germany all the rest will be comparatively easy. But let us imagine that we are unable to defeat the German spring offensive. Let us imagine that the Red Army will be forced once again to retreat, that we shall once again begin to lose territory, that the Germans will succeed in breaking through to the Caucasus: what then? In that event you know that Hitler will not stop at the Caucasus. He will go further—into Iran, Turkey, Egypt, India. He will join hands with Japan somewhere in the region of the Indian Ocean and stretch out his hands to Africa. Germany's oil, raw materials and food problems will have been solved. The British Empire will collapse, and the USSR will lose territory of exceptional importance. Of course, even in these conditions the USSR would continue the war. Let us presume that Britain and the USA would also carry on the struggle. But what would be our chances of victory? And when?... This at the choice: now or never!'

Churchill, who had listened to me throughout with a frown and his head on one side, at this point suddenly rose and with considerable agitation exclaimed:

'We shall die sooner than put up with such a situation!'

Eden, sitting to the left of the Prime Minister, added:

'I quite agree with the Ambassador. The question is just as he put it—now or never!'

But I continued:

'Of course, the Red Army is stronger than it was last year, and the German army weaker. Of course we shall fight savagely this year. But who can go bail for the future? Who knows whether Hitler has not some new military inventions? Some new, hitherto unknown gas? . . . And even if we leave aside the question of some "secret" weapon, Hitler after all has the active, if not always voluntary, assistance of his allies. Yet the USSR up to the present is alone bearing the whole giant impact of the Hitlerite military machine. The percentage of danger is growing greatly. But Britain and the USA are still pondering which year will be decisive—1942 or 1943?... Britain and the USA should also put their money on 1942, and should throw all their forces into battle this year . . . If that does not happen, a very dangerous situation will arise: while the "Axis" is fighting with both hands, the Allies will be fighting only with one. Such a situation should not be permitted in any event!'

Eden once again fully and completely supported me.

Churchill sat plunged in thought. Finally, he raised his head and said:

'Perhaps you are right. All the information I have points to the Germans preparing a blow eastward . . . Yes, you will have to withstand a terrible blow in the spring. We must help you. We shall do all we can.'

This india-rubber formula 'we shall do all we can' greatly disturbed me at the time. And not without justification. Later I shall describe in detail how barely, three weeks after the above conversation, the British Prime Minister began a stubborn campaign of sabotage against a second front in France, not only in 1942 but also in 1943.

The other conversation with Churchill about a second front which has fixed itself firmly in my memory took place in the summer of 1942—at the time when the great German offensive which we had expected during the conversation in March had already been launched in full measure. I put the question to the Prime Minister:

'Why do you consider that Egypt is best of all defended from the Germans in Egypt? It is quite possible to defend it near Paris. Everything depends on strategic calculations and the volume of force applied to the point of the blow.'

Churchill grew heated, and began warmly demonstrating that I was wrong. The more he said, the clearer it became that all his arguments bore the vivid impression of hot imperialist *emotion*, akin to the emotion which had inspired Kipling.

Churchill did not simply consider Egypt an important link in the system of imperial defence: he was patently in love with Egypt, with Arabia, with the northern coast of Africa, with all that at that time constituted the Mediterranean and Near Eastern theatre of military operations. Here lay his heart and his mind: and the names of Tobruk or El Alamein said much more to him than the names of Havre or Lille.

When I reminded Churchill that Britain and the USA in the communiqué of 12 June 1942 had promised to open a second front that year, he became very excited.

'The Germans have forty divisions in France,' Churchill asserted, repeating what he had more than once said to me before. 'The French coast of the Channel has been well fortified by them . . . On our side tremendous forces will be needed to overcome

German opposition in the event of an Anglo-American attempt to invade. We have no such forces at present. An attempt to make an invasion of the French coast at the present time would inevitably end only in disaster. The waters of the Channel would be red with the blood of our lads, while you would gain no benefit from it at all.'

I replied that our information about the situation in France drew a somewhat different picture. There were far fewer German troops there than the British believed, and qualitatively they were at a very low level: all the best units were concentrated on the Soviet-German front. The German fortifications on the Channel coast were as to 75 per cent the product of Goebbels' imagination. What really existed did not represent any serious obstacles for an invasion. The British and Americans had good chances of success: all that was needed was not to wait, not to postpone the decisive step to infinity.

When I had finished, Churchill said:

'At best the cross-Channel operations is fraught with great risk . . . There is much about it that is guesswork . . . The probability of extensive losses is very great . . . We are a small country, there are only 50 millions of us' (the Premier had once again forgotten the Empire) 'and we cannot throw away men's lives.'

'And do you think that we in the Soviet Union can throw away men's lives?' I said with irritation.

Churchill began assuring me that nothing like that was in his mind, but that Britain in this case must 'cut her coat according to her cloth'.

Churchill's arguments meant in practice that, as before, he was against a strategy of assault and in favour of a strategy of prolonged siege. True, the result of his strategy was bound to be the prolonging of the war and an increase in the number of human sacrifices and material losses of the Soviet Union, and of a number of other countries occupied by the Germans as well; but such considerations did not greatly worry the British Prime Minister. Now, twelve months after Hitler had attacked our country, it was clear to Churchill that the USSR was not going to collapse under the blows of the German armies, that it was capable of offering them serious resistance: and he became more tranquil. There was no necessity to come to Russia's aid at extraordinary speed in order to prevent a break-up of the Eastern front, which would have been disadvantageous for Britain; he could return to his imperial affairs, and in particular see to it that the Russians did not 'get above themselves'. In international politics the capitalist States are guided not by sentiments, not by generosity, not by any lofty ideals, but by crudely egotistical interests and not infrequently by very ruthless calculation. Whatever warm words bourgeois Ministers may utter, behind them always lurks the cold stone of their own advantage.

One must be fair to Churchill: he displayed quite exceptional firmness, consistency and skill in carrying through his line of policy, when working out jointly with the Americans their general strategic plans for the war. And as Churchill knew very well what he wanted, while Roosevelt, as we shall see in a moment, had no quite definite conception of how the war should be conducted, it was precisely Churchill—in spite of the tremendous superiority in strength of the USA —who managed for a long time, in fact, to control the military operations of the Anglo-American bloc. And this revealed itself most vividly on the question of a second front as well.

At that time, in the spring and summer of 1942, I did not know all the details of Anglo-American conversations on the problem which was so important for us. From various sources individual fragmentary facts used to reach me about the arguments between London and Washington on this question. But the general picture was already clear to me. I knew that Roosevelt was inclined to the speediest possible opening of a second front in Northern France, but that Churchill was stubbornly resisting. I knew also that prolonged and complicated negotiations were going on between them on this question, but their outcome was not clear to me for a long time. Only in mid-July was I finally convinced that in this London-Washington duel Churchill had been victorious, and I shall describe further on how I reached this conclusion. For the moment I shall make use of materials published after the war, in order briefly to describe what was really going on at the time behind the scenes in official Anglo-American relations.

4

Roosevelt and Churchill

In his war memoirs Churchill says: 'So many tales have been published of my rooted aversion from large-scale operations on the Continent that it is important that the truth should be emphasised . . . When I notice the number of books which have been written on a false assumption of my attitude on this issue, I feel bound to direct the attention of the reader to the authentic and responsible documents written at the time.'[1]

Very well, let us accept Churchill's invitation and study those basic documents which he quotes himself in his memoirs as proof of his 'innocence' of any organic antipathy to a second front in Northern France.

On 18 December 1941, twelve days after the Japanese attack at Pearl Harbour, Churchill developed his plan for the conduct of the war in a special memorandum. In it he examined in detail the steps which Britain and the USA should take in the Atlantic and Pacific Oceans, and then, proceeding to operations on land, sketched out the conditions which, in his opinion, would make it possible seriously to speak of opening a second front in Northern France. There were very many such conditions. Here they are:

1. If the actions of the British and Americans in the Pacific and Atlantic were successful;

2. If the British Isles would remain intact and more strongly protected against invasion than ever before;

3. If the whole West and North African shores from Dakar to the Suez Canal, and the Levant to the Turkish frontier, would be in Anglo-American hands;

1. *The Second World War*, Vol. III, p. 581.

4. If Turkey, though not necessarily at war, would be definitely incorporated in the American-British-Russian front;

5. If Britain the USA and the USSR had decisive mastery of the air;

6. If the positions of the USSR were strongly established;

7. If British and American troops had a footing in Sicily and Italy.

Now if all this happened, it would be possible to inflict a blow on the enemy in Northern France, and that not earlier than the summer of 1943.[1]

Inevitably the thought comes to one's mind: a strange way to prove one's 'innocence'! For was it thinkable at all that there should be simultaneously coinciding all the conditions set forth in the memorandum, even by the summer of 1943? And did not that mean that in substance Churchill was rejecting a second front in Northern France altogether, and was only hiding his attitude by piling up so many preliminary conditions? Really, for any normally reasoning person, the notorious memorandum of 18 December speaks not for but against the thesis which Churchill wants to demonstrate.

Churchill's memorandum was subjected to careful discussion in Washington, following which there was worked out an 'American plan' for the conduct of the war, at least for the next two years: it was markedly different from the British. Its essence was that in the spring of 1943 there should be an Anglo-American invasion of Northern France with 48 divisions (9 of them mechanised), of which the USA would provide 30 and Britain 18. The invasion would be supported by an air fleet of 5,800 planes, 3,250 of them American and 2,550 British.

The American plan provided in addition for an auxiliary operation, which received the code title of 'Sledgehammer', namely a landing in the autumn of 1942 on the French Channel coast, five or six divisions in strength: but only in one of two events—if the German situation in Western Europe became critically weakened, or if the situation on the Russian front became desperate.[2]

In justifying this plan, which later received the code title of 'Overlord', General Marshall, the Chief of the American General Staff, used the following arguments in its favour. It was important

1. *Ibid.*, pp. 582–4.
2. Sherwood, *The White House Papers of Harry Hopkins*, Vol. II, p. 525.

that the first great offensive of the Allied Powers should take place in Western Europe. Such an offensive could be prepared and organised there more speedily than elsewhere. The Allies there could make certain of local air superiority. It was easier than anywhere else for Britain and the USA to concentrate the necessary forces there. Thanks to the small distance from the base of the attack in Britain to the front in Northern France, the operation would require less tonnage, of which there was at that time a great lack. In such an invasion the USA, Britain and the USSR could combine their forces for a simultaneous attack on the common enemy. And here, finally, it was possible to give the maximum of support to the USSR, with the purpose of relieving the situation at the Soviet front.[1]

It will be seen that there was no sentimentality in Marshall's arguments. They bore a strictly business-like, military character. It was not accidental that the granting of aid to the USSR was mentioned last. The plan worked out by the American generals received Roosevelt's approval, and was energetically supported by Hopkins.

In comparing Churchill's memorandum and the American plan it becomes clear that Roosevelt and Marshall, even though they had rejected some of the numerous 'ifs' of the British Prime Minister and had recognised the desirability of 'Overlord', had nevertheless maintained the principal thesis of the Churchill memorandum, namely, the organisation of a second front only in 1943.

On 8 April 1942 Hopkins and Marshall arrived in London, and negotiated for a week with the British representatives headed by Churchill about a common Anglo-American plan for the conduct of the war. At first the British Premier was lavish in his compliments on the American plan, and declared his complete agreement with it: but nevertheless he thereafter began a systematic campaign of sabotage of the general line of policy laid down by Roosevelt and Marshall. Churchill asserted that the most acute and pressing problem of the moment was not assistance to the USSR but the peril of a link-up between the German and Japanese forces in the Middle East, and that it was there that British and American armies should be sent in the first instance. As however the British Premier's proposal met with strong opposition, not only from the Americans but also from some of the British,

1. *Ibid.*, pp. 524–5.

Churchill had to beat a retreat and solemnly to proclaim that 'the British Government and people would make their full and unreserved contribution to the success of this great enterprise', i.e. an Allied invasion of Northern France. This gave grounds for Hopkins to send Roosevelt an exultant cable to the effect that the British Government was in the main agreeable to the American proposals.[1]

But Hopkins' joy was premature. Churchill's statement at the end of the conference was on his part only a hypocritical manoeuvre. On 21 May the People's Commissar for Foreign Affairs of the USSR arrived in London. In addition to the conclusion of the Anglo-Soviet Treaty, discussed earlier, he wished—and this was his main task—to secure the opening of a second front in 1942. On 22 May there took place a long conversation on this subject between Churchill and Molotov in the British Prime Minister's study: I also was present. The People's Commissar, after briefly outlining the position at the Soviet front, pressingly demanded the earliest possible opening of a second front in Northern France, for the purpose of diverting at least 40 German divisions from the Eastern front.

Churchill replied in very great detail, with many particulars and historico-philosophic digressions: but the essence of what he said was very simple. Britain even together with the USA was not able in 1942 to organise an effective second front in Northern France, because allegedly they had not as yet a sufficient number of planes, landing craft and other military equipment. All that the Western Allies could do in 1942 was to intensify to the maximum their air bombardments of Germany and prepare energetically for an invasion of Northern France in 1943. The Premier supported his arguments, moreover, by stating that already the British and the Americans were tying down over 40 German divisions in Holland, Belgium, France, Norway and North Africa: was not this a very substantial contribution by Britain to relieving the position of the USSR?

Churchill's arguments aroused serious criticism from the Soviet side: but by the end of the discussion it was perfectly clear that the British Government would oppose in every possible way the creation of a second front in Northern France in 1942.

There remained only some hope of the USA, whither Molotov travelled on leaving London. On 29 May he arrived in Washing-

1. *Ibid.*, pp. 542–3.

ton, and had conversations there with President Roosevelt on various subjects, and particularly on a second front. Roosevelt proved, it seemed, more yielding than Churchill, and as a result a communiqué was agreed upon between the American and Soviet sides, in which there was a phrase: 'In the course of the conversations complete agreement was reached with regard to the urgent tasks of the creation of a second front in Europe in 1942.' On his return journey from the USA, Molotov interrupted his journey once more in London, and continued his conversations about a second front with Churchill. The latter agreed to insert in the British-Soviet communiqué about Molotov's visit the same phrase about a second front in 1942 that was contained in the American-Soviet communiqué. On 12 June both communiqués were published in Moscow, London and Washington. However, at the very moment of signature of the Anglo-Soviet communiqué, Churchill thrust into Molotov's hand a short memorandum which stated:

'We are making preparations for a landing on the Continent in August or September 1942. As already explained, the main limiting factor to the size of the landing force is the availability of special landing-craft . . . It is impossible to say in advance whether the situation will be such as to make this operation feasible when the time comes. We can therefore give no promise in the matter, but provided that it appears sound and sensible we shall not hesitate to put our plans into effect.'[1]

Rapidly running through the memorandum on the spot, in Churchill's own study, I made up my mind at once: 'Well, that means Churchill will open no second front in 1942.'

Molotov left for Moscow, and I began looking at what was going on around me with redoubled attention. I assembled all our most responsible military and Trade Delegation staff and, explaining to them the situation which had arisen, requested them very pressingly to follow any preparations which the British might be making for an invasion of Northern France in the autumn of 1942. Such an operation could not be improvised, it required great preliminary work both of a military and of an economic character. Such work could not be a complete secret, and its progress would not be difficult to observe in the factories and works, on the transport system, in the places where troops were disposed and so forth. For a month the comrades gave me

1. *The Second World War*, Vol. IV, p. 305.

precise information on the question which interested me, and by the middle of July it had become perfectly clear that the British Government was making no preparations whatever for landing a large-scale expedition on the French coast. This was of decisive significance. Then I tested their information by cautious conversations of a probing character with some of the members of the British Government. The sum total could no longer be a matter of the least doubt. The following is how it was formulated in my diary on 19 July 1942:

'My conversations with Churchill, Eden, Cripps, Beaverbrook and others, all that I have heard, seen and read here, lead me to the following conclusions:

'1. There will be no second front in 1942.

'2. Supplies by Britain and the USA to the USSR will be reduced (because of difficulties with the northern convoys).

'3. What are possible are a northern operation (Petsamo etc.), a raid on the opposite coast such as was mentioned during Molotov's visit (but I would not risk guaranteeing that it will happen), intensification of air bombardments of Germany and raids on the French coast (on condition of serious pressure from our side), the transfer of part of the British Air Force from the Middle East to our southern front (particularly if affairs in Egypt take a favourable turn for the British).

'Translated into plain Russian, this means that in the present year's campaign we must reckon only on ourselves . . .

'This must be taken into account in all our plans and calculations. This must be borne in mind for the future.'

In this spirit I cabled Moscow. I did not doubt that it would arouse an outburst of extreme and quite legitimate irritation in Stalin, an irritation which might rebound on myself as well (high authorities often do not like receiving unpleasant information from their men on the spot). But throughout all my work abroad I considered that the obligation of an Ambassador is always to tell the truth to his Government. All the more was it necessary to tell the truth on a question of such exceptional importance for our State and our people. On this occasion, however, everything went off comparatively smoothly, and Stalin's expression of dissatisfaction was confined only to an undeservedly rude reproof to me on quite a different subject.

My cable that in 1942 there would be no second front was more than justified. Today we know precisely that the ink was hardly dry on the communiqué of 12 June than the British Government began to get ready for sabotaging a second front not only in 1942 but in 1943 as well.

On 19 June, i.e. a week after the communiqué had been published, Churchill arrived in Washington with his advisers. He immediately presented a memorandum to Roosevelt which stated that the British Cabinet was against 'Overlord' in 1942 for two reasons: it did not believe in the success of such an operation, and it considered that an attempt to put it into effect would hinder the carrying out of 'Overlord in 1943'. Churchill then put the question: could the USA and Britain remain passive during the twelve months which remained before the beginning of 'Overlord'? And he answered: no, they could not. He went on to propose that they should 'study' the possibility of a military operation which later on received the code title of 'Torch'—an operation aiming at the conquest of French North Africa.

Stimson and Marshall objected to 'Torch', because it would require so much time, energy and resources that simultaneous preparations for 'Overlord' became simply impossible. One had to choose between one or the other.

Just in the course of these negotiations there arrived a cable about the fall of Tobruk (20 June). Churchill very skilfully exaggerated the military and political significance of this fact, and created in Roosevelt and his advisers the impression that it was necessary to take urgent measures to save the situation in North Africa. The British Premier did not succeed, it is true, in recruiting the President on this occasion as a supporter of 'Torch': but Roosevelt's resolution, so far as insisting on an invasion of Northern France in the summer of 1942 was concerned, was greatly shaken.

On 8 July, on his return to London, Churchill sent the President a long cable, the essence of which will be clear from the following passage:

'Not a single responsible British General, Admiral or Marshal of the Air Force considers it possible to recommend 'Overlord' as a practicable operation in 1942. Personally I am convinced that the occupation of French North Africa is the best means of relieving the position on the Russian front in 1942'.

The situation thus created was a very acute one, and in order to find a way out of the difficulty there took place in London from 16 to 24 July a further conference of British and American representatives. The basic question was, 'Torch' or 'Overlord'? The Americans (Hopkins, Marshall, Eisenhower) stood by 'Overlord'. On the contrary, the British, and Churchill first and foremost, asserted the impracticability of 'Overlord', and demanded preparations for the seizure of Northern Africa. By 22 July the negotiations had reached deadlock.

Thereupon Hopkins, who on his own admission was 'devilishly discouraged' by the firm refusal of the British to accept 'Overlord', appealed to Roosevelt.

And what did Roosevelt do? His conduct was characteristic in the highest degree.

Roosevelt made no attempt to save the American plan adopted in April: he did not even approach Churchill directly on this subject, although he constantly maintained a considerable personal correspondence with him. Roosevelt simply accepted the British opposition as an irrevocable fact, and cabled Hopkins and Marshall that some other land operation against the German troops should be found, in which American soldiers might take an active part in 1942 under all circumstances. As possible 'other operations', the President indicated—in order of priority—an offensive in Algeria or Morocco; 'Torch'; military operations in Northern Norway; support of the British operations in Egypt; American operations through Iran into the Caucasus[1].

After receiving such directives, it was no longer difficult for Hopkins and Marshall to come to an agreement with the British in London. The victory lay with Churchill, and it was decided that in 1942 the British and Americans would carry out operation 'Torch'.

At the same time it was decided that preparations for 'Overlord' in the spring of 1943 would continue—but this was now only a high-sounding form of words. On this subject Churchill says in his memoirs: 'American military opinion . . . was convinced that the decision for 'Torch' ruled out all prospects of a major crossing of the Channel into Occupied France in 1943. I had not yet brought myself to accept this view.'[2] Churchill here is patently departing from the truth. Field-Marshal Montgomery writes in his memoirs: 'When the North African project was approved, it was accepted that the cost in joint resources would mean not only that any hope of an operation in Western Europe in 1942 would have to be abandoned, but also that it would be impossible to complete the

1. Sherwood, *The White House Papers of Harry Hopkins,* Vol. II, p. 610.
2. *The Second World War,* Vol. IV, p. 581.

assembly of forces in England for a major cross-Channel assault in 1943.'[1] If this 'was accepted', can one imagine that Churchill did not accept it?

Involuntarily there arises the question, how is such strange (it would seem) behaviour on Roosevelt's part, in the negotiations on a second front between the British and the Americans, to be explained?

In order to reply to this question, one must have a clearer understanding of the personality of the American President himself: because up till now it has been wreathed in the mist of legend which greatly idealises the real Roosevelt. Before the second world war, and during the war, he was often represented as an extreme left-wing democrat, almost a Socialist, as a kind of Abraham Lincoln of the 20th century. Roosevelt was spoken of as a strong anti-Fascist and a warm supporter of the self-determination of nations. I well remember H. G. Wells in 1934, on his return from a visit to the USA, heatedly demonstrating to me that Roosevelt, without calling himself a Socialist, was in reality by his 'New Deal' opening the road to Socialism. The famous writer became most indignant when I said to him that in my view the 'New Deal' in reality was opening the road not to Socialism but to the growing together of the monopolies with the State apparatus, i.e. to the further strengthening of capitalism. This legend about Roosevelt, which strangely emanated both from the President's friends (who were proud of it) and from his enemies (who were terrified of it), established itself so strongly everywhere, including the Soviet Union, that for a long time it prevented a clear vision of the real Roosevelt.

Yet in reality Roosevelt was not quite like his portrait idealised by legend. Personally I had occasion to encounter him at the Crimea Conference of the heads of the Three Powers in February 1945, and to observe him at close quarters for nearly ten days. I also had several conversations with him in the lobbies of the Conference. And summarising my impressions of Roosevelt at that time, and comparing them with all that I have heard and read about him on other occasions, I have formed the following conception in my mind of the figure of the American President.

Roosevelt was undoubtedly a statesman of very great calibre—two whole heads higher than men like his predecessor in the Presidency, Hoover, or his successor Truman: but he was a

1. *Normandy to the Baltic*, 1947, p. 1.

statesman of a purely bourgeois kind. He had an acute mind, a wide sweep in action, vast energy. He saw much further than did other representatives of the American ruling class. He understood that in the circumstances of the thirties and forties of the 20th century the defence of the interests of that class required not quite usual methods, and he adopted them resolutely, often provoking noisy resistance on the part of more reactionary and more short-sighted circles of the American bourgeoisie. Against their will, Roosevelt had recourse to measures which appeared very radical, in order to save American capitalism at one of the most painful moments in its history (the world crisis of 1929–1933). But Roosevelt always was, and remained to the very end, flesh of the flesh of the United States ruling class, and his famous 'New Deal', as I have just said, only helped to strengthen American capitalism.

The bourgeois essence of Roosevelt revealed itself vividly in the sphere of foreign policy also. Before the war it was within his term of office that the USA adopted the Neutrality Act (1935) which was a real gift for the Fascist aggressors—because it forbade American citizens to sell arms to warring States, independently of who was the aggressor, and who the victim of aggression. It was precisely on account of this law that the USA refused arms to Ethiopia when Mussolini attacked her. In just the same way, in the years of the Spanish war of 1936–1939, the USA supported the Anglo-French policy of 'non-intervention'—which was an only slightly-veiled intervention in favour of General Franco, and resolutely refused to sell arms to the Spanish Republicans. The American Government conceived of its 'non-intervention' so widely that, when in 1937 there arrived in New York a shipload of 500 children evacuated from the Spanish Republic and proceeding to Mexico, they were not allowed to go ashore to continue their journey through the territory of the USA.

Of course, Roosevelt as an outstanding politician understood earlier than most the danger which Hitlerism represented for the world position of the USA, and he made the necessary practical deductions from this. He even ventured on such an unprecedented act as participation in the anti-Hitler coalition together with the Soviet Union—and up to this day the American diehards cannot forgive him for this. But, while fighting side by side with the Soviet Union, Roosevelt nevertheless remained true to his bourgeois essence, and this showed itself very obviously in his attitude to the question of a second front.

I have already said that the American plan for the conduct of the war, which was put forward by Hopkins and Marshall with the President's sanction at the Anglo-American conference in April 1942, took as its point of departure purely military considerations, and only reckoned with the demand of the USSR for the opening of a second front in Northern France as last on the list. Roosevelt considered Germany to be enemy no. 1, and wanted to defeat her first of all. Japan was for him enemy no. 2. However there existed in the USA at that time an influential group headed by Admiral King, commander-in-chief of American naval forces, which considered that enemy no. 1 was Japan. When in the summer of 1942, thanks to the resistance of Churchill to organisation of 'Overlord', it turned out that 12 months of preparatory work would be required if that operation were to be effected in 1943, i.e. twelve months of passivity externally at the various fronts, Roosevelt was alarmed. Might not the King group make use of this passivity in its own interests? Might it not be able to 'convince' the decisive powers in the USA that Japan must be considered enemy no. 1?

The struggle against such a danger could be carried on in two ways. It was necessary either to resist Churchill and secure the fulfilment of 'Overlord' in 1942—which was quite possible, bearing in mind the difference in the balance of forces between the USA and Britain—or to follow Churchill's lead, renounce 'Overlord' in 1942, and seek for some other front in Europe or Africa where American soldiers could now, immediately, in the autumn of 1942, join battle with German Fascism. Roosevelt chose the second path, because this was suggested to him by all the instincts, habits, calculations, hopes and conceptions of a *bourgeois* statesman.

That is how it happened that in the summer of 1942, on the question of a second front, victory was won by Churchill.

When today, after many years have passed, I turned over in my memory all the details of the struggle around the opening of a second front in those far-off days, I again and again put myself the question, how could Roosevelt and Churchill sign in June a communiqué about opening a second front in 1942, knowing full well that on its eve, in April, they had decided to organise a second front only in 1943? How could they assure us that they would open a second front in 1943, when they were beginning Operation 'Torch' in the autumn of 1942?

Churchill said to me more than once:

'The enemy should always be deceived. The general public may be sometimes deceived for its own good, but an ally should never be deceived.'

The negotiations about a second front in 1942 serve as a splendid illustration of how the bourgeois statesmen, not in words but in deeds, conceived of their obligations to their ally.

5

Churchill goes to Moscow

In the middle of July 1942 the Germans began an offensive against Stalingrad. Although the Soviet troops displayed great stubbornness and heroism in defending their position, the enemy nevertheless gradually drove them back more and more. On 15 July Boguchary and Millerovo were evacuated, on 19 July Voroshilovgrad, on 27 July Rostov-on-Don and Novocherkassk. Violent battles took place in the areas of Kletskaya, Tsymlianskaya, Kotelnikovo, Belaya Glina and a number of other points on the Lower Don. These successes of the German army aroused great alarm in the Soviet Union and beyond its borders. In Britain there once again raised their head all kinds of Cassandras, who again began to urge in every possible way that the Hitlerite army was invincible, that the Russians would not be able to take a stand on the Volga, that this defeat would finally undermine the strength of their resistance and that possibly they might begin negotiations with Germany for a separate peace. After all, the Bolsheviks did conclude a separate peace with the Kaiser in 1918!

The events at the Soviet front gave me no peace. My diary has the following entry for 19 July:

'A heavy week! Things at the front are very serious. True, Voronezh is still in our hands, and we have even begun to press back the Germans there. But the situation in the south is becoming threatening. We have lost Kantemirovka, Boguchary, Millerovo. The Germans say they have also captured Voroshilovgrad (Lugansk). I don't know how far this is true. There is no confirmation from our side. In any case, the German advance in the valley of the Don has been developing during this last week rapidly and successfully, and now they are clearly threatening Rostov. It is quite obvious that the Germans are making for Stalingrad, and that they want to cut the line of the Volga and cut off the Caucasus from the other regions of the country. If they were to succeed in this, the position would become critical. Will they succeed? Some intuition tells me they will not . . . But for the time being one cannot close one's eyes to the fact that at present we are face to face with a deadly danger to our country, to the revolution, to the whole future of humanity.'

The entry for 26 July runs:

'Another heavy week! Our troops are constantly retreating. The Germans are capturing one region after another. Rostov has fallen. The enemy has crossed the Don in its lower reaches near Tsymlianskaya. The Fascist hordes are coming nearer and nearer to Stalingrad. They are nearer and nearer to the Kuban and the Caucasus. Shall we really not be able to hold the Germans? Will they really, after all, cut us off from the Caucasus and consolidate themselves on the Volga? It seems simply a kind of nightmare out of a horror story.

'No, both intuition and cold calculation tell me that this cannot be . . . There must come a moment when the retreat ends, when fresh reserves are brought into action, when we shall be able to go over to the offensive against an enemy weakened by losses and by his long line of communications. And judging from everything, this moment would not seem to be far off.'

In such a situation I could not sit passively with arms folded, and looked for means of helping my people at least in some little way at this time of great misfortune. I have this entry in my diary for 21 July:

'At my last weekend in Bovingdon I thought over a plan of immediate action . . . What can I do to interrupt the dangerous lethargy of the British ruling group, to bring into motion the forces which are locked up here, to facilitate the birth of a second front?

'Thinking about this as I walked through the gardens, I came to the following plan:

'1. Stalin must seriously put before Churchill the question of the convoys and a second front, underlining that our people do not understand Britain's passivity at such a dread moment for us, and that if there is no second front in 1942, the war may be lost or, at the very least, the USSR will be so weakened that for the future it will not be able to take any particularly active part in the struggle.

'2. After Stalin has sent such a message to Churchill I shall speak in the same spirit at a private meeting of M.P.s and to editors of the London papers.

'I have asked Moscow about this plan. I await the reply.'

I attributed particular importance to my address to M.P.s. Until now we had appealed to Britain through her Government, and the results we had were not very favourable. Now we should appeal to Britain through a wider and more representative institution—her Parliament. Of course, such a method of conversation with Britain was somewhat unusual (though there have been precedents of this kind in British political life), and it might create diplomatic complications. However, the moment was too threatening, and I decided to take the risk: an exceptional situation required, or at the very least justified, the use of exceptional means for influencing it.

My plan was accepted by Moscow, and on 24 July a message came from Stalin (dated 23 July) which very sharply raised the question of the convoys, while on the question of a second front it said:

'I fear the matter is taking an improper turn. In view of the situation on the Soviet-German front, I state most emphatically that the Soviet Government cannot tolerate the second front in Europe being postponed till 1943.'[1]

Stalin's message was couched in somewhat milder terms than I would have liked, but it had a powerful effect. When I visited Churchill to hand him the message (I quote here from my diary for 24 July), 'he was in his siren suit and in a bad frame of mind, As it turned out later, he had just received unpleasant news from Egypt . . . Through grief Churchill had evidently overdone it a little with his whisky. This could be seen from his face, his eyes, his gestures. At times his head jerked in a strange sort of way, and then one felt that in reality he is already an old man . . . and that only a frightful concentration of will and consciousness maintains Churchill's capacity to act and fight.

'Stalin's message made the impression which I had expected on the Prime Minister. He was at once depressed and offended (particularly by Stalin's accusation that he was not fulfilling his own pledges) and there even seemed to pass through his mind the

1. *Correspondence, etc.*, Vol. I, p. 54.

thought that USSR might possibly leave the war, because quite unexpectedly he said:

'"Well, we've been alone before . . . We went on fighting . . . It is a wonder that this little Island of ours stood up . . . But . . ."

'"That is nonsense!" I sharply interrupted Churchill. "None of us have the least idea in our mind of ceasing to struggle. Our road has been determined once and for all—to fight to the end. But you must reckon with the realities of the situation . . . "

'Churchill grew calmer, but went on for a long time demonstrating that he was doing all he could, and that on the question of a second front the memorandum which he had handed to Molotov at the signature of the communiqué on 12 June remained in force'.

It was now necessary to carry out the second part of the plan—my address to the M.P.s. The Anglo-Russian Parliamentary Committee undertook to be the organiser. On 30 July, in one of the large committee rooms (but not of course in the Chamber), my meeting with the M.P.s was held at 3 p.m. I quote some extracts from my diary, dated the same day:

'There were about 300 in attendance—as "old hands" assure me, something without precedent in the history of this kind of meeting. Sir Percy Harris (Liberal) was in the chair. Among those present were Elliot, Hore-Belisha, Mander, Aneurin Bevan, Erskine Hill, and others. All three Whips were also there. Most important, old Lloyd George sat at the top table . . . This aroused a sensation. It "created an atmosphere", as Sylvester put it'.[1]

I was very well received . . . Then I was called upon to speak.

I began by saying that in the course of the war there had arrived 'an exceptionally dangerous moment, when Allies should sincerely and honestly, not fearing words, exchange views and find by common effort a way to save the situation'. Then I briefly described the course of operations at the Stalingrad front, where the Germans 'by means of a colossal concentration of troops, and in the first place of tanks and aircraft . . . have been able to break through our lines in a number of places, and during the past month have taken possession of the whole valley of the Don. The German advance has not yet been stopped, and consequently the Lower Volga and the Caucasus are threatened', I continued. These events were of the greatest importance not only for the Soviet Union but also for all the Allies.

1. Lloyd George's principal secretary.

Further, I put the question of how an unsatisfactory state of affairs at the German-Soviet front could be explained: and replied:

'Let me make an interesting comparison. In the war of 1914–1918 Germany never kept more than one-third of its armed forces at the Russian front, and the other two-thirds were tied to the Anglo-French front. In addition, Germany at that time was simply Germany, with a small number of Allies who were more a hindrance for her than a help. Russia in those years, also, did not have to worry about defending other parts of its territory. Yet you know what was the fate of Russia in the first world war. Now the situation is quite different. Russia of our day—the Union of Soviet Socialist Republics—has now been withstanding the pressure of 80 per cent of all the German armed forces for the second year in succession. In addition it is obliged to defend with large armies certain other parts of its territory. Furthermore, with whom is present-day Russia carrying on the war? With Germany? No, not with Germany alone, but in effect with the whole of continental Europe! Too often people leave out of account the fact that Germany at the present time controls the destinies and resources of over 300 million people, in the countries which she has occupied and in those which are her so-called Allies. Of course, there is an opposition within those countries, often there is sabotage, but all the same the Soviet Union is now having to fight a giant concentration of forces far surpassing the forces of the old Empire of the Kaiser. Here lies the main reason for such a dangerous moment having been reached in the course of the war!'

From this I drew the natural conclusion: in order to straighten out the situation, to emerge from a danger zone not only affecting the USSR but also all the Allies, the urgent creation in 1942, not in 1943, of an effective second front in France was essential. It was essential to create a single strategy of all the Allies, and urgently to mobilise their resources. It was time to take from the shoulders of the Soviet people at any rate some part of that disproportionate burden which it had had to bear during the preceding thirteen months.

I return to my entry in the diary:

'During my speech there was tense silence in the room . . . Only at times was it interrupted by loud applause—for example, when I said that the Allies most of all needed a single strategy. The same occurred when I observed that relying on the vast figures of the potential resources of the Allies was one of the most dangerous forms of complacency . . . When I mentioned that the question of the second front had been raised by us for the first time in July 1941, it was as though an electric shock had passed through the audience.

'After my speech there were questions—many of them, but hardly any hostile.

'Then Lloyd George took me away to his own room in Parliament. Megan came. It was already 4.15: the meeting had lasted a little more than an hour. Tea was served. We went on talking while we had tea. The old man said that throughout his long Parliamentary life he could not remember many meetings like today's—in the number of those present, in the strained attention of the audience, in the impression made on my hearers by what I said.

'"It is a good thing you were frank, almost brutal. It worked. You were in a difficult position, but you managed your job very skilfully: you went far enough in your exposition, without overstepping the framework of diplomacy . . . The M.P.s learned the truth from you. You know the Government feeds them on soothing syrup . . . "

'"But what can be the practical result?" I asked him.

'Lloyd George shrugged his shoulders. He himself perfectly understands all the importance of a second front in 1942 of all years . . . But Churchill is displaying a strange, incomprehensible passivity.'

I left Lloyd George with mixed feelings: I was satisfied that I had spoken at the meeting of M.P.s—it was my duty, and I had done it—yet at the same time I was feeling bitter at the realisation that, judging from all the symptoms, there would nevertheless be no second front in 1942. Lloyd George's scepticism only confirmed my fears.

Half an hour after midnight there was a sudden telephone call: the Prime Minister's secretary asked me immediately to come to No. 10 Downing Street.

I could not help being alarmed. What was wrong? What had happened? Some internal voice told me that this invitation to Churchill at night was somehow connected with the meeting—but how? I had not doubted from the outset that my speech to the members demanding a second front would cause dissatisfaction, and possibly even irritation, in the Government, and particularly in Churchill . . . Could it be that the Premier wanted to express his disapproval to me? And was it really such an urgent matter that an Ambassador had to be called in at one in the morning?

I continued in the words of my diary for 30 July:

'When I entered the Prime Minister's study, Churchill was sitting at the Cabinet table. He was in his invariable siren suit, with a black and grey variegated dressing gown over it. Eden, in slippers and a green velvet jacket which he puts on "at home" in the evenings, was sitting by him. Both looked tired but excited. The Premier was in one of those moods when his wit begins to sparkle with good-natured irony, and when he becomes very attractive.

'"Look at this: is it any good?" asked Churchill with a smile, passing a sheet of paper over to me.

'I ran through the document.

'It was the text of a message from the Premier to Stalin, beginning with the words: 'I am willing, if you invite me, to come myself to meet you in Astrakhan, the Caucasus or similar convenient meeting place. We could then survey the war together and take decisions hand-in-hand.'[1]

'"Of course it is good, and very good!" I responded after reading it.

'I should say so: a meeting between Churchill and Stalin might have very great consequences. And I supported the Premier's intention in every possible way . . . I enquired whether Churchill would go to Moscow if Stalin could not travel to the South? The Premier hesitated, but ended by giving me to understand that in the last resort he was ready to agree to Moscow.

'I promised immediately to communicate with Moscow, as Churchill intended to fly to Cairo on 1 August—he had urgent business there—and from Cairo would continue his journey to the USSR.

'Eden came with me to the door. When saying goodbye, he said as though in passing:

'"How good it would be if you could travel with the Prime Minister!"

'I replied that I should like very much to go, but that was a question for the Soviet Government to decide . . .

'Neither Churchill nor Eden had said a word about the meeting in the House of Commons. But all the same I have a certain feeling

1. *Correspondence, etc.*, Vol. I, p. 57.

that Churchill's message is in some way connected with the meeting—but how?'

Churchill's message went to Moscow that same night, and on 1 August there was already a reply from Stalin, which I immediately passed on to the Prime Minister. In it Stalin officially invited Churchill to come to Moscow at a date meeting his convenience 'for joint consideration of urgent matters relating to the war against Hitler, who is now threatening Britain, the USA and the USSR more than ever.'[1]

And so the question of Churchill's meeting with Stalin was decided. The practical preparations for the agreed step began. Eden informed me that it was Churchill's hope that I would accompany him during the visit to Moscow. I wanted to do this very much myself: it would be so interesting to participate in such an historic event. But Moscow requested me to stay in London. It was a clear demonstration of the Soviet Government's dissatisfaction with Britain's conduct on the question of a second front. Eden and Churchill understood it that way.

I was very worried about how the meeting between the heads of the two Governments would pass off. Knowing the character of both men. I was afraid that at the discussion in the Kremlin of such an explosive problem as a second front things might not become so acute between them as only to worsen the existing situation. I considered that, in spite of all the difficulties and disappointments, the tripartite coalition must be the foundation of our military and political strategy. Therefore, in order if possible to reduce the danger of a 'quarrel' between Stalin and Churchill, I sent off a long telegram to Moscow in which I described in detail the temperament, manners, tastes and customs of the British Prime Minister, and underlined in particular that, in addition to official negotiations, he liked to chat on the most varied themes 'purely privately', and during such conversations aimed at establishing closer understanding and contacts with his partners. This telegram evidently made a certain impression on Stalin, since, as will be clear from what follows, Churchill's meeting with him was in the long run 'salvaged' precisely by a 'private talk' of this kind.

Recalling now the circumstances of Churchill's visit to Moscow, I would like to clear up more the motives which prompted him to

1. *Ibid.*, p. 58.

such an unusual step. He says in his memoirs that the defeat suffered by the British Eighth Army at Tobruk and the neighbouring area of North Africa in June 1942 had made essential his personal presence in Cairo for the reorganisation of the British High Command in the Middle East. He goes on:

'We were all anxious about the reaction of the Soviet Government to the unpleasant though inevitable news that there would be no crossing of the Channel in 1942.'[1]

Translated into more simple language, thist mean that the British and Americans were afraid that the disappointment aroused by their refusal to create a second front in Northern France in 1942 might introduce too deep a division into the coalition, and might lead in the long run to a separate peace between the USSR and Germany. That my interpretation of the phrase I have quoted is the right one has been confirmed in substance by Churchill himself. It is not accidental that in his telegram to the British War Cabinet on 14 August, despatched from Moscow, he says among other things: 'There was never at any time the slightest suggestion of their not fighting on.'[2] And in his report to Roosevelt and the War Cabinet of 16–17 August, Churchill sums up his conclusions as follows: 'On the whole I am definitely encouraged by my visit to Moscow. I am sure that the disappointing news I brought could not have been imparted except by me personally without leading to really serious drifting apart.'[3]

However, in my recollection, there was one more essential reason which prompted Churchill to take the initiative as regards a meeting with Stalin, and in such an unusual form ('I am willing, if you invite me'). The British Premier says nothing at all about it in his memoirs, but nevertheless the reason was very real and pressing.

The great events at the Soviet-German front met with a profound and sympathetic response in Britain. It sprang from two sources, emotional and political.

The great mass of the British democracy was delighted with the heroism of the Soviet troops and the Soviet people, standing firm to the death against the terrible enemy. The ruling group thought with anxiety: 'If the Russians don't make a stand on the

1. *The Second World War,* Vol. IV, p. 409.
2. *Ibid.*, p. 440.
3. *Ibid.*, p. 450.

Volga, what will become of our possessions in the Near and Middle East?' Both followed with the greatest attention every event on the Soviet-German front, hotly discussed all the moves and counter-moves of the adversaries, made agitated guesses about the outcome of the giant battle. The newspapers were full of the most detailed information about its ebb and flow. The radio many times a day gave the communiqués about the battles, supplementing them with the comments (not always competent) of military correspondents. All the Soviet staffs in London, whether of the Embassy, the Trade Delegation or the Military Mission, were showered with continuing questions, the essence of which amounted to the question of all questions: would they or would they not hold out?

Particularly warmly did all these feelings display themselves when at the end of June 1942 there came round the first anniversary of Hitler's attack on the Soviet Union. The rulers of Britain and the City expressed their sympathy and good feeling, but 'in measured terms'. The 'national press' behaved in the same way, since it reflected at bottom their point of view. But the masses of the people at large gave full rein to their warmth and enthusiasm.

A wave of great meetings devoted to the anniversary and the problem of a second front rolled over the whole country. I attended myself, as guest of honour, at a meeting of ten thousand people at the Empress Hall in London, where the main speaker was Stafford Cripps, then a member of the War Cabinet. His speech was that of a friend to the USSR, and he received the loudest applause when he let it be understood that Britain was preparing a second front in 1942. In the feeling displayed, in the speeches, in the telegrams read out, the meeting was astounding. A greeting came even from the Archbishop of Canterbury. As we left the meeting, some of our Soviet comrades said:

'Almost like Moscow...'

Of course, this was to some extent an exaggeration, but all the same it was a significant assessment.

In other cities the same went on. I sent into the provinces, to be present at the meetings as guests of honour, all the responsible personnel of the Embassy. In particular, my deputy and Counsellor, K. V. Novikov, went to Birmingham, where Lord Beaverbrook was to speak. This meeting was particularly successful: it was held in the open air, and more than 50,000 people were present. The mood was one of enthusiasm. Beaverbrook sharply put the question of a second front. The meeting answered with thunderous applause.

But perhaps even more characteristic was the following episode. The Lord Mayor of Birmingham, Alderman Tiptaft, was in the chair, and in his opening remarks said:

'People talk about Communism . . . But if now we were to have a vote on that question, the majority of the country would probably prove to be Communist!'

The meeting responded with a thunderous 'yes!', and drowned the next words of the Lord Mayor in tremendous applause.

Of course, Tiptaft's words had to be taken 'with a grain of salt', but nevertheless . . . what must have been the public feeling for such a statement to be made by the Lord Mayor of Birmingham, the citadel of the iron and steel companies and the nest of Chamberlainism!

Such feelings continued to be expressed. Thus, on 12 August there was a great open-air meeting at Glasgow, at which over 20,000 people demanded the immediate opening of a second front. The same was the demand of many British trade unions—the South Wales miners, the London engineers, the Lancashire textile workers and others. On 25 October 50,000 people, at a meeting in Trafalgar Square in London, demanded that the Government should organise a second front without delay.

Most characteristic also were the scenes which daily could be observed in the most ordinary British pubs frequented by the workers. Friends and colleagues would be drinking, joking, talking about anything and everything. But then the moment for the news bulletin would approach. There would be a sudden silence and tenseness. The wireless would go on. The communiqué from the Soviet-German front would be read out, and people would listen to it with bated breath . . . Then the radio would be as often as not switched off: no one was interested in the rest of the information. Ordinary British people, not privy to the secrets of 'high policy', caught by their healthy class intuition all the historic significance of the battle on the Volga, as the decisive turning point in the course of the second world war.

At the same time a vast campaign for the opening of a second front was developing across the Atlantic. At the beginning of August there was a wave of mass meetings in the cities of the USA which put forward the same demand (75,000 people in New York, 20,000 in Detroit, etc.). The same demand was put forward by the Convention of the Automobile Workers (10 August), by the Convention of the Congress of Industrial Organisations of the USA (15 November), and by a number of other American trade union organisations. The same demand was energetically put forward by prominent politicians and cultural figures and other organisations.

Particularly symptomatic was the conduct of Wendell Wilkie, Republican candidate for President. As Roosevelt's personal representative he visited Moscow at the end of September 1942, and in an interview with an *Izvestia* reporter said that, in his opinion, the most effective way of winning the war by helping the Soviet Union was the establishment by the United States, together with Great Britain, of 'a genuine second front in Europe and in the shortest possible time which our military leaders will approve'. On his return to Washington Wendell Wilkie, in an interview with the American press on 14 October, confirmed his Moscow statement.

In such circumstances my speech on 30 July to a crowded meeting of M.P.s, and particularly the sympathy with which it was met by such an influential audience, showed Churchill that the demand for the speediest opening of a second front was becoming popular now in circles which he had seriously to take into account. It was urgently necessary to take steps to 'calm down' the agitation, and to prevent a further rise of the pro-Soviet wave which might threaten the military policy of the government. The Prime Minister's journey to Moscow, his meeting and conversations with Stalin, were a splendid 'mustard plaster' for distracting public passion from the slogan of 'a second front now!' This motive, in addition to the others I have dealt with above, played no small role, it seems to me, in the decision of the War Cabinet to sanction the Prime Minister's visit to Moscow. And it would seem that my appearance before the M.P.s on 30 July was the final straw which gave the British Government to understand that there must be no further delay with this measure.

The following day, 31 July, I had an important talk with the editors of the largest British newspapers. As my meeting with the M.P.s was 'off the record', I could not give information about it to the press, which would have been very important from the point of view of the struggle for a second front in 1942. In order to overcome this difficulty, I invited the chief editors of the London newspapers to the Embassy, and substantially repeated to them the speech I had made the day before in the House of Commons committee room. During the following days and weeks this found its reflection in the attitude taken up by the various newspapers to the burning question of the moment.

Somewhat later, in September, I had a long talk on the subject of a second front in 1942 with a group of American newspaper correspondents in London. This meeting also had useful consequences for us.[1]

I return however to Churchill's visit to Moscow. As I did not take part in it myself, I have no personal recollections of it. All the same, I consider it necessary even briefly to give an account of it, making use of Churchill's memoirs, corrected by what I came later to hear and learn from other reliable sources (the Soviet version of the meeting between Churchill and Stalin in August 1942 has not yet been published).

On 2 August Churchill flew to Cairo, and on 10 August from Cairo to Moscow. The route passed through Teheran, the Caucasus and Kuibyshev: severe battles were still going on at Stalingrad. The Premier was accompanied by a large staff, including General Wavell, (Chief of the General Staff), Marshal of the Air Force Tedder, and Sir Alexander Cadogan, Permanent Under-Secretary for Foreign Affairs. In addition, Churchill was accompanied by Averell Harriman, who was representing Roosevelt. The British and American guests arrived in Moscow on 12 August, and stayed there three days.

The first meeting between Churchill and Stalin was on 12 August, and lasted four hours. All present were in an extremely tense condition. Nor was this surprising: Churchill was giving a detailed explanation of the reasons which had led the British and Americans to renounce the opening of a second front in 1942. His arguments, however, as might have been expected, did not convince Stalin, who said in reply that evidently the British and Ameri-

1. In the work by Sir Ernest Llewellyn Woodward, *British Foreign Policy in the Second World War*, 1962, there is the following passage on pp. 198–9: 'Russian propaganda in favour of a second front continued, and M. Maisky went on arguing to Mr. Eden that the Russian army and people had been led to expect this second front in 1942. M. Maisky himself, to the knowledge of the Foreign Office, was trying to persuade newspaper editors in London to exert pressure on the Government. The Foreign Office, as earlier, thought it best to take no notice of these activities, unless M. Maisky went wholly beyond the limit permissible to an Ambassador. On September 18 Mr. Eden had to send for him in order to complain of a talk which he had given to a number of American journalists, and in which he had said that a second front in 1942 was not only necessary but "entirely feasible"'.

cans were simply afraid of engaging the German army face to face. This provoked Churchill, and he began asserting that the Russians, as 'land' people, badly understood all the complexity and difficulty of naval landings. There was no agreement between the two sides, and each maintained its own opinion.

Then Churchill developed to Stalin a picture of 'Torch' and the prospects which it opened. He writes in his memoirs: 'To illustrate my point I had meanwhile drawn a picture of a crocodile, and explained to Stalin with the help of this picture how it was our intention to attack the soft belly of the crocodile.'[1] Using the large globe, the British Prime Minister explained what serious advantages for the Allies would be represented by clearing the Mediterranean of the enemy. Naturally, the Soviet side could not agree with the British, but, Churchill writes, 'at least the ice was broken' and 'we parted in an atmosphere of good will'.[2] This opinion of the results of the first meeting was too optimistic. Already the next day, 13 August, Stalin handed the British Prime Minister a memorandum which stated:

'As a result of the exchange of views in Moscow on August 12 I have established that Mr. Churchill, the British Prime Minister, considers it impossible to open a second front in Europe in 1942.'

Pointing out further that the opening of a second front in 1942 was anticipated by the Anglo-Soviet communiqué released on 12 June 1942, that the Soviet High Command, in planning its summer and autumn operations, had counted on a second front being opened, and that the refusal to open it delivered a moral blow to all Soviet public opinion, complicated the position of the Red Army at the front and injured the plans of the Soviet High Command, the memorandum continued:

'I and my colleagues believe that the year 1942 offers the most favourable conditions for a second front in Europe, seeing that nearly all the German forces—and their crack troops, too—are tied down on the Eastern front, while only negligible forces, and the poorest, too, are left in Europe. It is hard to say whether 1943 will offer as favourable conditions for opening a second front as 1942 ... Unfortunately I did not succeed in convincing the British Prime Minister of this, while Mr. Harriman, the US President's representative at the Moscow talks, fully supported the Prime Minister.'[3]

1. *The Second World War*, Vol. IV, p. 433.
2. *Ibid.*, p. 435.
3. *Correspondence, etc.*, Vol. I, pp. 60–1.

On 14 August Churchill replied to Stalin with a counter-memorandum, in which he stated that the only possible second front in 1942 was 'Torch', that Britain was breaking no promise made to the Soviet Union, because at the time of signature of the communiqué of 12 June Churchill presented Molotov with a restrictive reservation, and that none the less the publication of the communiqué was useful, because it had misled the enemy. Churchill further objected to any public controversy as to the meaning of the communiqué of 12 June, since it might only reveal the differences between the Allies and thus injure their common interests.[1]

After such an exchange of pleasantries the atmosphere, naturally, could not be particularly cheerful. Even the big official dinner given in honour of the British guests in the Kremlin, with a multitude of toasts and good wishes, proved incapable of raising the temperature. The parting threatened to take place on a note of high disharmony, if at the very last moment Stalin had not recalled the British Prime Minister's fondness for 'private' talks. On the evening of 15 August he invited Churchill to drink a glass with him in his apartment. The two Premiers sat over this 'glass' nearly the whole night, almost to the very moment of Churchill's departure from Moscow. Conversations on business—the convoys, the communiqué, etc.—mingled fantastically with talks on the most varied philosophical, historical and personal subjects. After his return to Britain Churchill told me:

'It was a wonderful evening . . . Stalin's daughter came in—as red-headed as my daughter Diana—kissed her father and sat down to table. But she didn't stay long. Then Stalin asked Molotov to come, and made fun of him the whole time. He himself took charge of opening the bottles. Soon there was a big battery of excellent wines on the table. I did my duty by them, but capitulated when a sucking-pig appeared after midnight. But Stalin attacked it with all his energy . . .'

On their way back from Moscow to Britain, the Prime Minister again stayed for a few days in the Middle East, and got home only at the end of August. For nearly a whole month the democratic elements in Britain, which had been loudly demanding the immediate opening of a second front, had been living in expectation that the heads of the two Governments would reach agreement on such an important question. Very soon after Churchill's arrival,

1. *Ibid.*, pp. 61–2.

the British propaganda machine began widely popularising the following words in the communiqué with which the British Prime Minister's visit to the USSR had concluded:

'This just war of liberation both Governments are determined to carry on with all their power and energy until the complete destruction of Hitlerism and any similar tyranny has been achieved. The discussions, which were carried on in an atmosphere of cordiality and complete sincerity, provided an opportunity of reaffirming the existence of close friendship and understanding between the Soviet Union, the United Kingdom and the United States of America in entire accordance with the allied relationship existing between them.'[1]

These words were interpreted by Churchill's supporters as evidence of the fact that now there were no differences between the USSR and Britain even on the question of a second front. Our Embassy introduced the necessary corrective element into the tendentious interpretation of the communiqué by Government propaganda. Nevertheless, a certain confusion and misunderstanding made themselves felt among the mass of the people, and the struggle for the immediate opening of a second front lost part of its urgency and resolution. The visit to Moscow was now paying dividends to Churchill, in the shape of a certain weakening of internal pressure on this most acute question of the day. This made it easier for the Government to manoeuvre for the next two or three months, after which there began the great battle on the Volga, which was the turning-point in the course of the whole of the second world war, and which raised many questions of strategy in quite a new way—including the problem of a second front.

1. *Soviet Foreign Policy during the Patriotic War,* Vol. I, p. 181.

6

The Convoys

RELATIONS between the Allies in the summer and autumn of 1942, apart from the question of a second front, were seriously damaged also by the problem of the convoys, which became acute just at that time.

I wrote earlier that on 1 October 1941 an agreement was signed in Moscow under which the USA and Britain were to deliver military supplies of various kinds to the Soviet Union. The content of this agreement (i.e. the quantities, qualities and types of equipment) was satisfactory on the whole from the Soviet point of view, but its realisation came up against the *problem of transport* first and foremost. There were two possible routes from Britain and the USA to the USSR: the northern, through Murmansk and Archangel, and the southern, through Iran.[1] The first was shorter, and the cargoes using it could be delivered to the rail-heads of a comparatively developed network of lines. The second was much longer, and cargoes using it could be delivered to the terminus of one railway with a small carrying capacity. Naturally, both the British and the Americans at first decided to use the Northern route to the maximum. In fact, for about four to five months after the agreement had been signed (between October 1941 and March 1942), all the supplies to the USSR from Great Britain and the USA went through Murmansk and Archangel. Usually the convoys of merchant ships were assembled in Iceland or nearby

1. There was also a third route, through Vladivostok, which the USA could have used; but in the first place it was inconvenient, because it necessitated transporting the cargoes through the whole of Siberia and, secondly, within six months after Germany's attack on the USSR, it was interrupted because of Japan's entering the war.

and then, protected by warships—British alone, or British and American—were directed to the two northern Soviet ports, where they were unloaded and, after a short rest, the ships returned by the same route. The darkness predominant in such northern latitudes during the winter made these maritime operations particularly easy. Moreover the Germans, being very much occupied with the blockade of Britain, had not yet had time to regroup and select the necessary forces for interrupting the supplies to the USSR from the Western countries. As a result, the convoys during the first four or five months proceeded in tranquillity and had hardly any losses. The route across Persia at that time was used very little.

But from March 1942 onwards the position began to change. The Germans organised a base for their surface and submarine fleet in the Norwegian port of Narvik. They concentrated there a considerable number of submarines, which began patrolling the waters of the Barents Sea in the areas of the North Cape and Murmansk. Large surface vessels also appeared at Narvik—the famous battleship *Tirpitz* (40,000 tons) and the cruisers *Scheer* and *Hipper* (both of 13,000 tons). In the North Cape region, on land, a powerful air base was built up. In March 1942 the Germans began a systematic and severe crusade against the convoys proceeding to the USSR. The favourite place for this became the comparatively narrow passage between the North Cape and Bear Island (about 220 miles). The convoys were hunted usually by aircraft and submarines; but in reserve were the large surface ships, which had a great psychological effect. The very mention of the *Tirpitz* used to throw the British Naval Staff almost into a state of panic. As a result of these changes, the passage of the Anglo-American convoys to Murmansk and Archangel from March 1942 began to change into an ever more complex operation—all the more because just at this time the Polar night began to yield place to the endless Polar day.

On 1 March 1942 a convoy left Iceland which had the code title of PQ12. It had its own protection of an appropriate number of warships, and in addition it was covered by the main forces of the British Navy, headed by the battleship *King George V* and the aircraft carrier *Victorious*. As the British Admiralty, the head of which at that time was Admiral Sir Dudley Pound, reported, the *Tirpitz* emerged from the West Fiord, in which it was concealed, intending to intercept PQ12. However, it was observed by a

British submarine, and on 9 March the aircraft-carrier *Victorious* attacked it with air torpedoes. The *Tirpitz* managed to escape damage, but was obliged to return after a fruitless voyage to the West Fiord. As a result, PQ12 reached its objective without any losses.

Things proved worse with the next four convoys, which passed through the danger zone in April and May 1942. PQ13 was subjected to a powerful German attack by aircraft and destroyers, and lost 5 vessels out of 19; in addition the British cruiser *Trinidad*, which was part of the escort, was lost. PQ14 was caught in heavy ice to the north of Iceland, as a result of which, of its 23 ships, 14 had to return to Iceland, one ship was lost and only 18 reached a Soviet port. In PQ15 and 16 there were 60 vessels, of which 10 fell victims to German attacks—and with them perished the British cruiser *Edinburgh*, which was in the protective escort.

Naturally, war is war, and it had to be reckoned as normal that the transporting of war supplies to the USSR could not take place without losses. The problem was only how to reduce the losses to the minimum. But Churchill took a different road. As we know, in the spring and summer of 1942 he was carrying on a desperate struggle against the immediate opening of a second front in Northern France, a struggle in which Roosevelt had at first attempted to resist him, but then yielded. Churchill did not confine himself to this. In April 1942, basing himself on the losses suffered by PQ13, he began a campaign against the despatch of convoys to the USSR altogether—at least until the end of the Polar day, i.e. almost for six months. And this at the time when the Soviet Union was on the eve of suffering the great German onslaught which ended, as is known, at Stalingrad!

Churchill consulted Roosevelt on this question. The American President at first strongly objected to the intentions of the British Premier, underlining the perilous political effect which such a step would have in the Soviet Union. At the same time Stalin, in a message of 6 May, made an urgent request to Churchill to send off to the USSR in the course of that month the 90 ships which had accumulated at that time in the ports of Iceland. Under pressure from these two sides, the British Prime Minister was obliged temporarily to retreat, and three more convoys—PQ14, 15 and 16—were sent off in May. But this was only a temporary retreat. The melancholy fate of PQ17, the next convoy—a fate for which the British Admiralty bore entire responsibility—gave Churchill a pretext once again to raise a clamour about the temporary cessation of the convoys, and in the end to achieve his purpose.

PQ17 consisted of thirty-four merchant ships, and left Iceland on 27 June. Its escort consisted of six destroyers, two submarines, two anti aircraft vessels and eleven other warships of lesser importance. The convoy was covered by two British, and two American cruisers and three destroyers, under the command of Admiral Hamilton. Nine British and two Soviet submarines cruised along the Norwegian coast, anticipating the possible appearance of the *Tirpitz*.

Further to the west, under the command of Admiral Tovey, there were the main naval forces, including the British battleship *Duke of York* and the American battleship *Washington*, the aircraft carrier *Victorious*, three cruisers and a flotilla of destroyers. It will be seen that there was concentrated in the area through which PQ17 had to pass a powerful armada, capable of crushing not only the *Tirpitz*. But what happened in reality?

Churchill, being extremely interested in white-washing the British Government, describes the course of events in his memoirs as follows. 'In view of the heavy ice, the convoy passed to the north of Bear Island. The Admiralty gave Admiral Hamilton orders which prohibited his cruisers proceeding eastwards from Bear Island, unless the convoy were threatened by surface vessels of such strength that it would be incapable of fighting them. Admiral Tovey with his main forces was 150 miles north-west of Bear Island, with instructions to attack the *Tirpitz* if it made an appearance. On 1 July the Germans discovered the convoy, and on 4 July, approximately 150 miles to the east of Bear Island, sank four vessels. Admiral Hamilton with his cruisers still continued on a route near the convoy. At that time news was received that on 3 July the *Tirpitz* had left Trondheim, but where it was going remained unclear. The Admiralty thought that the *Tirpitz* aimed at destroying the convoy, which it would reach by the evening of 4 July. As Admiral Hamilton's cruisers were powerless against the *Tirpitz*, the opinion of the Admiralty was that the only way to save even part of the convoy was its hasty dispersal. Therefore on the evening of 4 July the Admiralty, on the personal responsibility of its chief, Admiral of the Fleet Pound, Chief of the Naval Staff, gave Admiral Hamilton the order that the cruisers should be despatched westward at full speed, while the convoy should scatter and proceed to Soviet ports independently. Admiral Hamilton acted with headlong speed and even excessive zeal: he not only despatched the cruisers westward immediately, but ordered the destroyers and other warships escorting the convoy to do the same. Thus the convoy, consisting of slow-moving merchant vessels with a speed of six or seven knots, was abandoned to its fate by the warships at the most critical moment. The *Tirpitz* in the end did not put in an appearance, but in return the German submarines and planes furiously attacked the defenceless merchant vessels. The result is comprehensible: twenty-three ships out of the thirty-four perished, and the remainder only reached Soviet ports by a roundabout route (some around Novaya Zemlia) in the end, after the greatest efforts and sufferings.'

That is how this outrageous affair appears even in the patently prejudiced exposition by Churchill.[1] Understanding that the behaviour of the Admiralty gives serious grounds for charges against Pound, the former Premier seeks to find 'extenuating' circumstances. He writes that the decision of the Chief of Naval Staff to recall the cruiser squadron commanded by Admiral Hamilton from the area through which the convoy was passing was explained by fear that in a clash with the *Tirpitz* the two American warships which were part of the squadron might be lost, and this might have had unfavourable political consequences in the USA. As for the recalling of the destroyers and other warships from the convoys' escort, Churchill considers this wrong, but explains them by unauthorised action by Admiral Hamilton, for which Pound bears no responsibility.[2] However, all these excuses cannot make any essential change in the assessment of the story of PQ17, as one of the biggest failures of the naval forces of Great Britain in the course of the second world war.

Naturally, the destruction of PQ17 aroused a very sharp reaction on the part of the USSR. On 18 July Churchill informed Stalin of the fate of PQ17 and, after setting forth in detail all the difficulties of effecting the northern convoys during the period of Polar day, informed him that the British and American Governments had come to the conclusion that it was undesirable to send off PQ18 in the immediate future. Instead of this, Churchill promised to increase supplies to the USSR in every possible way through Iran. On 23 July Stalin replied to the British Premier very

1. *The Second World War*, Vol. IV, pp. 234–8.
2. *Ibid.*, pp. 235, 238.

strongly that 'the British Admiralty's order to the PQ17 convoy to abandon the supply ships and return to Britain, and to the supply ships to disperse and make for Soviet harbours singly, without escort, is in the view of our experts puzzling and inexplicable'. Further, Stalin pointed out that deliveries through the ports of Iran could in no way make up for the discontinuing of the northern convoys, and that 'no major task can be carried out in wartime without risk or losses'.[1]

Our Embassy and the Soviet Military Mission in London were sharply critical of what had taken place. Both I and Admiral N. M. Kharlamov, the head of the Mission, as well as all our leading personnel, did not conceal our indignation in talks with British politicians, journalists, sailors and soldiers. In the end there was such an atmosphere in the capital that Churchill was forced in some way to react. He instructed Eden to arrange a consultation of representatives of the Admiralty and the Soviet side, so that Admiral Pound should explain to us the motives for his action and convince us that it was justified. Such a consultation did in fact take place on 28 July in Eden's room in the House of Commons. On the British side there were present Eden, A. V. Alexander (First Lord of the Admiralty) and Admiral Pound: on the Soviet side there were myself, Admiral Kharlamov and his deputy N. G. Morozovsky.

Feelings at the meeting ran very high, and this was at once reflected in the discussion. I will quote here some extracts from the entry in my diary of that date.

'Throughout the whole meeting, only Pound spoke and decided on the British side. Eden and Alexander throughout were either silent, or allowed themselves brief interjections, timidly looking at such moments to Pound. It seemed as though Pound was the teacher, and Eden and Alexander the pupils, whose highest wish was to get good marks from their teacher. A typical picture for the theme of mutual relations between Ministers and officials in Great Britain.'

Eden suggested that Pound should be called upon to speak first, in order to explain all that had happened. But before Pound could say a single word, I said (continuing my entry in my diary):

'The question is, when will the next convoy be sent off? It would be desirable to have a reply to this question from Admiral Pound'.

Pound obviously did not like such a question. Therefore he

1. *Correspondence, etc.*, Vol. I, p. 56.

acted the half-wit, and declared that in the last message from the Prime Minister to Stalin on 18 July it had been suggested that one of the high officers of the Royal Air Force should be sent to Moscow precisely in order to preserve the possibility of further convoys: but that unfortunately in Stalin's reply of 23 July this point had 'been left without any reaction'. Yet it was of exceptional importance: the possibility of convoys, in Pound's opinion, depended entirely on the possibility of 'making the Barents Sea dangerous for the *Tirpitz* . . . There should be a powerful air protection in the region of Murmansk'.

It was clear that the despatch of an officer was a pretext to gain time: therefore I invited Pound to say at once, at today's meeting, how many planes and of what type, in his opinion, should be stationed in the region of Murmansk to make the Barents Sea 'dangerous for the *Tirpitz*.' I would cable it immediately to Moscow, in two or three days I would have a reply, and everything would be settled. The convoy could then be sent off without delay. Pound did not like my proposition, and continued to insist on sending a British officer to Moscow. I retorted that there was a British Military Mission in Moscow headed by Admiral Miles, and his deputy was Air Vice-Marshal Collier: why should not Pound make use of them to get the information he required? But Pound rejected this proposition too. He absolutely needed to send a special man to the USSR: otherwise it would be impossible to bring about further delay. Then I made yet a further proposition: let Pound send his man to Moscow, but don't let's make the despatch of the next convoy dependent on that. To fix the date of such despatch, let us make use of the telegraph, I along my line and Pound along his. I return at this point to my entry:

'Pound nevertheless continued to be stubborn, muttering something under his breath. This made me lose patience, and I exclaimed with irritation:

'"I ask you to say, Admiral, how many planes after all should there be at Murmansk? Or don't you know?"

'This stung the Admiral, and reddening he said sullenly:

'"There should be six squadrons of bombers and four squadrons of torpedo-carriers".

'"Very well" I replied. "This very day I will ask my Government, and on receipt of its reply it will be possible finally to fix the date of the next convoy."

'Eden supported the method for clearing up the question which

I had proposed. Alexander did not object. Pound willy-nilly had to reconcile himself to it. . . .

'Now that the question of PQ18 had been settled, we went over to PQ17, Kharlamov, as a sailor, thought it necessary to have a serious talk with Pound about the best means of escorting the convoys through the danger zone. Inevitably the question arose of the reasons for the destruction of the last convoy, and Kharlamov in tactful but sufficiently definite terms declared that on that occasion the British Admiralty had made a mistake. The basis of the mistake was that the *Tirpitz*, even if it had come out of the fiord in which it was stationed, could not all the same have caught up with the convoy. The distance from the fiord to the convoy was too great. Consequently there was no justification for recalling the cruisers, and still more the destroyers.

'Pound listened to Kharlamov with obvious impatience. His face grew redder and redder. His whole appearance showed that he was thinking: "Don't teach your grandmother to suck eggs! Some green Soviet Admiral tries to give advice to me, a British Admiral! It won't come off!" '

' "What do you mean, a mistake?" Pound suddenly exploded. "I gave that order! I did! And what else should I have done?"

'Here Alexander intervened, and pronounced a fiery speech in defence of Pound and the Admiralty . . .

'This provoked me, and I said with emphasis:

' "No one denies the great services of the British Navy in this war, but . . . but even British Admirals are not without sin."

'Pound grew even more furious, and said angrily:

' "Tomorrow I shall ask the Prime Minister to appoint you instead of me to command the British Navy!"

'I burst out laughing and said that I had no ambitions for such a high honour.

'Eden intervened, and began asking "both sides" not to give way to excessive excitement. Then he added:

' "And so the Ambassador will ask his Government, and we shall see later what should be done."

'On this the meeting ended.'

Two days later I met Vansittart and told him about PQ17 and the meeting in Eden's room. He remarked not without malice:

'What are you surprised at? . . . Who is Pound? . . . A poltroon and a sluggard . . . If he has to take any action, he will find ten arguments not to do it . . . Or else suddenly, God forbid, something will go wrong ... These qualities are well known in the Fleet ... Do you know what his nickname is on the lower deck? "Don't do it, Dudley!" ... That's Pound all over.'

The protest from Moscow, the protest by Soviet representatives in London, Roosevelt's objection to the stopping of the northern convoys had their effect, and at the beginning of September PQ18, composed of forty ships, left Iceland for the USSR. This time the escort for the convoys was reorganised: in addition to the general coverage by the main forces of the navy, it was accompanied by 16 destroyers and a small aircraft carrier with 12 fighter planes. In addition, at Churchill's request, the Soviet Government sent to the north large air forces for the protection of the convoy in the Barents Sea. The Germans made a furious attack, mainly using their aircraft, but all the same twenty-seven ships out of the forty arrived safely at Soviet ports.

Then there was once again an interruption. From October to December 1942 the British and Americans, taking advantage of the night which had begun in the northern latitudes, began sending individual ships to Murmansk and Archangel without any escort: they were sent one after the other in such a way that there should be not less than 200 miles between any two ships. Only on 22 December 1942 did PQ19, consisting of 30 ships, leave Iceland, and after a sharp naval engagement off the North Cape, without losing a single merchant vessel, it arrived safely at a Soviet port.

In his memoirs Churchill gives an interesting table showing the movement of the northern convoys in 1941–2.[1] During these fifteen months (the convoys began after 1 October 1941) there were despatched to the USSR in all 283 merchant vessels (124 British and 159 American), of which 219 arrived safely at their destination. 64 ships, 23 per cent of the total, were lost on the way. These of course were serious losses, but not such as making the despatch of convoys ineffective. Such was the situation at the most difficult period of the war, when the Germans were trying to break through to Stalingrad, while the USA had not succeeded as yet in developing their military industrial potential to the full. In 1943 the problem of the northern convoys began gradually to ease, and in 1944 ceased to be serious. Moreover, by that time there had opened wider opportunities for the use of the southern route through the Persian Gulf, because thanks to the efforts of

1. *The Second World War*. Vol. IV, p. 245.

the British and still more of the Americans the carrying capacity of the Trans-Iran railway was greatly increased.

Concluding this chapter, I would like to say a word of thanks to those thousands upon thousands of foreign seamen, particularly British and Americans, who took part in the northern convoys. It was complicated, difficult and dangerous work. Nature herself made these voyages to Murmansk and Archangel, especially in winter time, a severe experience. In wartime circumstances, when there were added to the cold, darkness, fogs and storms of the Arctic, German shells, bombs and torpedoes, such journeys became doubly frightening. One had to possess great courage, resolution and endurance to undertake such a voyage. Of course, not all the seamen travelled on the northern convoys out of a feeling of duty and patriotism. But all the same there were great numbers of them who had the highest motives for their action, and some most distinguished received orders and medals of the Soviet Union. If one takes the mass of the foreign seamen as a whole, one must say without hesitation that they gave no small aid to our country at a time of misfortunes and sufferings, and thereby to the cause of the great and historic struggle of the freedom loving peoples against the Fascist aggressor.

7

The Red Cross

It was as though a great spontaneous tide had suddenly flooded into the doors of the Soviet Embassy . . . Only a few days after Germany had attacked the USSR, I received a cheque made out in my name for £60,000 from the Miners' Federation of Great Britain. Holding in my hands the covering letter, in which the leaders of that famous union, on behalf of hundreds of thousands of their members, expressed their anger at German Fascism and their sympathy for the Soviet people, I could not help thinking: 'Krassin was right.' And this is what I remembered . . .

1926. The great strike of the British miners in defence of their living standards. Its leadership in the hands of the Executive Committee of the Miners' Federation, headed by A. J. Cook, their General Secretary, a young and energetic left-wing trade union leader. The General Council of the TUC tries to support the miners by the General Strike, but on account of the half-heartedness and cowardice of its leaders does not push matters to their conclusion, and after nine days capitulates. The miners, however, don't want to bow the knee to the mine-owners. They decide to continue the struggle alone. Their resistance becomes a genuinely heroic battle. For six whole months 600,000 miners stand with folded arms, insisting on the satisfaction of their demands. However, the coal-owners, supported by the Baldwin Conservative Government, stubbornly refuse to make concessions. The position of the miners becomes more difficult day by day. The financial resources of their own union gradually become exhausted. The help given to the miners by the other unions cannot cover the expenditure on strike benefit. The strikers sell household effects, get into debt, go hungry. Their children during the strike are taken in by workers in other trades. There is gloom and anger in the mining villages. The Government, the coal-owners, the press denounce the strikers as traitors to their country. The miners don't surrender. But there is a merciless ruler in the world—hunger and its power attacks the strikers more and more deeply and painfully . . . Will they still be able to resist this deadly stage of their enemies for long?

But a new and important factor had appeared on the scene. The Soviet trade unions were holding out the hand of friendship to their British brothers. Among the Soviet workers—not only the miners—collections had begun on a large scale in aid of the British miners. The Soviet trade unions also voted large sums from their funds.

At certain intervals the Central Council of Trade Unions transferred these sums as they accumulated to the Miners' Federation of Great Britain. In all, during the strike, about £1,000,000 were transferred from the USSR to Britain. This enabled the British miners to continue their struggle and to end it not entirely at the mercy of the coal-owners (there could have been no question of a victory, given the balance of forces at the time).

In the autumn of 1926 I was present at a curious discussion in the study of L. B. Krassin, who at that time was Plenipotentiary Representative of the USSR in Great Britain.

Two members of the staff of our London Trade Delegation had said:

'We ourselves need so much, and have so little foreign currency. Are the Moscow comrades right in spending such large sums in foreign currency to help the British miners?'

Leonid Borisovich smiled and said:

'You can't approach this question in such a businessman's spirit. You must look further and wider. Yes, it's not easy for us at present to spend foreign currency in support of the miners in this country: but how is it you don't understand that the Soviet aid afforded them at this difficult time wins the hearts of hundreds of thousands and millions of British workers in our favour? It makes it more difficult just now for the Diehards to organise a crusade against the Soviet Union. It may later on lead to the British proletariat coming to our help, at a moment which will be difficult for us . . . Who knows what the future conceals?'

And now, fifteen years later, Krassin's wise words had been justified. How characteristic it was, in fact, that the *first* contribution after the German attack on the USSR had come from the Miners' Federation of Great Britain!

After this first contribution there came others, in a continuous and ever expanding stream, from trade unions, from the most varied organisations, institutions, groups and individuals. There were co-operative societies, schools, factories, small workshops, editorial offices of newspapers, artists' societies, cinema staff and officials of various Ministries. I recall very well Lord Woolton, the Conservative Food Minister, arriving at the Embassy with a cheque for £1,500 collected by the staff of his department. A little later, the Liberal Sir Archibald Sinclair, Air Minister, brought a similar contribution of £1,500.

In addition to these collective contributions there were countless gifts from individuals. Workmen, farmers, shopkeepers, intellectuals, housewives, sailors, policemen, school-children—all sent the Embassy their mite, whatever each could, wishing thereby to express their sympathy for the Soviet people and lighten even to a little extent the burden of suffering which had fallen to its lot. Sometimes the contributors said precisely what their money should be spent on—drugs for the wounded, the purchase of an ambulance, aid for orphans, warm clothes for the families of mobilised men and so forth. But in most cases people sent their money for the needs of the Red Cross in general, without indicating any special purpose. There were quite touching cases. Thus, two taxi drivers sent a few shillings every month, each time with letters wishing the Red Army speedy and decisive victories. I recall another remarkable case.

During the second Five Year Plan there worked at Grozny, at the oil wells, under a scheme for technical aid, a British oil technician Brian Montague Grover (such cases were frequent at the time). He fell in love there with a Soviet girl, the daughter of a local chemist, and wanted to marry her. But his contract ended, and he returned to England with a heavy heart. All his efforts to get permission for his sweetheart to go abroad were unsuccessful. Nor could he get a visa for returning to the USSR. Thereupon Grover acted like a real twentieth-century Romeo. He learned how to pilot an aeroplane, bought a second-hand sports machine, and in November 1938 flew illegally from Stockholm to the USSR, in order to fight there for the possibility of marrying the girl he loved and taking her away with him. He flew across the Soviet frontier without mischance, but his petrol supply was insufficient, and he had to make a landing on a collective farm somewhere near Kalinin. Here he was arrested, and sent to Moscow together with his plane. The investigation began. Grover quite frankly described the reasons which had led him to break the Soviet law. It was an extraordinary case, and a report was made to the highest authorities. Even in those severe times, the highest authorities thought it over. As a result, Grover was set free and permitted to marry and take his wife away to Britain. On their arrival in London, the couple visited me and asked me to transmit their gratitude to the Soviet Government for the kindness shown them. They also gave the press an interview in terms very friendly to us.

After that I lost sight of Mr. and Mrs. Grover. I heard only that Grover had gone away to work in one of Britain's African colonies, Kenya. And now suddenly this remarkable pair again appeared on my horizon. Soon after the German attack on the USSR I received from them a very warm letter, expressing their deep sympathy with the Soviet Union and informing me that they had organised a local collection in aid of the Soviet Red Cross. In fact, we received money orders from them several times, part of the general torrent of our collections, which exceeded during the first two years of the Soviet-German war (up to our departure from London for Moscow, of which more below) £650,000.[1]

The spontaneous flow of contributions faced the Embassy with a number of questions which had to be settled urgently and (quite often) independently.

The first question, however, was one of organisation. From the very beginning it became clear that the stream of contributions would be wide, prolonged and constantly expanding. Who should take charge of this entirely new branch of work at the Embassy?

At that time the Red Cross organisation in Moscow had had neither experience nor worked-out forms for this kind of activity. Regulations for foreign branches of the Soviet Red Cross were published only two years later, in 1943. It would have been

1. Much later I learned that Grover was unable to find work in his own profession in Kenya, and had become a fairly successful farmer. His family life was happy, and they had two sons.

possible, of course, to entrust its work to one of the Embassy secretaries: but this would have meant at once making the whole business bureaucratic, and greatly reducing the great voluntary element for which it opened the way. This was undesirable. It seemed to me more correct to take another path. It is very common in Britain that highly placed women should be at the head of funds similar to the Red Cross. The President of the British Red Cross ('The Society of the British Red Cross and the Order of St. John of Jerusalem', as it is officially called) is not the King but the Queen. Before the war the Aid for China Fund was headed by Lady Cripps, the wife of Sir Stafford Cripps. During the war, as will be told in greater detail later, the largest 'Russian Aid Fund' had Mrs. Churchill at its head. It therefore seemed appropriate to set up a fund in aid of the Red Cross of the USSR attached to the Embassy, and put my wife at the head of it. This would very much be in keeping with British customs, and would open the widest opportunities to the fund. For my wife, as Ambassadress, had connections and acquaintances which could be used in the interests of the fund, but were inaccessible either to a Secretary or even a Counsellor of the Embassy. This calculation justified itself fully as events turned out.

A. A. Maiskaya was 'regularised' as head of the Red Cross Fund at first by an Embassy order, and then later was sanctioned by the Red Cross in Moscow. Of course all her work was done in a voluntary capacity. A very small staff was got together to help her: at first consisting of one, later two and finally three, paid out of the Red Cross collections. Much was done to organise the office work of the Fund by V. P. Nadezhdin, a member of the Embassy personnel. Matters continued in this way until the middle of 1943, when after the publication of the regulations referred to earlier, Professor S. A. Sarkisov arrived in Britain as representative of the Red Cross.

I should say here that A. A. Maiskaya's work was energetically supported by the whole London Soviet colony. Everyone tried to do something to help, and this took the most varied forms in practice. The women of the colony, led by the wife of the head of our Military Mission A. A. Kharlamova, knitted, sewed, packed up and dispatched warm clothes for the Red Army and the civil population. The men, who constituted the majority of the staff of the Embassy, Trade Delegation, Military Mission and other Soviet institutions in Britain, gave help to the Red Cross in other ways: Admiral N. G. Morozovsky busied himself with 'pushing through' the Red Cross cargoes into the convoys for the USSR, the Embassy accountant Kuleshov carried on the tremendous work of registering the income and expenditure of the fund, workers in the Trade Delegation—I. T. Kachurov, A. I. Dubonosov, A. I. Mekhantiev and others—acted as technical advisers of the Fund when placing its orders with British firms, and so forth. Valuable help in establishing connections with British medical institutions was given by V. S. Grazhul, a member of the Embassy staff who was a doctor by profession.

Among the many sincere friends of the Fund among the British, I should like to mention here Dr. Geoffrey Vevers, Vice-Chairman of the Zoological Society of London. In the first world war he had been a British army surgeon in France; later he had become an expert in parasitology, and had published a number of scientific works on this subject. Later still he had transferred to the Zoological Society. Long before the war he had become a friend of the Soviet Union, and had twice been in our country. From the very first days of Germany's attack on the USSR, Vevers had thrown himself with unusual passion into the work of helping the Red Army and the Soviet people. He did a great deal to help the Fund to establish connection with various suppliers of drugs, medical instruments, materials, etc. He also supervised the quality of the materials acquired, and carried on tireless propaganda for aid to the USSR in British scientific quarters.

Another question which faced the Embassy was that of the best use of the money collected. On this subject A. A. Maiskaya had considerable correspondence with Moscow (the Red Cross, the Army Surgeon's Department and others) and received from them long lists of what was required for the front and for the rear. The Red Army's needs, of course, had first place. On the basis of these lists she distributed orders to the various British firms, since the production of medicines, medical instruments and apparatus was in private hands, as it is today. Sometimes there were serious complications as a result. Our Fund had to encounter the competition of a number of other funds for aid to Russia, which will be mentioned later, and also of the orders placed by British medical institutions. It was here that my wife was able to make good use of her responsible position as Ambassadress with a wide circle of connections and acquaintances. In the event of any difficulties she appealed to Mrs. Churchill, who always willingly helped her, or to members of the Government or leaders of the trade unions, and in the end was successful.

I will give one characteristic example. I have mentioned that Lord Woolton, the Food Minister, on one occasion came to the Embassy to hand A. A. Maiskaya £1,500 collected by the staff of his department. Just at that moment there arrived from Moscow a request for 200 tons of glucose. The British authorities could provide us with half this quantity, but 100 tons were still lacking. My wife knew that the Food Ministry also had glucose at its disposal. When taking the cheque from Lord Woolton, she complained to him that she could not find anywhere the necessary 100 tons. Lord Woolton very amiably promised her to arrange this; and in fact, a few days later the necessary quantity of glucose was received. However, Lord Woolton as we learned subsequently had some unpleasantness to put up with as a result of his action. It turned out that the 100 tons of glucose possessed by the Food Ministry was at that moment the last reserve of this commodity in Britain (glucose was usually supplied by the USA); but Lord Woolton thought it embarrassing to break his promise to the wife of an Allied Ambassador, and therefore fulfilled his promise in spite of everything.

Here I am obliged to make a small digression. In the book *My Darling Clementine* published in London, Mr. Jack Fishman, quoting the words of Lady Limerick, Vice-President of the British Red Cross during the war, states the following:

'"She (Mrs. Churchill) was also in frequent contact with Madame Maisky, the wife of the Russian Ambassador, and this involved her in dealing with a slightly embarrassing situation, because Madame Maisky used to come forward with long lists of requirements not necessarily related to the official lists from Russia." Where she got her information from, nobody knew, but she often said we must have this, that, and the other, and on the lists from Moscow there was no mention of these things; so Clementine had quite a job handling Madame Maisky.'[1]

Lady Limerick for some unknown reason was simply seeing complications where none existed. In reality there was nothing strange in A. A. Maiskaya's behaviour, and she more than once explained to Mrs. Churchill where she got her lists. The scheme of relations between the USSR and Britain in this respect amounted

1. *My Darling Clementine, The Story of Lady Churchill*, 1963, p. 248.

to the following: the Soviet Red Cross sent its official lists to the British Red Cross, and in addition sent *supplementary* lists to our Embassy Red Cross Fund, calculating that their cost would be covered by that Fund. However, when carrying out the supplementary requirements from the Red Cross, A. A. Maiskaya sometimes had to ask for the help of Mrs. Churchill in order to overcome difficulties arising from the privately-owned nature of the British drug industry.

Other organisations were set up—the National Anglo-Soviet Fund for Medical Aid, headed by Dr. Hewlett Johnson, Dean of Canterbury (July 1941): the Women's Anglo-Soviet Committee, headed by Mrs Beatrice King (September 1941): the Fund for the Relief of Women and Children in Soviet Russia, of which Mrs Henry Martin was secretary (October 1941): the Fine Arts Fund, of which Sybil Thorndike was President (December 1941): all these maintained contact through a Joint Committee for Soviet Aid. In addition, the General Council of the TUC had its own fund. The largest organisation was that set up by the British Red Cross, however, under the title of the 'Aid to Russia' fund, headed by Mrs. Churchill.

There can be no doubt that Mrs. Churchill as a person was sincerely absorbed by the work of her Fund, and did all that she could to help the USSR. In my diary I find the following entry for 16 March 1942:

'Churchill spoke with admiration of the Red Army, and of the vast increase in sympathies for and prestige of the USSR in Great Britain. He added with a laugh:

'"It's gone so far that my own wife has been completely Sovietised . . . All she talks about is the Soviet Red Cross, the Red Army and the wife of the Soviet Ambassador to whom she writes, with whom she talks on the telephone or speaks at demonstrations!"

'And then with a sly look, Churchill said:

'"Couldn't you get her elected to one of your Soviets? She really does deserve it."'

Mrs. Churchill, of course, was not elected to any Soviet, but when in the spring of 1945 she came to the USSR, she was received by the head of the Soviet Government, she made a long journey through the Soviet Union and she was decorated with the Order of the Red Banner of Labour. I believe she fully merited these acts of recognition on our part.

When my wife and I were leaving Britain in the autumn of 1943, we experienced much satisfaction in summing up the results of the activity of the Embassy Red Cross Fund.[1]

1. By the time of our departure from Britain the total sum collected by the Embassy Red Cross Fund over the two years was £650,000, and during the next two years up to the end of the war another £150,000 were collected.

In this connection it is interesting to quote the figures of collections by the other Funds which I have mentioned. They were:

	By mid-1943	*By the end of the war*
Mrs. Churchill's Fund	£3,000,000	£8,000,000
Hewlett Johnson's Fund	£250,000	£800,000
Trade Union Fund	£500,000	£700,000

8

The great turning-point

THOSE were difficult, very difficult days . . .

In May 1942 the Germans captured the Kertch Peninsula. On 3 July, after a second heroic defence lasting 250 days, Sevastopol fell. The whole of the Crimea was in Hitlerite hands. Our offensive on the south-western front, in the area of Kharkov, which began on 12 May, encountered a powerful counter-offensive of the Germans. The High Command of the front asked General Headquarters for permission to make a timely withdrawal, but Stalin refused. The offensive continued, and as a result the Kharkov group of the Soviet armies fell into encirclement by the enemy. With the greatest difficulty it broke through the encirclement and reached the northern Donetz, but its losses were very great. On 28–30 June the enemy began an attack on Voronezh and Stary Oskol. The Soviet troops offered a stubborn resistance, and the advance of the Germans on this section of the front was halted, but the situation remained extremely unstable. From the middle of July the military position began to take on a still more menacing appearance . . .

Now, many years later, we know that Hitler had been obliged to take note to a certain extent of the lessons of 1941, and to realise that he had not enough strength to carry on simultaneously a big offensive in three main directions—towards Leningrad, Moscow and the Ukraine—as he had tried to do in the first year of the war. Therefore in the campaign of 1942 he set himself more limited objectives: the capture of Leningrad, and the occupation of the Caucasus and the Lower Volga with their vast natural resources. The Führer was particularly hypnotised by Baku oil.

There were also other important considerations impelling him to direct the main blow southward: if Germany succeeded in reaching the Caucasus, there would open before her the intoxicating prospects of easy penetration into Iran, Syria, Egypt and India. The British Empire would suffer irreparable damage, while the Near and Middle East would become a province of Germany . . .

Yes, we know all this very well now. But at the time, in the spring and summer of 1942, we could only guess where the Germans intended to inflict the most serious blow.

Only by the middle of July did General Headquarters begin to understand the true intentions of the Germans. The course of military operations pointed ever more clearly to the enemy's centre of attention this time being the South. Only at the end of August did discussion begin at General Headquarters (on the initiative of the front) of organisation of a Soviet counter-blow in the South, and only in the second half of September were the first practical steps taken to put it into effect.

All that time the Germans were uncontrollably driving forward to the objectives which attracted them. Hitler formed two groups of armies—group 'A' which was advancing in the direction of the Caucasus, and group 'B' advancing in the direction of Stalingrad. By the middle of July the Germans, systematically pushing back the Soviet forces in spite of their stubborn resistance, reached the great bend of the Don. On 25 July group 'A' captured Rostov-on-Don and, developing its success, went on to occupy Novorossiisk, Maikop, the Mineralnye Vody district and at the end of September approached Mozdok. Here it met such strong resistance that it was obliged to halt its offensive without even reaching Grozny. In the Stalingrad direction fierce battles went on for a long time in the region of Kotelnikovo, Kletskaya, Kalach, but nevertheless on 23 August the Germans (General Paulus' 6th Army) succeeded in reaching the Volga for the first time, north-west of Stalingrad. All these were undoubtedly big successes for the enemy, but he did not achieve his main purpose: the Soviet troops, who had learned by this time the art of the war better, retained their fighting capacity. They fought well, but unlike the first months of the war never allowed themselves to be 'bottled up': at the suitable moment they withdrew and continued to fight on new lines.

From London I could not see all the details of this great drama, all the reorganisations, regroupings, replacements of one commander by another, which went on in the course of the battle: but the main lines of the developing picture were quite clear. The Hitlerites, sparing neither men nor resources, were furiously breaking through to the Volga and the Caucasus, while the Soviet men were standing against them to the death, fighting to the last man, bleeding to death—yet slowly, step by step, stubbornly clinging to every position, every hill, every rivulet, were retreating before this terrible avalanche of fire and metal. Willy-nilly there arose the question: what next? Would the Red Army stand fast before the accursed enemy? Would it hold Stalingrad? Would it defend the Caucasus successfully? . . . The more deeply the Germans lunged into the Don Steppes, the nearer they came to the Volga and the foothills of the Caucasus, the more torturing these questions became.

By the middle of September the Germans reached Stalingrad itself, and battles began on its outskirts. A fortnight later they succeeded in capturing the central and southern parts of the city. The Mamai Hill repeatedly changed hands. The front line passed through the territory of the Tractor Works, but the departments and workshops remaining in our hands continued to work, repairing damaged tanks, wrecked cars and guns put out of action in battle. 14 October was a day of particularly hot fighting: the struggle went on for every house, every floor, every staircase. The Germans succeeded in breaking through to the Volga in the city itself.

I have kept a copy of my letter to M. M. Litvinov at the end of October 1942. At that time Maxim Maximovich was Soviet Ambassador to the USA, and we exchanged views and news at every convenient opportunity. This letter gives a good picture of the feelings which the events taking place on the Volga aroused in me.

'This last month I live only with thoughts of Stalingrad,' I wrote to Litvinov, 'or more precisely, I am tortured by having to live through all that is going on there. A terrible picture, and yet a heroic one. I don't know whether there has been anything like it in history. I believe not. And I think, think and think without end: will we hold out on the Volga or not? Objectively the position would seem desperate. Goebbels is already shouting that Stalingrad has been taken, that there remain only individual pockets of resistance and that their liquidation is a matter not for the army but for police units. Goebbels of course is exaggerating, but from our communiqués too the situation looks critical. And still I don't believe, I cannot believe in the fall of Stalingrad! In the very depth of my heart there still lurks a spontaneous feeling that this is not the end. The very greatness of the heroism displayed at Stalingrad makes its continuation inevitable. If only this feeling is not deceiving me! . . . Perhaps in it is reflected that fact, full of the greatest historical significance, that our country has never in any conditions perished. I am sure she will not perish now either.'

The spring and autumn of 1942 were difficult for the Soviet Union. They were also difficult for Britain. Churchill writes in his war memoirs:

'I had now been twenty-eight months at the head of affairs, during which we had sustained an almost unbroken series of military defeats. We had survived the collapse of France and the air attacks on Britain. We had not been invaded. We still held Egypt. We were alive and at bay; but that was all . . . The fact that we were no longer alone, but instead had the two most mighty nations in the world in alliance fighting desperately at our side, gave indeed assurances of ultimate victory. But this, by removing the sense of mortal peril, only made criticism more free. Was it strange that the whole character and system of the war direction, for which I was responsible, should have been brought into question and challenge?'[1]

To the above there were added the vast difficulties at sea. During those twenty-eight months of which Churchill spoke, there were sunk a number of the largest vessels of the British Navy (including such capital ships as the battleship *Prince of Wales* and the battle cruisers *Repulse* and *Hood*). Every month, as a result of the activities of the German air force and the German submarines, there perished about 600,000 tons of merchant ships, with their personnel and cargoes. Even with the help of the USA, Britain could only with the greatest difficulty maintain its imports of food stuffs and raw materials at the minimum essential level.

In such circumstances the ground under Churchill's feet again temporarily began to shake. Arguments and differences broke out in Government circles on the conduct of the war. At the time I did not know all the details which were later so fully described by Churchill in his war memoirs, but their substance was well known to me.

1. *The Second World War*, Vol. IV, pp. 493–4.

One group of critics, headed by Lord Trenchard, put their main faith in the air arm. On one occasion I talked about this with Marshal of the Air Force Harris, He said to me frankly:

'If I had sufficient planes and pilots, I would win the war in the shortest possible time by destroying Germany to her foundations. But I haven't enough—that's the whole trouble!'

I began objecting, and pointing out that the notorious 'Douhet doctrine' considerably exaggerated the importance of aviation: but Harris would not agree with me at any price. He even quoted for me some concrete calculations as to the number of bombers and fighter planes which were necessary to crush from the air any possibility of resistance by Germany.

Another group of critics put forward the view that Britain, as had happened more than once in the past, should anticipate a prolonged war, and prepare for it appropriately both in the material and the psychological sense. In the autumn of 1942, Lord Hankey —one of the main representatives of the 'cunctatorial school of thought'—published a long article, in the *Sunday Times* if I am not mistaken, in which he demonstrated that the second world war would last not less than ten years.

A third group of critics, whose most outstanding representative was Stafford Cripps, considered that the whole machinery of leadership of the war should be radically reconstructed. He considered that the greatest possible element of centralised planning should be introduced into the waging of war. He proposed that for this purpose there should be set up a Directorate of War Planning, composed of Churchill as Minister of Defence and of his three highest advisers, who would not deal with any departmental affairs and would devote all their time and energy to the conduct of the war. The Directorate would have to work out war strategy and future military operations, replacing the Chiefs of Staffs Committee which then existed.

In every theatre of military operations there should be a single commander-in-chief, directly responsible to the Directorate. He should have at his disposal all arms in his region, and he should be assisted by a small joint military, air and naval staff for the particular theatre of operations.

Churchill disagreed with Cripps' plan, considering it impracticable. When telling me its essence, Cripps said:

'Winston thinks I am a dreamer and a utopian, but I am firmly convinced that my plan is the shortest road to victory.'

Cripps and Churchill could not come to an agreement. As a result, Cripps stated that he was resigning from the War Cabinet responsible for the general conduct of the war, but was ready to remain in the Government as one of the departmental Ministers. Churchill then appointed him Minister of Aircraft Construction, and Cripps remained in this post up to the end of the war.

All this internal struggle kept Government circles in a state of high fever for several months, and at one time there was even a question of a change of Prime Minister. But the general feeling, not only in ruling quarters but also among the general mass of the people, in the long run inclined to the conclusion that it was better not to make any experiments. The British have a proverb: 'Don't swop horses in mid-stream.' The spirit of this proverb triumphed in this particular case too.

One day at the end of September 1942 I had a long talk with Lloyd George. The old man was very worried by the prospects of the war, and frankly recognised the difficult position of the anti-Hitler coalition. Briefly going over the situation at each of the fronts, he concluded:

'Of course, every front has its importance, and some of our fronts are even very important: but all the same the most important today is what is going on in your country, on the shores of the Volga. This battle is truly of world importance. If you win it, Hitler and all his yes-men are done for. Not at once, not immediately, only in the long run, but still they are finished, finished for ever . . . But if you lose this battle . . .'

Lloyd George was silent for a moment, and then concluded with an effort:

'In that case I am frightened to think what will become of mankind . . . On the outcome of what is now taking place on the shores of the Volga depend the destinies of the world in the fullest sense of the word . . . I warmly wish you the most complete victory there!'

Two vivid and inspiring memories remain with me from those difficult and worried days—so strangely are the dark and the light interwoven in real life.

On one occasion Cripps invited my wife and myself to listen to the playing of the famous London pianist Myra Hess. It was agreed that we should first dine at a French restaurant in Soho, the foreign quarter in central London, and would then go to the flat of Myra Hess, with whom Cripps and his wife were close friends.

We met at the appointed time in Soho, had dinner, talking on various subjects, and were about to leave . . . Suddenly there was an unexpected howling of the sirens. A German bombing attack on London was beginning. After Germany's onslaught on the USSR the severe air attacks on Britain had ceased, but all the same from time to time Goering strove to remind the British that he had not forgotten them, and was ready to amuse them with his devilish toys as a sign of his attention.

What should we do? We could have stayed in the restaurant for the duration of the raid, in its bomb shelter. But we did not wish to deprive ourselves of the anticipated pleasure, took our seats in the car and drove to Myra Hess' flat in the north-western part of London. The journey was a fairly long one, and all the time bombs were bursting with a terrible roar first to the right, then to the left of us. Finally we reached the pianist's dwelling. She was in a very courageous mood, and said with joy:

'Well, thank goodness you have managed to get here! I was afraid that because of this stupid raid our musical evening would be ruined'.

She offered us a cup of tea, and then sat down to the piano. The bombs were continuing to fall, and pillars of flame were being thrown up in one direction or another. Myra Hess meditated for a moment, as though recalling something important, and then suddenly struck the keys. The sounds of Beethoven's *Appassionata* broke forth.

Myra Hess always played very well. But now, perhaps of the inner agitation aroused by the dramatic circumstances, she surpassed herself. The wonderful sounds poured in a passionate torrent, seizing upon one's mind and heart. We listened spellbound, not noticing the howling Junkers, paying no attention to the sinister sounds of the gradually subsiding raid.

When Myra Hess ended, we sat silent for a long time without moving. I thought to myself: 'If such things as the *Appassionata* exist on the earth, if people can rejoice so deeply in its wonderful harmony under the thunder of bombs and the howling of bombers, it means that all is not yet lost . . . It means we shall conquer!'

Another memory is of a somewhat different nature.

At the beginning of November 1942 a little group of Soviet Young Communist Leaguers came to London. There were three of them—Nikolai Krasavchenko, Vladimir Pchelintsev and Liudmila Pavlichenko. At that time the Allies were making great efforts to mobilise the youth of various nations for the struggle with the Fascist Powers, in a mobilisation spiritual as much as military. For this purpose there were organised large-scale international conferences of youth in the USA and Britain, at which our Komsomol trio represented the Soviet Union.

They visited America first, and the President's wife, Eleanor Roosevelt, was particularly kind to them: and from America they came to England.

Naturally, our Embassy provided the most friendly atmosphere for the Komsomol delegation and gave it every possible help in fulfilling its tasks. The delegation took part not only in the international youth conference in London, but also in a number of youth meetings up and down the country, telling them the truth about the Soviet Union and underlining the exceptional importance of a second front for achieving the speediest possible victory over Hitlerite Germany. Our young comrades everywhere enjoyed great attention, but particular attention was centred on Liudmila Pavlichenko. And this was quite natural: a student of Kiev University, she had become one of the best snipers at the Soviet front, and when she left to go abroad had accounted for 309 German soldiers and officers. She was greatly in demand during the reception at the Embassy on the occasion of the November anniversary in 1942. There can be no doubt that our Y. C. Lers did a great and useful work during their stay in the British Isles. The main thing was that they so well embodied the youth of the Soviet Union, fresh, strong, brave, profoundly confident of the future of their country and their people. This made a great impression, and many British people who came into contact with our trio said afterwards: 'A country which has such a youth cannot be conquered.'

On 14 November, by invitation of the International Youth Conference, I had to speak to the delegates about the world situation; and when today, many years later, I cast my eyes over the text of that speech, I am particularly struck by the spirit of optimism with which it was pervaded. I said: 'Your conference has opened at the time when very important changes are taking place on the world field of battle . . . We feel the first gust of a fresh wind breaking into the charged and difficult atmosphere in which the United Nations have been breathing up till now.'

Yet the speech was made even before the beginning of our counter-offensive at Stalingrad! Evidently at that moment the second world war was reaching its great turning-point, and everyone felt this on both sides of the front. Not by chance did Hitler, in his speeches of October-November 1942, twice scream hysterically: 'I shall not capitulate!'

On the morning of 20 November I received from Moscow an urgent message from Stalin addressed to Churchill. It stated:

'We have begun offensive operations in the Stalingrad area, in its southern and north-western sectors. The objective of the first stage is to seize the Stalingrad-Likhaya railway and disrupt the communications of the Stalingrad group of the German troops. In the north-western sector the German front has been pierced along a 22-kilometre line and along a 12-kilometre line in the southern sector. The operation is proceeding satisfactorily.'[1]

'At last!' was the thought that flashed like lightning through my mind. I was greatly excited, and almost danced with joy. I translated the message into English immediately, and took it to Churchill. He ran rapidly through the text, and, pondering over it, replied:

'That is magnificent news . . . If only . . . If only your offensive doesn't die away in a few days.'

'It won't die away!' I cried.

At that moment, of course, I really had no evidence of this, but I wanted terribly that that should be the case—and I could not imagine that Stalin would have sent such an optimistic message to Churchill without sufficient foundation. I remembered, though, how nearly a year before, on the eve of Eden's departure for Moscow, I had reacted to Churchill's doubts whether the forthcoming Anglo-Soviet negotiations would take place in Moscow, and not in Kuibyshev (I remind the reader that in December 1941 the Germans were on the threshold of the capital). I had then said sharply: 'Of course, in Moscow!' And I had proved right. Now I obstinately said to myself: 'I will be right this time too.'

Churchill's thoughts on that memorable day of 20 November were occupied with the Anglo-American invasion of Northern Africa which had just begun (more details of this later): and he began to talk about the conditional nature of all strategic calculations:

1. *Correspondence, etc.*, Vol. I, p. 77.

'Our landing in Algeria and other places turned out very successful, but the further development of operations since then brings us surprises and disappointments . . . The process is slower than we hoped and expected: we constantly discover difficulties which we had not anticipated.'

And then, wishing somewhat to soften the impression of his scepticism regarding the Soviet counter-offensive on the Volga, Churchill added:

'In any case, I warmly wish you the very greatest successes in the battle of Stalingrad!'

Thus began the great turning-point on the Volga, which was fated to become the turning-point of the whole second world war.

I shall not attempt to describe in detail the events at Stalingrad. They are well known, and several valuable works have been written about them.[1] However, for the better understanding of the story which follows I need all the same to dwell for a moment on the main stages of that remarkable battle.

On 19 November 1942 the units of the Red Army concentrated to the east and north-east of Stalingrad went over to a decisive counter-offensive against the German troops.

The Red Army's blow—and this perhaps may seem almost a miracle—took place suddenly. The Germans had not expected it. After a gigantic artillery preparation, Soviet divisions broke through the German lines on both flanks, and impetuously began to invest the 6th German Army under the command of General Paulus which had been operating in Stalingrad. By 23 November this Army had been enclosed in a ring, and by 30 November 300,000 Germans were firmly encircled by Soviet units.

Hitler tried to break through the Soviet encirclement from without, and free Paulus in this way. A powerful group of German armies commanded by Field-Marshal Manstein was hastily formed, and on 12 December it began a violent offensive against the Soviet troops surrounding Paulus from the direction of Kotelnikovo. But the attempt to liberate the 6th Army from its 'bottle' was a failure,

On 8 January 1943, in an effort to avoid unnecessary sacrifies and sufferings, the Soviet High Command invited Paulus to surrender, guaranteeing to all German soldiers, officers and generals

1. A. M. Samsonov, *The Stalingrad Battle*. Moscow 1960; *The Great Victory on the Volga*, edited by K. K. Rokossovsky, Moscow 1965 (both in Russian).

their safety, and after the end of the war a return to Germany or to any other country at their choice. But Hitler even now would not hear of any capitulation. As a result, Paulus rejected the Soviet offer.

On 10 January the liquidation of the 6th Army began. On 2 February the last remnants of the surrounded group of Hitlerites in the north of Stalingrad surrendered.

So ended the great battle which will remain forever one of the decisive battles in the history of mankind. The Red Army took prisoner 91,000 Germans, including twenty-four generals and about 2,500 officers. Hitler's hysterical screams and gestures on this subject only underlined all the more vividly the gigantic nature of the Soviet success.

Our successes did not end at Stalingrad. The Germans were now obliged hastily to evacuate the North Caucasus. The Red Army liberated Rostov-on-Don, Kharkov, Kursk, the Donetz valley and reached the shores of the Dnieper. At the other end of the front the Red Army broke through the blockade of Leningrad. The offensive of the Soviet armies continued until the end of February. Like some titan who had come to life, this workers' and peasants' army moved irresistibly westward, driving the Hitlerite hordes before it.

9

The War in Africa

SIMULTANEOUSLY with the great battle on the Volga, serious events were taking place in Northern Africa.

I have described earlier how in the autumn of 1940, immediately after the fall of France, Mussolini decided to seize Egypt and thereby inflict a painful blow at the imperial interests of Great Britain. The situation seemed to favour the Italian dictator: Abyssinia, Eritrea, Somaliland were already under his heel, in Libya about 200,000 Italian troops were disposed along the motor road stretching along the southern shores of the Mediterranean, and in Egypt the British at that time had only about 50,000 men, who, moreover, were seriously affected by lack of arms. In addition the Egyptian King Farouk and all his entourage were displaying unmistakable sympathies for the Fascist Powers, particularly for Italy, and did what they could to sabotage the defensive measures of the British.

On 13 September 1940 Marshal Graziani, who commanded the Italian forces in Northern Africa, began an offensive in the direction of Egypt, and four days later occupied Sidi Barrani, which was on Egyptian territory. However, for various reasons, among which no small part was played by differences between Graziani and Mussolini, this success was not further exploited, and there was a pause in the military operations which lasted nearly three months. The British took advantage of it. After transfering additional troops and weapons to Egypt, they began a successful counter-offensive at the beginning of December 1940, and by 8 February 1941 they pushed the Italians back to Benghazi, approximately half way between Alexandria and Tunis. At the same time

Abyssinia, Eritrea and Somaliland revolted, and with the energetic help of Great Britain they liquidated the 'East African Empire' of Mussolini.

In March 1941, to save his Italian ally, Hitler sent the first detachments of German troops to Northern Africa. The united German and Italian units went over in their turn to a counter-offensive pushed the British out of Benghazi and forced them to retreat eastward to the fortress of Tobruk. Here military operations again died away for many months.

Only in May 1942 were battles in North Africa resumed. The considerably strengthened German and Italian forces under the command of Rommel attacked the British, took Tobruk on 20 June and began to advance rapidly further eastward. By the end of July the British army had entrenched in the district of El Alamein, only about 100 kilometres to the west of Alexandria. The situation created was a very perilous one: but luckily for the British the German and Italian forces by this time were so exhausted and depleted that they were obliged to halt for a rest. The lull lasted about three months, and the British once again made good use in their own interests of such a fortunate pause. They brought more troops and arms to Egypt, and moreover completely reorganised their command in the Near East. At the end of August 1942, on his way back from Moscow to London, Churchill stopped at Cairo, personally visited the fronts, carefully studied the situation and then took resolute measures. General Alexander was put in command in the Middle East, while General Montgomery was put in charge of the Eighth Army, operating on the Egyptian front. Both these generals were considered to be the best of their kind in the British Army. The results showed themselves without delay.

On 23 October 1942 the Eighth Army took the offensive at El Alamein against Rommel's German and Italian troops. It proved very successful, and by 5 November the enemy was obliged to begin a retreat. Montgomery followed at his heels without giving him a breathing space. Demoralisation began in the ranks of the German and Italian troops: the Germans began seizing the means of transport and hastily withdrawing to the west, leaving the Italians to their fate. This naturally made the task of the British easier. Montgomery tirelessly advanced, while Rommel retreated without cease. On 4 February 1943 the Eighth Army crossed the frontier of Tunis from the east, and forced Rommel to abandon

Egypt and Libya for good. Henceforth these strategically and politically important areas came finally under the control of the British, greatly facilitating another big military operation which became known under the code title of 'Torch'.

From what I wrote earlier, it will be remembered that Churchill in July 1942 succeeded in winning the acceptance of 'Torch' (the invasion of Northern Africa) as the main Anglo-American operation for the winter of 1942–3. In August preparations for this began. The operation was an extremely complex and multiform one.

A large modern army had to be transferred by sea from the USA and Britain. Part of these forces were to reach the shores of Northern Africa direct from the USA, another part had to travel a shorter distance, if nevertheless sufficiently long, from Britain. At some point these two sections had to be united, and thenceforth to act on a single strategic plan. Secrecy had to be observed, at least for the most important stages of the operation, which in circumstances prevailing in the West was not easy. The fleet transporting the troops had to be protected against hostile submarines and planes. The neutrality of Franco Spain had to be assured. It was necessary to overcome—if possible without bloodshed—resistance by French generals and their troops, distributed through Tunis, Algeria, Morocco and formally recognising the authority of Vichy. Immediately after the occupation of the Northern shores of Africa it was necessary to organise the military and administrative government of the occupied districts. Lastly, it was necessary to complete 'Torch' as quickly as possible, since it was the necessary condition for 'Overlord' (the invasion of France), the fulfilment of which in 1943 at that time figured in the strategic programme of the Allies.

By the end of October, just at the time when the Eighth Army began its victorious advance at El Alamein, preparations for 'Torch' were completed in the main, and on 8 November 1942 the Anglo-American invasion of Northern Africa began. It took place simultaneously at Algiers, Oran, Casablanca, Dakar and some other ports. In order to facilitate the occupation, an 'American' character was given deliberately to the whole operation, up to the point that the British troops which were being landed wore American uniforms. It was thought that the French military in Africa would put up more easily with invasion by the USA, to which they had no particular hostility. On the contrary, they could not forgive Britain the bombardment of the French warships in July 1940. This calculation was justified to a considerable degree, and the seizure of the most important ports of French Northern Africa went off 'cheaply' for the British and Americans, as Churchill writes in his memoirs.[1]

Having landed, the British and Americans naturally attempted to develop military operations and consolidate their positions as quickly as possible. In Algeria and Morocco they were easily successful, but in Tunis things were otherwise. Hitler decided to offer serious battle in this French colony. Already on 9 November, i.e. the day after the beginning of the Anglo-American invasion, the first German units arrived in Tunis by air. By the end of November the number of German troops in Tunis rose to 15,000, and thereafter continued to increase, finally reaching 100,000. A large number of German planes and even tanks also arrived. As a result, Hitler succeeded in building up in Tunis a strong force by African standards, which under Rommel's command seriously retarded the completion of 'Torch'.

General Eisenhower, who commanded this Anglo-American operation, yielded to Rommel's superiority and gave up the intention of seizing Tunis at one swift blow, although the Anglo-American troops at one moment were only twelve miles from the city of Tunis. Instead, Eisenhower began accumulating forces and engaged in other preparatory measures requiring a longish period. This made it possible for Rommel to take the offensive and to push back the British and Americans, in spite of the fact that, as has been mentioned, the British Eighth Army commanded by Montgomery entered Tunisia from the east on 4 February.

'Torch' was not only of military significance it also had an extremely important political and administrative aspect.

The territories occupied by the British and Americans differed somewhat in their legal status. Tunisia was simply a colony, Algeria was a French Department, while Morocco was a Protectorate. Effectively, however, France was 'master' of all three States. Everywhere there were French garrisons commanded by French generals, and everywhere administrative authority was in the hands of the French, mostly again French soldiers. After the fall of France in June 1940 all her African possessions recognised the Vichy Government, and those in control of them displayed

1. *The Second World War*, Vol. IV. p. 564.

obvious hostility to Britain because of her destruction of the French Navy when it was in African waters. Therefore one of the most important tasks in preparations for 'Torch' was to bring over to the side of the Anglo-Americans the French troops and French administration in these possessions, or at any rate to neutralise them. In the prevailing circumstances the solution of such a problem, naturally, could be more easily tackled by American diplomacy rather than British. And in fact, in the autumn of 1942 Robert Murphy, a political representative of the USA, arrived in French North Africa. He began a large-scale effort to 'work over' the French military and administrative leaders, and achieved notable successes in this respect: not all of them agreed to put up with an Anglo-American invasion, but many were inclined to treat 'Torch' as the lesser evil in this situation.

But when the Anglo-American landing actually took place, there arose acutely the question of who was to be at the head of the political and administrative machinery in French North Africa. There could be no doubt that it must be a Frenchman—but who in particular? There were two candidates on the horizon at that moment, Giraud and de Gaulle. Giraud was a well-known French general, who had just made a sensational escape from German captivity, who understood little in politics and who oriented himself in the main on the USA. De Gaulle was the head of the Free French, a French patriot in the old style and a man of firm and independent character.

Roosevelt favoured Giraud, and wanted to see him as military and administrative head of Northern Africa. The American President was clearly unfriendly to de Gaulle, because in his opinion the latter displayed too much independence and obstinacy in his opinions and policy. But Giraud, whom the Americans on the eve of the invasion had even brought as far as Gibraltar, encountered from the French generals and politicians of Northern Africa such an icy reception (to be explained by various personal considerations) that there could be no question of appointing him the head of the machinery of government. As, on the other hand, the Americans would not hear of de Gaulle. In the end this post was given to Darlan, who was by chance at Algiers just at the moment of the invasion.

Darlan was an Admiral in the French Navy, a reactionary, a man of resolute character who enjoyed great authority in French leading military and naval circles, and violently anti-British in his opinions. This choice had little attraction for the British—the Left did not like Darlan as a reactionary, while the Right did not like him as an anti-Britisher: but for the time being Churchill had to put up with the situation created.

But democratic circles in Britain would not keep quiet. In Parliament, in the press, at public meetings they developed a wide spread agitation against the appointment of Darlan as administrative head of Northern Africa. They argued, not without justification, that the Allies had publicly declared that they were carrying on the war for the overthrow of the Fascist Powers, the liberation of the peoples and the establishment of the principles of democracy among them. Yet no sooner were these areas of Northern Africa liberated than the Allies were putting in power such a hardened reactionary as Darlan! How could this be reconciled with their political professions? The mistake must be immediately put right.

The campaign against Darlan was carried on at the same time in the USA, although on a somewhat smaller scale than in Britain: but this naturally raised the anti-Darlan wave still higher in the British eyes. Recalling those days Churchill writes in his memoirs:

'Passion ran high in England about the Darlan deal . . . Many of those with whom I was in closest mental and moral harmony were in extreme distress. All these emotions were fanned by the de Gaulle Committee and organisation in our midst. The Press gave full expression to this mood.'[1]

I can testify that Churchill not only does not exaggerate, he rather understates the strength of the indignation aroused in Britain by the Darlan affair: because he does not mention the reaction to it of the broad mass of the people, particularly the workers. It is worth noting that in ruling quarters too there were a few people who on account of Darlan's anti-British attitude were opponents of his appointment, and who therefore not only did not resist the democratic storm which shook the country, but even privately supported it or, at any rate, maintained the principle of friendly neutrality towards it. As a result the position of Churchill and his Government, who had officially sanctioned the deal with Darlan, proved very difficult.

And lo, at the very height of the political storm, the British Prime Minister received powerful support from the most unexpected quarter . . . Stalin!

1. *The Second World War*, Vol. IV, p. 572.

On 24 November 1942 Churchill sent the head of the Soviet Government a long message dealing with many different questions. In section 6 of this message he thought it necessary to apologise for the appointment of 'the rogue Darlan' as Governor-General of Northern Africa, and to reassure Stalin (whose disapproval he clearly expected) as regards the consequences of this step. On 28 November a reply message came from Moscow, in which the fourth paragraph read:

'As for Darlan, I think the Americans have made skilful use of him to facilitate the occupation of North and West Africa. Military diplomacy should know how to use for the war aims not only the Darlans, but even the devil and his grandmother.'[1]

When I handed Stalin's message to Churchill, the following scene was enacted. The Premier rapidly and without emotion ran through the first three paragraphs, dealing with Turkey, the convoys and the importance of personal relations between the heads of government: but, upon reading the fourth paragraph, he stopped, raised his eyes, thought for a moment and then, with tears in his eyes, exclaimed in moved tones:

'Oh Stalin, how grateful I am to you! You understand me so well!'

I knew that Churchill was a bit of an actor, and could in case of necessity, half-consciously and half-instinctively, bring tears to his own eyes: but nevertheless I could not doubt that at the moment he really was very moved. Soon after this, in order to allay the storm, Churchill was obliged to make a big speech at a secret session of the House of Commons. In it he quoted very effectively the fourth paragraph of Stalin's message. This made a tremendous impression, and the protests against the appointment of Darlan soon ceased.

Darlan remained, but the course of events very rapidly solved the problem facing Roosevelt and Churchill in its own way. On 24 December 1942 Darlan was shot dead. The man guilty of the assassination, Bonier de la Chapelle, a youth of twenty, was arrested and two days later executed. The circumstances of the whole affair remain unclear up to this day, and in particular what were Bonier's motives in shooting Darlan, and who was behind him. However that may be, Darlan's death disposed of an acute problem for the British and Americans. Churchill writes in his memoirs on this subject:

1. *Correspondence, etc.*, Vol. I, pp. 79–80.

'Darlan's murder, however criminal, relieved the Allies of their embarrassment at working with him.'[1]

In Britain the news of Darlan's death produced a universal sigh of relief, not only in democratic circles, but in those of the Government as well. I recall the conversation which I had at the beginning of January 1943 with Brendan Bracken, the Minister of Information.

'How did you meet the New Year?' he asked me.

'Splendidly,' I replied. 'I have had a wonderful New Year's gift: the blockade of Leningrad has been broken.'

And then I asked in my turn: 'And how did you meet the New Year?'

'Very well indeed,' he responded. 'I have also had an excellent New Year's gift: Darlan has ceased to exist.'

On the threshold between 1942 and 1943 new and fresh winds made themselves felt over the world for the first time. Although the great battle on the Volga was not yet over, the nightmare of Fascist oppression was beginning to disperse. Mankind's road to liberation from the menace of Hitlerite slavery began to show itself more clearly. The peoples raised their heads . . .

My diary has the following entry for 1 January 1943:

'A new year has begun, and we met it joyfully. Our feelings were quite different from those of a year ago. The main change is that during these twelve months we have measured up to the enemy at full height, experienced his strength and tested our own, compared our strength with that of the enemy and have become firmly convinced that we are the stronger. Of course much time and effort will still be needed to defeat him, but there is no doubt of the outcome. The whole question now is only this, not to break down ourselves in the process of crushing the enemy, and not to arrive at the finish in a state of complete exhaustion. Skilful manoeuvring will be needed for this—on the field of battle and on the field of diplomacy . . .

'One's thoughts involuntarily run ahead. First of all, when do we await the end of the war in Europe?

'I remain of my previous opinion which I expressed in October, that the end of the war in Europe can be awaited not earlier than 1944. And that if the Allies' affairs go well, i.e. if there is no split between them, or such friction as will paralyse the effectiveness of

1. *The Second World War*, Vol. IV, p. 578.

combined operations, and if a good second front in Europe is created in 1943. When particularly in 1944 one can expect an end of the war, it is difficult to foresee, but somehow I am inclined to think it will be in the spring or summer of 1944.'

Reading through this entry today, many years later, I cannot help comparing it with the actual course of subsequent events. It seemed to me then that victory would come approximately a year after the establishment of 'a good second front in Europe' (of course, on condition that unity between the Allies was preserved, as it luckily was until the end of the war). As in 1943 Britain and the USA opened no second front in Europe (I will deal with this later), the dates in my calculation were naturally postponed for a year. However, after the 'good second front' had at last been opened on 6 June 1944, victory came on 8 May 1945, i.e. eleven months later. Thus the 'formula' of my calculations was not far off the truth.

The impression created in Britain by the victory on the Volga was tremendous—and with inner contradictions.

All were amazed first and foremost at the astonishing heroism of the Red Army and the Soviet people. Churchill in his memoirs, recalling those days, writes of the magnificent struggle and decisive victory of the Russian armies. Less official and more objective people expressed their feelings much more vividly. Our Embassy was literally flooded with the most enthusiastic letters about the victory on the Volga. There were deputations from factory workers to express their greetings and their confidence in the defeat of Germany. Representatives of voluntary organisations, committees and groups of all sections of the people came to thank the Soviet people and the Red Army for their deathless achievement. Particularly touching were the visits from school children.

I remember one particular visit—from a group of children in an East End school. After the teacher had said a few words, a very pleasant small boy of about twelve got up and made a brief but intelligent speech on behalf of all the children in their school.

'We are so glad that you are beating those Nazis. We hate them. When we grow up, we shall fight them too.'

Then a little girl got up and told excitedly how she had already knitted three pairs of socks for 'our Tommies'. Tongues were loosened, and every member of the deputation tried to describe how much he or she hated the Nazis and what they were doing useful for the victory over them.

I looked at my guests, thinking: 'The victory on the Volga is saving you all from death, and opening the future before you . . . Perhaps you will live to see the victory of Socialism all over the world.'

When they were leaving I said to my young visitors:

'Remember one thing, children: the Red Army is a kind army, it wants everyone to be happy, and particularly children like you.'

In such circumstances ruling circles also were not stingy in expressing their joy and sympathy. My wife and I suddenly became 'heroes of the hour'; at social and diplomatic receptions everyone congratulated us, everyone poured invitations upon us, all tried to express their regard and their gratitude. The press and the radio were lavish with their praise for the Red Army, the Soviet people, the manners and customs of our country.

The Royal Society itself decided to make a commemorative gift to the Academy of Sciences of the USSR: the first edition of Newton's *Principia,* and Newton's letter as President of the Royal Society (which was already in existence) announcing its election of Alexander Menshikov as its member. Both gifts were presented to me in ceremonial circumstances, for transmission to the Presidium of the Academy of Sciences of the USSR.

On 23 February 1943, the twenty-fifth anniversary of the Red Army, the British Government publicly commemorated the date in the biggest hall in London, the Albert Hall. More than 10,000 persons were present, including all the top-level people in official Britain. There were appropriate speeches, appropriate congratulations, appropriate musical performances. Stalin sent the meeting a telegram of greetings.

I sat looking at all that was going around me and thinking:

'How fantastic life is! Could one have thought a quarter of a century ago that the heads of the City and of Whitehall would be solemnly celebrating the birthday of the Workers' and Peasants' Red Army, the terror of the bourgeoisie? Yet this has happened! . . . Truly you can never say "never" in politics!'

However, the great victory on the Volga had another, much less pleasant effect. One day at the beginning of February my wife was invited to a 'ladies' tea' in high society. There were present only the wives of British and Allied Ministers and foreign

Ambassadors, together with women prominent in public life. My wife returned in a state of great excitement.

'Can you guess what they talked about at this "hen party"?' she exclaimed.

'Probably Stalingrad,' I hazarded.

'Yes, of course, at first they talked about Stalingrad, and there was the proper dose of compliments addressed to us, but that was not the main thing. That was only a sort of before dinner *hors d'oeuvre*. But the dinner was something quite different . . . Nearly the whole time the ladies were discussing where it was best to go after the war for rest and relaxation!'

'Oh-ho!', I could not help saying. 'These noble ladies are rather anticipating events.'

'And how!' my wife continued. 'Most of them were talking like this: now, after Stalingrad, it is clear that the Germans will be defeated, and that in the very near future . . . So we should now be thinking not so much about the war as about what to do after victory . . . And the first thing that comes into their head is to go away somewhere, to forget the war as soon as possible and return to conditions and habits of peace time . . . But on the question of where it was best to go the ladies had a very lively discussion . . . There were various opinions, but the one thing they came together on was that it wasn't worth while going to the usual places in Europe—in France, Switzerland, Italy, etc. Europe after the war will be too ruined and disorganised still, there'll be too much still to remind one of the war and all its horrors . . . No, rest in Europe will not be very pleasant . . . It will be best to go to those parts of the world which were least affected by the war: and the general opinion in the end was that the countries of Latin America would be the best choice for rest and amusement.'

My wife's story of the 'ladies' tea' put me very much on my guard. A few days later, a short conversation gave me even greater concern. I had Duff Cooper to luncheon—a prominent Conservative, a former Secretary for War and First Lord of the Admiralty, one who had demonstratively resigned after Munich. He was an intelligent and cultivated man and a gifted writer, with whom one could have interesting discussions on current topics. This time Duff Cooper talked a good deal about the significance of the battle of Stalingrad, and made optimistic forecasts of the future. When we were saying goodbye, I asked him what he was now engaged on.

'I have returned to my David,' Duff Cooper replied.

I thought he was speaking of the famous painter in the days of the great French Revolution.

'What has so interested you in that French master?' I asked.

'Oh no,' Duff Cooper replied, 'it's not the French artist, but King David in the Bible . . . I began writing a book about him long ago, but the war made me interrupt it. I had to spend three whole years on quite different and more urgent matters . . . But now the situation is different, and I can come back to that ancient King of Judea.'

I was shocked. And so an intelligent and prominent politician and Member of Parliament considered that after Stalingrad he need not worry about the war any more, and might sit down to complete a book begun before the war which had not the slightest connection with the terrible events of the present day.

Both these facts which I have described forced me to look round more attentively, and then I saw a great deal which had previously escaped my notice. I will give some extracts from the entry in my diary for 5 February 1943:

'What is Britain's reaction to our victories? It's impossible to reply to this question in one word. For Britain's reaction to the Red Army's successes is complex and contradictory.

'The first thing that meets the eye is the general amazement at the strength of the USSR and the power of the Red Army. No one expected that after the painful trials of last summer we should have been able to preserve such a fighting capacity . . . This feeling is equally strong everywhere, both at the top and at the bottom of the social pyramid.

'The second feeling aroused by events in the USSR is the vast admiration for the Soviet people and the Red Army . . . But this feeling is of less universal nature than amazement. Among the masses the feeling of admiration is infinite and unquestionable. Here the prestige of the USSR during the last three months has risen incredibly . . . But the higher one goes up the social pyramid, the more the feeling of admiration proves to be mixed with various other feelings, mostly of a corrosive character.

'Take for example the intellectuals, intellectuals of all sorts, including Labour and democratic intellectuals. Their reaction to our victories is incomprehension . . . The British intellectuals have grown up in the belief that the best, most perfect, most effective system of government is bourgeois democracy . . . And suddenly, what an amazing turn of events! In this great examination by history it has turned out that the "Communist dictatorship" is giving quite astounding examples of courage and heroism, examples which far surpass all that could be demonstrated in this sphere up to today by the bourgeois democracy of Britain and the USA. How? Why? Through what cause? . . .

'Even more complex is the reaction of the British ruling classes to our military successes. On the one hand they are satisfied: it is a good thing that the Russians are beating the Germans so hard. It will be easier for us. We shall economise on our losses and destruction. Once more we shall achieve our ancient objective of fighting with other people's hands. But on the other hand the ruling classes are worried: will not the Bolsheviks become much stronger as a result? . . . And the greater become the successes of Soviet arms, the more profoundly are the hearts of the ruling group disturbed . . . So far the Red Army is at the approaches to Rostov. What the feelings of even the "Churchill group" will be when the Red Army is on the approaches to Berlin, it is difficult to say. I don't exclude unpleasant surprises.'

At that time the most important thing for us was the question of how the victory on the Volga would affect the opening of a second front in Northern France: would it accelerate it, or on the contrary put it off, Here is what is said in the same entry on this subject on 5 February:

'On this question there is again an inner division in the ruling group. On the one hand, it would like to postpone the opening of a second front as long as possible, so as to wait for the moment when we have broken Germany's back, and the Anglo-Americans can land "comfortably" in France and reach Berlin without great losses. But on the other hand, if Britain (and the USA) drag out the opening of a second front in the west too long, they may miss their chance and allow the Red Army to get to Berlin first. This they are terribly afraid of: the spectre of the "Bolshevisation of Europe" immediately rises before their imagination. Therefore the question of when to open a second front is becoming the main tactical question for the British and American Governments. From their point of view it should be done not too early and not too late, but just in time. But when is that to be?

The final conclusion is worded as follows in my entry:

'Britain and the USA will not open a second front in France in the spring, but will amuse themselves in the spring and summer with various secondary operations in the Mediterranean region (Sicily, Crete, the Dodecanese and so forth), Maybe they will invent some monster-Dieppe[1] in the north, but it is hardly likely that they will make any serious landing in France. It is unpleasant, but there is nothing to be done. One mustn't shut one's eyes to realities.'

1. At this small town, on the French coast of the Channel, the British had shortly before this carried out a brief and not very successful raid.

10

The Casablanca Conference

MY forecast proved regrettably accurate. It is essential to dwell in somewhat greater detail in this connection on the conference at Casablanca.

At the beginning of December 1942 Roosevelt had already proposed a meeting of the heads of the three Powers to discuss the most important problems of the war and the post war period. He suggested that it should take place approximately in the middle of January 1943, and that Northern Africa should be the area where they met. Churchill. of course, agreed immediately. But Stalin in a message to Roosevelt on 6 December wrote: 'This is so crucial a moment' (it was the time of the Stalingrad battle) 'that I cannot absent myself even for a single day.' Thereupon Roosevelt proposed that the meeting be postponed until 1 March 1943, but Stalin on that occasion too replied that 'front affairs simply would not let' him leave the USSR.[1] Instead of settling the questions which had arisen between the Allies by means of a personal meeting, Stalin suggested the method of correspondence. In the end the conference nevertheless took place at Casablanca, but only Roosevelt and Churchill took part in it.

It was held on 14–23 January 1943. The battle of Stalingrad was not yet over, but its outcome was already predetermined. This circumstance had the greatest influence on what took place at Casablanca. The state of mind of Roosevelt and Churchill during the conference can be characterised roughly as follows: 'The Russians are fighting splendidly; they will be able to settle their affairs themselves; we British and Americans can now busy our-

1. *Correspondence, etc.*, Vol. II, pp. 43–4.

selves with carrying out our own plans; all that is necessary as far as the Russians are concerned is to keep up their good spirits, for which it will be sufficient to send supplies on a sufficiently large scale, intensify the air bombardments of Germany and, of course, give them many fine promises.'[1]

The impress of such a state of mind lies on all the decisions adopted at Casablanca. In their joint message to the head of the Soviet Government on 27 January 1943, Roosevelt and Churchill wrote on the subject of these decisions:

'Our main desire has been to divert strong German land and air forces from the Russian front and to send Russia the maximum flow of supplies . . . Our immediate intention is to clear the Axis out of North Africa and set up naval and air installations to open (1) an effective passage through the Mediterranean for military traffic, and (2) an intensive bombardment of important Axis targets in Southern Europe . . .

'In addition we shall concentrate within the United Kingdom a strong American land and air force. These, combined with the British forces in the United Kingdom, will prepare themselves to re-enter the continent of Europe as soon as practicable . . .

'In Europe we shall increase the Allied bomber offensive from the United Kingdom against Germany at a rapid rate.'[2]

And that was all. But where was the opening of a second front in Northern France? It was nowhere. There was only a cloudy hint that the British and Americans would prepare their armed forces for such an operation, and await the moment when it would prove 'practicable'.

On 30 January Stalin sent a reply to Roosevelt and Churchill. In it he wrote:

1. Such were only my own summary impressions at the time. Today I can quote an indubitable proof that they were right. In the fourth volume of his war memoirs Churchill quotes his paper on questions of the general strategy of the war, which is dated 3 December 1942. It was the moment when Paulus had already been surrounded by the Red Army, but the outcome of the battle of Stalingrad was still not clear. There is the following passage in Churchill's memorandum: 'Recent most important events have altered, and are altering, the data on which thought on both sides of the Atlantic has hitherto proceeded. The Russians have not been defeated or weakened in the campaign of 1942. On the contrary, it is Hitler who has been defeated and the German Army which has been very grievously reduced. . . The demoralisation among the Hungarian, Rumanian and Italian troops on the Eastern front is marked. The Finns are no longer fighting, except for a few mountain troops'. (*The Second World War,* Vol. IV, pp. 588–9). If Churchill assessed the situation on the Eastern front in this way even before the crushing of the Germans at Stalingrad, it is easy to conceive to oneself what he thought after that defeat.

2. *Correspondence, etc.*, Vol. I, pp. 86–7.

'Assuming that your decisions on Germany are designed to defeat her by opening a second front in Europe in 1943, I shall be grateful if you would inform me of the concrete operations planned and of their time.'[1]

On 9 February the more precise information which he had asked for came from Roosevelt and Churchill: but it promised nothing satisfactory. It contained the following passage:

'We are also pushing preparations to the limit of our resources for a cross-Channel operation in August, in which Britain and United States units would participate. Here again, shipping and assault-landing craft will be the limiting factors. If the operation is delayed by the weather or other reasons, it will be prepared with stronger forces for September. The timing of this attack must, of course, be dependent upon the condition of German defensive possibilities across the Channel at that time.'[2]

The formulations used by Roosevelt and Churchill bore such an india-rubber character, and contained so many reservations, that I decided to have a personal talk on the subject with the British Prime Minister. This is what is written down in my diary for 9 February:

'"As regards the cross-Channel operation", Churchill said, "I really find it difficult to say anything definite at the present time. We British could find 12–15 divisions for this purpose . . . but as to the Americans . . ."

'Here Churchill made a gesture of helplessness, and said:

'"So far the Americans have only one division over here!"

'"What, only one?" I said in surprise. "You told me in November that there was one American division in Britain: has nothing really been added since then?"

'"Yes, that's how it is," Churchill responded. "Since November the Americans have sent over no more."

'"And how many American divisions do you expect by August?" I asked.

'"If only I knew!" Churchill replied in comic despair. "When I was in Moscow, I started with the belief that the Americans would by the spring of 1943 deliver 27 divisions to Britain, as they had promised. That was my point of departure in my conversation with Stalin. But where are they, these 27 divisions? . . . Now the Americans are promising only four or five divisions by August . . .

1. *Ibid.*, p. 89.
2. *Ibid.*, pp. 93–4.

If they keep their promise, the cross-Channel operation will be carried out in the strength of 17–20 divisions . . ."

'Churchill suddenly burst out laughing, as though he had remembered something very funny, and asked me:

'"How many men are there in an American division, do you think?"

'I replied with some surprise:

'"I don't know exactly, but I suppose it's probably 18–19 thousand."

'"Quite right", and Churchill laughed even more loudly, "if you reckon only the fighting men . . . But if you reckon the whole auxiliary personnel, there are 50,000!"

'I could not help gasping:

'"What do you mean, 50,000?"

'"Just that, 50,000!" Churchill exclaimed once more, and then with obvious sarcasm began to reckon them up. "There's nothing lacking in an American division! Well, of course, there's transport, the medical service, the quartermaster's department and so on. That's all quite normal. But listen to this . . . Two battalions of laundresses, one battalion of milk sterilisers, one battalion of hairdressers, one recreation battalion, one battalion of tailors, one battalion of cobblers . . . Ha-ha-ha! . . . We sent nearly half a million troops into Northern Africa, but that only amounts to 10 or 11 divisions."

'Churchill laughed once again, and added:

'"We British are bad enough in this respect, but the Americans are far worse."'

This conversation with the Premier finally convinced me that it was no use reckoning on a second front in Northern France in the spring of 1943. I still cherished a tiny hope, however, that perhaps it might be open in August or September. For this purpose it was necessary to shake up the British thoroughly, frighten them, and strike hard at that psychology of 'complacency' which began after Stalingrad to revive of its own accord, sometimes even at the base but particularly at the top of the social pyramid. It was with just this in view that I decided at least to utter a word of warning to our allies.

On 23 February 1943 there was open in London, with the active participation of the Soviet Embassy and the British Ministry of Information, a big exhibition entitled 'Twenty-five Years of the USSR and the Red Army'. In my speech opening the exhibition I said, among other things:

'However joyful our victories at Stalingrad, however valuable the successes of your Eighth Army in Africa, it would be the greatest mistake to think that Fascist Germany is already at the end of its tether. Unfortunately that is not yet so. The German military machine during the last few months has suffered a number of heavy blows, but it is not yet broken. It is still functioning, it is still strong. Fascist Germany still has many cards in her hands —territorial and other—with which she can play. And the Allied nations have ahead of them still a long and difficult road before they achieve their object of the complete defeat and destruction of the enemy. We can be satisfied with nothing less! . . . The road from Mozdok to Rostov and from Stalingrad to Kharkov was not a simple promenade for the Red Army. It was a path of difficult and heroic struggle.

'This word of warning seems to me particularly necessary because just now, in some places and in some circles, the victories of the Red Army are beginning to give rise to what I would call "optimistic illusions". In some places and in some circles people are beginning to think that the Germans are already on the run, that victory is just round the corner, that in virtue of this we can ease off a little and return to the feelings, habits and interests of peace time. Nothing is more dangerous than such a state of mind!'

Our exhibition was very successful and there were always many visitors. At the same time, as I have already described, the British Government arranged the ceremonial celebration of the 25th anniversary of the Red Army at the Albert Hall. There were words of gratitude and enthusiastic praise for the Soviet Union from all sides . . . but the business of invading Northern France in the spring of 1943 did not move forward in the least.

A telegram from Stalin to Churchill, sent at just this time, introduced a very strange discord on the background of this clearly unsatisfactory situation. In the first half of March 1943 the British Prime Minister sent to Moscow a film *Desert Victory*, which had been taken by British cameramen in Northern Africa. On 29 March Stalin sent the British Premier a message in which he wrote:

'Last night I saw, with my colleagues, the film *Desert Victory* you have sent us, and was greatly impressed. It splendidly shows how Britain is fighting, and skilfully exposes those scoundrels—we have them in our country too—who allege that Britain is not fighting but merely looking on.'[1]

1. *Correspondence, etc.*, Vol. I, p. 110.

When I brought Churchill this message, there was an almost literal repetition of the scene which I had witnessed a few months earlier, when handing over Stalin's message about Darlan: the British Prime Minister, with tears in his eyes, said in deeply moved tones:

'Our thanks to Stalin! He has judged our efforts aright!'

During these first months after Stalingrad many people in Britain, and not only in Britain, began thinking intensively of what the world should be like after the defeat of the Fascist aggressors. Previously, few had concerned themselves with such questions. The future was wrapped in mystery, no one knew how the war would end and who would be deciding the future destinies of humanity. In such an atmosphere all were concerned with the problems of the moment, and instinctively brushed aside those of tomorrow. Least of all did people want to build plans for world reconstruction after the day when the guns would fall silent.

Now, after Stalingrad, the situation changed sharply. Everyone in Britain believed that the Fascist Powers would be defeated: there was argument about when and at what price, but there was no longer any doubt about the final victory of the Allies. Hence naturally it followed that it would be the Allies who sooner or later would have to carry out post-war reconstruction on our planet. And this meant in its turn that it was the Allies who must prepare beforehand for the solution of such a complicated and gigantic task. It is not surprising that after the battle on the Volga ended statesmen, politicians, economists, writers, philosophers turned their attention to the problems of post-war organisation of the world, and began intensively discussing them and making their suggestions. I was also very interested in these problems at the time, and even sent the People's Commissariat for Foreign Affairs some considerations on the subject. Naturally, in the first half of 1943 I had quite a number of conversations on post-war themes with my British acquaintances of various shades of opinion and conditions. I will quote a few which I have more particularly remembered.

One day at the end of April 1943 I met Brendan Bracken at lunch. He was not only Minister of Information but a close friend of Churchill. After exchanging opinions on various current news, we touched on the question of how peace would be maintained after the end of the war. I cannot now recall who first raised this question, Brendan Bracken or myself. But we both seized on it and had a long discussion on the prospects opening in that sphere. I admit that at that time I had no fully clear reply to this most important question, and therefore I listened more than I spoke. But in Brendan Bracken's mind there was already a definite conception (even though not fully worked out as yet), which (as he did not conceal), for the most part reflected Churchill's views and inclinations. What did it amount to?

'The world which emerges from the furnace of this war', he said, 'will be a greatly ruined world, which will strive most of all to prevent any new war. How to assure it of a peaceful life . . .?'

Then Bracken developed a broad scheme on the following lines.

There should be set up a *supreme world council*, composed of the USA, Britain, the USSR and possibly China. It should have the responsibility for preserving world peace. In addition, there should be also set up, subordinate to the supreme council, three regional councils—for Europe, America and the Pacific. Each of them should be responsible for the maintenance of peace in its own region. If the regional council were unable to settle disputes between the countries of which it consisted, matters should pass into the hands of the supreme council. In order that the councils should carry out their functions, they would require a military force, which would be composed in the following way: each country would appoint a definite contingent of troops which the regional council could use in case of necessity. The same would be done by the Great Powers constituting the supreme council. All States, great and small, should conclude an agreement about the size of their armed forces. The leading body of the regional council should consist of representatives of all the countries to which its competence extended. Members of the supreme council could also form part of the regional councils if their possessions fell within the sphere of competence of any particular regional council. For example, the USSR might simultaneously be a member both of the supreme council and of the regional council for the Pacific, while Britain might be a member both of the supreme council and of the regional council for America.

Having set forth all this, Bracken asked me what I thought of such a world organisation.

'On paper', I replied, 'your scheme seems a very symmetrical and well-balanced one, but... But in practice undoubtedly various difficulties will appear . . . Here is one example, and a very important one: the structure of the regional councils provides for the representation of every country of that region in its central body. Here there can be no objections. But things are otherwise with the supreme council: it should include only three or four of the most mighty Powers. In other words, it provides for the setting up of a three-member or four-member directorate which in the long run will give orders to the whole world. This undoubtedly will arouse serious and sufficiently justified objections by other States: what then?'

Bracken admitted the justice of my remark, and began searching for ways of overcoming the difficulty; but the result was not very successful, because he still wanted to preserve in one way or another the dictatorship of the 'Big Three' in the future organisation of the world.

Then I asked him how he conceived of post-war Europe? Bracken replied that he would most of all like post-war Europe to be transformed into the 'United States of Europe'—but, of course, this could not be achieved all at once. Therefore Brendan Bracken considered that for the time being the regional council for Europe should consist of ten to twelve States and federations of States (such as, for example, a Balkan or a Danubian federation). France should be restored as a strong Power, but Germany should be weakened by separating Prussia from the rest of her territory. Poland and Czechoslovakia should be on friendly terms between themselves and also with the USSR.

'One question worries me greatly,' Brendan Bracken concluded. 'It is the relationship between the USA and Europe. The USA has no possessions in Europe, and therefore cannot be a member of the regional council for Europe, yet at the same time it is difficult to imagine Europe in the future without aid from America. We must find some form of association of the USA and Europe...'

'But perhaps it's not necessary at all?' I asked as though in passing (in conditions as they were then I had to be very cautious in my judgments on the USA).

'Oh no!' exclaimed my partner. 'Europe cannot live without America.'

On 12 May 1943 we had H. G. Wells to lunch. Here is the entry in my diary. 'We were only three—Agnia, myself and our guest...

We talked a lot on various subjects, but particularly on mankind's post-war future. Wells was underlining all the time that modern technique was transforming the world into a single complex, while the old psychology was tearing it asunder into dozens of nationally isolated channels. If this contradiction were not resolved, mankind would perish. Would it be resolved? Wells was not sure. He said:

'"Either the world will hurry forward in rapid leaps, or it will become a desert. There can be no third way."

'Wells pins his hopes to the USSR, but one feels that there are some "reservations" or other in his heart. It is not surprising. The muddle in the famous writer's head is amazing. The contradiction of which he speaks is a real one. The fact that he sees it shows that his mind is working on the right lines. But when it comes to how this contradiction can be resolved, there begins a real intellectual witches' dance. Wells suddenly proclaims:

'"We must set up a Fifth International!"'

Approximately one month after this conversation, Wells sent me the 'programme' of the Fifth International. It was a declaration of the 'Universal Rights of Man' consisting of eleven articles. They provided for child care, freedom to work, the right to earn money, the right to property, the right of free movement, the right to education and information, the right to freedom of thought, discussion and creed, personal liberty in the spirit of the British Habeas Corpus and freedom from violence. The declaration did not oblige a man to work, but guaranteed work for him if he wished. The declaration also gave a man the right to earn money, but prohibited buying, selling and hoarding for the sake of profit.

In his accompanying letter, Wells wrote:

'I hope for a world revolution (this at bottom is only the restoration of the materialist conception of history) which, in my view, does not at all require any profound alterations in the external and visible structure of human activity. 999 men out of 1,000 will only gain from a revolution founded on the principle of equality.'

I could not help shrugging my shoulders and thinking: 'I recognise my Wells: the very best intentions and an incredible muddle in his head!' However, I did not open a discussion with him, and simply sent his declaration on to Moscow.

I quote one more entry in my diary, dated 2 June 1943:

'Butler lunched with me. We talked a lot about post-war prospects in Britain (in addition to being Minister for Education at present, Butler is Chairman of the Conservative Party Committee on Post-War Problems). Butler expects that the future development of Britain will proceed on the following lines:

'1. A mixed form of national economy, i.e. some of the branches of the economy (electric power, the railways, maybe coal) will be nationalised, while part (road transport, sea transport, civil aviation, etc.) will come under "public control", and part will remain as before in the hands of individual owners.

'2. Gradually there will come into existence a "constitutional factory", i.e. one in which representatives of the workers will take part in the management. This idea, in particular is advocated by Butler's father-in-law, Courtauld.

'3. The educational system must be democratised, i.e. nearly all the "public schools" liquidated (but Butler still wants to preserve two or three of them) and the number of State grants for higher education should be greatly increased.

'I asked Butler:

'"So you want to lead Britain along the Fabian road?"

'Butler replied:

'"It's not a question of the name. You know that we British can do revolutionary things if they are carried out under the old title."

'Of course, Fabianism is not revolution. But for a Conservative it is almost a revolution. And Butler (who undoubtedly reflects the state of mind of the top leadership of the Conservatives) is evidently thinking about Fabianism, even though he doesn't want to name it.

'Then Butler talked long of the necessity of friendship and collaboration between our countries after the war, and towards the end asked:

'"If Britain proceeds along the road of what you call Fabianism, what do you think: will it help to strengthen relations between us?'

'"I think it will," I replied. It made a noticeable impression on Butler.'

... And one last entry in my diary, dated 3 June 1943:

'The Labour leader Herbert Morrison lunched with me. Somehow the conversation with Morrison also turned chiefly to post-war problems. Morrison developed ideas which I already knew from his speeches, published the other day in the form of a little volume *Prospects and Policies*. And the more Morrison spoke, the more strongly I could see the identity of his views with those of Butler. Of course, there are some distinctions in shades of meaning and emphasis, but in the main they stand on one and the same platform. Astonishing! Listening to Morrison, I thought how easy it will be after the war for the Conservatives to come to an understanding with the Labour Party on questions of the internal reconstruction of Britain—if, of course, the proletariat permits the Morrisons to continue their game . . . I fear it will!'

When I recall all these conversations today, I want to say that those I talked with at the time turned out to be bad prophets. Real, historical life did not adopt either the Directorate of a few Great Powers which so fascinated Churchill, nor the Fifth International of which H. G. Wells was dreaming, nor the 'constitutional factory' on which Butler based his hopes. Real life proceeded by other roads. So often are people mistaken in their anticipations. Nevertheless, I refer to all these views here in order to show what the atmosphere in Britain was like after the great battle on the Volga.

Although Churchill both publicly and in private talks promised a rapid completion of military operations in Northern Africa, events there proceeded, as should have been expected, much more slowly than was anticipated. Here there told both the reverses of Commander-in-Chief Eisenhower, and friction between Washington and London, and the military inexperience of the Anglo-American troops, the higher level of military command on the enemy side under Rommel's direction, and much else.

Matters went somewhat better when, at the end of February 1943, the British General Alexander was appointed to command the Tunis front (under the general control of Eisenhower). Two armies—the First from the West and the Eighth from the East—began concentrated military operations against the German and Italian forces in Tunis, which at that time had attained approximately 200,000 men. The main attack began on 22 April. On 2 May Churchill in his message to Stalin wrote:

'Since we entered Tunisia we have taken about 40,000 prisoners; in addition, the enemy have suffered 35,000 dead and wounded.

The casualties in the First Army have been about 23,000 and in the Eighth Army about 10,000. The total Allied casualties are about 50,000 of which two-thirds are British. The battle will be maintained along the whole front with the utmost intensity.'[1]

The attacks of the British and American grew ever stronger, the territory held by the enemy shrank more and more, his losses became ever greater and his position more and more hopeless. Finally, on 13 May General Alexander reported to Churchill: 'The Tunisian campaign is over. All enemy resistance has ceased. We are masters of the North African shores.'[2]

Thus, despite Churchill's 'optimistic' forecasts, operation 'Torch' dragged out for six whole months, and this played a most unpleasant part so far as the opening of a second front in 1943 was concerned.

In the post-war years great and still unfinished discussions broke out on the subject of the war in Africa in 1942–3. Churchill places a very high value in his memoirs on the battle at El Alamein and in Tunisia. Of the first he writes:

'It marked in fact the turning of "the Hinge of Fate". It may almost be said, "Before Alamein we never had a victory. After Alamein we never had a defeat."'[3]

About the second, he writes:

'No one could doubt the magnitude of the victory of Tunis. It held its own with Stalingrad.'[4]

Historians and politicians in the West have for many years developed and worked in every possible way on the thesis expounded by Churchill in the words just quoted. Some of them have gone so far as to declare that the real turning-point in the whole second world war was the two North African battles just mentioned, while Stalingrad occupies a secondary place. The most 'objective' of them were prepared to recognise Alamein-Tunis plus Stalingrad as the 'turning-point'.

However, in the light of the perspective of history, it is time today to make a more objective judgment of the true significance of various events in the course of the second world war. For that very reason, I do not intend by any means to decry the role of the military operations in Northern Africa. Undoubtedly Alamein and Tunis were big successes for the British and Americans, and

1. *Correspondence, etc.*, Vol. I, p. 126.
2. *The Second World War*, Vol. IV, p. 698.
3. *The Second World War*, Vol. IV, p. 541.
4. *Ibid.*, p. 698.

had their influence on the general course and outcome of the war. But I cannot help recalling here how Churchill himself, in his message to Stalin on 11 March 1943, said about the actions in Tunis that 'it is on a small scale compared with the tremendous operations over which you are presiding'.[1] The British Premier at that moment, at the very height of the Tunis battle, clearly understood the real relations and proportions. Then why later, when the guns were silent and he sat down to write his memoirs, did Tunis begin to 'hold its own with Stalingrad'?

No person today who is in the least objective can subscribe to such a statement. Things are quite otherwise. For if one compares the battle on the Volga with the simultaneous battles in Africa—whether in the number of forces engaged and losses borne, or as regards the scale of the military and political consequences, or the psychological effect on the peoples of the world, and particularly the peoples in the countries making up the Hitler coalition—only the hopelessly blind can see the 'Hinge of Fate' in the two African battles and not in the great battle on the Volga.

When the war in North Africa had at last ended by the middle of May 1943, there arose in all its acuteness the question of what was to be done next?

It might seem that the time had come to organise the invasion of Northern France. This was what Churchill and Roosevelt had promised when they began 'Torch'. They repeated their promise at the Casablanca Conference. But . . . The demoralising spirit of complacency which had raised its head so strongly in Britain and the USA after the Stalingrad battle was once more victorious. The leading part on this occasion, too, was played by the British Prime Minister.

On 11 May Churchill arrived in Washington, accompanied by a large suite of the highest leaders of the British armed forces, and met Roosevelt and his military and political advisers. On the eve of the meeting, on 10 May, Churchill sent a message while on the way informing Stalin that he was going to see Roosevelt; even earlier, on 6 May, Roosevelt had informed Stalin of Churchill's forthcoming visit—but neither invited Stalin also to come to Washington, or even to send his own responsible representative to take part in the conference.[2] Thus all the Washington decisions

1. *Correspondence, etc.*, Vol. I, p. 100.
2. *Correspondence, etc.*, Vol. I, p. 129; Vol. II, p. 64.

which were of very serious importance, were adopted behind the back of the USSR and only communicated to it after the event.

Just at this very time there was an extremely curious episode. Joseph E. Davies, formerly American Ambassador to the USSR arrived in Moscow, bringing Stalin a letter from Roosevelt dated 5 May 1943. In his letter the President expressed the wish to meet personally with Stalin on 'an informal and completely simple visit', somewhere in the area of the Bering Straits, accompanied by the most restricted number of people. Roosevelt proposed to bring with him only Hopkins, an interpreter and a stenographer. It was clear from the letter than the meeting should take place without Churchill. 'You and I would talk very informally and get what we call a meeting of minds.' Stalin replied to the American President on 26 May, and expressed his agreement with the proposal, but in view of the big summer offensive by the Germans which was then being awaited asked that the meeting should be postponed to July or August.[1] All this took place before the Soviet Government had been informed of the Washington decisions by the British and Americans.

On 4 June 1943, United States Ambassador in Moscow Admiral Standley handed Stalin a message from Roosevelt which had also been approved by Churchill, and which set forth these decisions. What did they amount to?

The plan for military operations during the remainder of 1943 provided for:

1. Intensification of the fight against the submarines.

2. Laying of preparatory ground work for entry by Turkey into the war.

3. The weakening of Japan 'by keeping up an unremitting pressure against her'.

4. The rendering of aid to the French armed forces in Africa in order to prepare them for the future operations in Europe.

5. 'To put Italy out of the war at the earliest possible moment.'

6. The intensification in every possible way of the air offensive against Germany and the countries occupied by her.

That was all.

Well, and what about the second front in Northern France?

On this subject Roosevelt's message said the following:

'Under the present plans, there should be a sufficiently large concentration of men and material in the British Isles in the spring

1. *Correspondence, etc.*, Vol. II, pp. 63–4, 66.

of 1944 to permit a full scale invasion of the continent at that time.'[1]

And so the second front in France was once again being postponed for a year!

I was unaware at the time of the details of the Washington negotiations which are set forth in Churchill's memoirs,[2] but, knowing the people who took part in them, I could easily imagine how the British Prime Minister demonstrated the necessity, after the victories in Africa, to develop operations in that Mediterranean which was so dear to his heart (after all, the Russians were beating the Germans even without a second front): and how Roosevelt, making a fiery speech about the necessity of giving help to Russia, was in the long run following Churchill's lead. Above all, it was as clear as daylight to me—and Roosevelt's message left no doubt of this—that on the main question of the moment, a second front or the Mediterranean, the Washington Conference had firmly replied: the Mediterranean.

It is not difficult to realise what an impression this reply made in Moscow. In his message to Roosevelt on 11 June Stalin wrote:

'It appears from your communication that the decisions run counter to those reached by you and Mr. Churchill earlier this year concerning the date for a second front in Western Europe ... Now, in May 1943, you and Mr. Churchill have decided to postpone the Anglo-American invasion of Western Europe until the spring of 1944. In other words, the opening of the second front in Western Europe, previously postponed from 1942 till 1943, is now being put off again, this time till the spring of 1944 . . . Need I speak of the dishearteningly negative impression that this fresh postponement of the second front . . . will produce in the Soviet Union—both among the people and in the Army? As for the Soviet Government, it cannot align itself with this decision, which moreover was adopted without its participation and without any attempt at a joint discussion of this highly important matter.'[3]

The tone of the message clearly indicated that the Washington decisions had aroused extreme irritation in Moscow. I was also indignant at the behaviour of Churchill and Roosevelt. Thinking over the situation which had been created, I could not help coming to the conclusion that the Soviet Government would not

1. *Correspondence, etc.*, pp. 67–9.
2. *The Second World War*, Vol. IV, pp. 706–10.
3. *Correspondence, etc.*, Vol. II, pp. 70–1.

be able to confine itself only to words, and that it must by some practical action demonstrate its dissatisfaction to the Allies. But how? On this subject I was not clear.

The reply to the problem which was worrying me came very quickly. A fortnight later there arrived from Moscow a telegram requesting me to fly urgently to the USSR to take part in the discussion of post-war problems, Although, as was mentioned earlier, I had in fact after Stalingrad devoted much attention to questions of the post-war organisation of the world, as Moscow well knew, nevertheless the sense of the directive I had received presented no mystery to me. The Soviet Government clearly wanted to indicate its dissatisfaction to the British Government by recalling me from London 'for consultations'—the most customary form in diplomatic practice on such occasions. I was even strengthened in my interpretation of Moscow's step when I learned before long that M. M. Litvinov, our Ambassador in Washington, had received similar instructions.

When I came to see Eden and, telling him of my instructions, asked him to arrange the possibility of a flight to Moscow for me, the Foreign Secretary grew very disturbed:

'Why is your Government recalling you for consultations just at this moment?' Eden asked bluntly.

I explained to him that in recent months I had worked a good deal on the post-war problems, and the time was now clearly approaching for their more serious discussion. What was there surprising in the Soviet Government recalling me for a time to Moscow to take part in the examination of these far from simple questions?

Eden heard me out with obvious disbelief, and said:

'No, no! Things are more serious. Your recall has political significance.'

And in front of me Eden rang up Churchill to tell him the news I had given him. Thus unexpectedly was my stay in London interrupted. And, as the future was to show, thus had ended my eleven years of work as Soviet Ambassador in Britain.

Part Five

★

Return to Moscow

I

London — Cairo

In the midnight darkness of 3 July 1943 I set forth from one of the aerodromes in Western England. I was seen off by my wife, my deputy A. A. Sobolev, who now remained as Chargé d'Affaires of the USSR, Admiral N. M. Kharlamov and a few other comrades.

At Gibraltar I was met by General MacFarlane, the commander-in-chief. I knew him from Moscow, where he had at one time been the British Military Attaché. He was in the British tropical uniform: in shorts and a 'hail and farewell' tropical helmet. He took me and my accompanying officer in his car to his official residence in the fortress. Although our Liberator was to take off again three hours later, nevertheless for that short time—such were the laws of wartime hospitality—I was allotted a special apartment in Government House as an important guest, and a military aide in the rank of Captain was attached to me.

At midday our Liberator again took the air and proceeded eastward. I knew that between Gibraltar and Cairo there was one landing-stage. Usually it was the aerodrome of Castel-Benito near Tripoli, but we did not seem to be approaching it. I went into the pilot's cabin and asked when we should arrive there. He replied: 'Oh, we won't be there at all.'

'Why?' I asked in surprise.

'At Gibraltar', the pilot explained, 'I had instructions to land not at Castel-Benito but a little farther on, at one of the military aerodromes in the desert . . . I don't know why.'

I could not help being put on my guard: in wartime one becomes particularly distrustful and suspicious. I only understood the reason for the change in the route the following day—but of that more later.

At about 6 p.m. the even course of the plane was suddenly interrupted. It began to circle and incline. I looked out of the window: far below, on the yellow surface of the desert, there were tiny white dots disposed in geometrical precision. It was the aerodrome at which we were to make our halt. A few minutes later our Liberator was running ponderously over the long concrete runway, amid the tents in which the personnel of the aerodrome were living, and which I had seen as white dots from above. We received a friendly welcome from the chief of the aerodrome and the other officers.

Then, once again at midnight, plunged in darkness, our Liberator took the air, and at 7 a.m. on 6 July arrived in Cairo without mishap.

At that time diplomatic relations between the USSR and Egypt did not as yet exist. There was no Soviet Embassy in Cairo. Therefore the British undertook to look after me while in the Egyptian capital. At the military aerodrome where our Liberator landed I was met by one of the secretaries of the British Embassy, Mr. Watson, who turned out to be a relative of Vansittart, whom I knew so well from my work in London. This at once established simple relations between us. Mr. Watson took me and my accompanying officer to the Embassy, where we had an entire three-room apartment for 'V.I.P.s' set aside for us. We took a bath, shaved, brushed our clothes and then, at the invitation of the Ambassador, Lord Killearn, went to have breakfast with him.

Lord Killearn was a very tall, broad-shouldered man of aristocratic appearance, with a noticeable paunch. Lady Killearn, a handsome middle-aged brunette presided, at table. There were also some others, in uniform or civilian clothes. The Ambassador amiably welcomed me, and presented me to his lady and to the guests. After the customary exchange of questions and answers about my journey, Lord Killearn suddenly with a melancholy expression and in sympathetic tones said:

'We have just had sad news: General Sikorski has been killed. Early yesterday morning he left Cairo by air for Gibraltar on his return journey from the Near East. On the way they had a landing at Castel-Benito. From there he flew to Gibraltar safely. But when his plane took off again from the Gibraltar aerodrome and had already gained height, something happened in it and the plane fell like a stone into the sea. They all perished. I fear the cause of the disaster will remain a mystery, because none of the passengers or crew were saved, and the sea at that spot is very deep: it will hardly be possible to raise the plane.'

For a moment there was a gloomy silence at table. Now it became clear to me why my plane had made its landing not at Castel-Benito but at the aerodrome in the Libyan desert. As Sikorski had left Cairo for Gibraltar on the same day that I left Gibraltar for Cairo, we should have been bound to meet at Castel-Benito if the usual route had been followed.

The British evidently feared that, in connection with the rupture of diplomatic relations between the Soviet and Polish governments which had taken place two months before, such a meeting might have given rise to some 'misunderstanding', and therefore decided to land us at different aerodromes. However, this was now only of academic importance.

When conversation was resumed at table, there was a long discussion about the reasons for the disaster, which, however, did not lead and indeed could not lead to any light on the mystery of the destruction of Sikorski's plane—since no one knew anything in effect except the very fact of the disaster.

I could not help remembering a conversation I had had with MacFarlane the previous day, and thought: 'Most probably the hand of the Germans is in this: is it difficult for them to smuggle their agent in among those thousands of Spaniards who daily come to Gibraltar from La Linea?' But I said nothing aloud. I had no facts to confirm my idea at that moment.

For various technical reasons our Liberator could proceed only in two days' time. I was glad of this delay, because I needed to settle in Cairo one important piece of business requiring a certain time.

After the battle of Stalingrad the Egyptian Ambassador in London, Nachat-Pasha, who until then had hardly 'noticed' me, suddenly changed his line of conduct, invited me to his Embassy to lunch, and began a conversation about how good it would be to establish diplomatic relations between our countries. I replied that I shared his opinion, and recommended that the Egyptian Government which at that time was headed by Nahas Pasha, the leader of the national-bourgeois party, the Wafd, should make a suitable proposal to the Soviet Government.

During the four following months a real comedy was enacted. The Egyptian Ambassador assured me all the time that he was making every effort to establish diplomatic relations between Cairo and Moscow, but every time he visited me made a request which could only spoil the whole affair. At first he wanted the proposal about mutual diplomatic recognition to come from the USSR and not from Egypt. When I rejected this, Nachat-Pasha, referring to instructions from his Government, began insisting that when diplomatic relations were being established the Soviet Government should in a special document undertake the obligation not to interfere in the internal affairs of Egypt. I laughed this ambition of the Egyptian Government out of court as completely incomprehensible, since the Soviet Government does not ever interfere in the affairs of other countries. A few days later Nachat-Pasha suddenly had a new and brilliant idea: let both Governments when restoring diplomatic relations exchange letters on this same subject, in connection with the dissolution of the Comintern which had just taken place. In doing so the Egyptian Ambassador referred to the Anglo-Soviet agreement of 1921, in which the Soviet side undertook not to interfere in the internal affairs of Great Britain. I explained to Nachat-Pasha the circumstances in which that agreement had been concluded, and finally said with some emphasis:

'Egypt is a quarter of a century late in recognising the USSR and in addition wants to get a bonus for it: that won't happen!'

All this dawdling had greatly irritated me, all the more because one felt in it the traces of the internal struggle then going on in Egypt. Nachat-Pasha was the creature of the then King Farouk, an extreme reactionary and a great admirer of Hitler and Mussolini. The Wafd Party was in opposition to the King, and relations between its leader Nahas Pasha and the Egyptian Ambassador in London—relations both political and personal— were very strained. Consequently, when I received a telegram recalling me to Moscow, the idea immediately flashed through my mind: 'Aha! When I pass through Cairo I will try and come to an agreement about diplomatic relations directly with Prime Minister Nahas Pasha.'

Now, finding myself in Cairo, I rang him up and asked for an interview. He responded very joyfully, and at once invited me to meet him at 6 p.m. I reached the house at the appointed hour, and I was brought in to a handsome drawing room in the European, I would even say Parisian, style. I had hardly had time to look round when on my right, beyond a door, steps were heard and Nahas Pasha impetuously entered or, more truly, rolled into the salon. He was a man of middle height, dark, with a lively face and uncommonly mobile hands and short, rapidly moving little legs. He was dressed in a light blue-grey suit, with a brightly-coloured tie with a big diamond tie-pin. The whole figure of the Egyptian Premier breathed the ease and brilliance of the Parisian, which by the way was not surprising: Nahas Pasha had had a French education, spoke French excellently and was an admirer of French culture.

'I welcome you on Egyptian soil!' he cried, stretching wide his arms as though he wished to embrace me.

I replied with corresponding amiabilities. After the inevitable questions about my health, my journey and so forth, Nahas Pasha was lavish in expressions of his highest admiration for the Soviet people, the Red Army and the victory on the Volga. Then he said:

'I am glad that a happy chance has brought you to Cairo. I very much want the speediest establishment of diplomatic relations between Egypt and your great country, but in our negotiations on this subject there have been some delays and complications . . .'

Nahas Pasha smiled significantly, and added:

'Not my fault . . . No, not my fault!'

This was a clear hint about Farouk and Nachat-Pasha. Then he smiled again significantly, and said, now quite transparently:

'Now you are here, and I am sure that without any barrier between us you and I will rapidly arrive at agreement . . . I will do it, whatever King Farouk thinks!'

Then we began discussing the practical steps. I proposed the following procedure to the Egyptian Premier. He sends me a letter as USSR Ambassador in Great Britain in which he informs me of Egypt's desire to establish diplomatic relations with the USSR; I take this letter with me, and on my arrival in Moscow immediately bring it to the attention of the Soviet Government; the Soviet Government replies to Nahas Pasha's letter by expressing agreement; thereafter diplomatic relations between the two countries will be considered established, and an appropriate communiqué will be published in Moscow and Cairo.

Nahas Pasha accepted the plan I had proposed, and we went on to discuss what his letter should contain. At the end I said to him:

'If you will allow me, I would like to give you some friendly advice: make your letter as clear and simple as possible. Say plainly in it that you want to establish diplomatic relations with the USSR, and do not try to put any supplementary conditions even in a veiled form. In that way we shall soonest of all arrive at our objective.'

'You are right,' he said. 'Tomorrow afternoon my letter will be in your hands. Please let me know at once whether it satisfies you completely.'

When I was already leaving, Nahas Pasha suddenly asked with concern: 'Have you had an opportunity to look at our lovely city?'

'Not entirely,' I replied. 'But I hope to do this tomorrow.'

'Would you like me to give you a guide?'

'Of course.'

Nahas Pasha clapped his hands in oriental fashion, and a young man of about twenty-seven came out of a neighbouring room. The Prime Minister presented him as a relative. 'He will show you all you wish to see,' he added, and we said goodbye.

When I returned from Nahas Pasha to the Embassy, Lord Killearn, meeting me in the corridor, asked as it were by chance: 'Well, did you come to an agreement?'

I understood that the British Ambassador very much wanted to know how negotiations for the establishment of diplomatic relations between Egypt and the USSR were proceeding; but I thought it unnecessary as yet to acquaint him with what was going on. Therefore I briefly replied: 'The matter is not yet completed'—and at once went on to other subjects.

The next day, 6 July, I had delivered to me in the evening the promised letter from the Prime Minister, in a vast packet with five large seals. The letter was in French, and completely satisfactory in its contents. Nahas Pasha declared in it that 'it would be illogical' if two States which were in the same camp of struggle for the cause of democracy did not maintain diplomatic relations, and expressed the firm hope that such relations would in fact be established between them most urgently. He laid down no particular conditions, only recalling that the Montreux Convention[1] for the abolition of capitulations had recognised a new international status

1. At Montreux in 1937 there was a conference of Egypt and the Powers which had enjoyed the privileges of a régime of capitulations in Egypt (USA, Great Britain, France, Italy, Belgium, Holland, Spain, Portugal, Norway, Denmark, Sweden and Greece), at which it was decided to abolish the capitulations.

for Egypt which excluded any political and juridical discrimination: adding that the USSR of its own good will had proclaimed the principle of equality of peoples.

So everything was in order. The decisive step had been taken in establishing diplomatic relations between the two countries. I lifted the receiver, and said to Nahas Pasha on the telephone: 'I am entirely satisfied with the contents of your letter. I do not doubt that it will make a good impression in Moscow.'

2

Moscow — London

At dawn on 7 July our Liberator once again took off. I had returned late from a visit to the American Ambassador's, had slept very little, and therefore was dozing for the greater part of the six hours' flight from Cairo to the next stop at Habbaniya. We flew over the mountains, plains and sands of Asia Minor, which passed by far below as on a cinematograph film. About midday we landed at Habbaniya. It was one of the largest air bases of Great Britain in the Near East, and around it had grown up an entire little town with a bazaar, a cinema, a craftsman's quarter, the editorial office of a newspaper and the other signs of civilised life.

My companion officer and I were given a 'V.I.P.' apartment—a small cottage of three rooms with a kitchen—and had a young lieutenant attached to me as an aide. However, the commander of the aerodrome upset us very much by telling us that we would have to stay a day or two at Habbaniya, as the weather was bad for flying in the region of the Caucasus, which we had to cross on the way to Moscow.

The two nights we spent at Habbaniya proved uncommonly exhausting: it was almost as hot and airless as by day. The thermometer showed 40° Centigrade. There were showers and ventilators in our apartment, and I made full use of both: but it was of little avail. Hardly had I gone to my hot bed when the sheet was soaked with perspiration, and I awoke in a state of painful languor, unable to find any rest. It continued thus until daybreak.

On 9 July, early in the morning, our plane set off for the remainder of the journey. The weather in the Caucasus region had improved. The engines were working well, and below us there rapidly streamed by the plains of Northern Iran, intersected here and there by mountains, the mighty range of the Caucasus, the Caspian Sea, Astrakhan, the brown Volga steppe, the Volga itself and finally Kuibyshev. Our Liberator landed here, we went out on to the green field in order to stretch ourselves after the tiring twelve-hour flight, drank a glass of our 'own' Zhiguli beer in the buffet, and then rose into the air again.

Another three hours of flight over forests, fields and cities of Central Russia, and then at last on the horizon, in the reddish rays of the evening sun, there began to glitter the golden church-domes of Moscow. After some complicated aerial manoeuvres, our Liberator turned sharply for the descent and landed at Vnukovo. Thank heavens, the long journey had ended!

I was met by representatives of the People's Commissariat for Foreign Affairs—K. V. Novikov, F. F. Molochkov and some other comrades. I congratulated the commander of the plane and the whole of his crew on the happy landing, and thanked them warmly for their splendid service on the journey. Then all the Soviet people got into the cars and drove off to the city. It was growing dark. The first stars were appearing in the sky, and the heart was singing: 'Moscow! Moscow!'

Moscow made a tremendous impression on me. It was still the stern Moscow of the war years. Food was being issued on ration cards, and there was not much of it: the city transport was inadequate, and frequently people were hanging in clusters around the buses and tramcars: electricity was being economised, and the lighting at night left much to be desired. The cleanliness of the streets was less than what one was accustomed to: large numbers of people, both men and women, were in military or semi-military uniform: in various places there remained the fortifications of the autumn of 1941: military units were marching almost all the time along the main streets of the capital...

Yes, Moscow was still wartime Moscow, the guiding centre of the greatest battle in history, and the people whom one met in private apartments, institutions, restaurants, public gardens and parks were all thinking and talking about the war. Its fiery breath penetrated that whole vast city, encompassing every one of its inhabitants...

I was at once at home in the prevailing atmosphere, and felt gladly that its basic note was profound optimism. Now things were quite otherwise from what they had been at my last visit in December 1941. Then one felt stern resolution, to stand fast to the death against the cruel enemy who was only a few tens of kilometres from the capital. Now the enemy was far from Moscow, retreating under the blows of the Red Army, and in the hearts of all Soviet people the spring was singing, and there rightly burned a flame of enthusiasm, inspiration, joy and confidence that complete victory was certain. I walked through the city in a joyful excitement, experiencing particular moments of delight when, in the evenings, I saw in the dark sky the many-hued volleys of artillery salutes, which only just before had begun to be practised.

I saw V. M. Molotov, K. E. Voroshilov, A. I. Mikoyan, M. I. Kalinin, N. M. Shvernik and other leading comrades. All of them asked me a great deal about Britain, about Churchill, about Anglo-American relations, and most of all about the prospects of a second front and the true intentions of our Western Allies. Now, too, I told the truth and only the truth, and the result was not too encouraging. My general conclusion amounted to this, that there would be no second front in 1943, that in British ruling circles fear of the ever more evident power of the USSR was growing, and that in the main we must reckon on our own forces. It was just then that there was beginning the famous battle of the Kursk salient, and all were awaiting with anxiety its development and outcome. I asked Stalin to receive me, in order to report to him direct on the British situation and all the problems connected with it: but he did not find it necessary to talk with me.

In Moscow I found also M. M. Litvinov, who, as I have told earlier, had been recalled from Washington simultaneously with myself, and we talked a great deal about the most varied questions. Maxim Maximovich and I had been great friends even from days of emigration in London, and I always liked to discuss with him the complex problems of international policy on which both of us were engaged. We also recalled the distant past—the days of our common exile in London before 1917—and discussed the events of the present day likewise.

I had many interesting meetings in Moscow. On one occasion I talked with a whole group of writers on various questions of current policy. I renewed my old acquaintance with P. I. Chagin, who was at that time in charge of the State Publishing House of Belles-Lettres, and undertook to publish the first volume of my recollections of childhood and youth, *Before the Storm*. I made the acquaintance of E. L. Lann, who visited me as reader of my reminiscences for the publishing house. We spent two hours together in my room at the National Hotel, talking not only about my manuscript, but also about many other interesting things. This first acquaintance on a business basis later developed into firm friendly relations, which were maintained right up to Lann's tragic death fifteen years later.[1]

I also saw A. N. Tolstoy. I had had dealings with him in the 'twenties, when I was editing the Leningrad journal *Zvezda,* while Alexei Nikolayevich, who had just returned from abroad, settled down on the shores of the Neva and was going through the first stages of getting used to the unaccustomed Soviet surroundings. I liked Tolstoy both as a man and as writer, we had many and frequent talks, and I noted with gladness how rapidly he was finding his orientation in this unfamiliar situation and standing more and more firmly on the soil of the new revolutionary Russia. Later I met Alexei Nikolayevich abroad once or twice, when he came on literary or public business. I became a particularly warm admirer of his talent when I read the first part of his novel *Peter the First*. Now, in 1943, Tolstoy surprised me pleasantly by his deep faith in victory, his inspiration and vitality.

I was very glad also to meet once more I. G. Ehrenburg. We were old acquaintances, also from the days of *Zvezda,* and I had followed his literary activity with great interest. I did not agree with Ilya Grigoryevich on everything, and did not like all his works. But I always admired his acute mind, his brilliant pen, his profound understanding of the West and his encyclopaedic and cultivated intelligence. I very much valued Ehrenburg's capacity for original thinking and taking untrodden paths. I particularly was fond of *Trust D. E., Thirteen Pipes, Julio Jurenito* and some other works. And in the period of the war, apart from his publicist articles, I was delighted with *The Fall of Paris,* which I consider one of the best works of Soviet literature. When I received the galley-proofs in London, I did all I could, fortunately with success, to ensure the speediest possible appearance of this novel in English. Talks with Ilya Grigoryevich were very interesting. He told me about what was going on at the front, where he used to spend so much time, and I told him about what was going on abroad, particularly in Britain and among the Frenchmen who had

1. In 1958 E. L. Lann committed suicide.

taken their stand under the banner of struggle against German Fascism. It was extremely valuable for both of us.

In the second half of August my personal destiny was also determined.

During the first weeks of my stay in Moscow there were some small conferences at the People's Commissariat for Foreign Affairs on the question of the post-war settlement, to discuss which I had officially been recalled from London. It was the light preliminary sounding made in the world of extremely great and complicated problems. No decisions were being taken. There were being made only summary headings for future research and elaboration. This work extremely engrossed me: it was most interesting in itself, and in addition was topical to the highest degree. There could be no doubt of victory, and discussions were only about when it would take place.

In connection with the problems of the post-war settlement I fairly frequently met Academician E. S. Varga. Evgenii Samoilovich took no part in the discussions at the People's Commissariat for Foreign Affairs, but I had known Varga for a long time as one of the greatest specialists in international economic questions, and cherished a great respect for his judgments and opinions. Therefore I liked, having 'ventilated' some question at a consultation in the PCFA, to go 'privately' to Evgenii Samoilovich and examine the same question once more with him: perhaps I would hear something new and interesting? Or I might discover in my previous arguments some mistake I had not yet noticed? And I must frankly say that such a 'testing by Varga' in many cases proved exceptionally valuable, and several times saved me from mistaken views. Later, when I had finally returned to Moscow and became Chairman of the Reparations Commission, I invited Varga to take part in it. I want here to express my deep gratitude to him for the valuable contribution which he made to the working out of the post-war programme of the Soviet Union.

One day, in the middle of August, I was sitting with Varga in his crowded little flat in the former Luxe Hotel, where he had been living for many years, and actively discussing with him the question of the size of the reparations which it would be realistic to expect from Germany. Suddenly the telephone rang: I was being urgently summoned by the People's Commissar for Foreign Affairs (I usually left at the PCFA the telephone numbers where if necessary I could be found). A quarter of an hour later I entered the People's Commissar's office. He met me with the words:

'You have been appointed Deputy People's Commissar for Foreign Affairs ... You will leave London and move to Moscow... We shall arrange for your flat and other living conditions ... You will be in charge of the problem of reparations: you will become Chairman of a special Government Commission on this question which is to be established, and with the Commission you will work out the programme of reparations demands which the USSR will put forward at the peace conference ... Are you satisfied with your new appointment?'

'Quite satisfied,' I replied.

'Have you any particular wishes in connection with it?' he continued.

'Yes, I have,' I replied. 'I should like to return now for a short time to London, collect my wife for whom in wartime conditions it will not be an easy journey to Moscow, and above all prevent the appearance around my name of gossip which may be quite undesirable and unprofitable for us.'

And I looked meaningly at the People's Commissar.

In the years of the great-man cult there were many cases when Soviet Ambassadors were unexpectedly recalled to Moscow and then vanished without a trace—either into the grave or behind the bars of some camp. Therefore in the West there had been created the impression that, once a Soviet Ambassador was recalled to Moscow, some unpleasantness or other was awaiting him at home. I wanted to protect myself against this kind of interpretation and suspicion, and put my request to the People's Commissar for that reason. Molotov thought for a moment, and then said:

'We shall discuss this.'

The next day he telephoned to me to say that my request had been granted.

'Only you will be permitted to stay not more than five days in London,' Molotov added.

This restriction was strange. In wartime conditions there were no regular communications between London and Moscow, with a precise time-table for the departure or arrival of trains or planes. To travel from Britain to the USSR one had to take advantage of some suitable occasion, which did not occur every day. Moreover, my wife's state of health did not allow her to fly. However, I did not begin arguing with Molotov, and decided to leave the question of the length of my stay in London to the natural course of events.

And so all was now clear. My London days had come to an end, and there was opening before me a long chain of days in Moscow. I was pleased: after many years of work abroad I was returning to my native country, and with the prospect of important and interesting work. At the same time it was a little saddening: so much of my energies had been put into my eleven years in London, where I felt that I was being useful to my country, and I wished so much to render her some further services before the end of the war, which now seemed no longer remote. I also had the feeling that, if I left Britain before Germany was crushed, a very important chapter in my ambassadorial work would remain unfinished . . .

However, all these elegiac thoughts and considerations retired modestly before the realisation of the great success which had fallen to my lot; and, full of vigour and good spirits, I began preparing for my forthcoming flight to London.

The most important part of these preparations were the tactics to be used on the question of establishing diplomatic relations between the USSR and Egypt.

It is hardly necessary to say that one of the first pieces of business which occupied me on my arrival in Moscow was the question of Soviet-Egyptian relations. The Soviet Government found the letter from Nahas Pasha which I had brought, quite satisfactory, and instructed me (since his letter was addressed to me) to reply to him on behalf of the Soviet Government that it agreed to the request of the Egyptian Premier for the establishment of diplomatic relations between the two countries. I drew up the text of such a reply, which was then approved by higher authorities. The letter was dated 26 July, and the main part of its text read:

'The Soviet Government is of the opinion that the establishment of normal diplomatic relations between the Union of Soviet Socialist Republics and Egypt would be an important contribution to the cause of strengthening the front of the nations united in struggle against Hitlerite Germany and her satellites, and equally would be in the interests of both countries. Therefore the Soviet Government willingly accepts your proposal to establish normal diplomatic relations between the USSR and Egypt, and is ready to exchange representatives in the shortest possible time . . .

'Bringing all the foregoing to the notice of your Government,

I consider it my duty to state that hereby diplomatic relations between our countries may be considered established.'

Then arose the question of how our reply should be transmitted to Nahas Pasha. It was considered inconvenient to send it by cable *en clair* direct to Cairo. It was decided to cable the text of the reply in cipher to our Chargé d'Affaires in London, A. A. Sobolev, and to ask him urgently to present the letter to the Egyptian Ambassador, Nachat-Pasha. And he—at least, we thought so—would as in duty bound immediately cable his Premier about the document he had received. The most cautious calculations led us to suppose that our reply would be in the hands of Nahas Pasha four or five days after it had been sent from Moscow.

A week went by, and there was no response from Nahas Pasha. This surprised me, but I did not wish to draw any hasty conclusions. Another week went by . . . and then another week . . . and still there came no news from Cairo. I could not understand what this meant, and racked my brains over the reason for such incomprehensible behaviour on the part of the Egyptian Premier. When it now turned out that I would have to fly to London, and moreover by the same route which I had taken on the way to Moscow, I firmly made up my mind to see Nahas Pasha once again, and carry through to its conclusion the process of establishing diplomatic relations between the USSR and Egypt. Therefore when leaving I took with me a copy of my letter to Nahas Pasha of 26 July, and also the draft of an agreement about the establishment of diplomatic relations between the two countries. Although from the general nature of the situation it seemed that Nahas Pasha must be desiring such establishment, nevertheless his incomprehensible silence aroused a certain anxiety in me, and when taking my place in the plane I was still not confident of the success of my mission.

I left Moscow on 22 August. This time there was no single plane at my disposal to fly the whole ten thousand kilometres from Moscow to London. One had to fly 'by relays'. I was not alone: Admiral N. M. Kharlamov, who had been recalled shortly before to make a report, was returning to London with me. I was pleased: there was someone to exchange opinions with during the long flights. A Soviet plane brought us to Teheran. We stopped twice on the way. The first was at Stalingrad, where I was simply thunderstruck by the giant cemetery of smashed tanks, armoured cars, guns, lorries and every other kind of military equipment remaining after the great battle. From the height of a few hundred metres the picture was frightening and demonic: it seemed as though the broad steppe, as far as the eye could reach, had bared iron teeth which threatened death to anyone daring to descend on it. The aerodrome was comparatively far from the city, the plane did not remain for a long time, and I had no opportunity to visit the ruins of Stalingrad. The second stopping place was at Baku, where we spent the night.

At Teheran, contrary to our expectations, we had to stay for twenty-four hours: the young Shah, who had in the autumn of 1941 succeeded to his father Reza-Shah (now in exile), wished to be perfectly polite, and invited me for a cup of tea. I visited him in his country palace, and we had a talk on purely social themes. On 25 August a British plane delivered us to Cairo. At the aerodrome I was told to my regret that Nahas Pasha was not in Cairo at present. It turned out that in the hottest months of the year the whole Egyptian Government moved to Alexandria on the coast, leaving in the capital only second- and third-grade officials. I then decided to go to Alexandria. N. M. Kharlamov welcomed this intention in every possible way, because he wanted to see the famous harbour of Alexandria with his own eyes: it was of particular interest to him as a sailor. The authorities in Cairo placed a small plane at our disposal, and on the morning of 26 August we flew from Cairo to Alexandria.

We were met at the Alexandria aerodrome by Nahas Pasha's personal aide-de-camp, Azis-Abeb. He was a tall and well-built Egyptian, in a red fez and gold-braided military uniform. He spoke English and French excellently, and was brilliant in his manners and amiable conversation. He immediately passed N. M. Kharlamov over to the care of the Egyptian sailors, while me he took straight from the aerodrome to the Prime Minister.

Nahas Pasha's residence was in a luxurious hotel on the very sea shore. I was brought into a large salon which served as his drawing room. A moment later Nahas Pasha himself hastened in. He greeted me as an old friend, and poured out the most elegant compliments addressed to the USSR, the Red Army, the Soviet Government and me personally. When this inevitable part of Oriental ceremonial was over, I asked Nahas Pasha: 'Did you receive my reply?'

'Yes, but only three days ago,' he replied.

'How, only three days ago?' I said in amazement. 'My letter was sent to you a month ago!'

'Quite true', Nahas Pasha said with an ironical smile. 'But you sent it through London . . . Well, but you know Nachat-Pasha . . .'

He did not finish the sentence, but from his gestures and expression it was clear what he wanted to say. Then Nahas Pasha clapped his hands, and his secretary came out of the neighbouring room. The Prime Minister said something in his own language, and a minute later there appeared on the table a folder of documents.

'Now look at these,' Nahas Pasha said to me.

They were the cipher messages which London and Cairo had been exchanging during the last month. All of them were in French, so that I could read them freely. I looked with surprise at him, and asked: 'Is your ciphered correspondence carried on in French?'

'Yes, in French', he replied. 'Our own language is not very well adapted for the purpose.'

That was it! I remembered that French was replaced by Russian in the correspondence of the Russian Ministry of Foreign Affairs with its personnel abroad only under Alexander III.

The cipher messages shown me by Nahas Pasha solved the problem over which I had been vainly racking my brains in Moscow. A. A. Sobolev had sent Nachat-Pasha my letter on 27 July, i.e. immediately after it had arrived from Moscow. The next day, 28 July, the Ambassador cabled Cairo that he had received the letter, but instead of transmitting its exact text by cable, he had confined himself to a very brief summary of its contents, adding at the end: 'The text of the letter follows.' Not having the original text, Nahas Pasha thought it inconvenient to raise the question for final decision by his Government. But the letter from London 'followed' extremely slowly, and reached Nahas Pasha's hands only on 23 August, i.e. almost a month after it had been sent from Moscow.

'So it turns out that Nachat-Pasha sent you my letter by ox-cart?'

'That's it, by ox-cart!'—and Nahas Pasha burst out laughing.

Then he continued:

'But directly I received the text of your letter, I immediately that very day, 23 August, sent you my reply. Here it is.'

And Nahas Pasha handed me a sheet of paper which I read through rapidly. In his reply the Egyptian Premier had noted with pleasure 'the complete agreement between our two Governments on the question of establishing normal diplomatic relations between Egypt and the USSR', and at the end of the letter said that 'the establishment of diplomatic relations between our two countries . . . must be considered as effected from this moment'.

'This is a copy of my letter,' he explained. 'The original was dispatched to London by airmail three days ago. I did not know that I would have the pleasure of seeing you so soon in Egypt, otherwise I would have kept back the original until your arrival. Please take this copy with you.'

I expressed my pleasure at this happy conclusion of our negotiations, and asked: 'From what date, then, shall we consider diplomatic relations between our countries established?'

Nahas Pasha thought for a second, and then said vivaciously: 'Let's reckon them established as from today, 26 August 1943. We have completed our negotiations today . . . and moreover today is our great holiday which all Moslems revere—Ramadan.'

Nahas Pasha went to the open window, and continued: 'Look out here . . . The whole city is beflagged . . . All the people are out in the streets, cheerful and happy . . . A good date for the beginning of relations between our countries!'

'Very well,' I said. 'Let 26 August 1943 be the date. I hope our descendants will remember this date with satisfaction.'

'Yes, yes: I don't doubt it!' exclaimed Nahas Pasha.

'Now we have one last quite small task,' I said. 'We have to agree the text of a communiqué to the press which will inform the peoples of our countries about this event.'

Nahas Pasha nodded, we sat down at the table, and ten minutes later we already had the text of the communiqué. The Prime Minister immediately handed it over to the typists for copying. It was agreed that it would be published simultaneously in Moscow and Cairo on 7 September 1943.

When all this had been done, Nahas Pasha said: 'And shouldn't we celebrate this happy event?'

'An excellent idea!' I replied.

Nahas Pasha again clapped his hands, and once more his secretary appeared. The Premier exchanged some words with him —and a few moments later the salon began to be filled with Nahas Pasha's closest collaborators. Then two footmen brought in glasses and bottles of . . . soda water!

'You will excuse me,' Nahas Pasha said with a gesture at the bottles. 'I suffer from an ulcer, and the doctors have categorically forbidden me to take alcohol.'

I replied with a polite joke that 'on a good occasion soda water may be no worse than champagne'.

He was delighted, and said: 'That's quite right.'

The footmen poured out the soda water, and Nahas Pasha gave a toast: 'For the happy future of Soviet-Egyptian relations!'

I supported his toast, we clinked glasses and drank them off.

Although there had not been a drop of alcohol in the glasses, Nahas Pasha suddenly became as lively as though he had drunk a Caucasian horn-ful of wine, jumped up, took me by the hand and cried: 'Come with me, I will show you how I live here!'

The Premier led me through his apartments, saying as we went from room to room: 'This is my study . . . This is my drawing room . . . This is my dining room . . .'

Finally, there was a closed door. He hurried up to it, obviously intending to throw it open. 'And this is my bedroom', he exclaimed.

This was too much. I instinctively made a defensive gesture, and slipped by into the neighbouring corridor.

Nahas Pasha accompanied me to the stairs, warmly shook me by the hand, and wished me in parting every happiness and success . . .

Kharlamov and I dined in a large Egyptian restaurant, and afterwards went to see the harbour of Alexandria. We had a special motor-boat placed at our disposal, and the British and Egyptian sailors accompanying us gave the necessary explanations. For two hours we inspected this famous port, which had served as the sea-gate into Egypt for five thousand years, from Pharaoh Djoser to our own times, and saw a great deal that was interesting, especially for Admiral Kharlamov.

During our tour I suddenly had an alarming thought. Nahas Pasha had told me that three days before he had sent the original of his reply to my letter of 26 July to Nachat-Pasha in London. He had only given me an unsigned copy. But what if Nachat-Pasha, on various pretexts, began delaying the immediate passing over of the original to me? I could stay in London only a few days, and during those few days I was bound to carry through to its conclusion the establishment of Soviet-Egyptian relations! The communiqué agreed by myself and Nahas Pasha must appear on 7 September. No accidents in this respect could be tolerated. What was to be done?

I decided to ask Nahas Pasha to sign the copy of his reply

which he had handed me that morning, and affix the appropriate seal. Let there be two equally valid originals. This would tie Nachat-Pasha's hands, and secure us from any possibility of a nasty surprise.

Our plane was leaving Alexandria for Cairo at 6 p.m. An hour before this I drove up to Nahas Pasha's residence. I was met by the same Azis-Abeb.

'I need to see the Prime Minister for a few moments,' I said in the friendliest tone.

Alas, Nahas Pasha was not at home, and Azis-Abeb did not know when he would return from some visit of inspection. What was to be done?

He began cautiously asking me what was the reason which made it so urgently necessary for me to see Nahas Pasha. I explained to him what I wanted, saying that this was war-time, the plane which was carrying the original of the Prime Minister's letter might be shot down by the Germans, the document would be lost, it would be necessary to duplicate it all over again, and the establishment of diplomatic relations between the USSR and Egypt would once again be delayed. Would it not be better to ensure ourselves against all possible unpleasantness by the means which I had thought of?

Azis-Abeb beamed. 'Oh, all this can be most easily arranged,' he exclaimed. 'Leave me your copy: as soon as the Premier returns, I will report to him, he will sign the document and I will send it to you in Cairo.'

'But tomorrow morning', I objected, 'I am flying from Cairo to London. I need to have the document today.'

'Nothing can be simpler,' Azis-Abeb said. 'It will be in your hands in a few hours.'

'For certain?'

Aziz-Abeb solemnly replied: 'I swear by Allah, blessed be His Name, that I shall keep my word.'

I will not say that that fully satisfied me, but there was no other way out. One had to take the risk. I handed over the copy of Nahas Pasha's letter to his aide, and flew to Cairo.

The same day, exactly at 10 p.m., the messenger of the Prime Minister knocked at my door. He had brought me by special plane a packet with five large seals. It contained the second copy of Nahas Pasha's reply, signed and appropriately sealed. I sighed with relief.

At dawn on 27 August N. M. Kharlamov and I flew off on the

British Liberator from Cairo to Gibraltar, and then on to London. The whole journey passed without incident. On the morning of 28 August we saw beneath us the bright green meadows of England. The plane landed on the same aerodrome from which we had taken off nearly two months before. Here we were met by our wives and colleagues.

Immediately on my arrival in London I informed Nachat-Pasha that I had the copy of his Prime Minister's reply. This cut off the Egyptian Ambassador from any means of creating further delays. The very next day he sent me the original. Now it was possible to publish the communiqué about the establishment of diplomatic relations which had been agreed between the two sides. At the last moment, on account of the difficulty of communication in wartime conditions, there was a slight discrepancy: the dates of publication were not fully synchronised. In Cairo the newspapers printed it on 7 September, and in Moscow on the 9th. But that was now a small detail. The main thing had been accomplished. Diplomatic relations between the USSR and Egypt had been renewed after a break of twenty-six years.

3

Return to Moscow

OF course, as I had anticipated, I was not able to settle everything in London in five days.

The British Government was most attentive and, wishing to make my return home as secure and comfortable as possible, suggested that my wife and I should travel by the same route which I had just followed, only not by plane but by sea and land. In the middle of September a large and well-guarded convoy of 30,000 troops was leaving Britain for India. We were offered a comfortable cabin on one of the ships in this convoy as far as Egypt, after which we could travel the whole way from Cairo to Teheran through Asia Minor by car, with the assistance and under the care of the British. I willingly accepted this offer, and the date of our departure from London was in this way settled. Preparations began. The greater part of our things were packed by my wife even before my arrival: she had set about this as soon as she had heard from me about my transfer to work in Moscow. But nevertheless something fell to my lot as well. The main problem was my library. It contained several thousand books, which we had accumulated during nearly twenty years of work abroad, and now they had to be sorted and packed for a long journey. As a result, there were thirty heavy boxes in our apartment which were to accompany us from London to Moscow.

The preparations for departure took other, more important forms as well. We said a friendly goodbye to the Soviet colony in London, all those comrades in the Embassy and Trade Delegation with whom I had worked for many years in good weather and bad. I will retain warm recollections of them to the end of my days.

We also bid farewell to those many foreigners, particularly British, who for many years had displayed their sympathy for the Soviet Union or maintained constant contact with the Soviet Embassy. These included Ministers and politicians, Members of Parliament and diplomats, people active in public life, writers and artists, journalists and trade unionists. As it was simply impossible to pay farewell visits to them all, and it seemed unsuitable to gather them all for a big reception at the Embassy in wartime conditions, I sent such people several hundred farewell letters, varying their contents according to the addressee. I received several hundred replies to my letters, many of them breathing quite sincere feelings of regret.

There were also personal farewell visits to people who were most close and sympathetic. Among them I remember particularly our visits to Bernard Shaw and his wife, to Sidney Webb who had recently become a widower, and to H. G. Wells. All of them were now aged people, who had grown old under our eyes, so to speak, and we feared in our thoughts that we should not meet them again. So it turned out.

It was particularly tragic with Mrs. Shaw. We visited the Shaws two days before our departure, which had been fixed for 14 September. Mrs. Shaw was very ill. In her early youth she had been thrown by her horse, and had injured her spine. Then everything seemed to pass off: but as years went on the old injury made itself felt more and more frequently, and no treatment was of avail. Now, at the age of ninety, Charlotte Shaw was a complete invalid: her frame was bent, she could not raise her head and spent the whole day in bed. But on our farewell visit she rose, dressed and came down into the drawing-room. She wished us the best in life, and recalled with deep satisfaction our eleven years' friendship. We said good words to her, too, in reply, but our hearts were sad and anxious. One could not help thinking: 'She is not long for this world.' The end came earlier than we could have expected. On the very day of our departure, an hour before the train left, we learned that Charlotte was dead. The first impulse was to go to Bernard Shaw and personally express our deep sympathy, but this was impossible: in wartime conditions one could not even think of postponing departure even for a few hours. Then I took a sheet of paper, and in a few heartfelt lines expressed all our grief and shock at the loss he and we had suffered . . .

When an Ambassador is leaving, a definite diplomatic procedure is observed. It varies somewhat according to his popularity, the length of his stay in the country where he was accredited, but most of all depending on the character of relations between that country and his own. In my case all the formal signs were in favour of organising a pompous farewell: I had worked eleven years in Britain, I was the representative of her powerful Ally in war, and I was well known in the British Isles. However, Soviet diplomacy has always striven to simplify as much as possible and democratise the diplomatic etiquette, the rules of which in the main were formed still in the epoch of feudalism. I have already described elsewhere how I had infringed strict 'protocol' on my arrival in London, by being the first to make ceremonial visits not only to Ambassadors but to Ministers as well. Now I also tried to arrange with Eden that all the 'farewell' formalities should be reduced to the absolute necessary minimum. In the end everything was limited to the King and Queen giving us their signed photographs, and Eden (because Churchill at that moment was out of Britain) arranged a farewell lunch for myself and my wife, at which there were present members of the Government and some other notables with their wives. At this lunch Eden made a speech in which he outlined the justification in history for the necessity of Anglo-Soviet co-operation.

On the eve of our day of departure I went to Hyde Park. In May 1917, when I was returning to Russia after the March Revolution, my last 'goodbye' to Britain was said in that remarkable park. I remember how after walking through it and thinking over all the years of my emigration, I had said:

'Farewell, my past! Now new and wide expanses are opening before me.'

Now, twenty-six years later, once again on the eve of my departure for Russia which had become the Union of Soviet Socialist Republics, I wanted once more to say goodbye to Britain in Hyde Park. Walking along its shady avenues and open fields, I thought to myself:

'How infinitely the world has changed during this quarter of a century! How Russia has changed! How changed am I myself! Then I was returning home as an unknown emigrant, but though I believed in the great achievements of my country I did not know exactly where, how and in what forms these would take place. Ahead was a cloud, true, one shot through with rosy gleams of light, but all the same a cloud. Now I am returning as an experienced diplomat of the Socialist Great Power, knowing well what his country needs, who will take part in building its future in the storms of the war and of post-war confusion. Life is sometimes more fantastic than a story, and I am glad that it has fallen to my lot to live through such a fantasy.'

We left London on the evening of 14 September 1943. Our departure was arranged in great secrecy: nevertheless, it turned out that many members of our Soviet colony were at the station, far more than had been planned. On the British side there were present the King's representative, Mr. Monck, and Mr. Harvey of the Foreign Office. In the semi-darkness of the black-out my wife and I rapidly shook the hands outstretched to us, and accompanied by wishes for a happy journey, took our seats in the carriage. A few moments later the train moved off at speed northward.

The next day, at 10.30 a.m., we were already in Glasgow. Half an hour later we were brought to Gourock, where lay the ship on which we were to continue our journey. We took our seats on the launch on which our baggage had already been loaded, and a quarter of an hour later were on board the vast liner, in which we had been given magnificent three-room accommodation on the top deck. Then we came out and began looking around. It was a typical autumn day in Scotland: grey sky, grey sea, raw air and a light mist in which clear forms and firm outlines seemed to swim and melt.

We set sail at 8 p.m. It was already dark, and it was in deepest night when we emerged into the ocean. It was stormy, and my wife, who was always a bad sailor, took to her bed at once. The following morning I came out on deck, and a majestic and awe-inspiring picture opened to my view. Eleven vast steamers were proceeding in line ahead, at intervals of 700-800 metres, the whole cortège stretching for nearly six miles. A dozen destroyers and corvettes on both sides accompanied the cavalcade, rushing ahead like bloodhounds and closing up the rear. It seemed as though some mighty fortress was moving over the sea, ready at any moment to reply with fire and metal to anyone who dared to attack it or hinder its advance.

The first officer approached me and began giving me explanations. Our convoy was carrying about 30,000 men to Africa and India. Its route would be the Atlantic, the Mediterranean, the Suez Canal and Bombay. It was composed of large passenger liners of various nationalities, requisitioned for war purposes. Our ship was the *Mooltan*, a liner belonging to the well-known British Peninsular and Oriental Line, of 21,000 tons displacement and 16 knots. It was carrying about 4,000 soldiers travelling to India.

We reached Gibraltar after five days, and then passed into the Mediterranean. During the next week the composition of our convoy changed. Some vessels left for ports in North Africa, which by this time was entirely and firmly in Anglo-American hands, while others came and joined the ranks of our armada. The composition of our guard changed: part of the destroyers and corvettes left, frigates, anti-aircraft cruisers and aircraft carriers joined us. We left Algiers and Bizerta behind. We passed by the rocky Italian island of Pantellaria, which had recently been seized by the Allies. Sicily and Malta were left behind. The wireless told us daily of events going on in the world, and in particular detail of what was passing on the various fronts. It was quite clear that after the battle in the Kursk Salient, the German military machine had had its backbone finally broken, and that the victory of the anti-Hitler coalition was quite assured. The only question was, when. And there was one more question about which at that time I began to worry more and more: would Germany be completely crushed, or would the war end in a compromise peace with her?

Sitting on deck, I thought a great deal about what the world would look like after the war: all the more because such thoughts were closely bound up with the work which awaited me in Moscow. I well remember that in my meditations a constant part was played by the problem of China, where Chiang Kai-Shek was still in power, and was supported in every possible way by the USA. And I could not help wondering how events would develop in that part of the world, say, in the next twenty-five to thirty years?

I thought much also about the problem of reparations to which I had to devote particular attention on my arrival in Moscow. I had several books with me on this question, read them carefully and drew my own conclusion from what I read.

The problem of reparations had a history of its own. It first arose in all its seriousness at the end of the world war in 1914–18. At that time France, which had suffered very greatly from the German invasion, insistently demanded compensation for the material losses, destruction, etc., which she had suffered, at the expense of the defeated enemy. But the rulers of France (and of the other Powers of the Entente), in the grip of the passions awakened by the war, were unable to display the necessary realism, and put forward a quite fantastic programme.

The total compensation which the Entente demanded from Germany was not so great in itself (30 milliard dollars, in instalments over fifty-eight years); but the trouble was that the Entente wanted to receive these reparations in cash—and not in German marks, but in some world currency like dollars, pounds or francs. In order to acquire this currency, Germany was forced frenziedly to develop her exports. Thereby she became a most dangerous competitor for France, Britain and the USA on world markets and even on the home market of these Powers themselves. An acute contradiction came into being, from which there was no way out: and Germany, playing on it skilfully, in the end got herself set free in effect from reparations altogether.

Having this historical experience before me, I thought out quite different lines on which the future reparations commission, over which I had to preside in Moscow, should work. I firmly resolved that the cash form of reparations should be completely rejected, and instead that compensation should be paid *in kind*, i.e. in factories, works, services, deliveries of commodities, food products, etc. Then I resolved that in determining the total of reparations we should confine ourselves rigidly to realities and, whatever the actual size of our losses, we should demand from Germany only what, given the necessary strictness, could be really received from her. Both these principles were, in fact, adopted as the basis of the Soviet reparations plan worked out by our reparations commission, later approved by the Soviet Government and in the end adopted by the Crimea Conference of the Big Three in 1945.

On 28 September, the fourteenth day after we had left Scotland, we arrived at last at Port Said. At the dockside in Port Said we were met by representatives of the British authorities in Egypt, who whisked us away without delay by car to Cairo. Here we were accommodated in the residence of General Wilson, Commander-in-Chief Middle East, known in common Army parlance as 'Jumbo'.

The three days we spent in the capital of Egypt were filled with all kinds of inspections, visits, acquaintances and, of course, the inevitable diplomatic luncheons and dinners.

We set off again at 7 a.m. on 2 October. All the details of our further journey were fixed during our stay in Cairo. Our route now was overland, by way of Jerusalem-Damascus-Bagdad-Kermanshah-Teheran-Tabriz and the Soviet-Iran frontier. Thus we were now to repeat by car approximately the same journey which, three months before, I had made by air. The British took responsibility for my safe passage from Cairo to Teheran (since at that time, throughout the region, there were no Soviet diplomatic institutions as yet), while in Teheran they would 'hand me over' to the Soviet Embassy in Iran. To accompany us from Cairo to Teheran I had attached to me a British colonel on mission. Our diplomatic couriers travelled with us. In all there were four cars and one lorry.

At 8 p.m. the same day we arrived in Jerusalem, and were put up in the grim building which then was called 'Government House'. Here was the office of the High Commissioner for Palestine, and here he lived himself with his family and his suite. At that time the post was occupied by Sir Harold MacMichael, who left the impression of a skilful colonial administrator in the typical British style. Judging from a number of symptoms, he was pro-Arab. This could be felt in his conversation, in the remarks of the members of his family and those of the company who gathered at their table. It was also characteristic that the servants at 'Government House' were entirely people of Arab nationality.

My wife and I, of course, were given a 'V.I.P.' apartment, and the Arab maid who came to unpack our hand luggage, began by asking:

'Of course you'll go this evening to King David?'

'King David?' my wife asked in surprise. 'What's that?'

An expression of the greatest contempt passed over the face of the maid, and then she condescendingly explained: 'King David is the finest hotel in Jerusalem ... There is going to be a big ball there tonight... The whole of society will be there!'

However, we displayed complete indifference to the information she gave us—which greatly lowered us in her eyes—and announced that we would go to bed immediately after supper, because we were very tired after the journey.

We left Jerusalem on the morning of 4 October and, after travelling without incident to Damascus and Bagdad, we arrived on the evening of the 8th at Kermanshah, a comparatively large city with a population of about 100,000, and were put up at the

Soviet Consulate. At last we were again amongst our own people, on a scrap of (at least juridically) our own territory! The little Soviet colony met us in friendly and simple fashion (a simplicity we were particularly glad of), entertained us with tasty Russian meat pies, and even for our recreation displayed their amateur art. At once we felt a kind of native warmth, for which we had been hungering when crossing the vast expanses of the British and Afro-Asiatic world.

In spite of the late hour, there came to greet me the Iranian Governor of Kermanshah, followed by the British Consul, the British colonel commanding the British forces in the Kermanshah district, and some other official personalities. It was already about midnight when I at last could get to bed.

We reached Hamadan, about eighty miles further on, next day. There were American units here, and the colonel commanding them offered to accompany us to Kazvin, where there were already Soviet troops. The road went through the mountains, but it was excellently constructed, and we moved ahead rapidly. At one spot, not far from the beginning of the Soviet zone, there was an American military camp. The American colonel insisted that we should lunch there. We were met in the most hospitable way by the officers, the food was excellent and the dining room light and roomy. Everything would have been perfect, but . . . the walls of the dining room were thickly hung with the pictures of naked beauties cut out of American gutter journals. When my wife came into the dining room with me, it was an embarrassing moment.

Not quite thirty kilometres from Kazvin, we crossed the border of the Soviet zone. At the border barrier there was a women's patrol, which checked our documents in friendly but businesslike fashion. We went into the Soviet border post, and I was struck by the picture: a young girl in military uniform was ironing her tunic. But the watch was maintained not only by women but by men as well. We spent about half-an-hour here, and exchanged the latest news in lively conversation.

At Kazvin, which at that time was an important centre of the disposition of Soviet troops, we hardly stopped at all. There remained only about 150 kilometres to Teheran, and we were in a hurry to get to the capital before nightfall. The local military authorities gave us the necessary escort, and a Soviet patrol on a speedy cross-country vehicle went ahead of our cars. Sixty kilometres from Teheran we were met by the Counsellor of the Soviet Embassy, Maximov, who was Chargé d'Affaires during the temporary absence of Ambassador A. A. Smirnov. On our arrival in Teheran, in the walls of the Soviet Embassy, the British colonel who had accompanied us from Cairo officially 'transferred' us to the care of the Soviet authorities. I thanked him sincerely for all his consideration for us, and for the excellent organisation of our journey from Cairo to Teheran.

So we were once more among our own people, and immediately began discussing our further route. We had to travel by rail from Teheran to Mianeh, where the railway then ended, and travel in cars for the remaining 180 kilometres to Tabriz. The baggage would not arrive at Tabriz for another two days, and we could make use of the time for rest.

We began with the Soviet Embassy. Its premises reminded one of a sumptuous feudal castle. Built by the Tsarist Government, it fully answered to the spirit of its epoch and the tastes of its former masters. The Embassy building stood in the centre of a large park, encompassed on all sides by a high stone wall. In the park were a lake with constantly fresh water, fountains, flower beds and a network of broad and narrow paths. In addition to the main building containing the offices and the apartment of the Ambassador, there were several other houses in the park containing apartments for the staff, the club and the canteen. Opposite the main building was a monument to A. S. Griboyedov. The author of *Woe from Wit* perished in Teheran over a century ago when serving as Russian Ambassador to Persia. It seemed to me only that the monument was too small and unexpressive. The creator of Chatsky and Famusov deserved a more impressive memorial.

On the morning of 13 October we left Teheran, and the following day arrived at Tabriz without incident. Here there were waiting for us two carriages with a marvellous conductor, skilled in all crafts, Grandpa David. We entrained rapidly, and the same evening set off. At midnight on the 14th our train crossed the Soviet-Iranian frontier in the neighbourhood of Djulfa. We were at last on Soviet territory, but it took another eight days before we arrived in Moscow. The war had greatly disturbed normal conditions, and particularly railway traffic. The trains went slowly. They stood for a long time at the halts. The usual routes were infringed, and connections between various cities, which had been direct, had become zig-zag in shape. We experienced this ourselves: when we arrived at Tikhoretskaya we learned that the direct route to Moscow was closed, and we had to get to the capital through Stalingrad. This made our journey longer, but in return gave us the opportunity to see the glorious city in its immortal heroic shape after the battle.

The train stood at Stalingrad for three hours. We were hospitably received by the local comrades and taken through the city. We saw with our own eyes the places which had become so familiar and so dear to us quite lately from the military communiqués: the Pavlov house, the Tractor Works, the Mamai Hill, the crossing at the Volga . . . The whole city seemed a mass of legendary ruins, roofless, with half-fallen walls, empty windows without frames, solitary chimneys. It seemed as though one could see through the whole city from end to end. Only here, on the spot, face to face with these relics of the great battle, did we begin better to understand and feel what had gone on here only a few months before, what an immeasurable quantity of will-power, energy, strength, resolution, self-sacrifice and devotion was required to live through all this, stand fast and crush the cruel enemy.

We left Stalingrad profoundly shaken by its vast historic drama, and at the same time profoundly inspired by that new gushing fountain of life which we could see at every step amid these sacred ruins.

On the morning of 22 October our train slowly steamed into its Moscow terminus. It was a grey autumn day, with rays of the sun, however, from time to time breaking through the darkling and rapidly moving clouds. We were met by representatives of the People's Commissariat for Foreign Affairs and our relations.

The long forty days of the complex and difficult journey from London to Moscow were ended. We were at home. Quite a new page of life was beginning.

Index of Names

(Dates given are only those relevant to the text)